OUT OF TOWN

THE COUNTRY HOUSE

OUT OF TOWN

THE COUNTRY HOUSE

EDITED BY PETER HYATT

images
Publishing

Published in Australia in 2006 by
The Images Publishing Group Pty Ltd
ABN 89 059 734 431
6 Bastow Place, Mulgrave, Victoria 3170, Australia
Telephone: +61 3 9561 5544 Facsimile: +61 3 9561 4860
Email: books@images.com.au
Website: www.imagespublishing.com

Copyright © The Images Publishing Group Pty Ltd 2006

The Images Publishing Group Reference Number: 663

National Library of Australia
Cataloguing-in-Publication entry:
Hyatt, Peter

Out of Town

Includes index.
ISBN 1 86470 150 1.

1. Country homes
2. Ecological houses I.
Hyatt, Jennifer. II Title.

728.047

Coordinating Editor: Andrea Boekel

Designed by The Graphic Image Studio Pty Ltd, Mulgrave, Australia
Website: www.tgis.com.au

Film by SC (Sang Choy) International Pte Ltd
Printed by Paramount Printing Company Limited Hong Kong

IMAGES has included on its website a page for special notices in relation to this and our other publications.
Please visit this site: www.imagespublishing.com

Contents

Introduction   6

Bishamon Float House, Japan   10
Suppose Design Office

Broadford Farm Pavilion, USA   16
Lake/Flato Architects

Canyon View Office/Guesthouse, USA   20
Kanner Architects

Carver Residence, Australia   26
Scott Carver Architects

Fritidsbolig, Finland   30
Todd Saunders & Tommie Wilhemsen

Hermitage Road Residence, Australia   32
Duc Associates Pty Ltd

House of Earth and Light, USA   40
Marwan Al Sayed Architects

House to Catch the Forest, Japan   46
Tezuka Architects and Masahiro Ikeda co ltd

Jackson Family Retreat, USA   52
Fougeron Architecture

Jai House, USA   58
Lorcan O'Herlihy Architects

Kerrisdale Farmhouse, Australia   62
Col Bandy Architects

Kropach/Catlow Farmhouse, Australia   70
Grose Bradley Architects

Les Abouts Residence, Canada   78
Pierre Thibault Architecte

Lookout House at Red Hill, Australia   82
David Luck Architecture

Malibu House 3, USA   90
Kanner Architects

Maunu Poolhouse, USA   98
Fung + Blatt Architects

Memoria Casa Schmitz, Chile   102
Felipe Assadi Arquitectos

Misonou House, Japan   108
Suppose Design Office

Podere 43, Italy   114
Labics Architettura

Retreat Summer House, Norway   122
Todd Saunders and Tommie Wilhelmsen

Richards-Ebert Residence, USA   126
Steven Ehrlich Architects

Ridge House, USA   128
Olson Sundberg Kundig Allen Architects

Smith Residence, USA   134
Patel Architecture

Solar Tube, Austria   140
Georg Driendl Architekt

Swann Residence, USA   148
Steven Ehrlich Architects

Texas Twister, USA   152
buildingstudio

The Fritz Residence, USA   160
OJMR Architects

The Keenan Tower House, USA   168
Marlon Blackwell Architect

The Moore Honey House, USA   170
Marlon Blackwell Architect

The Raveau House, Chile   174
Felipe Assadi Arquitectos

The Sinquefield House, USA   182
Barton Phelps & Associates

Wall-less House, Japan   186
Tezuka Architects and Masahiro Ikeda co ltd

Walla Womba Guest House, Australia   192
1 + 2 Architecture

Warabi Cottage, Japan   200
Opposition Architects

Wheatsheaf Residence, Australia   206
Jesse Judd Architects

Withers Residence, USA   212
McInturff Architects

Yakeyama House, Japan   216
Suppose Design Office

Index   222

Acknowledgements   224

PETER & JENNIFER HYATT

Introduction

Away from the urban centres and suburbs, where the city meets the country, housing can provide the great escape. Out Of Town houses are fluent, rather than necessarily affluent, responses to the environmental opportunity. They demonstrate the benefits of artful connection between habitation and habitat. With expanding cities and shrinking rural farmland, a new housing type has emerged that makes a critical link between suburban dwelling and country home. Between these two types and two worlds, is a hybrid of elegant simplicity.

The trend of big city housing requires serious re-evaluation from big, bigger, biggest towards inventive, sustainable design as good, better, best. Rural houses too have their particular stereotype. Environmental concerns and a growing sensitivity to the state of our planet have resulted in the principles of 'sustainable development'. Several of these projects show a deep and profound concern for the environment by harmonizing with it. Many are constructed in natural material (recyclable and bio-degradable) and utilize non-polluting and non-invasive construction methods. They represent a transition zone between urban where a very different, fascinating response is possible. They prove how functional, aesthetic delight is attainable and sustainable. They reverberate with ideas about nurture and nature, designed as sustainable objects that are brushed, never beaten, into the landscape.

Marlon Blackwell's Tower House and Honey House are adventurously tuned to site and need. With sculptural economy, Blackwell invites us to become part of the environmental fabric rather than separated from it. David Luck's series of black, steel-skinned 'boxes' float effortlessly among the scribbled eucalyptus trunks, yet their sharp, dark forms are clearly defined against the forest. Contrasting materials are evocatively used in the House of Earth and Light by Marwan Al-Sayed. Here he explores the solid and ephemeral—earthbound walls and the gossamer-like roof that "undulates gently to create an environment with its constant filtration of light and shadow that acts like a 'sky-painting', with the hopes of creating a modern, elegant desert tent".

The featured projects respond with a spirit of place that challenges size as a measure of substance. New suburban housing estates are outgrowing their allotments on an ascending scale of size that dwarfs need and practicality. The hidden cost of affluence is the irony of purchasing more but receiving less. There has been some vigorous elbowing and jostling for front row seats in cities in recent years. The rush for pre-eminence sees bulk make the kind of positioning statement that despoils the initial attraction.

By contrast, Out Of Town houses are spare in form, often constructed from pre-fabricated components, and reflect the shrewd transfer of an industrial or rural vocabulary. Smarter design speaks of economical, appropriate technologies and efficient materials/energy usage. The critical compass points of good design delight in the process of construction and environment. They are much less concerned with fashion than utility and flexibility. The Kropach/Catlow Farmhouse makes extensive use of inexpensive materials such as corrugated steel and simple technologies to assemble a filleted, climate responsive, pavilion.

Design that transcends catalogue and formula is within closer reach than is commonly understood. Fertile, strong ideas matched with optimism and craft are all evident in this work. There is a healthy difference and optimism about good ideas where relationships are fully made between people and place. These houses do more than sit lightly within their environment; they are responsive to the pleasures of light, breeze and outlook. Sustainable design is winning friends for obvious reasons, but it also threatens to create an energy conscious stereotype. Instead, it should occur as notes in the margin where a deep understanding and thoughtful response is forged between architect and client.

Mostly modest in scale, these houses are the big picture item underwritten by a keen economy of means. Ultimately such architecture speaks about a labor of love. Meaningful conversations between architect and client are helping to bridge this new territory. What is made to appear effortless and entirely natural is an art in itself and a tribute to the architects, who together with their clients, fully convert their opportunity.

7

SELECTED PROJECTS

1   Full view of house
2   Night view

SUPPOSE DESIGN OFFICE

Bishamon
Float House

Hiroshima, Japan

10

The Bishamon Float House comprises a residence and café. Located on a hill overlooking Hiroshima, it was built for a family of two and their pet dog.

Although surrounded by stereotypical houses built by well-known Japanese builders, the Bishamon Float House is distinctively different in that the house responds dynamically to its setting rather than being subordinate to it.

The architecture reveals a deep appreciation of nature as a source for creative and sympathetic response. The site is steeply sloping and consists of two layers: an upper section of about 3230 square feet (300 square meters) and a lower section of 1400 square feet (130 square meters). The middle section of the site was used for the house while the top 'arrival' section provides off-street car parking.

The three-story building is constructed of ferroconcrete with iron frames. The first floor is a café run by the owner of the building while the second floor, with a unique bridge, is the family's living space that includes a bathroom, kitchen and one wide room in the center.

The architect has created open and comfortable spaces on the second floor by taking advantage of soft sunlight reflecting off the leaves. At nightfall, directional lights are used under the building to accentuate its detachment from the earth.

Construction involved two pairs of slabs and a light roof, placed on six poles. These large steel frames resemble a giant swing and provide the means to project the Bishamon Float House as a floating box.

A simple structure in essence, the Bishamon Float House employs a sense of boldness to achieve its purpose of lightweight, dynamic projection into space above the city.

1

12

3   View of first floor café at night
4   Panoramic view from terrace
5   Approach bridge

13

6

7

6   View of house with approach bridge in foreground
7   View over surroundings from terrace
8   Full view of approach

<small>PHOTOGRAPHY: NACASA & PARTNERS</small>

8

1 Site plan
2 Wood decks allow circulation around all spaces
3 Alternating steel pipe column bays
4 Detail of steel window box at bath

Bounded by wild woods and a horse pasture, the pavilion and pool mediate the clearing between the two land features. An existing tree line delineates the grounds of the main house from those of the pavilion and pool and provides a visual scrim for the residence and a framed view through the adjacent horse pasture. Within the clearing, the pavilion gently hovers above the ground plane, funneling panoramic views from the structures to the nearby mountain range.

A covered deck serves as primary access to the building linking a grass lawn to the 60-foot (20-meter) lap pool. The glass walls of the communal space slide open and fold away, creating a flexible open-air shade structure during the warmer months while encouraging the prevailing wind conditions to naturally cross-ventilate and passively cool the space. Insulated roof sections lighten at the edges providing deep overhangs of corrugated galvanized steel, shading the outdoor deck spaces.

In addition to withstanding seismic loading, the pavilion structure is also designed to accommodate 125-pound (56-kilogram) per square foot snow loads, commonplace six months of the year. During these colder months, the space can be tightly sealed and warmed primarily by a wood-burning stove with supplemental mechanical heat. The structure offers the solitude of a Nordic family retreat and also serves as overflow accommodation for guests.

Simple materials and finishes reflect the rural context and recall the local agrarian vernacular. Organized in alternating 6-foot (1.8 meter) and 12-foot (3.6 meter) bays similar to a modern pole barn, crisp volumes clad in Ipe, a highly resistant air-dried Brazilian hardwood siding contain the utility spaces of the bath, shower room and support storage. These volumes float

Lake/Flato Architects

Broadford Farm Pavilion

Sun Valley, Idaho, USA

16

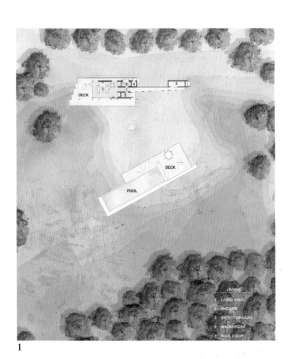

1

2

3

4

within a rigid steel frame system composed of oiled pipe columns and composite rafter flitches, clad in reclaimed Douglas fir.

Diffused light bathes the steam shower through the translucent acrylic panel, borrowing light from the clerestory windows above. It opens onto a private deck offering an outdoor showering experience. Bar cabinetry is hidden within the wooden volumes behind slatted doors, with interiors lined with birch plywood and flexible metro shelving to create an elegant and uncluttered space. Sustainable design practices are evident: passive solar heating, natural cross-ventilation, reclaimed Douglas fir, seventy five percent recycled steel content, non off-gassing foamed-in-place insulation, no VOC paints and high performance low E-glazing and recycled compact appliances and plumbing fixtures.

Integrated into the landscape, this simple shelter provides the family with an easily accessible retreat, immersing them as participants in the beauty of the seasonal changes in nature.

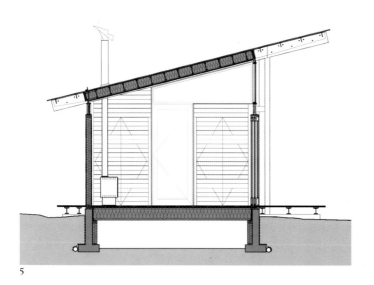

5

6

5 Building section
6 Covered deck at north end of pavilion
7 Detail of flitch rafter and steel tee purlins at eave
8 Plywood paneled ceiling plane floats over Ipe-clad boxes
9 Lift-slide doors roll back to allow open air space
10 Translucent ceiling panel borrows natural light for Ipe-lined shower

PHOTOGRAPHY: BRIAN KORTE

8

7

10

9

1   Site plan
Opposite:
     Northwest corner

KANNER ARCHITECTS

Canyon View Office / Guesthouse

Los Angeles, California, USA

20

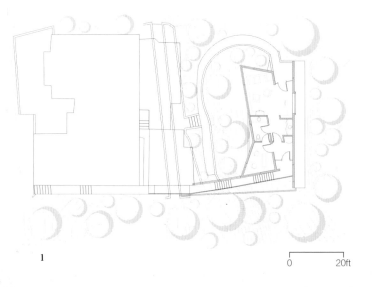

1

0   20ft

Located on a lush hillside behind a main residence, this small structure housing a psychologist's office/guesthouse is just a few steps away from home yet it feels like a protected sanctuary.

Solving the problem of an ever-frustrating commute, this home-office offers both privacy and convenience while enhancing the property's value. It also doubles as a guesthouse for visiting friends or family.

The owners insisted on a minimalist design: flexible, modern, and private but also warm and contextual. The structure's highly articulated form is composed of a series of angled cedar wall planes. Breaking the box into a series of angled walls allows the building to more effectively blend into its environment.

Each plan angle responds to room function, view corridors, light quality, and programmatic flexibility. The waiting room can also double as a guest room and has its own entrance. The main office space also has its own entrance and it can double as a living room. Both spaces have abundant views to the eucalyptus trees and lush landscape. A bathroom, entrance closet and small kitchenette round out the program.

Interiors are simple and take a back seat to the views framed by the large wood-trimmed windows. Staying with the natural palette of materials expressed on the exterior, the interior floors are maple. Ceilings, doors, windows and cabinetry are vertical grain Douglas fir. Walls are simple white painted drywall and lighting is suspended below the wood purlins on stainless steel cable tracks.

The new landscaping, steps and site walls tie in with the materials used elsewhere on the site. Broken concrete steps and retaining walls, bamboo hedges, red flax, liriope shrubs and young eucalyptus trees will one day mature to create a seamless blend with their older counterparts.

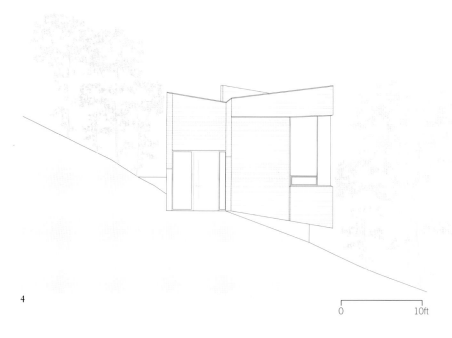

4

0   10ft

3   Patients' entrance
4   North elevation
5   Office/living room

23

5

6

8

7

6   Office
7   Bathroom
8   Stair leading to patients' entrance

Photography: John Linden

1 Top floor plan
Opposite:
  Arcadian fern glade with views toward south elevation and
  glazed box staircase

SCOTT CARVER ARCHITECTS

Carver Residence

MacMasters Beach,
New South Wales, Australia

26

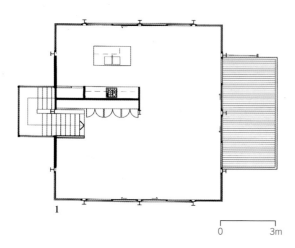

1

```
0          3m
```

Situated between a national park and the Pacific Ocean, the Carver Residence at MacMasters Beach is the modernist glass 'box' that makes the most emphatic site connection. Set amid lush forest and fern glade, the house soars into the bush canopy from its lightweight steel frame.

Although part of a suburban/rural growth 'belt', the house adopts a classic 'fishbowl' view of its surrounds. While neighbouring houses are part of the mass-market brick and tile anchored to bench-cut sites, the Carver Residence is pure tree house.

Inspired by a visit to Philip Johnston's seminal glass house at New Canaan, Connecticut architect Malcolm Carver has introduced his own searing minimalism to this Arcadian coastal site. Around one-and-a-half hours drive north of Sydney this exercise in rigour and restraint is sheathed in lustrous, self-cleaning glass and is the antithesis of adornment and high style.

Paying deference to the steeply inclined forest environment, the house sits lightly on its 10 galvanized structural-steel footings to allow the rapid reclamation of the site by native flora and fauna. The house has a modest footprint of 9 square meters (29 square feet), yet feels much bigger because of its transparency and free-flowing spatial arrangement.

The house has a total floor area of 163 square meters (1755 square feet) and has four double bedrooms with two bathrooms on the first level, with a connecting glass boxed staircase on the south elevation. The upper level contains the kitchen, dining/living area and balconies.

Its crisp, seamless exterior and the absence of eaves and roof gutters minimizes leaf and debris accumulation, vital against bushfires and virtually eliminates painting and maintenance. The galvanized

3

4

5

6

7

steel frame has already developed a tree-trunk patina that enables it to dissolve into its setting. By day the house reflects surrounding forest and sky and by dusk it becomes a lantern.

Complementing the floor-to-ceiling glass and outside/inside attitude, large sliding doors provide a free flow of cooling sea breezes and bush scent. Projecting balconies on the north entry elevation abut soaring eucalypts and angophoras. Filtered summer sun splinters through the treetops while winter light is trapped by the glazed expanses. Because of its elevation and bush setting, concealed internal roller blinds are rarely required for privacy or solar control. A slow combustion heater provides winter warmth.

The true 'tree house' nature of the house is best observed from the upper level where a great Australian landscape 'canvas' is created. The architect's rigorously framed image of pearly tree trunks and ocean views merge in this virtuoso example of careful craft as uplifting experience.

29

3   Every room receives priority treatment in its relationship to place
4   Meals preparation and kitchen with view south and west
5   Living room with frameless floor-to-ceiling glass looking east and south
6   Easterly view toward MacMaster's Beach and the Pacific. Lantern view at dusk when artificial light is finally required
7   Main entry facing north

PHOTOGRAPHY: PETER HYATT

1 Summer house in forest
2 Perspective
3 Rear view; outer room divides the house into two parts
4 Window slats at rear allow filtration of light at night
5 Conservation of trees is high priority. Trees border the very
 edge of the house.

PHOTOGRAPHY: TODD SAUNDERS AND TOMMIE WILHELMSEN (1); MICHAEL DAVIES (3–5)

TODD SAUNDERS & TOMMIE WILHELMSEN

Fritidsbolig

Åland, Finland

30

This summerhouse is situated on a group of islands in the Baltic Sea north of Stockholm. The 452-square-foot (42-square-meter) wooden house is in a small pine forest, 43 yards (40 meters) from the sea.

The objective of the design is to create a clear folding structure that moves up, down, over, and under through various spaces, creating fluidity through all areas of the house: the walls, floor, roof, roof garden, stair, and living spaces.

The house can be opened onto the outside room between the kitchen and bedroom to create one large room. This level provides views through to the pine forest beyond. From the top of the roof a panoramic view over the many islands around Åland unfolds.

A number of factors make this house environmentally responsible. The house is insulated with woven linseed fibers and all the wood is protected with cold-pressed linseed oil. All materials are from a local sawmill. The house is built upon pillars so that the natural landscape and tree roots will be preserved.

One of the most striking aspects of this house is its ingenious utilization of space. In opening all the glass doors to form one space for larger groups of people, the house assumes a multifunctional role. One can have breakfast on the terrace enjoying the morning sun; 20 people can sit along the front of the cabin watching the sunset or just as easily, dining facilities can be provided outside on the floor between the bedroom and the 'common room'. The idea was to create a space the architects had little control over but rather, invited the people using the space to express themselves as freely and creatively as they could imagine. A house without borders, is in many ways endless, and therefore always has a positive impact.

1

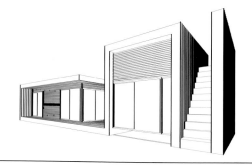

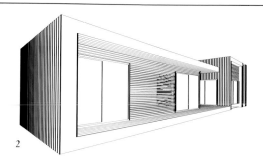

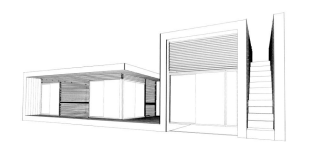
2

4

5

3

1   View from north at dusk with beacon tower
Opposite:
     North face reflecting in lap pool

DUC ASSOCIATES PTY LTD

Hermitage Road Residence

Hunter Valley, New South Wales, Australia

1

This home, set on a rural vine-growing property in the Hunter Valley has been designed to satisfy the needs of the client and the criteria created by its site.

It was intended that the building should sit lightly on the site and reflect the nature of the terrain. The slope of the site helped generate the exterior of the house. The slope was further accentuated by veranda columns at right angles. Entry is expressed as a bridge, and leads in a direct line to the gallery, which accesses all areas of the house.

The home has a post-and-beam structural system allowing internal and external change with minimal disturbance and reuse of the building components. Internal and external walls are modular and panelized. Services remain flexible to permit addition of new technologies or to retrofit at any time without major works. The building is designed to be low maintenance, with pre-finished components such as metal lined insulated sandwich panels, hot-dip galvanized structural members, and polished concrete floors.

The design intention is to provide a climatic environment, which evens out the extremes in temperatures experienced in the area. This intention is achieved using a number of strategies: The Ultra Floor method, while permitting speed in construction, gives a polished finish to ensure that solar control engenders passive thermal results. Floors are exposed to the solar rays in winter, and protected in summer by both roof and blade overhangs.

Full–height louvers to the gallery may be adjusted to allow or preclude solar access. The same louvers may be adjusted to allow the flow of air at a high level to exhaust through the louvers in the north wall.

Airflow can be accelerated by drawing air over a pond on the south side of the house and introducing pressurized airflow through floor vents. The same vents

carry conditioned air or air variations controlled by a building management system. In winter the gallery acts as a buffer air space. The south walls are glazed and set at a 10-degree angle to prevent reflections at night, thus preserving the view. The south wall is double-glazed.

The roof of the house has two insulated skins; 'papst' fans draw in and expel air to ventilate the void. The internal skin to the roof is an insulated sandwich panel with a pre-finished steel skin. The panels span the structural module.

Cross-flow ventilation is provided to all spaces. The east and west walls are the shortest and have few openings. The house is sited just below the crest of a substantial rise on the property. Over the rise to the north is the Great Northern Railway Line, and earth mounds have been placed on the north rise to protect the house from train-generated noise and to create wind protection for the lap pool.

Varying glimpses of the house are offered on approach from the entry to the property. The sense of arrival is heightened at night, provided by a softly illuminated water tower at the entry to the house. The tower enables some energy-free water pressure pumped from the under floor water tanks which are replenished by the roof catchment system. The tower also enables communication through satellite access and allows the building management system to collect and send data.

3

3   Insect screen enclosed deck
4   View from west
5   Cross section

4

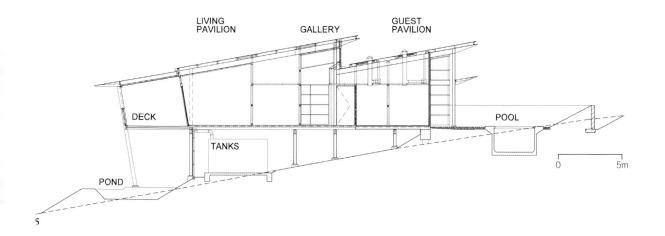

LIVING PAVILION · GALLERY · GUEST PAVILION · DECK · TANKS · POOL · POND

0   5m

5

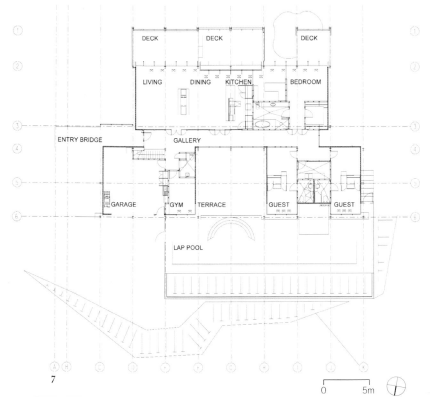

DECK   DECK   DECK

LIVING   DINING   KITCHEN   BEDROOM

ENTRY BRIDGE   GALLERY

GARAGE   GYM   TERRACE   GUEST   GUEST

LAP POOL

7

0   5m

Opposite:
    Kitchen; overhead unit above bench
    houses lighting and sliding glass
    track that separates kitchen from
    dining room
7   Main floor plan
8   Gallery
9   Pool terrace

8

9

10   View from north
11   House and lap pool with guest pavilion in the foreground

PHOTOGRAPHY: PETER HYATT

1   View looking north toward house with Squaw Peak mountain in
the distance
Opposite:
     View from entry to study/kitchen and living room bridge beyond

Alta Vista Park is a small residential enclave of architecturally distinctive modern houses including several Frank Lloyd Wright residences. The desert site is still only minutes from the urban core of Phoenix, Arizona.

Although primarily low and flat, the site offers dramatic views to the nearby Squaw Peak Mountains to the north and distant eastward views to Camelback Mountain. Native palo verde and ironwood trees; a few barrel cacti and a field of creosote bushes sparsely vegetate this arid suburban desert parcel.

The House of Earth and Light combines heavy, archaic desert walls with an ethereal and luminous lightweight fabric roof, capturing the abundance of desert light while mitigating its harsher climatic impact. The tension between heavy and light and between mass and space is a key conceptual strategy for this residence.

The solidity of the earthbound walls contrasts with the gossamer-like roof. Undulating gently between the metal trusses, a 'sky-painting' is created from the roof with its constant filtration of light and shadow. This concept was realized in the hope of creating a modern, elegant tent in the desert; one that attempts to open up for contemporary development in what the architect refers to as the 'fifth façade'.

The house is designed to bridge over a shallow, densely foliaged 'arroyo', or dry stream bed. This wash bisects the site and provides a cool, quiet place simulating a natural desert oasis harboring animal and plant life that includes small birds, jackrabbits and desert trees. The main living and dining room project directly over the wash to blend in with the natural life of the desert and take advantage of the natural breezes that flow through.

MARWAN AL SAYED ARCHITECTS

House of Earth and Light

Phoenix, Arizona, USA

40

3 Site plan
4 View of living room bridge over dry 'arroyo' wash
5 View from kitchen to living room bridge
6 View from kitchen

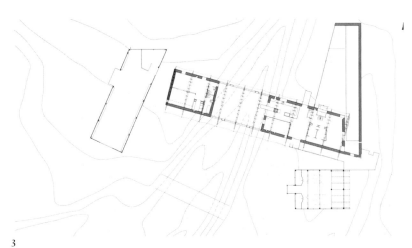

3

42

4

5

Emerging from poured-in-place concrete stem walls are thick 18-inch-wide (45.5-centimeter) poured earth walls. The thick solid walls contrast sharply with the lightweight fabric roof. A ventilated glass and steel bridge spans the wash oasis and is anchored by the monolithic walls forming the two main volumes on opposite sides of the wash. The poured earth volumes incorporate the entry, study, kitchen, bedrooms, and bathrooms.

All window and doorframes, steel trusses, and wall partitions, cabinetry and some light fixtures are custom-designed; additionally there is a custom glass tile and terrazzo entry floor, and cast glass bathroom sinks.

The furniture designed for the house includes an 8-foot-long (2.5-meter) magenta cast glass desk with American walnut cabinetry situated near the entry in the study. All custom cast colored glass work was carried out by Marwan's wife and glass artist Mies Grybaitis.

7

8

9

10

7 Night view from living room back to entry
8 Study and entry
9 Night view of lap pool outside master bedroom
10 View from master bedroom to pool beyond

PHOTOGRAPHY: BILL TIMMERMANN

1 Floor plan
Opposite:
    View from north

Located in the midst of a grove of red pines with heights exceeding 65 feet (20 meters) the House To Catch The Forest is a cottage that appears to be suspended. The underbrush is dotted with patches of sunlight filtered through the dense treetops. The owners, a married couple, used photographs to document the site's shifting transitions through the seasons.

In summer, the numerous trees surrounding the area obstruct the horizon and the ground is humid and covered with insects. Winter temperatures in this region can reach –68 °F (–20 °C) with a thick blanket of snow on the ground.

Taking advantage of the setting, the house was slightly elevated and designed to provide views of the treetops. A mountain and a flowing river are visible from the house, and looking higher through the tree trunks, a ridge of the mountain and the sky are visible. Because the walls and the roof are not parallel, resulting views are sliced. From under the eaves, the green landscape unfolds toward the valley.

The orientation of the valley dictated the building of the tube-like structure. The 16-foot (5-meter) ceiling traps the summer wind underneath it. The steep roof, built without a gutter, merges with the walls. Its sharp inclination prevents the accumulation of snow and falling larch leaves.

The unique setting of the house is made for simple living. The interior is almost totally devoid of partitions, although walls can be installed on both sides of the bathroom, if needed. Simple lines around the core of the house define the space that combines an atelier, bedroom, living, and dining room. The center core provides privacy despite the absence of partitions. The result is a seamless environment where reading, resting or taking a bath can be enjoyed within a single space. Heating is provided from an under-floor system.

Tezuka Architects & Masahiro Ikeda co ltd

House to Catch
the Forest

Chino-shi, Nagano, Japan

46

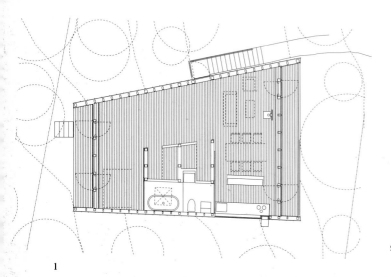

1

3

3   Cottage appears to float in forest. Roof tilt optimises view of treetops
4   View from north
5   Interior is one large space; kitchen, dining, living and atelier areas surround the center storage space

4

The varying ceiling heights facilitate aspects of everyday life. The bathroom ceiling goes down to 5 feet (1.5 meters), imparting a sense of intimacy to that area of the house, while a skylight above the bathtub permits views of the sky and surrounding trees.

The bedroom is also located under the lowest part of the roof, but its direct connection to the vast space of the atelier prevents feelings of confinement. The ceiling above the atelier is 4 meters (13 feet) high and the wide fiberglass-reinforced wall provides a space for creative activities. The volume above the living room, which faces the forest, is the largest.

The House to Catch the Forest attempts to merge the concepts of a multifunctional interior with a space that embraces the surrounding landscape.

5

6

50

7

8

6   Section of site

7   View toward entrance

8   Bathroom is separated from bedroom by sliding door

9   View from living area toward dining room and kitchen

Photography: Katsuhisa Kida

9

1 Site plan
2 Partial rear elevation at night

Located in the Big Sur area of Northern California, this 2,500-square-foot (232-square-meter) two bedroom house was built for a family to enjoy together on the weekends and holidays.

It is a modernist structure that sits lightly on the land, acknowledging the ecologically fragile nature of the site. Ten different consultants worked three and a half years to satisfy all the requirements of the local governing agencies that would have preferred to leave the site as it was—overgrown and uninhabited.

The house is composed of four volumes, all made of different materials, which are interwoven and interconnected to create visually and spatially complex exterior and interior spaces.

The steep walls of the canyon dominate the wooded site next to a creek. The house holds its own in this tall and cavernous place, neither dominating nor dwarfed by it. The main volume of the house runs parallel to the canyon with a butterfly roof and glass corners that reach out to the sky and the light at the open ends. The thin roof sits delicately above a band of extruded glass, connecting to the roof structure with thin rods, invisible on the exterior. At the corners of the

Fougeron Architecture

Jackson Family Retreat

Big Sur, California, USA

52

1 Redwood Grove
2 Road
3 Creek

1

0   64ft

3

4

3   View down canyon from level 2 deck
4   Front elevation
5   Front elevation at night
6   View across bridge to library
7   View across living area to kitchen

5

6

house, two-story clear windows frame the views of the redwoods and the sky at the ridge of the canyon. This volume is clad in standing seam copper.

On the front, the second volume is a single-story structure that includes all the service functions for the house and acts as buffer from the dirt road, which leads to the other houses in this old subdivision. It is clad in yellow Alaskan cedar that is turned in three directions acting as a rain screen, a fence, and a railing. The material is left untreated so it will age naturally, becoming silvery gray.

The back of the house is open to views of the creek with a custom steel and glass volume inspired by the glass conservatories of the 19th century. The fourth volume of the staircase is both the seismic structural brace for the house and a visual foil to the shimmering and transparent volumes surrounding it. It is clad with gray integral color stucco that wraps inside and out.

On the ground floor, two bedrooms at opposing ends of the house enclose in the middle the two-story communal living space. This space comprises the fireplace room—a homage to the architecture of Bernard Maybeck—and the loft library above. The 15-foot-high (4.5-meter) windows in the bedrooms dissolve the corners of the spaces, bringing light and views into the bedroom and living spaces of the house.

55

On the second floor, the space is open, with the library and communal sleeping room separated by glass panels from the two-story bedrooms below.

A combination of transparent glass and extruded channel glass reflects and dapples the light on the inside, creating an ever-changing interior with a warm play of light and shadow throughout the day.

7

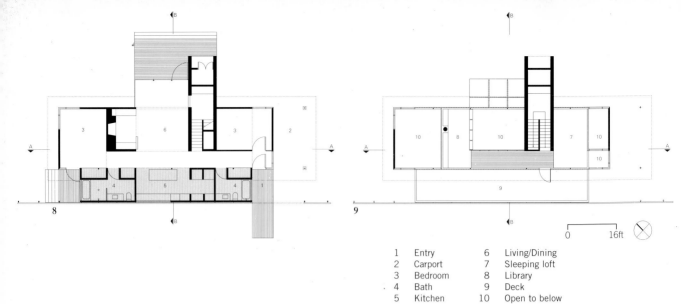

1	Entry	6	Living/Dining
2	Carport	7	Sleeping loft
3	Bedroom	8	Library
4	Bath	9	Deck
5	Kitchen	10	Open to below

8   Level 1 floor plan
9   Level 2 floor plan
10 Living area from stair landing above
11 Master bedroom

PHOTOGRAPHY: RICHARD BARNES

56

10

1   Projection wall
2   Swimming pool
3   Front entrance

LORCAN O'HERLIHY ARCHITECTS

Jai House

Santa Monica, California, USA

58

Sitting on a gentle slope overlooking the Santa Monica Mountains, the Jai House is a study of the interaction between building and landscape and celebrates 'architecture of removal' by stripping away spatial excess, revealing an authenticity of construction and craft.

The building is designed to blur the boundary between landscape and structure. The primary level, which houses the main public space, is conceived as a linear bar that acts as a buffer to Mulholland Highway. This level engages the earth at one end and floats above the landscape at the other, opening completely to the views of the canyon beyond. The primary level houses the living, dining, kitchen, two bedrooms, yoga studio, and outdoor rooms. Extending the interaction between inside and outside is a 75-foot (22-meter) lap pool that slides through the building and public spaces. The pool and deck are an extension of the living room.

The upper volume, which is at a 90-degree angle to the primary level, houses the master bedroom suite that frames the view toward the Santa Monica Mountains. The bathroom area is open to the master bedroom.

The client's brief stipulated that the house include space for exclusive yoga retreats. The yoga room is at the east end of the house and is separated by an outdoor room, seamlessly engaging the interior design. The exterior material of the primary level is smooth-troweled plaster with glass walls. The upper level is also smooth-troweled plaster but with a dark coffee-bean color.

1

2

3

4

5

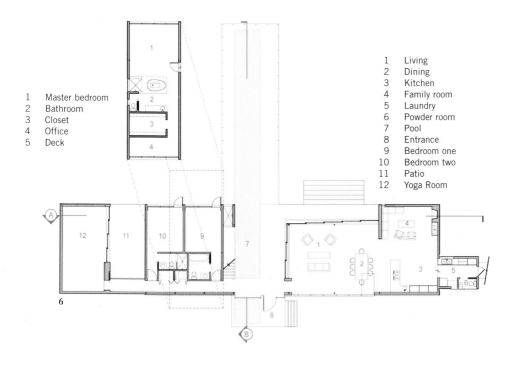

1   Master bedroom
2   Bathroom
3   Closet
4   Office
5   Deck

1   Living
2   Dining
3   Kitchen
4   Family room
5   Laundry
6   Powder room
7   Pool
8   Entrance
9   Bedroom one
10   Bedroom two
11   Patio
12   Yoga Room

7

8

4   Rear entrance
5   Living room
6   Floor plan
7   Exterior shower
8   Interior chair

PHOTOGRAPHY: JOHN COOLIDGE

1   Dual pavilions viewed from northwest
2   View of farmhouse from south

This simple farmhouse located on a low ridge, on a sprawling 148-acre (60-hectare) property overlooks the river flats and billabongs of the Ovens River. It is a working property where the owner takes a keen interest and a hands-on role in the running of an efficient, small-scale beef cattle farm. The farmsheds represent an integral part of this activity and form part of the main structure.

An intriguing building that is almost obscured from the controlled arrival sequence, it only truly reveals itself once the visitor is captivated by its prominent location and has explored its spaces. The planning is simple and develops a strong connection with both the immediate and distant landscapes.

The external skin uses the simple concept of a tent fly. Sliding screens allow the building to be manipulated to respond naturally to rapidly changing climatic conditions. The major axis of the building (north and south along the ridge) creates long walls to both the eastern and western aspects. Perforated metal screens that match the wall profile slide across all window openings in these façades and can be manipulated to respond directly to seasonal swings.

The Kerrisdale Farmhouse is adaptable to the changing seasons. The sliding screens ensure the building can be closed up and secured assuming the persona of a nondescript shed when the owners are away. The concrete slab provides the building with a basic thermal mass as the background to the easily manipulated skin system. The mechanical equipment is only required to deal with the extremes.

The reasons for going into the bush are reinforced by the spirit of the building that embodies oneness with nature. It is a serene house to be in because it is at peace with its location and can be manipulated to respond to the changing external climate through natural systems.

COL BANDY ARCHITECTS

Kerrisdale Farmhouse

Yea, Victoria, Australia

62

1

64

3

3   Kitchen/dining area
4   Entry looking northward
5   Site plan

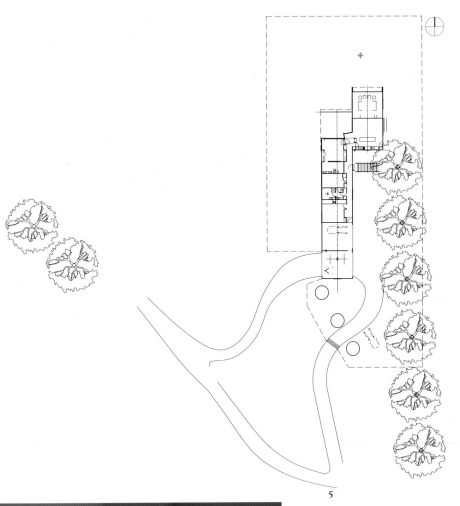

65

6   Lounge
7   Main veranda
8   Kitchen

7

8

9

68

9   Bathroom
10   Main bedroom
11   View of main bedroom from veranda

Photography: Peter Hyatt

10

1 Site plan
2 Steel frames cantilever over sloping ground projecting
   a sense of the house hovering over the landscape

The genesis of the Kropach/Catlow Farmouse is the small rural agricultural structures found throughout the farming landscape of Australia. A simple repeating portal frame, direct fixed steel cladding and elementary roof form for rainwater collection, characterize these structures. Scattered over the land, glinting in the sun with their silver patina marking the land in ad hoc composition, these structures with their rudimentary rectangular plan and section allow for a multitude of functions: tractor accommodation, shelter from the storm, winter housing, animals or hay bale storage. Whatever their function, these 'tin sheds' are embedded in the collective memory of Australian bush-dwellers.

The house is conceived as a platform, or more correctly, a veranda in the landscape. The veranda is fundamental to the culture of Australian housing—it is a place of transition—from outside to inside, from sunlight to shade, from public to private, and from the vastness of the landscape to the intimacy of the room. The plan is linear with the bedrooms to the east and living spaces to the west. This linear arrangement allows all rooms to face north toward the sun. The living spaces are framed with sliding glass doors to all sides to enable the veranda to extend spatially beyond the house.

GROSE BRADLEY ARCHITECTS

Kropach/Catlow Farmhouse

Byron Bay, New South Wales, Australia

70

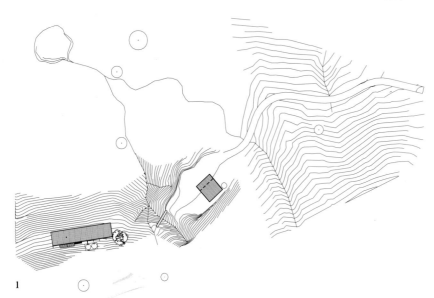

1

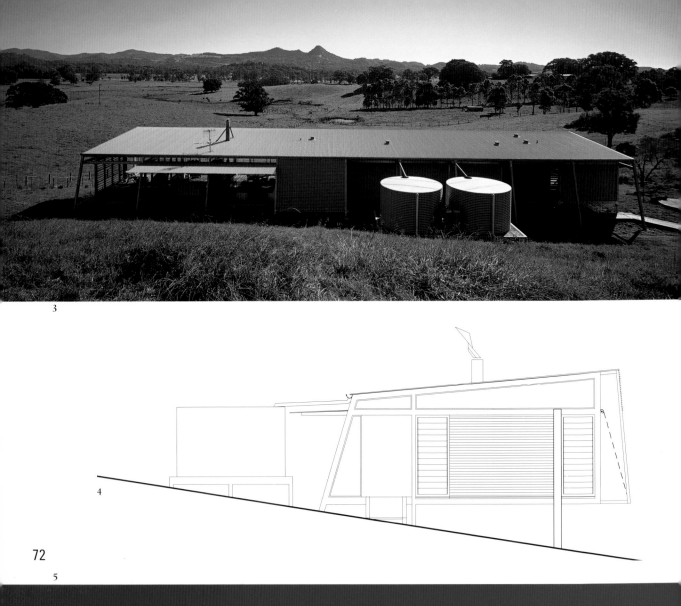

3

4

5

The sun control to the north is moderated by fixed aluminum angles spaced to allow winter sunshine deep into the house and to exclude the more intense summer sun. Along the length of the north elevation are external adjustable planar blinds, translucent and reflective to ensure the north sun heat is deflected. The translucency provides daylight illumination inside. These sun control devices are located in an inclined zone perpendicular to the roof pitch.

Rainwater is delivered to the steel corrugated tanks via the skillion roof's direct water collection at the lower edge of the roof.

The architecture relies upon the articulation of detail to ensure that the vision of an overly simplistic shed is avoided. It is the romantic Arcadian context that allows an architecture of authenticity; utility blended and working with the landscape.

6

3   Monoslope roof allows rainwater to be collected and stored
4   East elevation
5   View from north
6   Wide glass façades effortlessly merge outside with inside

7   Floor plan
8   Kitchen opens to view
9   View from bedroom
10   Hall
11   Main bathroom
Following pages:
    Living room

PHOTOGRAPHY: PETER HYATT

7

74

8

1 South elevation
2 South view
3 East terrace
4 East elevation

Modeled by the last glacial stage and the retreat of the Champlain Sea waters, this region is a boundless plain of rich soil known as the St Lawrence Lowlands. The clients were delighted at the view of this site, edged by a river and dominated by a dense pine forest. Its landform was formed over time by the flow of the river. The site is accessible through the plain and a gentle grade leads to a wooded plateau before reaching the river. On the riverside, a small glade covered with ferns adds to this scenic beauty.

The project layout required a minimum distance of 100 feet (30 meters) from the high water position of the river. Water supply is provided by an artesian well. An environmentally friendly wastewater treatment system using bacteria to filter and degrade water impurities is used.

The clients wanted a country house. As art collectors, they expressed the desire to have great spaces in which their pieces can be exhibited. They were also sensitive to the idea of furnishing the house with sculptural elements.

The flexible plan has three distinct parts: a privacy zone, a public zone and, between the two, a circulation zone.

The privacy zone includes the master bedroom and bathroom, the kitchen, and a shared bathroom. The generous fenestration offers plenty of brightness and permeability to those spaces and opens onto a large peripheral porch. A veranda overhung with ferns supports the indoor/outdoor harmony joining the kitchen and a winter garden. A lightweight roof seems to be floating over that privacy zone.

PIERRE THIBAULT ARCHITECTE

Les Abouts Residence

Saint-Edmond-de-Grantham, Québec, Canada

78

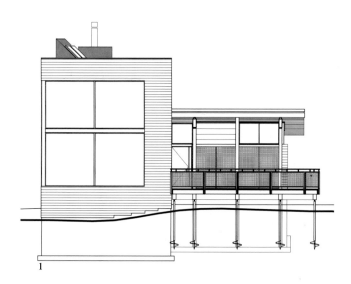

1

2

3

4

5

The public zone includes the living room, a library, and the guest rooms. This large two-story volume will be the receptacle for works of art. The guest rooms and the library sculpt the space: the rooms hang from the roof in a cubic volume and the circular-shaped library is perched up on steel stilts.

Wood is largely used: structurally for the clerestory framing walls and the post-and-beam system; and aesthetically for its warmth and mellowness, inside as well as outside. In total, interior spaces occupy 2500 square feet (232 square meters).

5   Entrance patio
6   East view
7   Main entrance
8   Roof plan
9   First floor plan
10   Ground floor plan

PHOTOGRAPHY: ALAIN LAFOREST

6

7

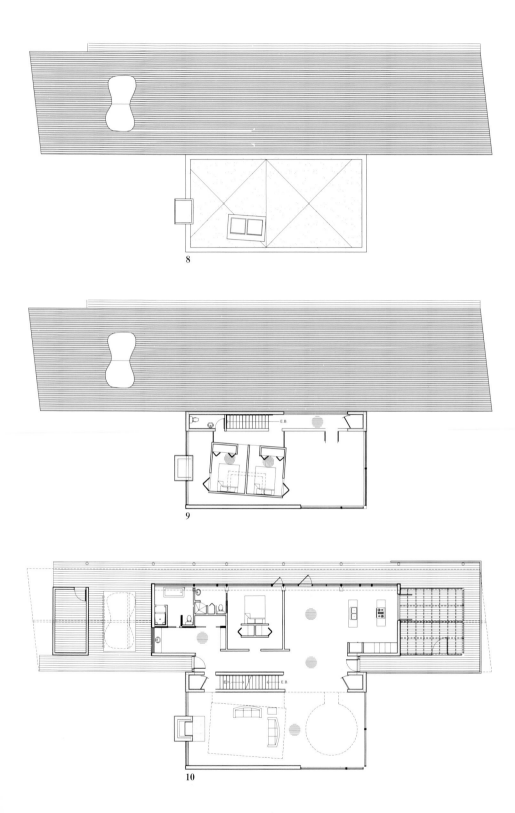

8

9

10

1   View out of living room with operable walls
Opposite:
    Exterior view of living room

DAVID LUCK ARCHITECTURE

Lookout House
at Red Hill

Red Hill, Mornington Peninsula,
Victoria, Australia

82

1

Lookout House is located on the Victorian Mornington Peninsula, one hour's drive from metropolitan Melbourne through the flat southeastern suburbs and up the slow rise into Red Hill. Across the Arthurs Seat escarpment the journey ends in a gravel and leaf-strewn driveway. Along the boardwalk, a glimpse of Port Phillip Bay beckons. Once inside the dwelling, the view from the ramp is delightful although obstructed by a detached section of the building toward the fully glazed end.

The glass skin is punctured by a steel bridge that leads into the main room, twisted on axis to true north and on axis back to the city of Melbourne. Window openings in this room are on all the cardinal points. The large solid tectonic wall and floor planes are tilted and open. The use of plate glass, steel sheets and sliding walls accentuate the modernist theme

Behind the minimalist object, a sense of intellect, hope, and the spirit of Australia pervades. The exterior's black walls blend with the darkness of the night and merge with the black walls of the interior. The interior's artificial lighting has an exaggerated theatrical effect.

The Lookout House unites the ancient landscape with modern Australia. The ramp is symbolic of the culmination of the journey from the city, and also acts as an enclosed veranda linking and opening up to the functional rooms on the east and shutting out the sun's heat from the west. A *tatami*-proportioned and spatially still bedroom cantilevers out to the east. The ceilings, bed canopy and bed laying space are of the dimensions of the sleeping body. Sliding doors delineate the platform edge against the native grasses and wildflowers outside. A 26-foot-long (8-meter) glass meter box kitchen becomes an aquarium workspace for living, invoking a sense of being at one with nature, under the tree canopies. The main room with mixed living, dining, bedroom and terrace functions is at the end of the ramp. Movable walls with inbuilt sofas expand and contract, exploding the myth of 'lifestyle lounge suite concepts'.

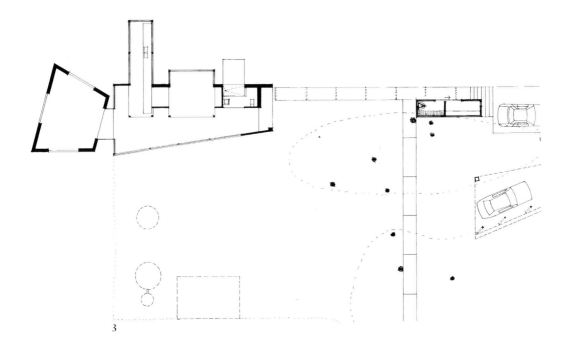

3

4

3 Plan
4 Front entry
5 West elevation with minimal glazing

5

8

Opposite:
    View from top of ramp into living room
7   View from top of ramp looking into kitchen and bedroom
8   View from top of ramp looking back toward entry
Following pages:
    East elevation

PHOTOGRAPHY: PETER HYATT

7

1   Site plan
Opposite:
      Courtyard entrance with cantilevered soffits

KANNER ARCHITECTS

Malibu House 3

Malibu Hills, California, USA

1

```
0          50ft
```

While he chose the name *Simpatico Sem*, a mix of Italian and Tibetan which intimates the spiritual blending of mind and soul, the owner of this 4,200-square-foot (390 square-meter) modern home in the hills of Malibu, California, might just as well have named it Phoenix. This would describe how the home rose and today stands majestically on the very site where the same owner lost his home in the great Malibu fire of 1994, 10 years before.

Essentially two cubes linked by a staircase, the house's simplicity counters the complexity and wildness of the surrounding rugged hills. The house's extruded modernist composition is a reaction to many conditions of the project: the site's linear topography; a desire for massive window openings to take in spectacular views of mountains immediately outside, and the ocean in the distance; the need for fire resistance (no overhangs, tile exterior); a requirement for xeriscape, and client/architect preference.

The stair and breezeway connect the two-part plan, with kitchen and garage areas on the south end, living room and study placed on the opposite end. Bedrooms are upstairs with descending canyon views. The house is positioned to receive maximum sunlight with expansive windows in all rooms. From the master bedroom, the client has vistas of the mountains, canyons and the ocean beyond.

A mere 25 feet (7.6 meters) wide, the building's lean profile provides excellent cross-ventilation of abundant sea breezes. The layered composition of the west elevation allows for large dual-glazed openings with numerous projections designed to shade the glass.

The home's interior is a blend of cool and warm. The main floor, with its common spaces, has a floor of concrete pavers. The bedrooms upstairs are carpeted. The presence of marble (white, blue and matt-black) and cherry on both levels tie together the whole.

The home's stark contrast to the site is intentional – it is an honest expression of its resilience. It is an object subject to immense weather conditions, fires, winds, floods – it is a home designed to observe and view nature and never again be consumed by it.

3

3   View west toward entry courtyard
4   Dining room
5   South façade at dusk, zen garden in foreground

4

5

6

6   Kitchen with center island
7   Master bedroom with terrace
8   Living room, stainless steel and concrete fireplace
9   West and east elevations
Following pages:
    Courtyard, view south toward Pacific Ocean

Photography: John Linden

8

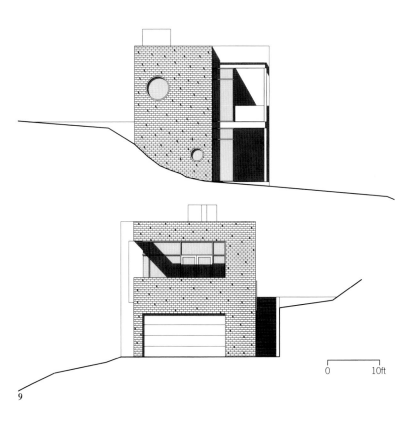

9

0   10ft

1   Site plan
2   Pool house bath interior

Across several levels of broad lawn from a rambling
1950s post-and-beam house at the foot of the San
Gabriel Mountains stands an old stable. Its weathered
redwood boards and battens, deep with the grooves of
age, recall the dusty corral that once adjoined it.

The corral gone, a cool blue pool now rests, punched
into the plane of a concrete deck. Crisp and modern,
rectangle upon rectangle, the deck and pool reside
in a clearing of a deodar cedar grove. The pool is
visible from the house, but remains distinctly
detached from the hospitality that it represents.
A new owner with a busy entertaining agenda
devised a strategy to bridge the gap between
house and pool.

The architects introduced another rectangle,
perpendicular to the pool, to address the house.
A floating wooden egg-crate trellis intersects the far
end of the barn. This now shares the spotlight with
the pool, and defines a shady dining spot. The
trellis also overhangs the pool's deep end where
a plastered bench allows one to relax in the water
under semi-shade with a cool drink within reach.

A section of the old barn interior was transformed
into guest quarters. A polished concrete floor sets
off the drywall, closet, and daybed. A simple
kitchen was introduced. Everything was in place
to satisfy the guest except for a bathroom.

With the most minimal alteration to structure, the
architects created an L-shaped space with a skin
of salvaged, obscured, glass panes fitted into a
structure of canted shelves and notched struts,
and capped with a band of frameless clear glass.
A corrugated steel roof free-spans from the rear barn
wall to the fascia board.

Fᴜɴɢ + Bʟᴀᴛᴛ Aʀᴄʜɪᴛᴇᴄᴛꜱ

Maunu Poolhouse

Altadena, California, USA

98

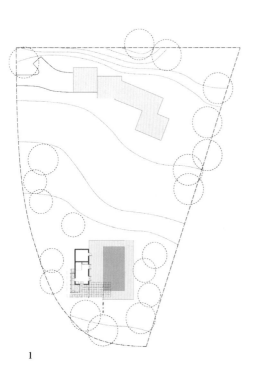

1

As no sewer line or septic system is within reach, an incinerating toilet is used with gray water drainage for the sink and shower. Exposed copper piping supplies solar-heated water for the shower and sink. A layer of cement fiberboard and a sliding panel with a small amount of wood detail at the shower and sink complete the enclosure.

The play of light through the day and seasons filters through the translucent glass with foliage peeking under the corrugated ceiling. A light, lean, translucent, and breathing structure, the Maunu Poolhouse gently merges with the pool and as easily, with the forest-clearing setting.

3

4

3   Egg crate trellis over dining area and portion of pool
4   Pool house exterior with view of shower
5   Long view of pool house
6   Guest room interior

PHOTOGRAPHY: TIM STREET-PORTER (2, 4–6); ALICE FUNG (3)

5

This country house is on 11 acres (4.5 hectares) of land at Calera de Tango, southwest of Santiago.

The site is framed by views of the Andes to the east and coastal mountain ranges to the west and features abundant eucalypts and small fruit tress. The fruit trees served as inspiration for the architects in determining the levels of the house.

The house, which includes living room, dining room, two bedrooms, two bathrooms, sauna, basement and swimming pool, was designed for a couple with no children.

The architect's aim was to create a contrast between the land and the 'artificial' nature of the building by incorporating several volumes. The lower volume, a concrete box 3.2 feet (1 meter) high and 9 feet (2.7 meters) wide, houses the swimming pool and the basement and also serves as the house's foundation. Looking out over the treetops, the first volume contains the public rooms, including a geometrical structure made from glass and native alerce wood, derived from a large evergreen in the cypress family native to the Andes mountains. The second volume is of reinforced concrete.

FELIPE ASSADI ARQUITECTOS

Memoria Casa Schmitz

Calera de Tango, Chile

102

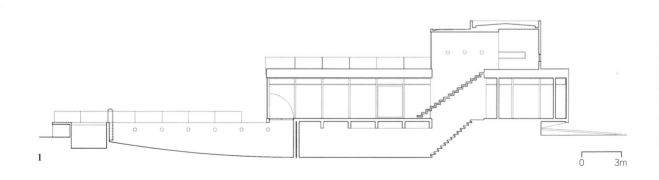

1

0   3m

1   Section showing three levels of house
2   Swimming pool

3   Kitchen; furniture allows
     communication with living room
4   West façade. Main room hangs over
     glass volume of living room
5   Main entrance over south façade
6   Glazed volume roof is also a terrace on
     the first floor
7   Second floor plan
8   First floor plan
9   Basement floor plan

3

4

5

6

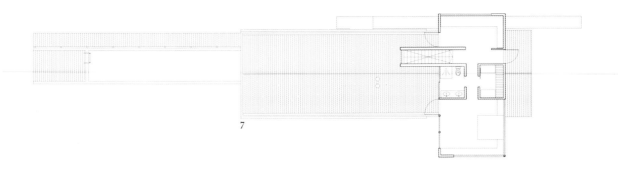

7

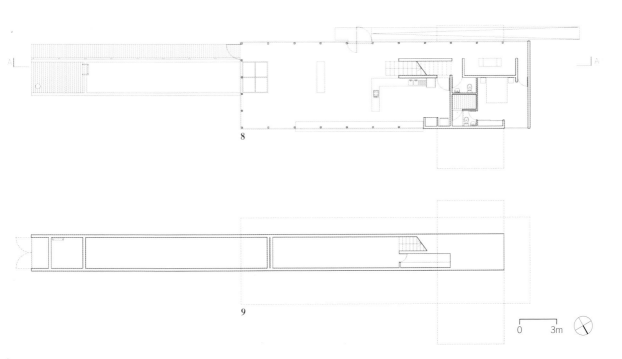

8

9

0   3m

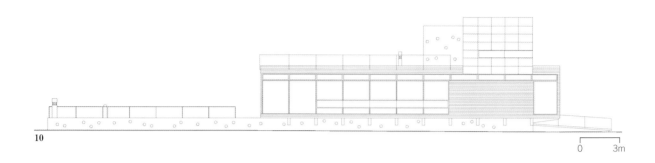

10

0 3m

11

12

13

10   North façade plan
11   North façade
12   Living room with view of pool ahead
13   Living room with forward views of
       kitchen and stairway

PHOTOGRAPHY: JUAN PURCELL

1   Full view of house
2   North elevation
Following pages:
    East elevation

One hour from Hiroshima city, this house with a studio was built for a family of three. Although there is an adjacent house on the west side, the Misonou House faces a rural landscape and benefits from being surrounded by fields in the other three directions.

The family's wish was to 'live in nature' as much as possible. To this end, elements of structure were compromised to accommodate opening the house to its environment. This is achieved, by the absence of corner pillars, creating a wider vista of uninterrupted space. The minimal structural elements promote a feeling of weightlessness: as if the house were suspended.

The definition between interior and exterior is treated as fully integrated rather than merely a scenic option for indoor life. The Misonou House uses a 'sash' style corner treatment without obvious reinforcement. There are few geometric materials and objects in the house to conform to the room shape, enhancing the sense of blending harmoniously with the environment, in this case, the surrounding fields. Once doors and windows are opened this sense is fully achieved as the veil that separates structure and nature is dissolved.

Thermal comfort is addressed in a number of ways. Easily ventilated in warmer months with large opening doors and windows, in winter the concrete floor's thermal mass provides valuable passive heating as low-angled sun penetrates from north, south, and west. A water-heated under-floor system, in combination with direct solar gain achieves efficient, year-round energy performance.

An unusually high degree of physical comfort and sensory pleasure is achieved by the combination of outdoor characteristics and indoor comfort. Using simple and direct energy management strategies, The Misonou House embraces nature deep into its existence.

SUPPOSE DESIGN OFFICE

Misonou House

Hiroshima, Japan

108

1

4

5

6

4   Toilet
5   Living room
6   Upper floor
7   Entry

PHOTOGRAPHY: NACASA & PARTNERS

113

7

Opposite:
    Detail of south façade

Built in the late 1930s, Podere 43 was part of a thorough reclamation project of the marshy areas of low-lying Maremma, in southern Tuscany in the province of Grosseto. The overall project envisaged building 45 identical and progressively numbered farmhouses, the typological pattern laid to Marcello Piacentini's design. Consisting of three functionally independent central cores, the biggest and main one was to be turned into the farmhouse, while the other two were to be used as a barn and a tool shed, with an oven, a pigpen, and a dovecote.

The site, the nature of pre-existing elements and the client's wishes dictated the overall arrangement of the 1-hectare (2.4-acre) estate and created a starting point for the analysis of the relationship between the architecture and the landscape.

The farmhouse is now the country house of a young couple with two children. Rather than use it just as a weekend residence, the requirement was also for a place to meet and gather with parents, friends, and relatives.

Almost the entire ground floor space of the house and the former barn serves as a communal area where family and friends interact, while the more secluded second floor where the bedrooms are located, offers privacy.

The project impacted on the three existing buildings in different ways: the farmhouse, the most complete and formal of all, and the only one suitable for living in, retained its historic character. The barn and shed were redefined completely, both becoming part of the landscape. The geometrical structure against a backdrop of ploughed fields conveys a feeling of merging the artificial with natural and outdoors with indoors.

LABICS ARCHITETTURA

Podere 43

Albinia, Grosseto, Italy

114

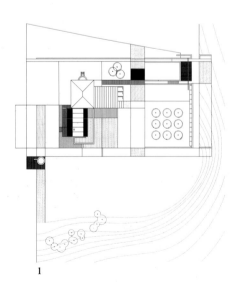

1

3

4

5

3 Living room wooden deck with fireplace
4 Elevation
5 Detail of pool
6 Entrance and car park

117

6

7   View of south façade and steam bath
8   View of living room facing kitchen
9   Section
10   Living room and winter garden

7

118

8

11   Section of fireplace
12   View of south façade
13   Guest annexe

Photography: Luigi Filetici

120

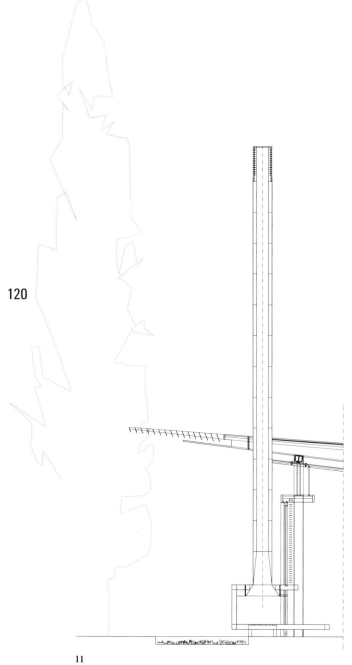

11

12

13

1   Axonometric perspective
2   House merges with surrounding trees
3   Structure is raised above ground level to impart
    a 'suspended' feeling

Nestled in woodlands beside one of Norway's most spectacular fjords, the architects built this cabin as a summer retreat for themselves and their friends. The site is a two-hour drive from Bergen in Hardanger, only 262 feet (80 metres) from the shoreline of the lake and only 32 yards (30 meters) from the forest, a stream, and a 98-feet (30-meter) high waterfall, and is accessed by crossing an old stone footbridge.

The site is also 262 feet (80 meters) above sea level, thus creating a dramatic relationship to the large fjord in front.

The purchase of the spectacularly beautiful site and the construction of the cabin were funded by the architects themselves to attract clients to their work. In this sense it is experimental, but it is also very popular. The result is a design that is, without compromise, an expression of Saunders' and Wilhelmsen's architectural vision.

The retreat was divided into two parts: one for eating and sleeping with another smaller room to be used for whatever the user desired. A long, narrow floating outdoor floor connects these two parts. This outdoor floor made the space twice as large by connecting the two buildings so that in the summer, one could walk barefoot from one building to the other. The front elevation faces the fjords and the inner space toward the mountains creates an area that can be complemented by a small fire in the evenings.

The architects put the structures together with added help from a carpenter. The house is environmentally friendly and is insulated with recycled newspapers. All the surrounding trees were conserved and integrated into the design. The interiors are minimalist. Low levels of technology are supported by natural gas with candles as the main evening light source. During the summer months, this area of Norway has only about four hours of darkness.

Todd Saunders & Tommie Wilhelmsen

Retreat Summer House

Hardanger Fjord, Norway

122

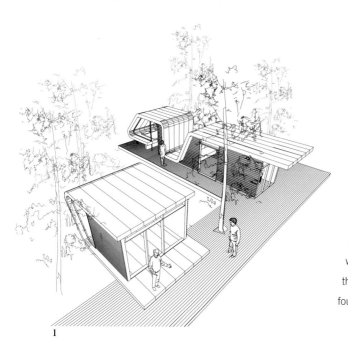

1

2

3

4 Panoramic view over fjord provides constantly
  changing views
5 Floor plan
6 Courtyard in between the two structures
7 Treated terrace floor permits one to walk around
  barefoot
8 Simple and elegant interior. Birch plywood floor
  continues to form wall and ceiling
9 Corner windows open up to fjord views

PHOTOGRAPHY: BENT RENE SYNNEVÅG

4

124

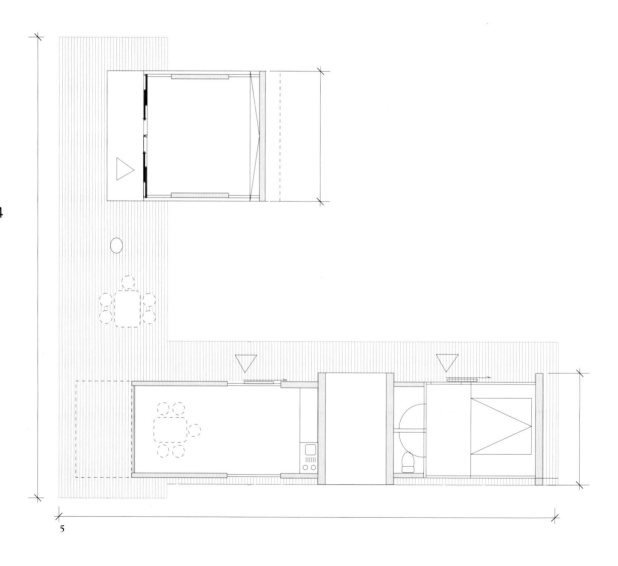

5

6

From the large outdoor terrace, the unfolding views are almost hypnotic. The site has a distinct spiritual feel to it, with the cool, dark forest to the rear but dazzling vistas of light toward the front. Sitting quietly and taking in the beauty of the constantly changing landscape of mountains, clouds and fjord throughout the day fascinates and enthrals.

7

8

125

9

1   View facing the town of Telluride
2   St Sophia Mountains by moonlight
3   Roof forms emulate mountains
4   Trusses supported on local stone columns
5   Upper level
6   Lower level

PHOTOGRAPHY: MICHAEL EBERT

This 5000-square-foot home is made up of soaring glass and strong geometries that capture the magic of this majestic mountain setting. The house in plan is composed of an interlocking series of six sided diamond-shaped modules. This repetitive planning principal includes four Colorado stone columns supporting a structural roof truss system of recycled fir timbers. Corner-butted glass captures carefully framed views of Mt Wilson and the St Sophia Range of the Rocky Mountains.

The vision of the owners was to build a home where guests were welcomed to enjoy the breathtaking views, while remaining comfortable, private and non-congested. The house includes the master bedroom as well as three additional independent suites for guests and grown children.

STEVEN EHRLICH ARCHITECTS

Richards-Ebert Residence

Telluride, Colorado, USA

126

1

2

3

4

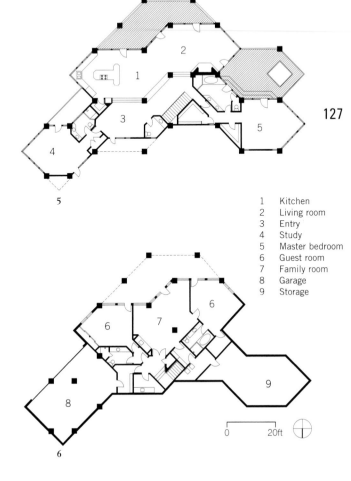

5

6

1 Kitchen
2 Living room
3 Entry
4 Study
5 Master bedroom
6 Guest room
7 Family room
8 Garage
9 Storage

0   20ft

1 View from below the ridge
2 Entry

An undulating hilltop ridge offered an opportunity to design a house that limited its contact with the earth while maximizing visual connections to nature. Situated in a semi-arid conifer forest in eastern Washington, the house is conceived as a series of rooms that spring from three stone piers to bridge the natural undulations of the ridge. Stretched along the ridge's edge, the rooms touch only the highpoints, and open to views of the forest and meadows on either side of the ridge.

Designed for a family that wanted to enjoy the experience of the natural setting in all seasons, the house is purposefully open to the surrounding landscape. The casual lifestyle is picked up in the informal layout of the house and in the use of natural and understated interior finishes. The entry and stairs to the main level are located in the central stone pier. Inside, the spaces are open and interconnected. The kitchen, dining and living rooms are one big space with floor-to-ceiling windows; bedrooms are clustered together in a less open portion of the house. A small, detached wood-clad box, 'the fort', is accessible via an outside bridge. It serves as a home office and is the one concession to privacy, emphasizing the separation of family life from business life.

The exterior is clad with horizontal wood siding and stone, materials selected to merge the house into the landscape. Limiting the building's contact with the earth preserved the visual qualities of the ridge and its disturbance of the natural landscape.

OLSON SUNDBERG KUNDIG ALLEN ARCHITECTS

Ridge House

Eastern Washington, USA

128

1

3   Deck with living area beyond
4   Bridge connecting main house to fort
5   East elevation

6   Living/dining/music area
7   Master bedroom
8   Living/dining/music area floats above ridge line

PHOTOGRAPHY: PAUL WARCHOL, BRUCE VAN INWEGEN

6

7

PATEL ARCHITECTURE/Narendra Patel AIA

Smith Residence

Bighorn Canyons, Palm Desert, California, USA

The Smith House is an emphatic expression of its rugged desert site. Located at Bighorn Canyons in Palm Desert, California, it offers a dramatic view of the Santa Rosa Mountains and the 13th fairway.

The timeless beauty and universal appeal of stone have inspired architects since the beginning of civilization. 'Harmony in nature' was the design philosophy of this house. The goal was sensitive integration of unique architectural image within the natural design environment.

The house is set deeply into the earth berms and designed to appear solid and anchored from the street side. This desert home turns a weather-toughened stone-clad face to the street and provides sheltered forecourt to the owners and their guests.

The exterior of the house is composed of different architectural forms covered with stone, copper, wood, and glass. The entry door is located past the circular drive court and is approached by crossing a wooden bridge over the front water feature. Just across the threshold, this seemingly dense and solid house offers nearly unobstructed views of the fairway and mountains. The living room patio extends beyond large pocket doors. The views and the walls carefully control perspectives.

Instead of separate living, dining and family rooms, the house has one large room that provides the free-flowing living space, and two master suites. The kitchen is an extension of the living area separated by a cantilevered counter. The sense of spaciousness is heightened by the contrast between a 10-foot (3.5-meter) ceiling and a 14-foot (4-meter) high exposed wood beam ceiling radiating from the center point to the outside. The heavy log beam ceiling with saguaro paneling intensifies the impression of an ancient ceremonial space adopted for contemporary use.

The pool area has large decks and covered patio areas. Outcropping of boulders around the house and some inside the house blend harmoniously with the surrounding desert.

1

2

3

1   Exterior of house is designed to appear solid and anchored from the street side. Materials used are natural stone, log columns and copper roofing

2   Great Room has large pocket doors that open to the outdoor living area. Log beam ceiling resembles a giant wagon wheel that continues from inside to outside

3   Pool is designed to become part of the surrounding desert landscape incorporating large boulders and native plants

4

5

4 House is strategically positioned to maximize energy efficiency and shelter from summer sun. Log trellis overhang creates protection for the glass and gives dramatic shadow and light effect
5 Outdoor living room is designed to encourage 'resort living', a term that implies spending as much time outdoors as indoors
6 Heavy log beam ceiling and wood floor is combined with large boulders in the Great Room

7

7   Master bath has extensive use of natural stone slabs, glass blocks, skylights and mirrors

8   The Great Room is a concept of open spaces. Dining room, living room, bar and kitchen all open to each other, yet have their own place

9   The seemingly dense and solid house offers nearly unobstructed views of the fairway and the mountains

PHOTOGRAPHY: NICOLA PIRA

8   9

GEORG DRIENDL ARCHITECTS

Solar Tube

Döbling, Austria

Solar Tube was built in Döbling, a quiet, rather wealthy residential area with mostly single-family homes on the northwestern outskirts of Vienna. The 14,000-square-foot (1300-square-meter) property is narrow but long, with a lush tree canopy.

Before the design process commenced, the characteristics of the location were considered: the sun's position, the number of hours of sunlight and other weather aspects were some of the factors taken into account.

A 'solar tube' is generally a small light-and-heat captor installed on the roofs of houses. In this case, the entire house serves as a collector, open to light and heat on all sides. The wooded site has enabled the architect to use generously glazed elevations, sloping or curved in various parts. Since the roof and floors are also partly transparent, the core of the house works like an integrated atrium. The glass 'tube' that forms the uppermost level helps cut heating costs in winter. Apart from its energy-saving virtues, glass also offers intimacy with the surrounding nature by simulating the feeling of living in a tree house. It is a symbiosis between nature and architecture.

Solar Tube was built in only five months. Fast-paced construction was possible due to the usage of mostly prefabricated or in-stock units and base materials, reinforcing the notion that custom-designed and manufactured elements do not necessarily produce better results.

Overheating in summer is avoided by the surrounding trees as well as by a special ventilation system that works like a chimney. In winter the heating costs are minimized because of the building's

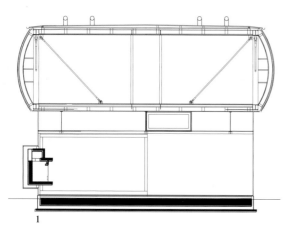

1

1   Cross section
Opposite:
    East elevation

3 View from east
4 Front view from street
5 View from west
6 Longitudinal section

3

142

4

compact coat, designed to absorb high amounts of sun energy. Helping conserve energy further, the defoliated trees in winter allow the sunlight to shine through the glazed façade and roof.

Seeing Solar Tube from the street is a unique experience. The remarkable shape and the glass façade of the house attract passersby, although the façade facing the street is more secluded to afford more privacy compared to the sides facing the garden. The core of the house, the integrated atrium, is open to all sides. Even from the ground level one can see through to the sliding roof, because of the partly transparent floors. To ensure uninterrupted views, the bedrooms on the uppermost level are reached through a suspended walkway. The spirit of the interior embodies open living. Because the architects designed the integrated furniture in the kitchen, library, cupboards and bathrooms, it is in perfect harmony with the design of the building itself.

5

143

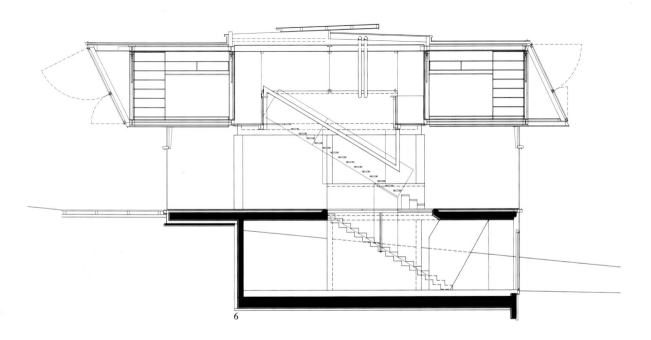

6

7

8

9

7   Living room terrace with view of second floor
8   Second floor; view toward bedroom on south
9   First floor living room
Following pages:
     First floor

Photography: Bruno Klomfar (p. 141, 5, 8, p. 146–147); James Morris (3, 4, 7, 9)

145

1   Site plan
2   Initial sketch concepts
3   Front elevation

This residence, perched atop a narrow mudstone ridge in California's Santa Cruz Mountains, is a blend of rustic simplicity and technological inventiveness.

The open floor plan allows for flexible space suited to the owner's informal lifestyle and to the musical events that they frequently host. The concrete slab floor, conforming to the flattened ridge top, forms the organizing and structural spine of the house, doubling as a solar thermal mass. With front and rear doors to the house open, the mudstone-colored slab becomes a link in a pre-existing ridge-top hiking trail.

The house, square in plan, is essentially a gable-ended post and beam structure. Its exposed posts, beams, and rafters are hand-hewn pine from Colorado and locally milled redwood ceilings. The design strikes a balance between the rustic, gable-ended portions of the house and the simple cube-shaped central space. Traversing the space, a gossamer, steel-truss bridge links the two upper bedroom lofts.

STEVEN EHRLICH ARCHITECTS

Swann Residence

Scotts Valley, California, USA

148

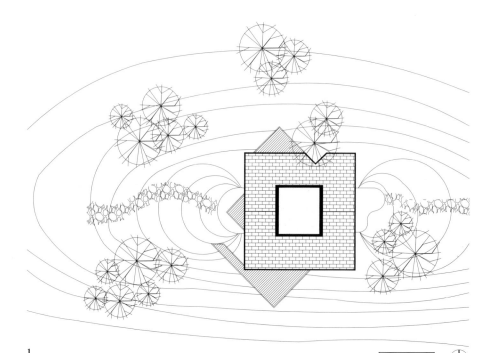

1

0   20ft

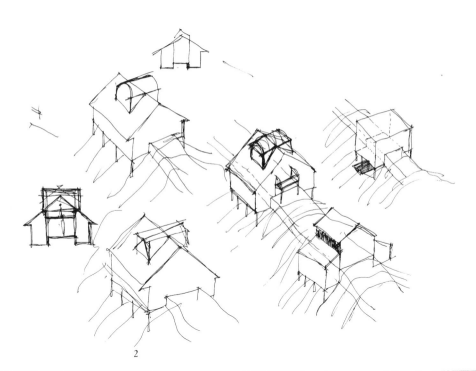

2

4

5

6

4   Steel-truss bridge
5   A fire at sunset
6   Concrete spine acts as thermal mass
7   House straddles a steep ridge

PHOTOGRAPHY: LAWRENCE MANNING

7

1 West elevation with carport
2 View from south
3 Floor plan

This house, a 45–minute drive south of Dallas, is used for frequent weekday visits and longer weekend stays. The owners, avid bird watchers with an abiding love for the ranch, are restoring some of its areas by reintroducing wetlands, native grasses and indigenous bird populations. The retreat acts as guest quarters and a beginning point where visitors can set out on loosely defined nature trails meant to offer a heightened appreciation of the landscape.

The main structure, oriented on an east–west axis, sits between hardwoods and an open meadow. The west entrance is situated between the woods and a smaller stand of live oak that shades the entry and west carport from the afternoon sun. This west parking area has a steeply angled 2x cypress screen—a 'flag'—that announces the retreat's presence for arriving guests. A similarly constructed angular screen surrounds the rooftop mechanical units.

The structure's roofs are supported by a 12-foot (3.6-meter) on-center post-and-beam system that allows them to float above the main body of the building. This offers a 2-foot (0.6 meter) band of clerestory that extends inside the house to provide an abundance of natural light.

A wood stoop and small pedestrian bridge of industrial metal decking connects the front entry to guest parking at the project's west end.

An 8-foot-wide (2.4-meter) sitting porch runs most of the main building's length along the north side to face the woods. Between the tree line and the house there is an open lawn of buffalo grass. It is the only manicured part of the landscape and is the play area for the family's grandchildren. The west side of this lawn is bordered by a water trough and birdbath. This trough is on axis with the main entrance.

BUILDINGSTUDIO

Texas Twister

Rey Rosa Ranch, Texas, USA

1

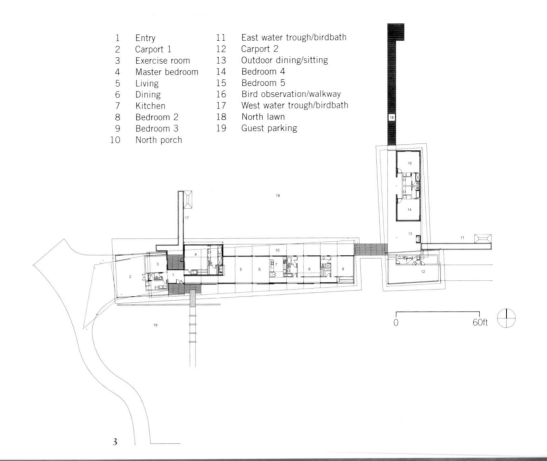

1	Entry	11	East water trough/birdbath
2	Carport 1	12	Carport 2
3	Exercise room	13	Outdoor dining/sitting
4	Master bedroom	14	Bedroom 4
5	Living	15	Bedroom 5
6	Dining	16	Bird observation/walkway
7	Kitchen	17	West water trough/birdbath
8	Bedroom 2	18	North lawn
9	Bedroom 3	19	Guest parking
10	North porch		

0   60ft

3

4

5

6

The north sitting porch connects the two-bedroom guest quarters to the main structure by a wood bridge. This bedroom wing, constructed of double brick walls, forms the eastern boundary of the open lawn.

Another double carport, for ranch vehicles, is at the east end of the complex. In between the carport and the guest bedroom structures is an outdoor dining porch with a fireplace. Here, another water trough and birdbath extend east into the landscape toward a complex of Quonset hut outbuildings.

The guest quarters' cantilevered concrete walk extends north, turning into a raised boardwalk and continues into the woods. This deck ends at the top of the scrub trees to become a bird–watching platform.

The building is post-tensioned slab-on-grade with glulam beams and steel columns forming the main structure. The walls are constructed of 2x wood framing with industrial aluminum siding and brick masonry for its exterior wall sheathing. Interior walls are painted gypsum board. Ceilings are an exposed wooden structure and floors are of sealed concrete.

7

155

4 North elevation and porch
5 Interior view of living and dining rooms with kitchen beyond
6 Interior view of guest bedroom
7 Bird watching platform viewed from below
Following pages:
    Outdoor dining porch and guest wing

9

158

9   Interior view of living area with entry beyond
10   View from southwest
Opposite:
     View along south elevation

<small>PHOTOGRAPHY: TIMOTHY HURSLEY</small>

10

1   Two wings connected by living spaces
Opposite:
    A New-Century modern home

This new single-family residence of 2600 square feet (242 square meters) is composed of kitchen, dining area, living room, office, three bedrooms, and two-and-a-half bathrooms. The site is a flat, irregularly shaped lot at the end of a cul-de-sac in a neighborhood containing a variety of styles and references to the preferred typical suburban desert subdivision architecture.

The house is designed for a retired couple with the need for guest bedroom suites and a large communal space for the living, dining, and kitchen areas. To achieve a feeling of simplicity within conventional means, it was decided that planning and construction must be straightforward and the character of the house reflect a strategy of both enclosure and openness focused toward the main outdoor space. Two simple volumes are connected together to define a corner with one wing containing the guest bedrooms, and the other containing the master suite. The two wings are connected at the main living, dining, and kitchen space.

Hallways are located along the east and south sides of the two wings and help to define the laterally spaced rooms, which can be closed off from the circulation zone with large sliding walls. The rooms all access the outdoor pool/courtyard space from large sliding glass walls.

The materials and finishes used throughout the house are exposed concrete block walls, natural stone veneer walls, plaster-over-wood framing, concrete floors, walnut cabinetry, Gascogne-Blue limestone floors in bathrooms, translucent glass panels, Montauk-Black marble counters in the kitchen, and Venetino-White marble countertops in the bathroom and on the kitchen island.

OJMR ARCHITECTS

The Fritz Residence

Palm Desert, California, USA

160

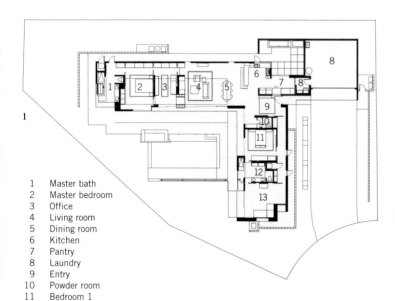

1   Master bath
2   Master bedroom
3   Office
4   Living room
5   Dining room
6   Kitchen
7   Pantry
8   Laundry
9   Entry
10   Powder room
11   Bedroom 1
12   Guest bath
13   Bedroom 2

3   All spaces have indoor/outdoor qualities
4   L-shaped plan provides privacy to guest and living spaces
5   Residence sits at the end of a cul-de-sac

4

162

3

5

164

6

6   Dining/kitchen area is main hub of house
7   Powder room is elegantly detailed
8   White marble and black concrete add visual contrast
Following pages:
    All spaces are oriented toward vast outdoor area

Photography: Ciro Coelho

7

8

1 Sketches of orientation, views and articulation
2 Sky court view to west
3 View from northeast

PHOTOGRAPHY: RICHARD JOHNSON

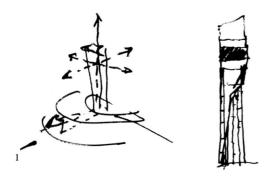

MARLON BLACKWELL ARCHITECT

The Keenan Tower House

Fayetteville, Arkansas, USA

168

2

The Keenan Tower House is located on a hickory and white oak-wooded, west sloping hill in the southwest corner, the high point, of a 57-acre (23-hectare) tract of land near Fayetteville, Arkansas.

The owner's requisite was a vertical structure that would rise above the 50-foot-high (15-meter) tree canopy and provide views of the surrounding Ozark mountains, in homage to his childhood memories of happy times spent in a tree house built by his grandfather.

The 82-foot (25-meter) high tower structure functions as a residential retreat with programmed levels including a utility room, foyer/bathroom/kitchenette, living/sleeping room, and a skycourt.

The structure is designed to maximize both horizontal and vertical views. An open-air vertical sequence rotates up from a ground level of pecan shells, through the tree canopy, intertwined through filtered light and shadow, to the foyer level where light and view are lost, and then regained, upon entry into the light-filled living/sleeping room above. Here continuous steel frame windows provide 360-degree views of the surrounding foothills and plains of Oklahoma. The expansive horizon is emphasized through a 10-foot (3.5-meter) room height. A fold-down stair leads one to the skycourt above and here, views are controlled to the horizon through the specific placement of openings.

The steel tube tower structure is clad with a disengaged 2x6 vertical white oak fin lattice around the stairwell. The lattice affords views of the tree canopy, filters light, and blends with the rich vertical textured bark of oak and hickory trees native to the site. This organic condition is contrasted with the 'white' cladding of horizontal standing-seam steel panels that enclose the east elevation and the upper program elements.

All wood floors, decks, and wall assemblies are of locally milled white oak. All mechanical, plumbing, and electrical lines are channeled through one vertical chase wall that also serves as structure for a small dumbwaiter. Local river and creek stone articulates the ground at the base.

3

1   Roadside view at dusk
2   Southeast view

June Moore is a beekeeper. The prized sourwood honey produced in beehives in the adjacent forest is sold along country roads and at local markets. In 1998, June wanted to add two structures—an apiarian structure for processing and storing honey and a carport/outdoor work area. The inverted metal wing roof of the carport is a counterpoint to the roof forms of the existing June Moore House.

Primary architectural elements were developed to allow the Honey House to evolve from within. The ordering methods of modern beekeeping and its ongoing domestication of bee activities and behavior were also considered. The modern four-sided hive box is organized as a series of shallow orthogonal frames that articulate and separate the brood chamber below from the 'super' (honey chamber) above. Movable frames allow the stored comb honey to be removed without upsetting the brood chamber. While the Cartesian frames delimit the space of bee activity and make it manageable, they have virtually no effect on the constructed organic patterns of the bee colony's day-to-day activities. The tense interplay between the efficiency of the beekeeper's equipment and the bees' willingness to adapt to it is central to the continual production of honey and the survival of the colony.

Experience had dictated that local craftsmen were often hard to keep on the job due to a variety of hunting seasons including squirrel season, deer season, and turkey season. In order to control costs and ensure timely construction, the primary architectural elements were conceived as a kit of parts. This facilitated the fabrication of the elements in Arkansas for shipment to the site. The crew from Fayetteville assembled the entire structure on site in one month.

Marlon Blackwell Architect

The Moore Honey House

Cashiers, North Carolina, USA

170

1

2

3   Axonometric
4   Honey display wall
5   Detail of honeycomb wall

PHOTOGRAPHY: RICHARD JOHNSON

The structure's single most prominent and complex architectural element is a unique load-bearing steel plate and faceted glass wall that acts to organize the storage and display of honey, filter natural light, and provide a rich mosaic of reflections of the surrounding foliage. The multiple spatial configurations within the wall exhibit transparency, translucency, and opacity, depending upon one's perspective, the season of the year, and the time of day. The wall is both frame and edge—a frame that reorders the view, an edge that becomes the view.

172

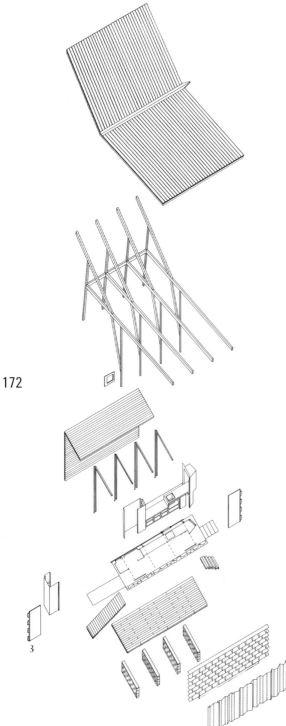

3

4

1   East façade
2   Main access; bridge facing hill towards main area of
    house flanks working area
Opposite:
    Main corridor. Diagonally formed wall provides view
    toward the Andes mountain range

FELIPE ASSADI ARQUITECTOS

The Raveau House

Between Santiago and Farellones, Chile

174

Located off the road between the city of Santiago and the village of Farellones, this house offers spectacular views of the magnificent mountain range beyond.

The sloping site, which declines to the Mapocho River, ultimately defines the two main volumes that make up this house. One section, which holds the sleeping quarters, follows a jagged line that descends to the river. It is crossed by another section that holds the dining and living quarters, separated by a terraced area that from the interior of the house offers the first views of the landscape beyond.

The house is situated on 60 pylons 328 feet (100 meters) above the river. The pylons protect the house from natural water erosion on the sloped site. The house is principally constructed from onsite reinforced concrete, structural steel, and pine coated with tar paint.

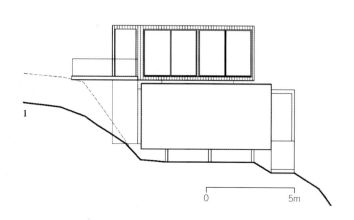

1

0   5m

2

4

4   Connection between approach ramp and horizontal volume of house
5   Approach ramp; floor and lateral wall are covered in steel
6   Dining salon

5

6

7   Main access plan (second floor), studio and entrance level
8   Ground floor (first floor) rooms level
9   Kitchen and view toward hill
10   Main bathroom with view toward valley
11   Main façade

178

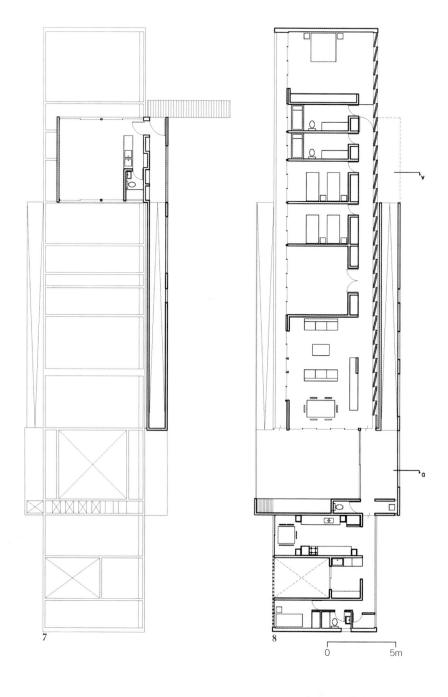

7

8

9

0   5m

10

11

13   14

12   Intermediate space separates bedrooms and lounge
13   View of central space dividing the house's functions and salon enclosure
14   Guest bathroom
15   North façade

Photography: Guy Wenborne

15

1   Aerial view looking south
2   Public rooms from river road
3   Site Plan
4   East wing

This large vacation house is the centerpiece of a 1000-acre (404-hectare) rural retreat and ecological study center. It is perched on a wooded limestone bluff overlooking the Osage River in the rolling Ozarks. Part lodge, part family compound, duality is the theme of the 22,000-square-foot (2044-square-meter) building. Bedroom suites and major rooms arranged to merge with surrounding nature frame an arcaded courtyard.

New facilities are sited for minimal disruption of the natural terrain and farm operations while surrounding woodlands and meadows undergo restoration. The old farm compound is prominent upon entering the site. Arriving through the woods, the road turns abruptly to enter a parking court. The central entry portal is the dominant feature of the front of the house. Moving into the stone-paved platform of the courtyard, the view of the river unfolds below. Roads and trails lead visitors from the house to explore surrounding nature.

The building's program reflects a complex initiative and the plan responds with a graduated structure of spaces. Clusters of rooms frame the central court. Lined by arcades on three sides, the courtyard functions as the most public interior space (based on Rosselino's piazza in Pienza). Most other spaces are entered off the courtyard and its entry canopy is designed as an acoustic reflector for musical performance groups and speakers. Glass enclosures expose interior volumes to view from all sides and long sight lines connect distant points. In winter, an overhead glass door closes the portal to allow interior circulation around the courtyard. On the west, two-story bedroom suites are split by tapered walkways that give private routes into the woods. Sitting rooms and screened porches cantilever over the forest floor, softening the building's landing and merging inside with outside.

Shed-roofed volumes project from the bluff, each interacting differently with the outdoors. The gallery/living

BARTON PHELPS & ASSOCIATES

The Sinquefield House

Osage County, Missouri, USA

182

1

2

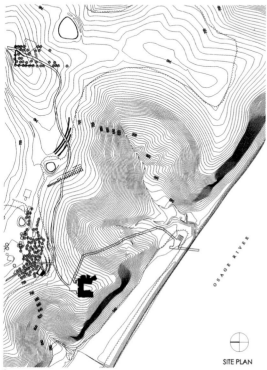

3

SITE PLAN

4

5

6

7

room extends furthest, along an axial clearing, to frame a view of the river's southerly arc. The dining room pushes into the woods, its slanted window mullions tilting with the tree trunks beyond. In the billiard room, glazed corners give non-axial views out and back into the house.

The stone masonry front and lower story anchor the building to the rock on which it is built. On three sides the battered masonry base lifts the light, wood-sided envelopes of the mostly single-story composition above the sloping site. On the east, masonry walls drop off the bluff to enclose a mezzanine exercise room and lower level swimming pool. Entered at the low end of its folded ceiling, the pool space rises to give views out amid a grove of stone piers that support the voluminous wood and glass forms above. A natural limestone bank supports a rough stone stairway that links the lower garden with the central courtyard.

Heating and cooling are produced by an extensive 'groundsource' well system that transfers constant ground water temperature to heat pumps distributed in attic spaces. Pool water is heated by groundsource and kept covered when not in use. Glazing systems are thermally broken metal frames with inch-thick insulating glass. Louvered arcades reduce summer heat gain. Domestic water is supplied by wells on the property and septic systems with sand-bed filters release clean irrigation water. Fire sprinkler and hydrant systems are fed from the pool and farm pond.

5   South elevation
6   Courtyard with mist over river
7   East wing
8   Interior's wide glass expanses offer views over surroundings

Photography: Timothy Hursley, Arkansas office

185

8

1 Site plan
2 Stairs to rooftop
3 View from north; ground floor has no walls

The Wall-less House is located in the Setagaya-Ku district of Tokyo, on a large site secluded from a densely populated, residential neighborhood. It resembles a retreat villa in the countryside and is completely open to the landscape and environment.

Occupying just 20 percent of the site, the house leaves ample space around it for a truly open, continuous space: a wall-less house. Using a lightweight steel, load-bearing frame structure, the axial loads are distributed through only a utility core in the center and two thin columns, therefore opening the living space to the outside completely on all sides. The floors seem to float in air, surrounded by the trees for greenery and privacy.

TEZUKA ARCHITECTS & MASAHIRO IKEDA CO LTD

Wall-less House

Setagaya-ku, Tokyo, Japan

186

2

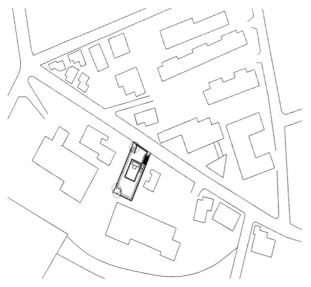

1

4

5

4   Initial sketch
5   View from bedroom
6   View from garden
7   Stair to second floor
8   Living room; sliding doors can be opened to incorporate garden with interior

6

7

8

9

10

11

9   View of garden from living room
10 Bathroom
11 Kitchen at core of house sustains earthquake seismic loads
12 View from rooftop

PHOTOGRAPHY: KATSUHISA KIDA

1   Western deck as formal address to view beyond
Opposite:
    Ceiling opening to north floods space with filtered light
    through forest canopy

The pristine Tasmanian coastal bushland, resplendent with native fauna and flora, is the site for the Walla Womba Guest House. Extremely remote and practically inaccessible, this guesthouse is a hidden retreat conceived as an escape from the pressures of contemporary urban living.

The property is environmentally autonomous and not connected to town power, water or sewer. Solar power has generator backup, rainwater is collected for household uses, and waste is dealt with on-site. Two raised, subdividable pavilions share accommodation and living functions. The bushland experience is central to the design, which literally opens up living spaces to the bush.

The building is planned around two raised parallel pavilions linked by a central circulation spine. The east–west axial configuration is based around the simple criteria of solar orientation, specific view lines, and conventional programmatic relationships.

The ability to connect with the forest and water from within the house was paramount, with the aim of offering the user an intimate yet comfortable Australian bushland experience. Large, external sliding doors, view-framing windows, the extension of living spaces to decks and careful spatial orientation all heighten the experience.

The inverted and simplified roof form evolved from the owner's desire for a curvilinear shape that allowed the roof to lift toward the northern aspect. Low visibility from the water was another consideration achieved by orienting the roof pitch away from the water, through judicious selection of colours and materials and also maintaining the landscape buffer zone between the house and the coast.

I + 2 ARCHITECTURE

Walla Womba Guest House

Bruny Island, Tasmania, Australia

192

1

The structure is a composite galvanized steel and timber frame and is bushfire resistant. The colors of the external materials are influenced by context: deep grays for steel and sheet cladding, and other 'natural' finished metals blend with the bushland setting.

Hardwood floors, neutral carpet and off-white painted plasterboard heighten the experience of the exterior from within and complement the natural Tasmanian timbers used in joinery and custom furniture.

Internal spaces are configured into a conventional linear, bi-nuclear plan containing essentially living/public functions in one roofed pavilion and sleeping/private functions in a second, linked by a third, low-roofed spine. The living room configuration maximizes sun and expansive views. Bedrooms gain other specific views. Decks are located with consideration to sun, views, shelter, and relationships to external pathways and the shoreline.

3

4

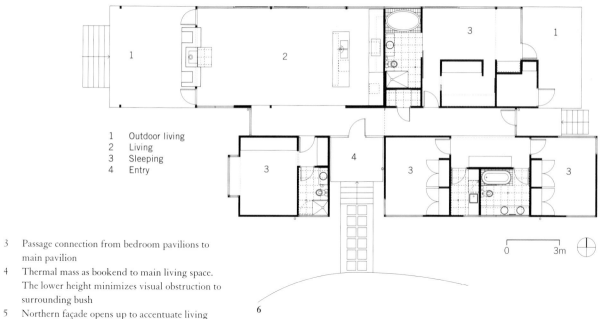

1 Outdoor living
2 Living
3 Sleeping
4 Entry

3 Passage connection from bedroom pavilions to main pavilion
4 Thermal mass as bookend to main living space. The lower height minimizes visual obstruction to surrounding bush
5 Northern façade opens up to accentuate living space as veranda
6 Floor plan; 3 pavilions linked by passage

6

0   3m

5

7

7   Water view from master bedroom
8   Sweeping roofs provide visual interest and concealed gutter system
9   Cross section through house as linked pavilions
Following pages:
    House sits delicately poised in coastal bush setting

PHOTOGRAPHY: PETER HYATT

8

1 Sleeping
2 Living

9

0   3m

197

1 Site plan
2 North elevation; overlooking Mt Asama
3 East elevation; random opening on wall
4 East elevation; floating volume on sloping hill

Warabi Cottage is situated in a wooded area of Karuizawa, a town developed over the past century into one of Japan's most renowned resort areas.

The client was a landscape architect working in the city whose desire was to live in the woods, enjoy nature and secluded time away from busy urban life.

The site is located on a sloping hill and from the highest point, Mt Asama, a mountain symbolic to the local residents, can be viewed. The design objectives of Warabi Cottage were to utilize the sloping characteristics of the site and consider the surrounding forest.

Simple high ceiling space oriented toward Mt Asama, visible during the winter season, was the client's brief. Thus the living floor area was raised 10 feet (3 meters), the point at which Mt Asama was best visible. Since interior columns obstruct the view outside, the structural solution was to form a frame of wood beams and columns at the 3 foot (900 millimeter) pitch on the concrete box. In order to float the main volume of the house off the sloping hill, two concrete beams are cantilevered from the main concrete box.

Each frame is connected by a steel rod tie bar and is reinforced by the steel flat bar. These wooden structures were placed on to the concrete beams to form the simple rectangular box floating from the sloping hill. The main cottage space has a 13-foot-high (4-meter) interior volume, allowing loft space and a work area on the mezzanine level.

The location of windows on the sidewall is intended to maximize views of the surrounding wooded area through randomly placed openings. The concept of deliberately limited window openings is based on the idea of *Shakukei* (borrowed background scenery often used in traditional Zen gardens).

The overall impression this cantilevered cottage on a sloping hill projects could be interpreted in two ways: as a full-scale tree house or as a bird nest, at one with nature and the surrounding woodlands.

OPPOSITION ARCHITECTS

Warabi Cottage

Karuizawa, Japan

200

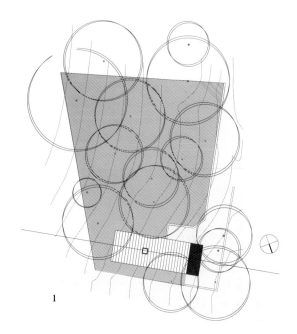

1

2

3

201

4

5

202

5   Night view
6   Entrance canopy
7   Section of site
8   View to Mt Asama from loft

6

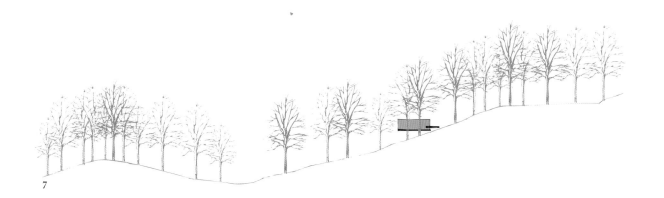

7

8

9

9 Kitchen
10 *Shakukei* window
11 Open bathroom
12 Terrace view from living room

Photography: Yusuke Abe

10

11

12

1 Arrival point with stepped floating deck that provides a
  disciplined edge to the roofline
2 Vividly stained plywood interior contrasts with charcoal
  steel veneer

Jesse Judd Architects

Wheatsheaf Residence

Wheatsheaf, Victoria, Australia

The Wheatsheaf Residence investigates the nomadic nature inherent in the holiday unit. Nestled in 10 acres (4 hectares) of abandoned messmate forest, the extruded form sits both comfortably within, and distinct from, its monoculture environment. The house examines the typology of the ephemeral, a stressed skin structure that seems to be spontaneously relocatable, perhaps informed by the Airstream trailer, an aircraft hull, or the folded steel bus stops that dot Melbourne's southeastern suburbs.

The scheme's two parts function as both discrete and integrated elements, grounded in rudimentary internal planning. Consisting of two folded planes, the experience of the house is about the section cut. The front and rear elevations reveal the planar skins, extruded as a simple platonic gesture. The side elevations divulge little more of the womb-like interior, appearing as the simplest temporary vernacular, a corrugated iron lean-to, complete with veranda.

The primary material is simply formed corrugated steel, a floor that becomes wall and then roof. The use of black allows details to fade away—more emphasis is then placed on the main gesture. This main curved plane within the living area is lined internally in plywood, stained a red/orange that emphasizes both the warmness and the timber patterning of the ply. A train-carriage aisle/hallway connects the main space with three linear bedrooms, a severed exposition of the overall platonic volume, expressed through a primary magenta parallel entry. Ply is also used for key joinery surfaces, but here is stained a gray-brown, more akin to the surrounding forest.

1

2

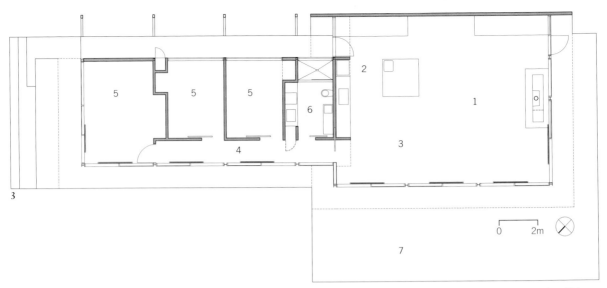

3

<table>
<tr><td>3</td><td>Floor plan</td></tr>
<tr><td>4</td><td>View from rear and south elevation. The house is framed by a row of steel ribs that emphasizes the enfolding skin</td></tr>
<tr><td>5</td><td>Stained ply interiors provide a lightweight lining that reinforces the razor thin steel profile</td></tr>
<tr><td>6</td><td>Entry sequence reveals the house designed in this section rather than the more conventional plan</td></tr>
</table>

Following pages:
  Steel shell visually retreats into the forest's recesses and allows red-stained interior to become centerstage

PHOTOGRAPHY: PETER HYATT (1–3, 5, 6); PETER BENNETTS (PAGES 210–211)

1	Living
2	Cooking
3	Eating
4	Walkway
5	Sleeping
6	Bathroom
7	Deck

4

The contiguous timber deck is clad in rough sawn turpentine, cut from the demolished former piers of the Wooloomooloo wharf on Sydney Harbour, and hovers uneasily over the forest floor, allowing the native wildlife to run freely under foot.

The Wheatsheaf Residence is raised above the ground; an expressed steel structure contains a deck-platform at a controlled height so it does not require a balustrade.

This is architecture as surface: three-dimensionally smooth, yet sufficiently complex to be legible through our increasingly "logo-ized" world of visual codes and conventional signs.

5

6

This tiny house, designed for a University of Maryland professor of Art History, occupies a wooded 10-acre (4.5-hectare) site in rural Southern Maryland. The client, who grew up in New England in a house designed by Dan Kiley, asked for two things—a simple cabin in the woods, in the spirit of the Kiley House, and the proper setting for a commissioned artwork, a sun drawing by artist Janet Saad Cook.

The cabin exists in two asphalt-shingled, tightly functional wings. The Saad Cook piece is in the middle, in a metal and glass room that bridges the wings. This space, which also houses the living and dining areas, is designed around the artwork. Here, the sun drawing projects reflected images, which change with the movement of the sun and clouds, onto a wall—an ephemeral response to place, time, and architecture. The glass wall is to the north, and the second-story bridge that connects the two wings runs in front of it. This allows the south wall to receive the projected image on a billboard-like surface, which itself allows south light in only at the floor and ceiling.

McInturff Architects

Withers Residence

Accokeek, Maryland, USA

212

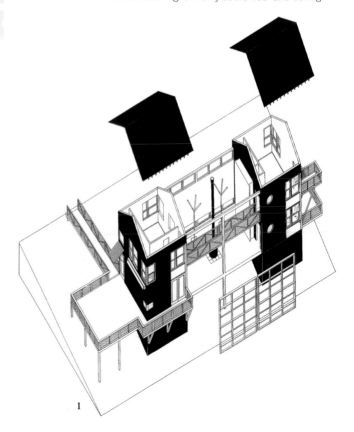

1   Axonometric
2   View from downhill

1

3

4

5

3   Great room with kitchen beyond
4   South wall with sun drawing
5   Entry façade

PHOTOGRAPHY: JULIA HEINE

1   Open and airy spaces are special characteristics of house
2   Entry
3   Second floor bedroom

The House at Yakeyama is located on a hilltop, in the village of Kure, a 40-minute drive from the city of Hiroshima. Located in a serene, wooded area, on a picturesque site, the house resembles a country villa.

The design concept's foremost objective was to fuse design with nature. To take advantage of the characteristics of the site and the panoramic view toward the south, the floor level of the house was raised 3 feet (1 meter) off the foundation. The suspended nature of the floor level provided excellent views of the surrounding elements: nature, the sky and trees, from within the house.

The elevated floor was built in the traditional Japanese 'Taka-yuka' form, permitting good ventilation and protection from rainwater, insects, and vermin.

SUPPOSE DESIGN OFFICE

Yakeyama House

Hiroshima, Japan

1

2

3

4

5

6

7

4   Living room
5   Bathroom
6   South elevation
7   Stairway

PHOTOGRAPHY: NACASA & PARTNERS

INDEX OF ARCHITECTS

Index

Barton Phelps & Associates, USA　　　　　　　　182
www.bpala.com

Col Bandy Architects, Australia　　　　　　　　62

buildingstudio, USA　　　　　　　　152
www.buildingstudio.net

David Luck Architecture, Australia　　　　　　　　82
www.users.bigpond.com/david.luck

Georg Driendl Architekt, Austria　　　　　　　　140
www.driendl.at

Duc Associates Pty Ltd, Australia　　　　　　　　32
www.ducassociates.com.au

Felipe Assadi Arquitecto, Chile　　　　　　　　102, 174
www.felipeassadi.com

Fougeron Architecture, USA　　　　　　　　52
www.fougeron.com

Fung + Blatt Architects, USA　　　　　　　　98
www.fungandblatt.com

Grose Bradley Architects, Australia　　　　　　　　70
www.blighvollernield.com.au

Jesse Judd Architects, Australia　　　　　　　　206
www.jessejudd.com.au

Kanner Architects, USA　　　　　　　　20, 90
www.kannerarch.com

Labics Architettura, Italy　　　　　　　　114
www.labics.it

Lake/Flato Architects, USA　　　　　　　　16
www.lakeflato.com

Lorcan O'Herlihy Architects, USA　　　　　　　　58
www.loharchitects.com

222

Marlon Blackwell Architect, USA   168, 170
www.marlonblackwell.com

Marwan Al Sayed Architects, USA   40
www.masastudio.com

McInturff Architects, USA   216
www.mcinturffarchitects.com

Olson Sundberg Kundig Allen Architects, USA   128
www.olsonsundberg.com

OJMR Architects, USA   160
www.ojmrarchitects.net

1 + 2 Architecture, Australia   192
www.1plus2architecture.com

Opposition Architects, Japan   200
www.opposition.jp

Patel Architecture, USA   134
www.patelarchitecture.com

Pierre Thibault Architecte, Canada   78
www.pthibault.com

Scott Carver Architects, Australia   26
www.scottcarver.com.au

Steven Ehrlich Architects, USA   126, 148
www.s-ehrlich.com

Suppose Design Office, Japan   10, 108, 216
www.suppose.jp

Tezuka Architects and Masahiro Ikeda co ltd., Japan   46, 186
www.tezuka-arch.com

Todd Saunders and Tommie Wilhelmsen, Norway   30, 122
www.saunders.no

Acknowledgements

Invention, investment and risk apply to all of these featured projects prepared to challenge convention. The selected work is the expression that presents itself for the camera and viewer's pleasure. It captures surface and (hopefully) substance, light, shade, context, and detail.

From the comparatively anonymous, hard working contractors to motivated clients and architects, these houses represent a willingness to create an incremental climate change towards livelier, lovelier buildings.

The Images Publishing Group Pty Ltd (Australia) provides a major voice in the recognition of architecture from around the globe. IMAGES' coordinators Joe Boschetti and Andrea Boekel deserve special praise for their willingness to surmount numerous obstacles in pursuit of a quality production.

Bringing together such a collection of work requires a curatorial eye and ear and it is our privilege to help reveal the efforts of talented teams unified in their purpose to set standards, not boundaries.

Peter and Jennifer Hyatt
Project editors

224

DATE DUE			
Dec 18 68			
GAYLORD			PRINTED IN U.S.A.

YALE UNIVERSITY PUBLICATIONS
IN ANTHROPOLOGY

NUMBER 54

KAPAUKU PAPUANS AND THEIR LAW

LEOPOLD POSPISIL

REPRINTED BY

HUMAN RELATIONS AREA FILES
PRESS

1964

Reprinted from the 1958 edition

Library of Congress Catalog Card Number: 64-20560

Published simultaneously in Canada by Burns & MacEachern, Ltd., Toronto

Printed in the United States of America

PREFACE

LAW is one of the traditional categories of Western culture which generally has not been discussed in the anthropological studies of other people. This monograph presents an analysis of the structure and function of law in a Kapauku Papuan confederacy of the interior of Netherlands New Guinea, an area which is relatively unaffected by the legal ideas of Western civilization. The analysis of law is based on an investigation of the confederacy as a whole as well as an inquiry into the legal systems of all of the confederacy's subgroups, such as lineage, sublineage, village, household, and family.

The purpose of the monograph is to demonstrate with the help of the Papuan data the effectiveness of a theory of law formulated on the basis of a comparative study of thirty-two cultures and a survey of an additional sixty-three. The cultures in the sample range from very simple ones such as those of the Bushmen and the Yaghan to the complex cultures of the Inca and the Chinese.[1] The theory analyzes phenomena which traditionally have been regarded as law (see for definition Webster's New International Dictionary: Neilson and others, 1940: 1401), and abstracts the essential common features of these. Thus it isolates four attributes which help to differentiate law from other social phenomena such as political decisions, purely religious taboos, and customs in general. After thus analyzing the structure of law, the primary interest is directed toward the dynamic aspect of law and its relation both to the smaller group in which it is upheld and to the larger society as a whole. Through this approach, the writer has arrived at a theory of the relativity of law and custom.

To achieve the above objective, the writer presents first a general ethnographic picture of a Papuan culture. Whereas the first part of the monograph concentrates upon the individual and his conception of the universe, the second part deals with Kapauku society and its subgroups. Thus the discussion of law is properly related to the legally relevant aspects of religion, politics, economy, and customs in general both of the society as a whole and of its subgroups. In testing the theory of law, special attention is given to the analysis of authority and leadership, and to the decisions of specific disputes and the motivations underlying them, 176 of which decisions are described in the third part of the monograph. Against this material the theory is tested in the fourth, or last, part.

The research. The Kapauku Papuans of the interior of the Netherlands New Guinea appear to comprise one of the most suitable societies in which the research could have been conducted for the following reasons:

1. The society is one which has not yet been affected by Western ideas of law.

2. A virtual absence of chieftainship as well as of formalized legal procedures, and

---

[1] The intensively studied cultures have the following geographical distribution: Africa 6, Asia 4, Europe 3, North America 5, South America 5, Oceania 9.

3

denial of the presence of any authority and law by the Europeans challenged several of the hypotheses in the theory.

3. The people like to talk about disputes and feel no embarrassment in revealing the names of the parties to the disputes.

4. The linguistic analysis had been completed and therefore the writer was able to study the language from a well written textbook (Doble, 1953).

The material for this monograph was collected during a period of twelve months starting in November, 1954. The writer was escorted from Paniai Lake, where he was brought by an amphibian plane, to the Kamu Valley by a police patrol consisting of Papuan police led by the white police commander from the Tigi Lake area. The Kapauku were informed that the writer intended to stay for one year in order to study their customs and language. When the small expedition reached the Kamu Valley, an area which had not yet been brought under the control of the Dutch Administration, the natives staged a great welcome party, presented the writer with a pig and invited him to stay with them. They offered him a nice piece of land through which ran a creek springing from the foot of the Kemuge Mountain, and promised help in building his house. Because of this enthusiasm and the suitability of the area, the writer decided to accept the offer. With the assistance of the natives and police, he built himself a house between the villages of Botukebo and Kojogeepa. The police escort left the Kamu Valley after four days and a native police boy who remained to protect the writer returned after two months. The house site had several advantages. Besides offering cool drinking water, its location outside of the village territory may have slightly lessened any influence the writer's presence may have had on the village. It also prevented the writer's identification with only one village, and allowed informants from other villages free access to the writer's house. On the other hand, its proximity to the two neighboring villages enabled the author to visit them frequently as well as facilitating close and continuous observations of the life of the natives.

Because there were no reliable interpreters available, the writer had to master the Papuan language. After three months of study, he could converse on the current topics of daily life. In six months, his knowledge of the language became satisfactory for research purposes and its concentrated study was ended.

Since it is a custom in the Kapauku culture for adolescent boys and young men to come to live for a long period of time with a rich man and because a white man is considered particularly wealthy, the writer became "adopted" by forty-eight Papuan boys. In return for their daily food, the boys and young men served as messengers, informants, and carriers of supplies (Pl. 1). As the writer's presence in some people's homes would have often interfered with a violent dispute, the boys also were used in collecting many of the data on legal cases presented in the third part of the monograph.

Being completely fluent in the language of the people, the writer became a participant observer during much of his stay. In this role he worked, played, ate, and on several occasions spent the night with the people. He participated in the various festivities, danced three nights in the feast house on a jumping floor, taking notes on the behavior of the participants as well as recording the texts of the songs. The writer's participation in the daily life finally led him to the battlefield in the role of a neutral observer. Having friends on both sides, he was not in danger of being shot and was able to take still and moving pictures of the fighting.

In addition to the participant observer's approach, the writer used informants extensively. About 160 individuals supplied data on general Kapauku culture and on legal cases in particular. There were two different types of sessions with the informants. In the afternoon a single man was invited as a guest and treated to food and tobacco. This type of informant spoke about personal matters such as his life history, his particular financial transactions, possessions and sales, his attitude toward specific native leaders, or his experiences in war or in legal disputes in which either he himself or his close relatives were participants. During these private sessions most of the material on legal cases, sorcery, and local gossip was accumulated.

In the evening the writer made use of a group of informants numbering from five to twenty at a time. Sitting by the fireplace they "taught" the writer, as they used to say, the Kapauku way of life. During these meetings notes on history, philosophy, religion, politics, law, and economics were secured and texts of legends and myths recorded. The several informants present at the same time corrected each other's generalizations and discussed the various controversial issues, thus providing the writer with more reliable data, different opinions, and such variations as are due to personal and residential factors. Some of the informants were so intelligent that the writer sometimes forgot they were Papuans and argued with them as if they were his European or American professors.

Collecting data on genealogies provided the writer with a crude measure for testing the reliability of the individual informants. If their statements about more distant relatives were substantiated by the data supplied by other informants who were closely related to the same relatives, the original informants were considered reliable.

The writer's relations with the people assumed a more formal basis when three of the prominent headmen[2] asked him to become their best friend. Thereafter the writer received the most intimate information as well as the secrets of the three men. It was as if a new world opened up. The writer started to comprehend the emotional problems of the Kapauku men, their attitude toward Europeans, their "Weltanschauung." He felt their fears and was allowed to become a partner in their joys. He became aware of the local gossip and acquired a knowledge of the identity of the local "cannibals" and sorcerers.

Whenever possible, the writer recorded native texts. Thus he obtained full versions of myths, legends, songs, political and judicial speeches, magical and religious rituals, spells and prayers. The favorable research situation also allowed the use of questionnaires and of Rorschach tests.

There is little literature on the Kapauku. What is available are a few short articles

[2] Names of the three best friends: Ijaaj Jokagaibo of Itoda, Ijaaj Ekajewaijokaipouga of Aigii, Ijaaj Awiitigaaj of Botukebo.

on specialized topics written about the Kapauku in regions other than the Kamu Valley (de Bruijn, 1939a–c, 1940), and a book on the Mountain Papuans (le Roux, 1948–51) in which generalizations are so broad and nonspecific as to preclude its use as a source of data on the Kapauku. A few additional sources disclose nonobjective impressions about the Kapauku of the Paniai Lake region.

ACKNOWLEDGMENTS

The research among the Papuans of Central Netherlands New Guinea which has resulted in this monograph was generously financed by the Ford Foundation. However, the Foundation is not to be understood as approving by virtue of its grant any of the statements made or the views expressed in this volume. I am grateful to the Administration of Netherlands New Guinea for inland transportation, protection, and support during the period of the research.

This study was originally presented to the faculty of the Graduate School of Yale University in partial fulfillment of the requirements for the degree of Doctor of Philosophy. I am particularly indebted to Professor Cornelius Osgood, my adviser, for his encouragement and advice during the course of my research and for the constructive criticisms and constant aid connected with the preparation of this volume. Without his backing and help, this monograph might not have been written.

I wish to express my thanks for the assistance of many: R. den Haan, for his understanding, refreshing correspondence, and support during my research; Marion Doble, for help in learning the Kapauku language; Professor Floyd G. Lounsbury, Professor W. S. Laughlin, Professor George P. Murdock, and Pauline Schwartz, for helpful advice and suggestions; and Shirley P. Glaser, for the maps and drawings in this monograph.

Finally, I thank Ijaaj Jokagaibo and my many Kapauku informants for their friendship, protection, and instruction in their language and culture.

Yale University, 1958   LEOPOLD POSPISIL

CONTENTS

	PAGE
Preface	3
Acknowledgments	6
Part One: The Kapauku World and the Individual	13
Introductory Statement	13
The Universe and Its Creator	16
Introduction	16
Good and evil	17
Ugatame	17
Spirits	18
Man	19
Magic: the relation between spirits and man	24
Animals	32
The relations of animals and men	32
The relations of animals and spirits	33
The world of plants	33
The relations of plants and spirits	34
The inanimate world	34
Conclusion	34
Life of an Individual	35
Pregnancy and birth	35
"Aejoka stage"	38
"Peu joka stage"	38
"Joka stage"	40
Adolescence	44
"Juwo, a pig feast"	47
Marriage	52
Adulthood	56
Senescence	59
Death	60
Conclusion	62
Part Two: The Ijaaj-Pigome Confederacy	63
Introduction	63
The Ijaaj-Pigome Confederacy	64
Geography	64
Population	67
Food Quest	68
Social Structure	74
The phratry	74
The subsib	75
The lineage	75
Political Structure	76
Leadership	77
The concept of freedom and independence	77
"Tonowi, the authority"	79

7

PAGE

The Best Friend Relationship... 86
War.. 88
The Sublineage.. 95
    Land Ownership... 97
    Social Structure... 100
The Village of Botukebo... 101
    Population... 101
    Social Structure.. 102
    Economy... 104
    Political Structure... 107
The Household... 110
    Residence... 110
    Daily Life.. 112
    Economy... 114
       Individualism.. 115
       Production... 118
       Distribution.. 121
       Investment.. 131
       Consumption... 131
The Family.. 132
    The Nuclear Family.. 132
    The Polygynous Family... 135
    Adoption.. 136
    The Extended Family... 137
       Kinship behavior.. 137
       Kinship terminology... 139
PART THREE: RULES AND DISPUTES IN THE KAPAUKU SOCIETY........................ 144
Offences against Persons.. 145
    Murder.. 146
    Attempted Murder.. 149
    Manslaughter by Accident.. 149
    Battery... 152
    Attempted Suicide... 153
    Sorcery... 154
    Taboo... 155
       Personal taboos... 156
       General taboos.. 156
    Lying... 159
    Relations between the Sexes... 161
    Incest.. 164
    Adultery.. 167
    Divorce... 172
Offences against Rights in Things... 176
    Ownership of Land... 176
    Trapping and Hunting Laws... 182

PAGE

Ownership of Movables... 184
    Theft.. 184
    Theft of a pig.. 192
Destruction of Property.. 196
Liability for Property.. 197
Ususfructus... 200
Intestate Inheritance.. 201
    Intestate inheritance from a male............................... 201
    Intestate inheritance from a woman............................. 203
    Intestate inheritance by a minor............................... 203
    Inheritance of bride price..................................... 204
    Concluding remark on intestate inheritance..................... 204
Testament... 205
Contract.. 208
Sales Contract.. 209
    Sale of land... 209
    Sale of crops.. 210
    Sale of pigs... 211
    Sale of chickens and dogs...................................... 214
    Sale of houses... 215
    Sale of movables... 215
    Agency in the sales contract................................... 215
Barter.. 216
Pig Breeding Contract... 217
Land Lease.. 218
Credit.. 219
    Daba loans... 219
    Waka jaedai loans.. 226
    Kadee jaamakii loans... 228
    Nogei jegeka menii loans....................................... 228
Loan of Movables.. 228
Labor Contract.. 228
Gifts... 229
    Gift of land... 229
    Gift of movables... 230
Forcible Seizure of Property...................................... 230
Offences against and by an Authority............................... 232
Delicts by an Authority which Exploit his Power to Pass Decisions......... 232
Delicts against the Power of an Authority.......................... 234
Delicts against Society.. 243
PART FOUR: KAPAUKU LAW... 248
The Form of Law—a Problem of Methodology.......................... 249
The Attributes of Law... 257
    The Attribute of Authority..................................... 258
    The Attribute of Intention of Universal Application............. 262

PAGE

The Attribute of Obligatio... 264
The Attribute of Sanction... 267
    Corporal sanctions... 268
    Economic sanctions.. 269
    Psychological sanctions....................................... 270
    Supernatural sanctions.. 271
    Self-redress.. 271
    Cases without sanctions....................................... 272
  Conclusion.. 272
Legal Levels... 272
Legal Dynamics.. 278
Justice.. 285
The Relativity of Law.. 288
CONCLUSION.. 290
BIBLIOGRAPHY.. 293

ILLUSTRATIONS

PLATES

Explanation of Plates AT END
1. A Young Informant, Ijaaj Akaawoogi
2. The Kapauku Country
3. A Kapauku Village and House
4. Scenes of Food Production
5. Pictures of the Pig Feast
6. Views of a Kapauku War
7. A Tree Burial and a Kapauku Headman
8. Kapauku People and Scenes

TEXT FIGURES

	PAGE
1. The Western Part of Netherlands New Guinea	12
2. Chart Showing Status Curves of the Sexes	60
3. The Kamu Valley and the Wissel Lakes	65
4. Political Structure of the Ijaaj-Pigome Confederacy	85
5. Sublineages in the Southeastern Kamu Valley	96
6. Plan of the Village of Botukebo	103
7. Diagram Showing Social Control in the Family	115
8. Diagram of the Attributes of Law	263
9. Diagram Illustrating Legal Dynamics	279

TABLES

	PAGE
1. Demography of the Five Full Member Villages of the Ijaaj-Pigome Confederacy	67
2. Demography of the Village of Botukebo	102
3. Financial Status of the Residents of Botukebo	107

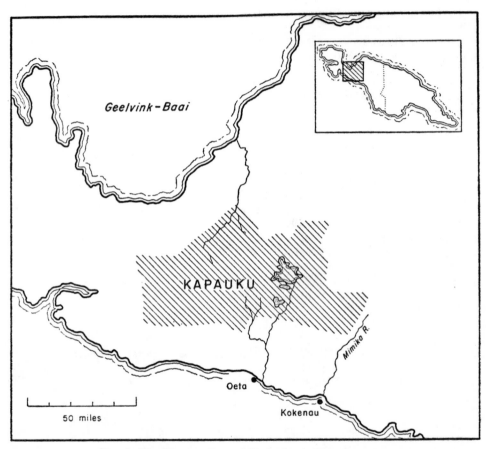

FIG. 1. The Western Part of Netherlands New Guinea.

PART ONE: THE KAPAUKU WORLD AND THE INDIVIDUAL

INTRODUCTORY STATEMENT

KAPAUKU is a name applied by the coastal people of southwestern Netherlands New Guinea to a tribe of about 60,000 Mountain Papuans who inhabit an area in the Central Highlands located between 135°25' and 137° east longitude and 3°25' and 4°10' south latitude (Fig. 1). The Moni Papuans who live to the northeast of this area named them Ekari. The people call themselves "Me" which means "the people."

The males average 151.2 cm., while the average female stands 142.1 cm. high. Their heads are brachycephalic, the average index being 80 for males and 81 for females. Their faces are broad (facial index for males 78; facial index for females 76) and their bodies are well proportioned. Heavy brow ridges as well as deeply depressed roots of broad noses with straight bridges and depressed tips lend to the males a fierce look. This is even more accentuated by the wreath of black beard left growing on the peripheries of the massive jaw and on the angulated zygomatic arches (Pl. 7, *bottom*). The full but not everted lips are often spread in a broad grin which dispels the impression of ferocity and shows two rows of wonderfully healthy teeth. The people have dark pigmentation, their skin ranging from deep dark brown to bronze. The babies and small children are of a light bronze color. The hair which varies from kinky through curly to wavy is red-blonde in about thirty-five per cent of the children. It tends to become dark brown at the age of about fifteen years. However, the writer has observed many males and females in their twenties and thirties who still have reddish hair.

The country of the Kapauku is rugged with high mountains (some peaks attain an altitude of 14,000 feet) and deep valleys. In the northeastern part of the territory there are three spectacular lakes—Paniai, Tage, and Tigi—which are arranged in a line from north to south (Pl. 2, *bottom*). To the west there is a fourth residuum of an old lake—the swampy, flat Kamu Valley, dotted with small lakes, the waters of which are led southward by the winding Edege River. The valley floor lies 4,500 feet above sea level, and the surrounding mountains rise to peaks well over 9,000 feet. The temperature in this valley reaches about 28°C. at noon, between two and three in the afternoon with the arrival of a short tropical storm it drops to about 20°C. and is then followed by a mild, warm evening. During the night the air cools off, and toward morning the temperature may drop to 6°C.

The dense vegetation of the virgin forests which cover the higher reaches of the mountains includes a great variety of tall hardwood evergreens, some soft wood trees, several species of pandanus palms, bamboo, rattan, shrubbery, various vines, and many kinds of flowers, weeds, and grasses. The bottoms of the valleys are, as a rule, swampy. The floor of the Kamu Valley is covered with tall grass and reeds which from a distance give an impression of a green carpet. The native fauna consists of several species of marsupials, rats, wild pig which has been introduced, cassowary birds, several species of birds of paradise, parrots, hawks, a few lizards, and some non-poisonous snakes. In the Kamu Valley the game is so scarce as to provide only a small supplementary source of proteins in the native diet.

In this environment of rich soil, luxurious vegetation, but paucity of animals, the Kapauku live by horticulture. With their neolithic polished stone axes, they clear patches of secondary growth forests and build fences around the areas in order to protect the growing crops from wild, as well as domesticated, pigs. The newly cleared land is burned over and on the following day a variety of crops is planted by means of a planting stick. The Kapauku raise sweet potatoes, sugar cane, several species of greens which resemble spinach, bananas, taro, gourds, cucumbers, and three different species of reeds, the young shoots and buds of which are eaten. Recently introduced tobacco and manioc are grown as well.

The domesticated pig forms the important source of proteins in the native diet. Apart from supplying food, pig breeding constitutes the only way to become rich and to acquire prestige, achievements which in turn enable a man to become an influential politician. The animal when young is kept in the house where it shares a room with the woman who is raising it. When about four months of age, it sleeps under the elevated floor of the native plank house. It is free to roam the country and to look for the food which forms a supplement to the sweet potatoes fed to the pig twice a day.

The Kapauku devote some of their spare time to hunting, trapping, and gathering. These activities, practiced in the Kamu Valley more for enjoyment than as daily work, add necessary proteins to the predominantly vegetarian diet. The hunting is done with bow and arrows, and the most common trap is a snare which is used for catching wild boar, rodents, and marsupials as well as birds. The gathering of a great variety of bugs, larvae, frogs, reptiles, fruit, as well as wild plants supplements the products of agriculture and hunting.

The fishless rivers and lakes offer to the natives an abundance of crayfish, tadpoles, water bugs, and dragonfly larvae, which the native women catch in oval or circular nets. From time to time, men may enjoy diving for crayfish or spearing them with a contrivance consisting of a reed shaft with a seven-pronged hardwood tip.

Kapauku material culture is very simple. There is no pottery, weaving, use of metal, sculpture, or painting. Basketry is limited to the manufacture of braided rattan armlets. The natives distinguish themselves, however, in stringmaking and netting. The inner bark of several species of shrubs and trees provides them with necessary raw material. String is rolled on the thigh by men as well as by women. While women use a coarse string for the manufacture of utilitarian goods such as fishing nets, rough net bags, and string skirts, the men devote more time to the production of fine strings which are utilized in making purses, net bags, shoulder nets, and ornamental dance nets. This activity constitutes the people's main artistic expression. To make their products even more pleasing, they use yellow and red orchid stems as a wrapping on the string of the net bags, thus producing colorful designs on the finished artifacts.

The native dress is a very conspicuous one because it is scanty. While women wear a sort of skirt made of strands of inner bark or of string, the men adorn their bodies with a penis sheath made from a long, orange gourd closed at the top with a fur stopper. This cover for the genitals is held in position by a belt braided of inner bark string. Both sexes wear their net carrying bags suspended from the top of the head.

Polished stone axes and knives as well as flint flakes and bone needles are the only manufactured tools of the Kapauku. As weapons, the natives use bows and arrows tipped with hardwood or bamboo points. Spears do not serve as weapons in this society.

The Kapauku of both sexes adorn their bodies with shell and teeth necklaces as well as with hair pins decorated with feathers of parrots and birds of paradise. The tall trees in the jungle are used for the manufacture of dugout canoes and planks.

The natives live in rectangular plank houses with roofs made of thatch or bark. The house has an elevated floor covered with palm bark and has an open fireplace of stones in the center of each room. Save for some pegs and wood racks, the house is void of any kind of furniture. While men of the household sleep in a common room, every adult woman should, ideally speaking, have a room for herself and her children.

A native patrilocal household consists of two or three monogamous or polygynous families, the male heads of which are usually closely related. A cluster of about fifteen houses forms a village which is ideally exogamous. Since the Kapauku are organized into many exogamous patrilineal totemistic sibs, and because a village is composed of the male members of the same sib with their in-marrying spouses, we may regard the village as a patri-clan community (Murdock, 1949: 68). Several villages are united into a political confederacy which represents the largest unit in the political organization of the Kapauku. While the confederacy becomes engaged in frequent wars in which its male members fight as a unit, warfare almost never occurs inside this group.

Wealth plus skill in oratory constitute the prerequisites for assumption of the political leadership of a village. Because the wealth of an individual changes with losses and successes in pig breeding as well as with the age of the individual, the political structure of the village and confederacy is in constant flux. New individuals are elevated to village leadership only to lose their positions some years later to younger or more successful pig breeders. One of the village headmen through his influence and the number of his followers and allies achieves a position which amounts to the territorial headmanship of the confederacy. The native leaders maintain order by application of an unwritten common law which forms the basis for decisions informally rendered.

The Kapauku believe in and practice a capitalistic economy in which money, credit, sales, and savings play an important role. Individualism is more pronounced in this culture than it is even in the West. There is practically not a single piece of property owned by more than one individual. Even the ownership rights of wives and of children eleven years old are clearly defined and distinguished from the rights of other members of the family. In the economic sphere, the individual is largely independent and there are few regulations that restrict him in his activities.

In their interpersonal relations, all people consider themselves equal. There are no castes, slaves, or social classes. The position of women is not greatly inferior to that of the men. Obedience is achieved mainly through inducement rather than by forcing on someone the behavior desired. The people are realistic in their outlook, placing little emphasis upon ceremonialism and the supernatural. Perhaps the most outstanding trait of their personality is a quantitative approach to the universe. Their highly developed decimal mathematical system which enables the people to count into thousands is one of the manifold manifestations of the quantitative orientation of the culture. They place value upon higher numbers and larger volume. The emphasis upon quantity may assume forms which come as a shock to a Western observer. My informants when confronted with a magazine picture of a smiling girl failed completely to react to her beauty. Instead they started to count all her teeth.

THE UNIVERSE AND ITS CREATOR

Introduction. Unlike Europeans, the Kapauku do not separate supernatural and natural phenomena. Their world, created a long time ago by Ugatame the creator, is composed of five main categories: spirits, men, animals, plants, and inanimate substance. Since this section serves to present the Kapauku view of the universe, we shall not employ the traditional category of religion to set off some phenomena from others. Instead, the attempt will be made to follow the above mentioned categories and their mutual relations as closely as possible. Let us begin with a short version of a legend.

"Once upon a time we were small dark people. We lived in this country because Ugatame determined so. We had no pigs, no sweet potatoes, no rats, and no shell money, but we were a healthy people. Death, disease, and flies being absent, we were immortal. Once upon a time a young girl came to our country from the coastal region (north coast) where she had been living with her parents. She was a tall white woman, much taller than we were. Wherever she went, she distributed pigs, rats, sweet potatoes, taro, shell money, and menstrual blood. Thus she came, carrying a canoe, to our Kamu Valley. At Magidimi she lost the canoe and one of our men proposed to find it for her. But instead he raped the young girl. As a consequence the canoe disappeared into the ground. The girl became angry. She castigated the man and gave him a piece of wood, saying: 'Because you all are bad, beating and raping people, I give you flies, death, and darkness. You take it.' Then she left for the Mapia region where she married a very tall man and they both left for the southern coast on their way to the land of the girl. Having boarded a canoe they departed. We do not know where they went. The people say they went to the sun and moon. In the distant future they may return. The two were Ugatame."

To the Kapauku, his country is part of the flat world, limited by the solid bowl of blue sky ("*epa maida*, on the blue") making a circle where the sky touches the earth. The sun travels on the inside of the inverted blue bowl during the day. In the evening it slips under the edge of this bowl and travels back from west to east on the outside of the sky ("*epa wado*, blue over"), thus bringing night. Emerging in the east again, it marks a new day. There is no underworld below the surface of the earth; there is just rock and soil.

Beyond the blue of the sky exists a world similar to ours—the land of Ugatame, the creator of earth, man, spirits, and of the laws of nature, as well as of all that occurs. "He created because he wanted to do so." He is the only being with true free will. All events in nature, all men's actions, disease, death, and accidents are predetermined by him. There is no true chance and there is no true cause. Everything is bound in a sequence of events predetermined by Ugatame. "Why then are you angry with the man who killed your brother? His action was determined by Ugatame," the writer said to a Kapauku. "Because Ugatame determined it, I am unable to control my anger. When I do control it, it is not because I choose to do so, but because I am afraid of my enemies; this fear I cannot control as I cannot control anger." The psychological motivations for actions, drives, anxieties, needs, and emotions seem to be conceived by the people as a compulsory force by which the creator enacts his will.

Good and evil. To pursue this trend of thought even further, we may inquire into the nature of evil and good. Since both are determined by Ugatame, he then must be the source of them. Informants readily confirm this idea and they do not understand why we are astonished by this notion. "Evil, *peu*" and "good, *enaa*" are not substantives in the Kapauku language. They are not absolute phenomena. The criteria for good and evil are always relative to subject and object. The same action may be good from the point of view of the actor and bad for the object. To say that "*puja peu*, the lie is bad" actually means that it is bad to lie to us but that it may be good to lie in order to defend our group against another group. To deprive a man of his personal liberty, an act unheard of in the native culture, seemed an exception to the rule. My informants claimed such an action to be "*peu umina*, bad altogether." The only instance of this deprivation they experience was the "white man's jail." At first they asserted such deprivation to be bad for everyone. Only later, the writer found out that even this unbelievable "crime" was not, after all "bad altogether" or bad absolutely. The people were willing to admit it must be good from the point of view of the white man.

Ugatame. The essence of the universe is the unfolding of the scheme "*ebijata*, drawn up," by Ugatame. As a being, he is inconceivable to the people. This statement, strictly speaking, is false in three respects. Ugatame is neither "he," nor "being," nor "is." Ugatame is not of masculine sex, nor are "these two" a singular phenomenon. The nature of the creator comprises both sexes, as we have already seen in the introductory myth. Moreover Ugatame "are" not people, animals, spirits, or anything—they are two, everything, and nothing—inconceivable, incomprehensible, their dual sex being manifested by the sun and the moon. "Are the sun and moon Ugatame?" the writer asked. "No, they are not." "But you called them so." "Yes, we do, but they are not Ugatame, we cannot see the latter as we do the sun and moon, and we cannot comprehend them." The moon and sun are manifestations of Ugatame, images which human beings can perceive. The creator is omniscient, omnipotent, and potentially omnipresent. He never punishes man; how could he when all events are determined by him? Men do not fear him. Their relation to Ugatame is similar to that of a child to its father. They do not make any offerings. They just ask and pray, for "good" events—good to the individuals praying. Ijaaj Jokagaibo of Itoda concluded that prayer probably has been also predetermined by Ugatame, thus it is not distinguished from other realities.

· *Spirits.* Ugatame created not only earth, animals, man, plants, water, and sky, but also spirits which are phenomena with a different existence from our own. To the Kapauku, these beings form a natural and indispensable part of the universe. Sickness and death, like success and failure in a man's life, are explained by the actions of these beings. They follow definite natural laws. They can be conquered by man. Having been created along with the rest of the universe by Ugatame, they are a realization of Ugatame's "creative determination." The *"enija*, spirit,"* is usually invisible, but it may appear to a man in a dream or during the day in a vision assuming a form traditional in type. There are many "species" of spirits, each one having a distinctive manifestation. Their essence is immaterial. Most people see them as shadows among the trees when they make a scratching or whistling noise. If an *"enija"* is seen by a man in a friendly mood, in a dream or as a vision, the man is believed to have acquired power over it. Ijaaj Jokagaibo saw the spirit Tege, one of the most feared and lethal beings, in the form of a handsome young man sitting at noon on a boulder in the jungle and holding the bow and arrows with which he kills people. Jokagaibo knew right away from its appearance that it was Tege and tried to talk to it. But the spirit disappeared. After a few years it came back, this time in a dream, and it started a conversation with him. By obtaining the proper vision and performing the prescribed magical rites, he acquired control over it.

All spirits combine evil and good functions, and all of them have a definite sex. A spirit is not a singular being. It is a species. To have Tege as a guardian spirit means that one commands a whole army of these beings. Guardian spirits are used in curing magic as well as in sorcery. In the former, they chase away other evil spirits; in the latter, they are the aggressors. During the day the various spirits are believed to roam the virgin forests and the mountains, while at night they attack people, slipping into them, according to the less sophisticated informants, through the mouth, or according to more intelligent people, immaterially penetrating the body as two shadows might fuse together. A spirit, by its singular-plural existence, at the same time is mortal and immortal, destructible and indestructible. A shaman can destroy Tege but in its plural aspect it would continue to exist, making its appearance in the singular form in many cases as sickness.

The Kapauku make use of these spirits to explain natural phenomena. Thus clouds, although clearly recognized as vapor, are believed to be a spirit's special habitat. Rain is said to be caused by the female Abeguwo, a spirit who urinates down on the people. Stars are the lighted ends of cigarettes smoked by the spirits in the blue sky. Thunder is the flatus of a spirit. And earthquakes are caused by a mythical beast Awega, who beats the earth with its tail. The latter is not a true spirit, but in the Kapauku world it occupies a place intermediate between spirits and animals. It has a form and behaves like a huge python and actually is closer to animals in its essence.

Man. Man is a combination of spirit and matter and thus he stands between the animal kingdom and that of spirits. He is composed of the material substance, the man-animal, and of the spiritual component, the soul proper. During the day the spiritual substance and the material one coincide, and the mental processes, such as memory and conception, are cooperative efforts of soul and body. On the other hand, dreaming is always an experience of the soul. The soul leaves the body and wanders around having its own faculties of "spiritual perception and spiritual conception."

These two realities are reflected in the Kapauku epistemology. If one says, "It is so and so," that notion is based upon sensual perception and spiritual conception. The question "Is there an Ugatame beyond the sky?" requires the proper answer, "I do not know." An answer "I know there is . . ." would refer to a spiritual perception (in a dream) or to a sensual perception about which one is completely sure. Thus when the writer asked an informant "Do you know whether there is an Ugatame?" the answer was, "I do not know." Ugatame is imperceptible sensually, as well as spiritually. To get a positive answer on the Kapauku notion of Ugatame, the writer had to ask "What do the Kapauku think, is there an Ugatame?" By such a question the writer referred to the third category of knowledge —the spiritual and bodily conceptualization which, in this case is based neither upon spiritual nor upon sensual perception and is linked with cultural tradition. Thus there are two realities in this world, a material and a spiritual, which correspond to the dual aspect of man—to his body and to his soul. Kapauku also differentiate, more exactly than we do, between perception, *epi kai*, and conception, *dimi gai*.

If we combine the two cognitive processes with the two realities we would expect to get a fourfold classification of notions: the bodily perception referred to as *"ani dou,* I see," *"ani juwii,* I hear," etc.; the bodily conception to which the term *"ani dimi gai,* I think," would correspond; the spiritual conception *"ani ipuwe enija gai,* my soul thinks (in a dream)," and finally, spiritual perception, *"bagume dou,* to dream." Nevertheless this logical scheme, which we would expect to exist, is inconsistent at one point with the actual Kapauku epistemology. There is never a pure "bodily" conception without spiritual assistance, i.e., activity of the soul. In the scheme above, bodily conception should be substituted by mixed bodily and spiritual conception. Thus while the soul by its own thinking in a dream is independent of the body, the body itself is always dependent upon the soul in the process of conceiving. Consequently we have to correct the above scheme as follows: bodily perception, mixed bodily and spiritual conception, pure spiritual conception, and spiritual perception.

The cooperative effort of the body and the soul, of the material and the spiritual, is not only the essence of thinking, but also of life itself. When the soul leaves the body for a prolonged period of time, the body dies, or as the Kapauku says, "I die." What do the Kapauku think of life and death? Is there any concept of "eternal life" in the people's philosophy? Who is "I?"

When a baby is born, it is just a man-animal without a spiritual counterpart. It becomes a true human being with the advent of the soul, an event which coincides with the baby's manifested capacity to think and to speak meaningful sounds. This occurs when the child is about eighteen months old. At that time the formation of a new human being is completed. Accordingly, the life of a man means a symbiosis of the soul and the body. "To live" is expressed in Kapauku *"umii tou,* sleep remain"; "sleep" refers to the spiritual, and "remain" to the bodily existence (remain in the material sense).

The soul is a true spirit. The Kapauku are at a loss if asked about its shape and size. They would say, "It may be like the body in which it dwells. It may be a translucent counterpart of the body. It may change with the growth and aging of the body." But these statements are made simply to satisfy the interrogator's curiosity. Since the essence and importance of a soul is its spirituality, which is imperceptible, the shape itself may be a deception of the senses. Thus the reference to "a departed soul eating a man, walking, causing disease, or helping" is meant in an incorporeal sense although materially expressed. During the day the soul stays in the body of the individual. At night it leaves and wanders around experiencing the things we dream about. Thus the body can and does exist without a soul. This condition exists during the first months of one's life, while a person is sleeping, and finally when one is in a coma or about to die. In all these instances according to the Kapauku, when the mind is away, there is an absence of mental activity. Only the prolonged absence of the soul causes the body to die—death being essentially the cessation of cooperation between spirit and matter.

The Kapauku believe that there is no underworld, no land of the soul. The soul simply leaves the body and proceeds to the virgin forest where it stays during the day. At night it may return and linger around the houses in the village. Its relation to the world of living people is determined by the type of disposal of the body. If a corpse is placed in a tree in a small hut with an opening in front and with the corpse's face directed to the house of the mourners, the soul of the deceased is believed to become a guardian spirit of the relatives who reside in that house and who pray to it. The tree house consists of a platform made of sticks and poles tied by vines to the tree's branches. On the platform, walls are erected. These are made of pieces of wood stuck vertically into the platform. The structure is thatched over with grass and foliage (Pl. 7, *top*).

It is felt that a man should have a burial proportionate to his importance. Accordingly there are several forms of disposing of the dead. But all apply the principle of the window which induces the soul to become a guardian spirit to the dead man's relatives. Interment of a corpse, bound with vines in a squatting position, with the head above the ground is used to dispose of young people, children, or individuals who were considered unimportant during their lives. The head is usually covered over with a dome of branches and soil, and a small window is left in front of the face. A circular fence around this structure keeps out the pigs.

A rich man, on the contrary, is abandoned in a squatting position in a specially constructed house on stilts, the walls of which are made of planks and the roof of bark. The opening of this structure is directed toward the house in which dwells a relative who wants the departed soul as his helper.

Like other spirits, a soul guardian spirit reveals itself as such in the protégé's dream. It helps the man with white and black magic. It brings him luck in his economic endeavors and it fights the attacking evil spirits. In his dreams, a man may be taught new magical formulae, ways of making a fortune, and avoidance of dangers including even those of which one is unaware. The man on his part only prays to the guardian spirit. There are no offerings, and no magic is directed toward the soul.

Interment with the head of the corpse above the ground also facilitates revenge by the departed soul on a sorcerer or a man who, strange as it may seem, may have caused the death by breaking a taboo himself. The writer was fortunate enough to participate in one of these burials. A small boy died of bacillary dysentery. His father, a headman of the village of Botukebo and a famous warrior, charged that his son died because a man from another clan failed to give the father money for killing a common enemy. This should have been paid in precious Kapauku cowries but the culprit gave only poor cowrie shells which had been brought in by white men. The breaking of the supernaturally sanctioned duty to reward the warrior in good currency caused the death of the warrior's son. The father took all necessary steps to punish the offender. He repeatedly instructed his child to go and punish the guilty one. The little boy in his last agonies promised the father to kill the man. After the death, the parent buried his son in a shallow grave with the head protruding above the ground, and with the face and the aperture in the superstructure of the grave directed toward the village of the "killer." We stood in silence above the grave when the father knelt in front of the face of the boy and addressed him for the last time: "You know that you have died because of the unpaid blood reward. The blood of the killed enemy choked you and appeared in your feces. You have promised to punish your 'killer.' Now is the time to go to the guilty one and kill him. There you go my son!" And the father, his eyes full of tears, pointed in the direction the boy was facing.

Relatives bury their dead in graves provided with windows only if they loved them very much and their affection was reciprocated during the life of the deceased. If there is any reason to suspect the departed soul might turn against the mourners, then complete interment, or abandoning of the corpse in the house on a special platform resembling that of the stilt house of the rich man, or cremation takes place. In the case of interment, the corpse is buried in a squatting position with the head covered completely by earth. As a result it is believed that the soul will be prevented from taking revenge on the relatives.

The corpse of an important man whose relatives fear the departed soul is abandoned in the house where he dies. The corpse is then placed on a stilt platform as mentioned above. Similarly, the departed soul of a woman who dies in childbirth is considered dangerous and is disposed of in the same way.

A man killed by an arrow in war, in a dispute, or in an ambush, requires a special kind of burial. Because his soul is expected to punish the killer, the arrow is left in the wound. Thus, by the principle of association of the corpse with the enemy's weapon, the soul is induced and enabled to find the owner of the missile and take revenge. A simple platform, made of two lengthwise poles connected with short crosspoles and supported by four forked sticks five feet in height serves as a proper place of disposal. The structure has nothing to do with the soul's revenge, however. In case of accidental shooting or execution the same structure is erected, but care is taken to remove the lethal arrow from the body, break it, and hide it in the bush, thus disassociating it from the corpse and preventing the departed soul from harming the one who caused the accidental death or the execution.

The spiritual aspect of man is dual. While the soul constitutes the main part of the spiritual aspect, a man also possesses a shadow. During the life of an individual, "*aija*, the shadow," is passive. It just stays near the man; there is no communication between it and the body or the soul. Only after death does the shadow become an active spirit called *tene*. Thus death is not simply a permanent separation of soul and body. It also involves a very delicate process of transfiguration of the spiritual component of man. During life, the good and bad nature are united and are possessions of the "body and soul"—the "I." With the severance of the tie between the two, the malevolent spiritual potentialities of the individual separate themselves from the more positive ones and associate with the departed shadow or *tene*. Although this departed shadow behaves in the same way as does the soul, it differs in its appearance and nature. The *tene's* image shows an etheric, dark outline of the dead man as a detached shadow but without any of the details which one can detect on the soul's image. While both the *tene* and the soul can and do help and harm people, the soul is basically good natured. Its negative actions can always be termed "punishment," while the *tene's* are mischievous. The soul and *tene* both heal. Both help people in distress. But while the soul's help is directed in its action toward the profit of the protégé, the *tene's* action is motivated either by its own present or future advantages or by the harm such an action would bring to other people. In sorcery, one usually asks the *tene* for help. In white magic, one prays to the soul. Generally speaking, people fear the *tene* but feel at ease with the departed soul. The two spirits are not dependent on each other in their actions. They may act independently in a given situation.

Ijaaj Kagajtawii of Aigii of the South Kamu Valley died. The sons built a nice stilt house for the corpse and mummified it by driving a pointed pole through the rectum as far as the neck and by piercing the cadaver with arrows to let the juices and blood flow out. For such a wonderful burial, the sons expected the soul and the *tene* to become efficient guardians and helpers. But it happened that three children of Ijaaj Tideemabii of Kojogeepa, the oldest son of the dead man, died. Tideemabii saw the *tene* of his father in a dream and the *tene* did not address him. Thus it became apparent that the father's *tene* was the killer of Tideemabii's children. The enraged son destroyed the corpse house of Kagajtawii as a reprisal for the murders. After this no further deaths occurred in the family. This absence of more deaths has been attributed to the departed soul of the father whose own *tene* caused the deaths. As a reward for this protection attributed to Kagajtawii's soul, the sons put up the father's skull on a pole facing their house. Thus the departed soul stays at their home and helps, while the *tene* of the same person is said to roam the dark virgin forests of Kemuge mountain and be very hostile to the relatives of the deceased man.

From the above we can conclude that the *tene* is not simply a departed shadow. The shadow not only is passive during a man's life, but is also considered not to be endowed with any definite spiritual properties. It is called "*aija*, the shadow," during a man's life, while after its departure it is called *tene*. On the contrary, "*okai ipuwe enija*, the soul," bears the same name prior to and after the death of the individual. The shadow never experiences dreams, while the soul does. The Kapauku never pray to the shadow during their own lives but they do pray to their own souls for such help as luck in business and protection against disease. Thus it is the impression of the present writer that a *tene's* properties are not simply those taken away from the soul. The latter retains all it had prior to death. A *tene's* spiritual properties are something like a malevolent spiritual reflection of the soul's attributes. Thus death not only separates soul from body, and kills the latter, but it also gives birth to a new phenomenon, the *tene*. Consequently death among the Kapauku is not only a destructive force—it also creates. Because its creation is so terrible, the people have a greater reason to fear death than we do. They abhor death because it not only destroys the body but also creates the evil *tene*.

The Ego concept.—Having discussed death we must turn, finally, to our next problem, the Kapauku concept of life and of "I," the individual. The life of a man starts in the womb. The sperm fluid initiates the growth of the fetus in the mother's body and after the birth it increases the flow of milk. To stimulate the female body to reproduce, one has to have frequent sexual relations. One or a few sporadic relations cannot bring about pregnancy. In the legal field, this notion plays an important role in adultery cases. The fetus and a small baby live without cooperation of spirits of their own. Nevertheless, within the mother's body, and after birth through the mother's breast feeding, the individual "in the making" is under the influence of the mother's soul. The child lives in anticipation of the advent of its own soul. Through the rest of life, soul and body cooperate, and this cooperation is "*umii tou*, living;" the "*tou*, body stays in material space," and the word "*umii*, to sleep," signify the separate existence of the soul. A Kapauku man is not the simple sum total of the two entities, body and soul. His "I" is not the body because he can lose parts of it and still live. "I" is certainly not his "*okai ipuwe enija*, his soul," because he prays to it and it has its own dream experiences. *Ani ipuwe enija* can be translated as "I, the owner of the spirit" or "the spirit owner of myself." It is the opinion of this writer that the latter meaning more clearly symbolizes the Kapauku outlook. The spirit "owns me," rather than vice versa.

If "I" is neither body nor soul, if dreaming is the experience of the soul, and "I" functions just during the day, then the latter concept must refer to the nature of the daily functioning of man's two components together, which is the thinking "I" as the determinator of actions. Thus the essence of "I," the mental process, is the cooperation of soul and body. "Body stays, soul dreams, and body-soul lives."

Magic: the relation between spirits and man. Having discussed spirits and man we may now inquire into the nature of communication between the two. We have already dealt with the guardian spirit institution which enables almost everyone to make contact with the spirits. Nevertheless there are more formalized relations between spirits and men which are carried on by special individuals. While all death and sickness are regarded as caused by evil spirits—wealth, success, and health may be brought to an individual by his guardian spirit. To manipulate the spirits of both types one has to command knowledge of the formalized behavior that is believed to control the spirits and sometimes be able to accomplish the desired task even without their help. Such formalized behavior is called magic and the specialists in it are shamans and sorcerers. The first term is applied here to a man using "white magic," the latter to an obnoxious individual employing "black magic" for selfish reasons. The Kapauku also make the differentiation, calling a shaman "*kamu epi me*, white-magic-know man," and "*kego epi me*, black-magic-know man."

Shaman.—A shaman, or *kamu epi me*, is always a middle-aged man or woman, in good health. An old, weak individual shows by his physical condition that he cannot take care of his own health, and certainly cannot be helpful to others. A young individual, in his or her "teens," would lack the experience necessary for successful performances. All the shamans the writer saw were healthy, muscular, athletic-looking people, usually rich and successful in their economic and political pursuits. Personal success is proof to the Kapauku of a man's power. How can a man who is not capable of acquiring good health and financial prosperity for himself help others to the same things? A shaman must also be a fast talker with a convincing voice and respectable behavior. He commands spiritual powers which an ordinary man lacks. He usually has more than one guardian spirit. To be a shaman one must have as helpers not only souls and *tene* of the dead relatives, but also an important spirit, as for example Tege, the horrible demon of the woods, Madou, the water spirit, Ukwaanija, the wife of Tege, or Makiutija, the ghost of the earth. These spirits are effective as helpers not only for chasing away other evil spirits but, by having power over them, the shaman obviously can cure a man whose sickness has been caused by one of the species he commands. Thus a Kapauku looks for a shaman helped by Madou when he believes the latter is the trouble-maker. Ijaaj Ekajewaijokaipouga of Aigii, the headman of the Ijaaj-Pigome confederacy had five departed souls and *tene*, and twelve different evil spirits as his helpers. Being an excellent speaker, muscular, healthy, very rich, and a political leader as well as a brave warrior, he was considered one of the best curers in the valley.

The profession of shaman is open to everyone irrespective of sex, position, or age. Nevertheless, only individuals with the above mentioned qualifications tend to be recognized by the society. One becomes a shaman not by learning but because of the power that comes through dreams and visions in which one acquires spirit helpers and is taught by them specific cures. Dreams also tell the shaman the nature of the disease of a particular man and prescribe a suitable cure. The society recognizes a man as a shaman when he performs several successful cures and tends to have the above mentioned characteristics. A shaman has no supernatural powers himself. The cure is performed for him by his spirit-helpers. They tell him the formula in dreams, or they possess the shaman and talk through his mouth in a high-pitched voice and like a machine-gun that is firing. Other people listen to the talk and interpret it, the shaman in this case acting as a medium. The advantages associated with shamanism lead everybody to envy the lucky man. He is most respected. From his activities, he derives only friends and no enemies. For a single cure he is paid from two to six true Kapauku cowries. His political and legal authority, if he happens to have any, become more prominent with his success in the field of magic.

White magic.—From the functional point of view we can divide white magic into preventive magic, curative magic, countermagic, rain stopping and rain making, profit making, love inducement, and war magic. From the teleological aspect we may distinguish magic affecting groups and magic affecting individuals only. Although the specific performances are "revealed to individuals by spirits" and differ one from the other, we may abstract some observances which recur over and over again. The following elements are met in many magical rituals:

1. Magically important plants. A Ti plant top resembling a broom and called *"ude kopa"* is believed to be endowed with power to chase away most of the spirits. It has also a divinatory function. A knot is made on the ends of the leaves and the broom is shaken during the performance of a ritual. When the knot is shaken lose, one is sure of the cure's success and of the departure of the evil spirit.

Most of the spirits are associated with a specific species of tree, bush, or flower. The shaman makes use of these during a ritual to influence the spirit. For example, *"otikai*, tree top," a broad leafed evergreen tree, sometimes fifteen feet high, is stuck into the ground and a ritual performed around it when the Tege spirit is involved. The spirit should be pleased and listen to the shaman.

2. Offerings are made to induce the evil spirit to leave. Fire, foliage of magically significant trees, intestines of rats and small birds, and gall bladders of pigs are the objects used for this purpose. We may notice here that Kapauku do not waste too much in pacifying the spirits.

3. Offerings, if not hung on a pole in the type of magic affecting a group, are always

thrown into the tall grass behind the back of the shaman. He does not look back at the offerings lest he disturb the spirit who is about to accept them.

4. Shamans always talk in a fast, machine-gun-like fashion, and often in a high-pitched voice, interrupting the talk by breathing in with a hissing sound. They almost always stand during the performance while the individual patient is seated.

5. The shaman may chase away evil spirits by moving magical plants and glowing embers counterclockwise, followed immediately by clockwise circles around the head of the seated patient or around a group of standing persons.

6. Spitting on embers or just any place has an effect similar to the circles described above.

7. Water has a purifying force. Shamans, as well as patients, apply it freely to different parts of their bodies during a performance. Some shamans and patients even take a bath during or after the cure.

8. Every magical procedure the writer observed started with a prayer by the shaman to the creator and to his guardian spirits asking for help with the magic. After this came the main part of the ceremony including magical spells, offerings, spitting, encircling, beating the bush and the sick man with the *"ude kopa*, Ti plant"* and the using of bow and arrows. During this part of the magic, either an offering bundle is prepared by placing leaves, ferns, intestines, and embers in one bundle of leaves, or the appropriate single offerings are immediately thrown into the jungle or placed on a pole or stump. In some rituals there is a third part comprising purification rites, consisting of an application of water to the bodies of both patient and curer followed by the throwing of the offering bundle into the bush in the manner previously described.

9. As a part of their magical performances, some shamans extract an *"enijaka agijo,* evil object"* which had been placed in the body of the sick man by the spirit. They do this by means of sleight of hand, using a piece of charcoal, a small stone, a human bone, or a hair; they may even bite the patient and spit out his blood, declaring it to be the spirit's evil substance. These performances, although presented in a way to deceive an audience, are in essence just performances of contagious magic. The spirit is believed to cling to an object recognized by the older experienced people to have been introduced by the shaman. After the "extraction," the object is thrown away.

10. Toward the end of an act the shaman may also recapture the patient's soul which, although still lingering around, is about to depart. He does this by catching the end of the *ude kopa* and then placing this magical broom on the head of the patient saying, "Stay, do not depart." This is done only after the evil spirit has been expelled.

11. A shaman may become possessed by his guardian spirit. He falls into a trance and speaks in a high pitched voice about the cause of the disease and its proper cure. An assistant interprets what the shaman says.

12. Dreams may be used by some magicians as a part of the treatment. During the act, the shaman falls asleep. The assistant suddenly screams and grabs the shaman, thus waking him up. The latter, still half asleep, shouts a few words. These

words are interpreted by the assistant in the same way as a spirit's message during
a possession.

The above elements are used in the categories of magic which follow. Shamans
differ in the selection of elements and in their own peculiar choice of the wording
of a magical spell, of the way they use their bows and arrows, and of repetition and
sequences of the techniques. They also differ in eloquence and knowledge of the
lore, and in the selection of paraphernalia.

Preventive magic is used when one man suspects another individual of sending
an evil spirit to kill him. He prefers having the magic performed prior to the onset
of the disease. The procedure is almost exactly the same as in magic used for the
curative purposes described below.

Curative magic is used after a man has been attacked by an evil spirit which
tries to scare away the soul. The shaman tries to expel the spirit by bribing it with
offerings and frightening it away by his power. This type of magic is the most
common of all the categories discussed. All the techniques and the general sequence
outlined above are employed. At the end of the process, the shaman makes recom-
mendations about the continuation of the treatment of the patient. He may suggest
another practitioner. Very often he asks the sick man for an expression of generosity
as a condition for complete recovery. This is usually a pig-killing and free distribution of the meat to the public. The sick man may also be requested to set aside a
certain quantity of cowries for his son's inheritance.

Counter-magic takes place when a man is believed to be a victim of sorcery.
The objectives are twofold. Not only should the patient be relieved of the spell
and rid of the evil spirit but counter-magic should be used to send back the evil
spirit to kill the sorcerer. Since this is considerable to ask of a spirit, the performance
is more elaborate, the bribes are more numerous, and greater generosity is required.
Kapauku call this type "*kego ekigai*, to untie the black magic."

Rain-stopping magic is a very simple affair. It falls within the scope of imitative
magic. A branch may be cut and placed in the house to dry; with its drying the rain
is supposed to "dry out" too. Through the evaporation process, water in a bamboo
container induces rain to stop as well. Also, ashes will serve for the same purpose
when thrown into the rain; they stop it by "drying it out." Since rain is caused by
spirits, these activities are communications between the spirits and man.

Rain-making magic consists simply of a spell.

Magic for economic profit, such as earning much shell money and thus gaining
prestige, is used by the giver of a pig feast at two occasions. One is the day when the
people gather to start the construction of the dance house and the other the night
prior to the *putu duwai naago*, the day when pigs are slaughtered and the pork
sold. At both occasions the magic can be divided into two parts: a prayer by the
feast owner to Ugatame, to his guardian spirits, and to his own soul to make the
feast a success, thus bringing him much shell money and prestige; and the magic
performance itself, consisting of an offering of rat's intestines to influence the "flow
of cowries."

In the prayer, Ugatame is asked to create cowries for the man who prays and thus to change any bad destiny he might have originally ordained. Here is the text of the prayer made on the night before the pigs are slaughtered:

Mege ebijata me, ekina ebijata me, Ugatame nadouje!

(Creator of cowries, creator of pigs, creator look upon me!)

Ekina pame taime mege pame taime, owa imouda kapa mijo nauwigou.

(You who gave birth to and made pigs, you who gave birth to and made cowries, from the roof top descend down for me.)

Ekina ugataine, mege ugataine, naugaije!

(Wanting to create pigs, wanting to create cowries, create them for me!)

This prayer is expected to help the ensuing magic to be successful by calling on the help of Ugatame. The magical spell which follows the prayer is directed toward acquiring shell money and has nothing to do with the creator, the soul, or the guardian spirit. At the time of the construction of the dance house, a prayer is made after an "*onage*, willow-like tree," has been cut to be taken to the site of the dance house as part of the rite. The formula is uttered over the stump of the freshly cut tree and the rat's intestines are placed thereon. Then the feast owner and his companions, shouting and yodeling for joy, carry the tree to the village. There, on the building site, the tree is stuck into the ground, together with the Ti plant next to the main front post which carries the ridgepole. In this place a hole is also dug, a new spell pronounced, and again rat's intestines are deposited, this time in the ground. The hole with the offering is closed by placing a forked stick in it which serves as one of the supports of the jumping floor structure.

During the evening preceding the day when pigs are slaughtered and pork is sold, the pig feast giver prays again (using the above text) and utters a magical spell, this time depositing the rat's intestines in the bush.

Love magic is made by introducing a small piece of *janebo*, a tiny flowering plant with violet blossoms, into a fruit or a cooked sweet potato, which is then handed over by the lover to the chosen person. The latter, after eating the food, is believed to become magically attracted to the person who gave the food and to fall in love with him or her. No spirits are invoked in this kind of magic.

War magic makes use of two pieces of paraphernalia, either *jape daagu*, a highly polished stone with white veins in it, or the green branches of the *bii* tree. Both objects are used to prevent one from becoming sick or dying from an arrow wound. The simple magical rite consists of licking either of the articles mentioned above and rubbing them in slow motion over one's body. These rites are not directed toward preventing one from being hit or toward healing one's wound. They are performed by the warrior to repel an evil spirit trying to enter the body through a wound, or to expel the spirit after it has taken hold of the wounded man's body and has manifested itself in fever, blood poisoning, or some other agony. The belief is that one cannot magically prevent being wounded by a missile. Being wounded depends entirely upon the enemy and the skill of the warrior in avoiding flying arrows. One uses magic against evil spirits only. These spirits, manifesting themselves by the above symptoms, try to kill the man whose body they have entered by expelling his soul. They are sent by the enemy and are the latter's guardians and helpers.

Group magic rites differ from the ones used in the cases of an individual in that some of the above outlined ritual elements are not effective in the group type at all. Also some rites have to be modified because of the fact that there are many persons who act as patients or who otherwise profit from the act. Thus, in the case of group magic when many individuals from the same political or social unit—such as a political confederacy or a village—are believed to be attacked by an evil spirit, the elements of water purification, soul recapture, extraction of an evil object, treatment with the Ti plant broom, *ude kopa*, and the squatting of the patients are eliminated. Other ritual observances are modified to suit the changed situations. Encircling with *ude kopa*, rat's intestines, glowing embers held by the shaman and moved around the heads of the individual patients, are all changed to the encircling of the whole group of gathered kinsmen. On this occasion the shaman is walking rather than standing in one place and he carries the mentioned paraphernalia altogether in a bundle, thus saving time and energy. In the case of war magic with intent to affect many persons at the same time, the shaman rather than the individual warrior becomes the performer of the rite. He does not touch the individuals with the "*jape daagu*, charm stone," but merely carries it around the group while uttering the prescribed spells. Some of the functional categories of magic discussed never appear to be used in the group rituals; these are the love and profit making, rain making and rain stopping practices.

Sorcery.—"*Kego tai*, black magic," requires its own specialist, "*kego epi me*, the sorcerer." Like the shaman, he usually is a healthy and wealthy individual of either sex. The decline of his bodily strength and wealth mean an eclipse of magical powers in his case also. Similar to the shaman, the sorcerer makes use of spirit helpers, *tene* and evil spirits. He acquires these through dreams the same way the shaman does. But unlike a shaman, the sorcerer possesses personal maglignant powers, independent of any evil spirit. These enable him to kill persons or animals by simply looking at them, mumbling the deadly spell, and thus transforming his evil intentions directly into a lethal blow. Consequently in the Kapauku hierarchy of beings, a sorcerer stands above the average man. An individual obtains recognition as a specialist in this profession after he succeeds in "killing" people known as his personal enemies. An individual's death, after having been threatened by the sorcerer, is sufficient proof of the latter's power and action. The fear exhibited by other people toward the sorcerer brings him advantages in legal disputes, in love rivalries, and in trade. The specialist is well paid (six Kapauku cowries). Nevertheless, unlike a shaman, the sorcerer is hated by most of the people. He may experience ostracism and even death administered by the hand of a relative of his victim. A sorcerer's crimes do not end with the death of his victim. He is said to return to the victim's grave during the night and devour the corpse. By this action he prevents the *tene* of the murdered man from taking revenge.

Using as a criterion the nature of the killing agent, black magic can be divided into three categories. One category we may call sorcery with the help of an evil spirit. The second is called "*bido dou*, strong look," because the performer uses his personal power directly, without relying upon the help of another spirit. This we may call direct sorcery. The third is a category which includes practices in which both the personal power of the shaman and spirit helpers operate. These categories can be further subdivided in accordance with the nature of the act. In this way the original three categories can be subdivided into imitative, contagious, and simple spell performances.

1. Sorcery with the help of a spirit. Black magic of the first category employs an evil spirit. The sorcerer does not use his personal power but by means of a spell asks his helpers, such as *tene*, to go and kill a man. In the first subdivision of this category, imitative magic with spirit help, the practitioner may use an "*ude kopa*, Ti plant broom" and ask his supernatural helper to bring the soul of the enemy and deposit it on the broom. Then, with a quick motion, the sorcerer seizes the end of the broom, thus catching the soul, and crushes it by blows of an ax applied to the Ti plant. When Tege is a helper, the *otikai* tree magically associated with him is cut and stuck into the ground. Then the sorcerer, while mumbling a magical spell, cuts the stem by a blow of his ax. Tege is supposed to kill the enemy in a way similar to that by which the *otikai* tree is cut. If other spirits are the helpers, their magical trees are used instead.

Contagious magic with a spirit's help makes use of things somehow associated with the enemy, such as the latter's fingernail clippings, hair, feces, arrow, track, spittle, blood, or food waste. The sorcerer casts a spell over these things, relying again upon the help of an evil spirit which kills the victim. A jaw of a dead sow, an offspring of which is kept by the enemy, is subjected also to a spell and placed in a forked branch of the *otikai* tree. The tree, being associated with Tege, induces the spirit to take revenge and kill not only the sow's offspring but, by the principle of contagion, also the pig's owner.

In the magical rites of the simple spell with spirit help, the performer asks his assisting spirit to bring death to the enemy. There is no other elaboration necessary. This type of magic is not considered especially effective.

2. Direct sorcery. "*Bido dou*, the black magic of the strong look," makes use of the personal destructive power of the sorcerer without reference to his helping spirit. In the imitative subdivision of the category of direct magic, the practice with "*ude kopa*, Ti plant broom," described above, is also used. This time the sorcerer himself approaches the hut of his future victim, stands still at night at the corner of the house, stretches out his hand with the broom, and orders the soul of the sleeping man to come and sit on the end of the pandanus. The rest of the act is the same as described under the category of magic with the help of a spirit. The sorcerer's direct order issued to the soul and his nonreliance on the help of a spirit differentiates the two otherwise identical performances. The practices with magical trees associated with a given spirit obviously do not fall under this category because the very use of the tree implies the spirit's help.

Direct contagious magic is performed over objects in some way associated with the victim. The performances are identical to those of contagious magic with spirit help. The only difference is in the spell where no reference is made to any spirit. The rites involving the use of trees magically associated with a spirit are ruled out because they imply the spirit's help.

The sorcery of the direct, simple spell is believed to be the most dangerous and it requires also the best sorcerers to undertake it. They wait for their victims in ambush, being hidden in the tall grass or in the jungle; or they observe victims who work in their fields, walk on the paths, fish in streams, or chat at their houses or at pig feasts with other people. In his hideout, the sorcerer stares for a long time at the victim and then he pronounces his spell which destroys one part after the other of the condemned person's body. The spell also stipulates the time of the future death:

Aki ki kabokajaweega uno gaati umijake kabokajaweega

(You, I have made you to die, in ten nights of sleep I have made you to die)

Akija migoka bokajake, pekakaa bokajake, akija bokokaa bokajake

(Your head having died, eyes having died, your chest having died)

Akija badokaa bokajawejake, akija ganeka kabokajawega.

(Your feet having died, even your arms I have made die.)

Male sorcerers are reputed also to kill game simply by looking at it and uttering a spell. They need no arrows for hunting. An informant told the writer in secret, however, that some of the sorcerers are "crooks" who steal animals from traps of other people and claim they were killed by their magical power.

Ghouls.—Men and spirits are not separated one from another by a rigid barrier. There are beings in the Kapauku universe which combine the properties of the two categories and stand somehow between them. We have already discussed the sorcerer who kills magically by his own power, thus having qualities which otherwise belong to the world of the spirits. Another transitional being is called "*meenoo*, the ghoul." The Kapauku word is a compound of "*me*, man," and "*nai*, to eat." This being is a known living woman who usually has already given birth to three children. While she was asleep her soul was expelled from her body by the ghoul spirit who takes its place. Starting with the night of this transformation, the woman leads two lives. She lives, works, and acts as a normal human being while awake and in the presence of other people. When not observed she changes into "*doudiutija*, a dog with the ghoul spirit," or "*kegoutija*, a hawk with the ghoul spirit," and roams the countryside looking for people who walk alone along the paths, or work in their gardens. After a suitable individual has been located *meenoo* changes back into the woman and waits in ambush for the victim. She jumps on him from behind and beats him with a stick over the head and other parts of the body. Interestingly enough, the wounds thus inflicted never bleed, they only swell sometimes. The victim may be beaten to death on the spot or he may have enough power left to escape and die later. *Meenoo*, in the woman's form, flees the place of the crime. During the night, again in human form, she returns to the fresh burial site of her victim who meanwhile has been buried by his relatives. There, the ghoul digs up the grave and feasts on the corpse. This continues for several nights until the cadaver is consumed.

The ghoul as a spirit is immortal. By killing the woman, one kills just the body while the spirit survives and together with the woman's "*tene*, the departed shadow" may take revenge upon the killer. It is also better to know where the ghoul spirit resides than to turn it lose by killing the woman and then have to expect that another normal woman will be turned into a monster. Therefore, *meenoo* are never killed as is often the practice with sorcerers. People are too afraid to retaliate. It is also an imbedded custom that a married woman should not be punished by anyone else than her husband.

The Dutch authorities told the writer about cannibalistic practices of the Kapauku. Also the people themselves pointed out recent cases of cannibalism. All the instances reported to the writer which he has closely investigated brought out nothing more than the belief in ghouls. By a careful checking of the graves of several recent "victims," the writer discovered that the graves had never been disturbed. Moreover, the individuals claimed by the people to be victims of the above described murderous assault, and later of endocannibalism, died of natural causes like dysentery, pneumonia, or heart attack. The writer saw two corpses on which the shaman pointed out places where the victims had been fatally struck by the ghoul. In neither case could the writer detect any swelling or laceration. All the accusations of ghoulism and the talk about this subject, were considered a deep secret by the informants, and thus the situation recalled the witchcraft complex of central Europe during the Middle Ages. It is the opinion of the present writer that all the cannibalistic stories about the Kapauku, at least in the Kamu Valley, refer to a belief in ghouls rather than to true cannibalism.

Animals. Animals follow man in the Kapauku hierarchy of beings. Except for the dog, they are only living bodies without a soul. There are several loose categories within the animal kingdom. Some of the more important animals are not classified with any other and have only names of their own: as for example the pig, dog, and cassowary bird. Besides these the Kapauku recognize the "*woda* class" in which all larger mammals, rodents, and marsupials are classified together. The "*jina* class" comprises all the creeping and crawling things like lizards, snakes, caterpillars, and worms. Sometimes the name is loosely applied to most of the insects. The "*bedo class*" denotes every flying animal with the exception of insects. Thus birds and bats are classified together, while the cassowary bird, a relative of the ostrich, is usually not called *bedo*. The name *bobaga* is applied to all the species of butterflies and moths, and *pune* to flies.

Animals reproduce like man and have the same bodily functions. Their life cycle, however, is recognized to be very different in many cases. Thus the dragon fly starts as a small larva, *tanu*, grows into a large one, *jukuga*, then transforms itself through the pupa stage into the adult insect, *gepou*. The transformation is a natural one determined by the laws of Ugatame.

The relations of animals and men. Man eats the animals, domesticates them, and thus exploits them economically. Animals, unless serving as hosts to evil spirits, are harmless to men, except for dogs and wild boars which may become dangerous in self-defence. Another relation between man and animals is actualized by the spiritual component of some human individuals. Thus, with the ghoul, the spirit migrates from the body of a woman into the body of a dog or hawk. A departed *tene* of a woman enters and may live in the body of "*wogijo*," a swift. *Wiguuwii*, another small bird, is believed to be often the host to a man's *tene*.

The relations of animals and spirits. A variety of evil spirits may reside in some individuals of the animal species that are traditionally associated with various types of spirits.

We deal here with a pure residence concept. "*Pugaago*, a bright colored parrot," is by no means Tege, but this evil spirit of the woods often resides in it. Similarly, "*togi*, a mud hen," is the host of Maneta, the horrible water spirit; "*aaga*, a large red-plumed parrot," lends his body to Ukwaanija, the wife of Tege, who calls out to people through the beak of the bird "*me bokai, me bokai*, man shall die, man shall die*," thus predicting her next exploit. Ukwaanija may also reside in "*tuubo*, a large hawk.*" The huge fruitbat, *daaijai*, may shelter Adaa, the wood spirit. Maneta, the water demon, stays also in the body of "*ou*, a reddish-colored water snake," and Makiutija, the spirit of earth, wears the disguise of "*bego*, a huge lizard." Lizards and snakes are believed to be especially infested with spirits. Therefore, they are inedible, and usually killed on sight. The only exception to this rule is the python, which is "harmless" and considered a delicacy of the Kapauku menu.

The dog stands above the rest of the animals, and because of the duality in its nature, it is actually closer to man than the animals. It has a soul similar to man's. The relation of the dog's soul and body is analogous to the relation of man's soul and body. Because of this similarity, the dog is not eaten. In Degeipige in the South Kamu Valley, it may be buried in a tree like a man, or it is simply dumped into a cave or a crevass in the limestone. The dog's departed shadow, *tene*, is harmless to people. It only roams the woods and barks during the night.

The world of plants. Plants are different in many respects from all other categories discussed so far. They do not move, they are believed to have no sex, and they reproduce from seed which may be compared to an egg, but with the difference that the seed is only a separated part of the plant's sexless body. The organism does not shelter a soul. It has only the material body which is recognized as different from the flesh of both animal and man. It grows, matures, gets old, and dies. Except for tabooed species, plants are exploited by man and animals without being able to defend themselves. Man uses plants as food, fuel and as raw material for his building and industries. Although the species associated with the spiritual world are used in curative magic as charms, plants are claimed not to be used at all as medicine. Certain species are tabooed to be eaten or even cut. Breaking of these taboos is followed by automatic punishment as determined by Ugatame. Some of the taboos are linked with sex. The *kugou* and *jigikago* types of large green bananas are tabooed to females during their fertile years of life. In the same way "*teto*, a deep red type of sugar cane" and "*apuu*, a vine bearing potato-like tuber" are taboo to those women. It is believed that the husband would die if his wife should break the taboo. *Kuugai*, a palm with horizontally arranged crown leaves, and *kujaa*, a huge, thick-stemmed, leaf-bearing tree, are tabooed to be felled. It is believed that a violator will become stricken with a serious illness.

The relation of plants and spirits. A group-magic rite may consecrate a tree and establish an ownership relation between the tree and a spirit. Cutting such a tree would provoke the anger and revenge of its supernatural owner.

In the above case, the relationship is activated only by the spirit while the tree is just a passive phenomenon. Nevertheless, there are plants in the Kapauku universe which are active and affect the spirits rather than vice versa. Some plants, already discussed, are traditionally associated with certain species of spirits and are believed to have some power which controls them. By the shaman's manipulation of these plants, the spirits are induced to obey the wishes of the expert. *Ude kopa* and *jukune*, another Ti plant, occupy a special position among the plants mentioned because both have a generalized power which controls most of the supernatural beings and compels them to help with white magic in case the first plant is used, and with black magic if one uses the second.

The inanimate world. Rocks and soil and water are considered dead matter created by Ugatame as the basic substance on which the worlds of spirits, men, animals, and plants should exist. The blue of the sky belongs to the same passive category exploited by all classes of beings discussed up to this point. Besides providing man with stones for tools, soil for growing plants, salt for eating, and water for drinking, the inanimate world provides one more type of material of great use to man. It is the *jape daagu*, the polished stone endowed with magical power to cure a man, when he is hit by an arrow, by preventing an evil spirit from entering the body through the wound. This charm, and a cave or a mountain top used by a spirit as a habitat, are the only inanimate objects which have a relationship with the realm of spirits.

Fire is a queer phenomenon. It does not fit anywhere into the classification of beings that has been discussed. It gives heat and light, it cooks the meals, burns the rats in their holes, and clears the fields of bush, but it also hurts and burns people to death. There is probably a spirit in it, the Kapauku say. What kind of a spirit nobody knows. Ashes are called the feces of the fire, thus suggesting a relationship to the animate world.

Conclusion. With the discussion of the inanimate phenomena we have finished the survey of the Kapauku universe. We have investigated the creation and structure of the world, the nature of its laws and beings as they are conceived by the people. We have gone into philosophy, religion, and magic in order to formulate a basis for the understanding of the discussions to come. The logical sequences of notions which have been presented in this section of the monograph are by no means the property of all the Kapauku living in the Kamu Valley. The knowledge of such lore differs from individual to individual according to age, sex, intelligence, and interest. A young boy would have as his spiritual possession just a small part of what has been presented.

LIFE OF AN INDIVIDUAL

Pregnancy and birth. "My wife is pregnant, and we expect a baby in two moons," said Jokagaibo of Itoda. He was very proud and only wished it might be a son. Men usually like to have as many children as possible, especially boys. "A boy would be a good warrior. He would help me with the field work, settle down in my house or nearby, and support me in my old age. He would be strong and back me up in all the quarrels with other people." These were some of the reasons why Jokagaibo desired a boy rather than a girl. This preference does not mean that a girl would not be welcome. On the contrary, she would represent a future source of income in the form of the bride price paid for her. This would go to her mother and to her brothers, who could then buy wives for themselves. Thus, we may say, Kapauku definitely like to have many children, and half of them male and half of them female if possible. The preference for boys plays a highly important role only if there are none in the family or only a few.

The pregnant woman is very dear to her husband. Because she carries his baby she belongs to him more than she does prior to or after the pregnancy. For this reason it is almost unheard of to grant a divorce to a woman while she is pregnant. Should she run away with another man, the peaceful settlement which usually follows the breaking up of a marriage would be precluded and a war would be the outcome. While she is pregnant, the wife is helped to carry heavy loads by her husband. He admonishes her not to overwork. Nevertheless, she is not considered a sick person, and she works until the delivery of the child. On the contrary, a married woman who cannot become pregnant is considered sick. An evil spirit is residing inside her and preventing the conception. The proper thing to do then is to call in a shaman to perform curing magic with the top of the Ti plant.

As much as pregnancy is valued in married women, it is considered undesirable and shameful among the unmarried girls. If it does happen, there are two ways to prevent disgrace being brought on the girl and her family: either a marriage takes place, or the girl uses mechanical techniques of abortion. She massages her abdomen and hangs herself by her hands from a tree. This treatment seems to be so efficient that most informants could not give me a single example of a birth out of wedlock although some of the girls marry quite late and most are sexually promiscuous prior to marriage.

In anticipation of the imminent birth, the prospective father gets ready for the occasion. He tries to snare some giant rats or larger marsupials in order to have some meat for the feast which will celebrate the birth of his child. If he does not have pork and cannot shoot or trap any game himself, he travels to other villages and tries to buy pork, rats, or marsupials from other people. Some fathers are caught by surprise and have to look for the meat after the arrival of the child.

While the husband is combing the country in search of meat, the prospective mother asks some experienced older woman, usually her own mother or other close female relative, to assist her at the birth. When the pains start, the chief assistant squats behind the woman in labor and comforts her. The other women helpers, usually about three in number, stand by to receive the child. The scene takes place in the open, a few yards from the house of the husband or that of the wife's parents. Male and female onlookers may stand around, only the children being chased away. Should there be any difficulty during the delivery, a shaman is called to perform the usual *ude kopa* curing magic. The child is received by the assistants who pour a little water over the child to wash and protect it from the possible influence of evil spirits. When the mother feels strong again, she cuts the umbilical cord. This is placed in the bush and is not subjected to any kind of magic. The afterbirth is placed by the mother on leaves and deposited on some branches and made into a bundle supported by two forked poles standing about five feet high. This structure is erected in the bush near the house by which the delivery occurred. The newly born child is put into a rain mat of pandanus leaves, and this in turn is wrapped in a net. The child is suckled immediately after the birth.

Should the mother and child die, both are buried in the normal way described in the previous chapter. If only one of them dies, specific rules have to be observed in disposing of the body. A stillborn child must be placed in a tree house which is usually carelessly constructed. If the child survives the mother, the latter is abandoned on a platform in the house where the delivery took place and the baby is given the breast by the father's or mother's close female relative. If the baby has a physical abnormality or is mentally deficient, it is nonetheless saved and nursed to adulthood. Should it be born with teeth, although not a single case is known, it would probably be killed because of the belief in *"enija joka*, child of an evil spirit." This is also the case when twins of opposite sexes are born. The female is always killed for the same reason as a child with teeth. In such a situation, the method is to pour water from a gourd into its mouth and nose, thus suffocating it. The execution is done by a male relative, but never the father. The little corpse is buried in a tree in the same way as is a stillborn child. Because there is a belief that an evil spirit has entered the woman and begot the second female twin, curative magic must be performed on the couple to expel the intruder for good.

The birth ceremony is held a few days after the delivery of the baby. The new father gives a feast in which he functions as host. It is considered appropriate to treat everyone who comes with pork or meat from a *"woda*, a large rodent or marsupial." The host should have at least eight large pieces of pork, each weighing about six pounds, or ten *woda*, ready for this occasion. He and his father cook the meat in a cooking mound made of fern and pandanus leaves tied together in a bundle into which preheated stones, meat, and edible greens are deposited. The cooking is done in the front portion of the Kapauku plank house which is the common quarter for all the males of the household. When cooked, the meat is cut into small pieces by the host and distributed to the male guests squatting around the place where it is cooked or outside of the house. The food is handed to the females through a hole in the partition between the rooms. The guests eat, joke, and gossip, as well as discuss serious political and economic affairs; in the evening some experts in folklore may tell legends and myths. The people may remain long into the night, some of them even sleeping in the house of the host and returning home the next day. The feast is not only a celebration of the birth of the child, but it is also an occasion for increasing the prestige of the host through his manifestation of generosity. He and his father are not supposed to eat. They, as proper hosts, just cook and distribute the meat. "The birth ceremony was like a small pig feast; there were so many guests that I felt ashamed not to be able to give them more than I did," boasted Jokagaibo of Itoda the day after he gave a feast celebrating the birth of his daughter. The more guests there are and the more food distributed, the greater the prestige of the father. People will talk for quite a time about the successful celebration.

Because the Kapauku men say it is hardly fair for the husband to get all the prestige from the event of the birth of the child, the wife is compensated by the privilege of giving her own feast. She does this a few days after her husband's ceremony at her parents' home, where she is presented with the meat necessary for the occasion. The ceremony is analogous to that described above with the exception that it is the wife who this time functions as hostess. She cooks the meat in her mother's room and distributes it first to her female guests who sit or squat around the cooking mound, and then to the males in the men's room to whom she hands it through the aperture in the wall. Unlike her husband, the wife is not banned from eating. It is her father and brother, the providers of the meat, who do not participate in its consumption.

The birth imposes only a few restrictions on the parents. The mother is forbidden to leave her room for about three to five days. For about seven days it is taboo for her spouse to fell trees, burn them, plant sugar cane, build fences, or take a long walk. There are no food restrictions for either spouse. All these taboos have been set by Ugatame, and their neglect would cause the newly born child to become sick.

The baby is put into a rain mat of pandanus leaves. This, in turn, rests in the woman's large carrying net. Wherever the mother goes, the infant is carried along in her net. The baby is never washed; it is cleaned only with leaves and the mat is replaced when it becomes bad. Feeding occurs whenever the baby is hungry and cries. The breast is given to the child and the nipple is introduced into its mouth. To get a better flow of milk, the mother may apply pressure to the breast and thus satisfy the hunger of her offspring. The baby may even be forced into sucking if it does not eat enough.

The child is comforted whenever it cries. It is hugged, petted, and in the evening the mother emits a purring sound by letting the air flap the tip of her tongue to put the child to sleep, a Kapauku version of the lullaby.

An individual receives his name from a close male relative such as a father or father's brother. A child may be named any time from his birth until adolescence. The name reflects some attribute of the recipient or a fact somehow connected with his birth. Thus the name "Kamutaka" is constructed from the words: "*kamu tai*, to perform a white magic," and "*ka*, with." A shaman had to be called in to help with the delivery of this baby. Awiiwiijaaj is a compound of *"awii*, a dry period," and *"wiijaaj*, a parrot." The boy was born in a period of dry weather and the father, looking for meat, could only bag a parrot. Gaajaduu, a female name, recalls the fact that the first *"woda*, marsupial" cooked for the birth ceremony was wrapped in the leaves, *imouda*, of the *gaajaj* tree. Nevertheless, there are many people whose relatives have failed to assign them a name. They are called: "second son of so-and-so," "granddaughter of so-and-so," or "younger brother of that man." Thus "Ekajewaijokaipouga" means: Ekajewai—the name, *joka*—son, *ipouga*—second born son to the wife of Mr. Ekajewai.

"Aejoka stage." *"Aejoka*, the babyhood stage," ends when the child starts walking. When the baby is approximately eight months old, the pandanus mat is discarded and the child is carried in the hands or wrapped in a net (Pl. 8, *top right*). It is often placed in a sitting position on the shoulder of the mother with its legs spread around her neck. The child keeps its balance by holding on to the mother's hair and she supports it by one hand. Elevated above the heads of all adults the baby looks down upon rather than up to the people it meets, goes to pig feasts, travels to the fields where its mother works, participates in the dances of the adults and even swings part of the night on the jumping floor. If it happens to survive all these experiences, it is subjected, with the advance of the next *"peu joka* stage," to the weaning process, a gradual prolonged affair lasting even more than one year. In addition to the mother's milk, the child is given juice of sugar cane, chewed for it by its mother, and later pre-chewed sweet potatoes as it drinks less and less mother's milk. Then taro and banana are fed to it, and by the third year of its life, the child eats practically everything that the adults do, but softened, cooked, peeled, and sometimes chewed for it by the mother. With the birth of a sibling whose arrival everybody welcomes except the frustrated older child, this process may become more abrupt. Nevertheless, even then the transition is rather gradual, and everyone understands and sympathizes with the neglected child.

"Peu joka stage." During the period of life called *peu joka*, which extends from the time the child starts walking to its seventh year of age, boys and girls are entirely under the control of the mother. It is primarily her responsibility to watch over them, to socialize and discipline them, and thus to prepare them for the next period during which more profound distinctions between the sexes are made. The father seldom interferes with the mother's care and education of the children. When a child cries, the father may become angry at the mother and scold her. Should something undesirable happen to it, the mother may be admonished or even severely beaten by her husband. She is supposed to show children how to behave and to explain to them the necessity for acting in a certain way. For mischief she may admonish them, scold, or even spank them a little. The father very often takes the side of the child and reprimands or even physically punishes the mother for being too severe or unjust.

The children of both sexes sleep with their mother in *"kugu*, the woman's quarter." She makes their only garment, *jokaka moge*, a small and short apron consisting of strands of the inner bark of a tree, which covers the genitalia and the back. The children follow her to the fields, watch her make nets and fish in the stream or a pond. Thus, by observation and informal instruction, the children are introduced to the skills they will have to master during the next developmental stage.

One of the first things the children must learn is bowel and bladder control. When a child starts walking, the mother points out the proper places in the bush near the house and carries it there every time it needs to attend to these natural functions. After a lapse of time the child is encouraged and praised for taking care of its bodily necessities itself. If it defecates or urinates at home, it is scolded and later even spanked. Noisiness and aggressiveness are controlled similarly, first by admonition and explanation and later by scolding and light spanking. When the frustration from the punishment is too great, the child may throw a mild "temper tantrum." The parents consider this behavior to be beyond the control of the child. They never beat and maltreat it but try to reduce the sorrow through affection and through fondling. Very frequently the sorrowful child is lifted onto the adult's shoulders and lovingly carried around. When it stops crying, it is rewarded by further affection.

The child, like the adult, eats three main meals a day. On these occasions, it is taught the basic etiquette: not to cough, blow its nose, spit, or talk about bodily necessities and sex.

Because children of both sexes play together, the mother encourages them to wear their aprons and mildly scolds them "*aki ego beu*, you are not even ashamed," if they discard their garments. Toward the end of the "*peu joka* period" of life, they may even be slapped for not being modest in dressing and eliminating.

The child is not only a recipient of advantages and favors but is also induced to work a little and is praised for helping with some small tasks which are performed in a playlike fashion. It fetches water, stones and leaves for cooking and brings dry twigs and branches to feed the fire. The mother makes a small "*ebai*, fishing net," with a circular frame which a child of either sex carries into the swamps and shallow waters. There, under the direction and supervision of the mother, by dragging the shallows with the tiny contrivance, it fishes for dragonfly larvae, water insects, tadpoles, and eventually for crayfish.

During this period of life there are no maturation ceremonies save for the occasion of the first haircutting. The father is in charge of this task and he uses a bamboo knife for completely shaving the head of his eighteen-month old child. The hair is hidden in the bush to prevent a sorcerer from using it in his profession. After the head-shaving, a feast is given by the proud parent who treats everyone who comes to cooked pork. This ceremony has no magical connotation; it is only a celebration of the child's growth and health.

Although the older *peu joka* spend much time with their mothers, they play most of the day in groups composed of siblings and other children. The small gang hikes around the village, fishing, collecting insects, and watching small pigs. To make it possible for the small child to participate in these group activities, the mother delegates her power to supervise, with the tacit approval of the father, to an older sibling of the child or to his (or her) parallel cousin. The individual entrusted with the care of a younger child is then fully responsible and is punished should anything happen to his charge. This gang situation, coupled with the father's giving the boy a bow and arrows, marks the point where the lives of the two sexes become progressively differentiated, to come closer together only in old age. Thus, at the close of the *"peu joka* age," the child has a sense of responsibility, manifested by regularly supplying the household with water, stones, and leaves for cooking. He also has some fundamental knowledge about work in the fields, animal husbandry, and fishing.

"Joka stage." Now the child is prepared for a period of life marked by an abrupt increase in education, self-control, and the inculcation of law and heterosexual behavior. It is no more referred to as *peu joka* but the sex connotation is often prefixed to the word *"joka,* the child." Thus we hear: *"Anaa jagamo joka okai jukuga kei maagodo epi,* my female child; she really knows how to fish for dragonfly larvae." The *joka* period distinguishes itself sharply from the previous one by the segregation of the sexes. Especially for the male child, this is a time of profound change and basic reorientation. Until this time his activities had been linked primarily with those of his mother and younger siblings. He slept, played, and worked with children of both sexes, but he associated only with female adults. He wore the same garments as his little sister, he went fishing with the net and collected insects as only the women do, he slept in *"kugu,* the women's quarters," and in general acted as a female rather than as a male.

Approximately at his seventh birthday, he experiences a radical change in the educational efforts of his parents, who start to focus upon transforming this female-like individual into a male. Now the little boy is invited by his father to spend the night in the men's room. In the beginning, the boy sleeps a few nights with the father and then returns to the mother's quarters. As time goes on, he sleeps more and more often with his father. Finally, spending the night with the mother becomes the exception to the rule. Also, he eats with the menfolk of the household, gets a stronger bow from his father, and abandons the fishing net. His apron is exchanged for a small *"koteka,* a penis sheath,"* made of a long gourd held in position by a string which goes around the waist of the little body. Then, wearing the garments that adult Kapauku use, the boy is teased into more prudishness in the presence of women.

At this time the mother's command vanishes and for it is substituted more intensive control by the father. He scolds more severely and even uses a stick to make the son obey. Nonetheless, the punishment is never harsh. The father is usually lenient with his son, and it is primarily the child's love, respect, and admiration for the parent which are the stimuli for the boy's education. The child's training is never over-intensified and is more sporadic than constant. Often it depends on the boy whether he will follow the parent to the field where he will be taught to clear the underbrush, to cut trees, and build fences. Every now and then the father and son will spend an afternoon in discussing the value of different types of currencies, pig raising, current prices of different merchandise, and the way to become rich. These abstract discussions, illustrated by the father's own experience, are enjoyed by the eagerly listening boy, who is already aware of the importance of economy and wealth. The parent also enjoys these talks which help bolster his own ego. He tells his son about his exploits and success which, because modesty is a value in this culture, he cannot discuss with his male relatives or friends, and which his own wife, if told, would not believe anyway.

The boy is ready to learn the skills his teacher has mastered. Making bows and arrows, rolling string on the thigh, making nets, roasting gourds for penis sheaths, polishing stone axes and stone knives, and chipping flint by percussion are a few of the many subjects a Kapauku man-in-the-making has to study. When the opportunity arises and a new house is needed, the boy may learn how to cut trees, to split logs, and to use an ax and two wedges to make planks. He may also be permitted to help with the construction of the house itself. Jobs requiring great strength are not taught until the boy reaches about fifteen years of age. Then he is shown how to hollow out a huge log with an ax and shape it into a canoe, how to smooth the floor of the canoe with the same tool changed into an adz, how to make holes for the long vines which are used for pulling the craft to the lake or river and for mooring it. It is also at this time that the boy, for the first time, tackles the soil of the valley's bottom lands to carve out a drainage ditch with a wooden, leaf-shaped, spadelike tool. Hunting with bow and arrow, setting traps, and cutting up of the animals, though explained by the father, are practiced in the adolescents' gang in a playful way until the boy becomes an expert in these arts. During the long evenings the boy listens to myths, legends, and actual history told and discussed by the adult members of the household; thus he acquires the awareness of the time perspective which helps him make sense of his life.

A Kapauku must not only be educated in all the skills and knowledge of his group but in order to become a real man he must acquire the necessary independence which is so important in this culture. The father gives his son a garden plot and encourages him to work on it for his own benefit. The boy soon brings home a crop harvested in his own garden and, by distributing the food, he functions as a host to the rest of the family. Providing food for one's own father is, for a Kapauku of eleven years, an important act which gains recognition from the older folks. "Today we have eaten my son's sweet potatoes and *idaja* (a green similar to spinach)," the proud father tells his friends in his son's presence, making the boy feel important and equal to the adults. Gradually the son starts his own finances; he plays the role of creditor and debtor to some close relative such as his father, older brother, or cousin. It is a great event for a small "capitalist" when he is given a pig by his rich father. This act lays the foundation for his future economic independence. If he is successful in raising and breeding the animal, he may start on his way toward the career of a "*tonowi*, a rich man and authority in the village."

Courage is one of the attributes of Kapauku independence. This is believed to be partially inherited and partially inculcated, and a serious effort is made by the father to make his son a brave warrior. Fortitude is developed first by a mock fight with sticks between the father and son. As time goes on the fighting grows more serious, and the boy if not skillful enough receives quite a beating. Finally, the real art of war, shooting well and avoiding flying arrows, is taught when son and father discharge war arrows at each other. This training is a serious affair; an inattentive pupil or teacher may even be killed in the practice.

Part of the education is left to the older boys, who, in a playgroup, teach their young companions archery, trapping, hunting, climbing rocks and trees, netting, oratory, folklore, and all the tricks and games of which a Kapauku youth can think. The group of boys roams the swamps and practices shooting into "*edege*, a parasitic spiny plant with a tuberous stem." A ball made of grass, tied together with rattan and set afloat in the stream may provide a moving target for the young archer. A more elaborate game of shooting is called *maki wagii*. In this game two targets of bamboo screens, plastered with mud, are set about forty meters apart. The gang separates and the boys shoot reeds back and forth counting the hits. Fortitude is tested in another game, *kimu kopa gokijai*, a fight between two groups of boys who beat each other over the head with long thin sticks of reed, bamboo, or tree branches. The favorite game is "*kimu tii*, play war," between two parties fighting with bows and blunt arrows or reeds provided with a soft end section. To keep the war a game, the "warriors" are usually recruited from two neighboring villages of the same political unit; but sometimes boys from hostile clans may get mixed up in the fight and the play may turn into actual war and people be killed. Hunting rats is also a pleasant pastime as well as an educational experience. The skillful boy is rewarded by admiration from the girls who are given his kill. The young hunter is tabooed from eating his first seven bagged specimens of each of the following animals: rats, birds, marsupials, and large rodents. To avoid sickness and to gain friendship, he presents this game to his sister or some other favored girl. Thus he not only gets recognition as a good hunter, but also gains approval for his generosity, the highest value in the culture.

There are games imitating hunts, disputes, legal processes, and marital troubles. These are enacted as dramas or comedies. The plays draw a wide audience consisting especially of the unmarried girls and the married men. Even old people will listen to a comedy and enjoy the numerous jokes and the comical performance of the actors. A path or empty space in front of a house may serve the young artists as a stage. In case there are visiting boys staying in a house overnight, the men's quarter is utilized as the scene for the play which may continue long into the night. One by one the people in the audience and the actors go to sleep, only to be wakened by a new joke and laughter which slowly gives way to the silence of the night.

The girl who has passed her seventh birthday does not experience anything comparable to what the boy goes through. While for him the "*joka age*" means a profound reorientation and change from a basically feminine role into that of a man, she simply continues the role she has played with a logical intensification of her education. There is no change for her in sleeping quarters, neither is there a trans-ference of authority. Her mother still punishes her in the old way, although she may use more slapping than before. Her dress changes slightly from a short bark apron to a skirt of full length reaching to her knees. In other words, while this state of growing represents a crisis and a strain for the male, for the female it is simply a quiet period of preparation for the next and crucial period in her life.

The little girl follows her mother to the fields and learns how to weed, plant sweet potatoes and other vegetables, how to harvest, cook, roll string on the thigh, and make nets with or without a bone needle. She continues to fish with her small net, but as time goes on her net is made larger and larger and, finally, she goes into the deeper waters after crayfish. She learns also to navigate a canoe by pushing it with a long forked pole, avoiding sunken logs and whirlpools in the river. This skill, when mastered, she utilizes in fishing and transportation as well as for pleasure. It is amusing for her to go by boat when she is captain and the boy plays the passenger's role. The hunting accomplishments of her brothers are matched by her when she brings home delicacies such as dragonfly larvae, tadpoles, water bugs, and mole crickets. Like the boy, she too is tabooed from eating her first seven crayfish which she presents to her brother in expectation of admiration and of future remuneration of a fat bird or a rat.

Because the *"jagamo joka*, girl" is to become a lady with responsibilities of her own, her parents try to make her as independent as possible. Her father gives her part of his field which is marked as her responsibility by sticks pushed into the ground, thus making *"medeke*, boundary," between "her plot" and those which her mother or sisters work. She does not own the land; it is hers only to care for. She plants the sweet potatoes, does all the weeding, and finally brings the produce home, cooks it, and with pride presents the food to her father and brothers.

She sells some of the produce of her industry, such as nets and string, and thus accumulates her own savings. She may also conclude a contract with her father to raise a piglet for him. After the grown pig is sold or slaughtered, she has a right to ask for *mune*, a payment in shells or beads, for watching and feeding the animal. Although her monetary position is far less important than that of her brother, her ability to earn money and through her diligence and hard work to possess some savings brings her admiration from the older people and makes her more attractive to future suitors. Ijaaj Bunamabii of Botukebo, a bright young girl of about eleven years, is so known for her skill, savings, intelligence, and industry that already some older boys and young men have their eye on her and are waiting until her breasts start to grow, a mark of the marriageable age. Her father is tremendously fond of her. He likes to go walking with her and even in an all male gathering, he tolerates her sitting next to him or even on his leg. He once boasted to me: "I have never punished her in her life, she is so good."

Gangs of young girls are as common as those of young boys. They hike together, go to a neighboring village for a dance, and visit overnight with friends, providing they are granted permission from their parents. The girls play many games together.

A string game, *gaa do gaa*, is enjoyed by several of them playing at the same time with one string. Each pattern they make has a meaning and a story that goes with it. As another pastime, the girls make a ring from a long willowlike tree branch and bounce it back and forth. Among the many entertainments, one finds the girls playing in the sand or mud, making small fields and disputing the boundaries, drawing pigs in the mud and cutting them up. They also play jew's harps given to them by older boys (Pl. 8, *bottom right*). As do all the women, the girls like to dance and do not miss any opportunity to go to a feast. They also join the boys in their play, functioning either as the laughing audience for the drama performances or as active participants in the rat hunts when they stamp the rats out from the grassy area and in the war game when they collect stray arrows.

Adolescence. The period of life which in our culture is called adolescence comes to the Kapauku boy as a smooth continuation of the previous "*joka* period" with no dramatic changes comparable to the reorientaton he went through when seven years old. A grown boy, sufficiently strong, rather independent, and about fourteen years of age is referred to as "*agana*, the young bachelor." At this time he is considered to be a man with full responsibility, an individual on whom the household can rely for economic contributions and on whom the village as well as the political unit can count as a warrior. He has acquired all the skills needed in agriculture and the knowledge of fundamental industries such as bow and arrow making and netting. He has mastered hunting, trapping, and pig raising, but his knowledge of folklore, laws, religion, magic, ethics, and especially the art of "business administration" is still superficial and incomplete. The developmental stage of *agana* provides for the acquisition of this higher knowledge as well as for filling in gaps which might have been left in his basic training. The educational task is no longer the exclusive responsibility of the father. Since the boy has become rather independent, having his own fields, money, credit, and debts, and possibly raising a pig, he himself may choose his teacher from among several individuals. If his father happens to be a wealthy and successful man, the son is most likely to recognize him as the best source of education. In other cases he may select one of his wealthy close relatives to teach him what his father cannot teach. Thus a boy of fourteen may leave his home and go to live for a period of time, sometimes as long as a decade, with his older brother, maternal uncle, parallel cousin, or other relative. He may even make a more radical decision and join an important "*tonowi*, rich man and headman," who in exchange for farm work and allegiance will feed the adolescent and give him the desired instruction. Thus it happens that a *tonowi* may have five or more students in his house—the Kapauku version of a university.

In the life of a Kapauku, adolescence has another important but more agreeable function—matchmaking. After the separation of the sexes during the "*joka* state," they are again drawn together, but this time for different reasons, with different assumptions, and usually over the protests of the members of the older generation. The gang of boys, formerly concentrating entirely upon hunting, sports, and games, becomes now something like a pack of wolves; they are still hunting, but now not only quadrupeds; "*api*, the adolescent girl," with grown breasts becomes their primary "prey." The mentioned change in the physical appearance of the girl, which comes with her thirteenth year of age, defines her as marriageable. Adolescence for the female lasts from this time until her marriage. While for the boy, this age is that of growing emancipation from the supervision of the father, for the girl it means the reverse. She is not only watched by her mother, but her father and older brothers become authorities on such subjects as permission to visit with people, to see some boys, or to go to feasts. By this time the girl knows all she needs for her life except for her future role as wife and mother. These notions are acquired at the time of the first menstruation, which makes the girl a fully marriageable woman. Since menstruation occurs later than the enlargement of the breasts, its onset finds some girls already married.

While there is no puberty ceremony for the boys, menstruation is an important event in a girl's life. " *Daba owa*, a hut," made of a simple oblong wooden frame leaned against two posts and thatched over with grass and branches, is built for her by her father, brother, parallel cousin, or, if married, by her husband. She stays in the hut for two nights and two days during her first two menstrual periods. All this time she is kept company by two or three older women, her closer relatives, such as mother, older sister, brother's wife, mother's sister, or father's sister. The women bring her food and instruct her in marital duties, birth, care of children, and especially in the observance of taboos.

The taboos of a woman of childbearing age fall into two categories, one connected exclusively with the puberty ceremony and the other consisting of food taboos to be obeyed until the beginning of the menopause. She is forbidden to sleep during the puberty ceremony, otherwise she will have nightmares. She is not allowed to hear or tell legends during her first two menstrual periods, otherwise her future husband will die; neither is she allowed to leave her thatched hut for the stated time because she would become very ill. Should she wash or comb her hair during the puberty seclusion, death would be her supernatural punishment. At the same time she is also prohibited from eating any kind of birds, rodents, marsupials, banana, sugar cane, Kapauku beans, manioc, and some kinds of caterpillars lest sickness result. During the rest of her life, or actually until the arrival of the menopause, taboos are placed on eating *teto*, red sugar cane; *apuu*, a vine bearing potato-like tubers; and *jigikago* and *kugou*, the two types of large green bananas. Should she violate any of the above prohibitions, her husband would die and she, most probably, would be executed by the enraged "in-laws."

After the ceremony is over the girl hides the leaves with the menstrual blood in the bush to prevent a sorcerer from harming her by contagious magic. Menstrual blood is considered a symbol of fertility and is not contaminating. Men have an aversion to it, feeling ashamed and even sick should they see it. The Kapauku believe menstruation has nothing to do with lunation "because women get it at different times and their periods vary in length."

The girl discards *dugaa moge*, the inner bark skirt, and puts on *danii moge*, a garment similar to a skirt which consists of a rope belt from which bark strings hang down. These are brought together, passed from the front between the thighs, and tucked under the belt in the back, thus forming a kind of bark string wrap.

A young athletic-looking man with regular features, black hair and reasonably dark skin, who jokes most of the time and is known as a good hunter, dancer, and singer would make the ideal mate for most of the maidens. Young women are thought to be overselective and irrational in evaluating a man. "Wealth, bravery, generosity, eloquence—such things are not considered by them at all," complained a thirty-five year old wealthy headman of the Pigome clan. "You can never figure them out, they think differently than men do. A man who has red hair and lighter skin is mocked, although he may be generous, wealthy, and brave. The whiter men (albinos) can scarcely find a mate at all."

To meet the standard set by the women, men have to endure such hardships as combing their hair, putting on necklaces, armbands, and noseplugs, buying a new carrying net and a new penis sheath, and plucking their facial hair with a stone knife. "And after you have borrowed money to buy those things and spent time in pain while a couple of stupid fellows pulled your beard, you find out that she does not like you anyway," complained the headman.

Not only the young maidens are selective; the young men also have their preference for good-looking girls with strongly built bodies, thick thighs and calves, and large breasts. "My girl has breasts as large as the head of this boy," boasted a young Don Juan while his less fortunate friends listened with glittering, dreamy eyes. On the other hand, older men simply look for a healthy and industrious woman, not caring about her thighs.

Hearing the above complaints of the men, the girls defend themselves: "Who would like to marry a man with gray hair, fifteen kids, and five wives already? Because we can have only one husband we have to be careful about selection, while they can take any woman. If they do not like her, they marry again." We may conclude, then, that it is hard for a Kapauku man to get a girl but it does not involve too much risk, while the reverse is true for the opposite sex. Both sexes meet while participating in their gang activities or attending feasts. A boy stares at a nice-looking girl and then tries to attract her attention by joking with his own companions. When he catches her admiring look, he becomes bolder and may present her with a necklace, armlet, or hairpin with plumes of a bird of paradise. If she should secretly give the boy a cooked sweet potato, it is a proposal for a date always involving sexual intercourse. Another blunt way of courtship is to approach a lonely girl in the field and just ask her for coitus. A handsome boy has a good chance that the young lady will give her consent.

"The Kapauku women are more sexual than men," claimed most of my male informants. "They even ask you for intercourse. They are never satisfied with their husbands. They look for other men. They commit adultery and thus cause most of the wars in which men get killed," Ijaaj Awiitigaaj of Botukebo told me. "All women are bad. Do you know Dimi Oumau who is married in Mauwa? Well, once

I went to visit her husband and he was not at home. . . ." Since this involves living people, we had better stop at this point and conclude that extramarital intercourse is a rather common pleasure for many married women. They do not feel sorry for it and have no bad conscience. This, of course, does not necessarily mean that they would boast about it. They even have to keep pre-marital love affairs secret because they would be punished by their fathers and brothers and their lovers might be fined three or four cowries. If the known lover is a wealthy man or a boy from a wealthy family, the parents close both eyes and let the young people alone. Nevertheless, they try to induce the young man to marry their daughter and to pay a good price for her.

Though many of the beautiful daughters of the Kamu people are promiscuous, there is no prostitution for money. Girls who are too promiscuous are punished by their parents and are sometimes even shot with an arrow through the thigh. This is because a wealthy man would hesitate to marry such a girl through fear of having domestic troubles later on, which in turn means the probability of a lower bride price for her parents and brothers.

"*Juwo, a pig feast.*" Most of the heterosexual acquaintances that develop into love affairs and often into marriage have their beginnings at a "*juwo,* a pig feast," which is the most important event in the economic and social life of all the Kapauku. It constitutes a unique opportunity for both sexes to meet, joke, and become acquainted with each other, and it provides for institutionalized channels through which the process leading to marriage can be initiated.

The complex of events which we call here "*juwo,* a pig feast," starts as an idea in the mind of an important and wealthy man. "I have a couple of sows with litters of pigs now. I think I should have a pig feast when they are grown," said Ijaaj Ekajewaijokaipouga of Aigii to the writer one evening.

"Why do you have to have a pig feast? Pig feasts cause you a lot of trouble, expense and worry. Why don't you just sell the pigs or the meat and collect the money?" the writer asked.

"If I just sell I would get lots of money, but people would not think too much of me. They wish to dance and sing. They wish to meet with other people. My parallel cousins and the men of my village told me just the other day, 'It has been a long time since we have had a pig feast in Aigii. You are a *tonowi,* you should do something about it so that other people will see that we do better than they!' So I must have a feast."

"Why do you not let them sponsor the feast if they desire it?" the writer asked.

"But I am a *tonowi.* They know it. And besides this, I do not want Iibii to have a feast. He tries to be more important than I, anyway."

Thus Ekajewaijokaipouga was really more worried about his political prestige than about the profit he could make on meat. By giving a feast one not only sells meat and earns money, has fun in dancing and singing, gains prestige from the success of the event and from one's own generosity, and performs what we may call a "patriotic and moral" deed, but one also undermines the popularity of political rivals as well as shames the traditional enemy—the people from another political confederacy. The decision to give a feast is followed by calling on other people to hear their opinions. In this way the initiator, called now "*maagodo juwo ipuwe,* the real pig feast owner," finds two or three other individuals who will join him in the sponsorship of the feast and so become "*juwo ipuwe edadai bagee,* pig feast owners, helpers." They are usually his relatives of the younger generation (his father's sister's son's son, half brother's son, brother's son, father's brother's son's son, father's brother's son's son's son, etc.), or sometimes, they are the younger individuals from the same generation (younger brother, father's sister's son, etc.). The main owner with his helpers urges young or poorer people to volunteer for plank-making, post-cutting, and rattan-collecting—necessary activities in the construction of the dance house.

To assure success of the whole enterprise, the building of the dance house is initiated by a magical rite performed by the main owner of the feast. Early in the morning he leaves for the woods and there, over the stump of a freshly cut *onage* tree, he executes the "money-increase magic" as described in the first chapter. Then he carries the tall tree to the selected site, which is now filled with the building materials, and plants it along with "*ude,* Ti plant," at the place where the main front post will stand. The second part of the magic follows in the manner previously described. To participate in making a success of the pig feast, the helping owners plant their Ti plants as well. However, while the main owner of the feast has the right to the front post, his helpers have to be satisfied with posts in the back.

The building process starts with the construction of the jumping floor, the main part of the edifice. Its frontal dimension of about seven meters and the lateral one of about five meters are determined by the owners and then staked out. The many boys of the village and the owners' friends start the work by sticking short forked branches into the outline defined by the stakes, and placing between them stumps with their roots down. Both serve as foundations and support for the spring platform. The roots of the stumps, sitting horizontally on the ground, prevent the structure from sinking into the mud. Into the forks and to the upper ends of the stumps, the floor's frame is tied with rattan. The strong elastic poles which cross the area are lashed on the frame, thus producing a floor for the dancing platform. The rest of the structure consists of posts, vertical planks serving as walls with ventilation cracks every twenty-five centimeters, and rafters thatched with thorny leaves of an agave-like plant. The height of the building is about five or six meters. This main section of the building is called *emaida.* In front of this structure there is usually but not always an "*akagau,* vestibule," formed by the extension of the lateral walls and of the roof of the *emaida.* This additional space is closed in front by a few posts and planks. Its plan is an oblong the width of the jumping floor and about three meters in depth. A door about two and a half meters wide in the front walls of the *emaida* and *akagau* provide the necessary entrance into the building. The enclosed porch is for protection of the onlookers against rain and is a place where fires are built to warm the dancers during the cold night. The jumping floor is elevated about forty centimeters above the ground. While most of the poles composing it are lashed closely together, there are a few gaps of about forty centimeters in width left along both lateral walls to be used as pits for small fires which provide some additional heat and light during the dancing at night.

After the dance house is completed, people erect the *"juwo owa,* feast houses,*"* one for each owner of the feast. Four walls of perpendicular planks stuck into the ground delimit an area about six meters wide and ten meters long which is protected against the rain by a sloping roof made of rafters with a thatch of leaves of an agave-like plant. Along the back wall of these structures there are small rooms, corresponding to the number of wives of the house's owner. The feast house serves as a dormitory for the guests, as a storage space for the owner's pigs, and as a place where meat is either sold or distributed or cooked and eaten. The meat of the pigs that are butchered in this house is stored, prior to its sale or distribution, in the rooms of the wives. The wives keep their own shares of the meat in the same place.

A long and highly significant dancing period of about three months duration follows this preparation. During this time, groups of men and women may come from any village to spend the night participating in a dance. This practice is called *"ema uwii,* going to the dance house,*"* and is enjoyed by all Kapauku irrespective of their sex or age. "Tonight all the men of Botukebo are going to have a dance at Bunauwobado. Many girls have promised to go with us," a young man told me jubilantly. This was a men's dance where the men do the singing and dancing and the girls and women go along to carry torches which provide light and heat for the dancers. Being served in this fashion is no monopoly of the men. Women announce their dances in the same way, and then the men are expected to reciprocate.

To exploit the situation fully, the dancers have to meet the aesthetic demands of the opposite sex. The boys wash themselves in the creek, comb their hair, take their own or borrowed fancy bows and arrows, put on armlets and insert bright flowers, red Ti plant leaves, and decorative twigs under their armlets and also put them into the carrying net which is suspended on their heads by a strap running over the highest point on the skull. They decorate their hair with a cassowary headdress resembling an Indian war bonnet, and they stick hairpins which hold the gorgeous plumes of birds of paradise in their coiffures. Girls in turn, being tabooed from washing and combing, compensate by putting on a new *"moge,* the loin wrap,*"* and placing as many necklaces and trade beads as they can collect and carry around their necks. Some girls wear so many necklaces that the latter give an impression of heavily beaded breast plates.

Prepared in this way, the men gather in the afternoon on a clearing in their village to launch their forthcoming escapade with *"waita tai,* a counterclockwise circular dance"* in which the whole group, yodeling in a barking fashion, called *juu tai,* runs around and around with bows and arrows in their hands. The women join in by running on the periphery of the circle with lifted hands, shaking their breasts by jumping and swinging at the knees. After such a wild dance, the group starts to run to the village where the dance house has been built (Pls. 5, *top*, 8, *bottom left*). Because this journey may take four or even more hours, the excited Papuans, in order to release their energy, perform *waita tai* several times during the run. Near sunset, the group arrives at its destination.

Yodeling and cheering, they come running into the village and *waita tai* in front of the dance house. Next comes "*tuupe*, a clockwise, circular, trodding dance" in which the people are pressed against each other and, while singing, prance on the ground in fast short steps. Then they rush on to the jumping floor of the dance house to sing an "*ugaa* song." It starts with the familiar barking cheers while the people, standing in one place, bend their knees in a very fast rhythm, thus making the floor go up and down. After about three minutes they slow down, almost stop, and a man sings a solo which his helper answers in counterpoint fashion. This solo, lasting about two minutes, is followed by the chorus with which the dancers finish the "*ugaa* song." Then they immediately start rocking the floor and barking again to introduce another one. The females, joined now by others from neighboring villages, walk with lighted torches in counterclockwise fashion around the central group of the singing men on the dance floor. So it goes on and on without stopping through the night. No wonder that after such a performance most of the people cannot move for a couple of days, and that toward morning their voices are reduced to a whispering hoarseness which gives way only after a lapse of several days.

The "*ugaa* songs" have a definite meaning. In them the solo singer may propose friendship to a man, urge contributions to his own bride-price collection, ask his best friend for a gift, or express sorrow over the loss of a close relative. Besides songs with such meanings, there may be one directed to a specific girl who is present in the dance house. In such a "*waka ugaa*, courting songs," the singer declares his love to the maiden and proposes a marriage:

"Meekamude, *kaauwije Aigiijake, kaauwijee Aigiijake jagepaapa kauwijee no, ou waoo*." Meekamude, let's go because of you to Aigii, let's go because of you to Aigii, to the "*jage* pandanus," do let's go because of you (the words *ou waoo*, symbolize the sound of pandanus in the wind).

In the above text, Meekamude, the beauty of the South Kamu Valley, is asked to join a boy in the Aigii village at a place where "*jage* pandanus" grows. Though not made explicit, love and marriage are implied in the song.

The words of this "*ugaa* song," except for the sound of the pandanus *ou waoo*, are sung by the lover and his helper only. While this duet is a composition of the singer, the second part or the pandanus sound is traditional and chanted by the whole chorus. The same proposal may be sung in many other traditional variations such as: "water *ugaa*," "wind *ugaa*," "rain *ugaa*," etc. The particular type selected is determined by mentioning the subject in the text of the duet, and is followed in the chorus by the appropriate words symbolizing the associated sound. While carrying a torch, the girl listens to the song in which her name has been mentioned. If she rejects the proposal of the boy, she promptly leaves the jumping floor and goes home. If she continues going around with the flaming light, she has accepted the offered love and later during the night the pair steal away and run to the boy's village. The close male relatives of both young people meet and try to make arrangements for the payment of the bride price for the girl who is already living with her future husband.

Most of the young people are not interested, however, in concluding an early marriage. Thus the above pattern for proposing marriage serves only a few individuals who happen to have serious intentions. For the majority, the dance provides an opportunity to meet and joke with members of the opposite sex and eventually arrange for a love affair with marriage as its possible consequence.

The light is dim in the dance hall and the place is crowded beyond imagination. Thus, the girls with torches have to push their way through the multitude, passing between the dancers at the center of the floor and the onlookers, who stand, squat, or sit along the walls. The situation gives a boy plenty of opportunity for getting acquainted with a girl, for joking with her, or even for molesting her without punishment. The "young lions of the jumping floor" may mock the girls to attract their attention, and stand in their way in order to be pushed aside, thus gaining an opportunity to retaliate in kind after the girls have circled the place. The boy feels successful if the victim screams, fights back, slaps him, or pushes him in turn. A rebuke, avoidance, or a bad look, however, is interpreted as the lady's displeasure, and the suitor looks for another object of affection.

The bright-colored plumes of the hairpins worn by the boys provide another aid to flirting. Girls are anxious to get these and, while passing the boys, they snatch them and plant them in their own hair, only to be deprived of the ornaments during the next circle when the encouraged boys take their chance. It happens frequently that torches go out and darkness suddenly obscures the vision of the crowd. This moment is fully exploited by a bold boy who grabs the passing maiden by her breasts. Though struck between the eyes, slapped by other girls, and possibly knocked down on the floor by older and stronger individuals of the weaker sex, the boy feels fine, and is most happy while thinking how he will boast about his deed to the other less "fortunate" fellows.

The greatest triumph for a boy comes when a cooked sweet potato is pushed secretly into his hand by a passing girl. A date has been asked for and sexual relations promised by this small token of love. From then on, the boy watches his date to see when she leaves the dance house. He follows her into the darkness to spend the whole or part of the night collecting the highest reward the dance provides. Later the couple, separated again, steals back into the dance house or joins groups of tired people around their fires in the vestibule or in the feast houses. The flickering of the fires, the humming of the voices, and the lullaby of the songs coming from the dance hall hug them both in a dream world where their souls relive the sweet events their bodies have just experienced.

Within a few days after the completion of the dance house, the owners have *putu duwai naago*, the day when they determine the date of the main feast. The occasion is actually a feast in itself when *"ipuwe bagee,* the sponsors," kill about eight pigs and distribute the cooked meat to all the people who come. The killing is done in the feast house shortly after the sunrise. Throngs of people come from all directions, running, yodeling, and jumping over the bottomless puddles of the swamps. Each group representing a village, a lineage, or even a confederacy performs *waita tai* and *tuupe* dances in front of the dance house and afterwards dances on the jumping floor (Pl. 6, *bottom*). After a few songs, each group moves out to make room for others who are already yodeling and dancing outside. Around nine o'clock in the morning, raw meat is distributed to all male visitors. Then cooking mounds are made for the preparation of entrails, fat, and less choice meat. These, after being well steamed, are cut up and distributed to women and girls squatting in the outside of the *juwo owa.* In the afternoon, the owners of the pig feast convene and determine the day of the *juwo degii naago,* the last and the main day of the whole sequence of the celebration. Different opinions are expressed, advisors enlighten the "convention" on the customary procedures and, after some arguments and heated debate, the owners settle for a day anywhere between sixty and 480 days from *putu duwai naago.* As an aid in remembering, "Job's tears" are strung or knots are made, by the sponsors, on a string which is hung in the men's quarter of the sponsors' houses. From then on, every morning the owner takes away a seed or unties one knot. While time passes, the pigs scheduled to be slaughtered are growing fatter. The night dances taking place in the dance house reach their climax during the night preceding the *juwo degii naago* feast. During the first half of the last night, the men dance and the women circle the floor with torches. During the second half of the night, the men provide the dancing and singing women with light.

The main feast starts about one hour after sunrise when the sponsors kill their pigs (Pl. 4, *bottom*). During the whole morning, people come even from far-away places with their hogs to be slaughtered, with shell money for purchasing pork, with salt, strings, nets, and bamboo containers to be sold. Although every arriving group goes through *waita tai, tuupe,* and *ugaa* dances, the day is devoted to business and earning shell money. Groups of buyers cluster around a place where a pig is being cut up, offer their shells in exchange for pork, or wait to get a piece of meat as a payment from a debtor. People argue about the value of individual shells, bargain about the price of the merchandise, and dispute the quality and volume of the pork throughout the day. Everybody enjoys the occasion (Pl. 5, *bottom*). In the afternoon all is over. The visitors, sometimes numbering as many as 2,000, leave in groups for their villages. They are rich in meat and experience and poor in money. For many of the people, the day has meant fresh meat and a prospect of good food for the next two days. For the owner, it has been a day of economic profit and status enhancement. And for young lovers, the day has meant plenty of opportunity to look at each other, admire new garments or necklaces, and even to arrange new dates.

Marriage. After her breasts enlarge and the girl is about thirteen years old, she is marriageable. The boy must wait until he is seventeen or eighteen years old. It is considered immoral to marry prior to these ages, and people believe that the violator's "*epo peu kai*, vital substance deteriorates," that disease sets in, and death may result. Coming of age is not a pleasant experience for many girls. Although they date the boys they like, dance, and visit people, joke and laugh most of the time, the threat of being eventually forced to marry a rich old man is always too real to permit full enjoyment of the events. This is especially true when the brother expects a large bride price for his sister and hopes to use it for buying his own wife. Father, mother, and brother try to induce the girl to marry such a rich individual, and they are seldom interested in her own preferences. The brother, especially, acts as if he has forgotten his love for his sister. Since it very rarely happens that the choice of the brother and the sister coincides, the former tries, by talking, beating, or even by shooting an arrow through her thigh, to persuade his unfortunate sibling to marry the rich man. In one case a girl bled to death after the artery in her thigh had been unintentionally severed by her infuriated brother. However, when a girl is determined, no one can force her into any marriage. There are some socially recognized ways for her to resist. She may elope with her lover, and his parents and relatives may try to settle the affair by offering a reasonably high bride price to the girl's family. She may also simply escape into the woods and hide away for many months until the rich man loses patience and marries another woman. In her hiding, she is supported by friends, maternal relatives, and lovers. The willingness of a woman to marry an individual is very important not only because the wedding depends on it, but also because the marriage itself can be dissolved by the woman any time through the same channels as outlined above.

The boy, on the other hand, is free from all pressure and may marry anyone who accepts him. His only problem is to raise sufficient funds for the bride price. In marrying, he has two alternatives: the approved ethical one; and the unethical, nevertheless practical, elopement. There are about four proper weddings to one elopement (on the evidence of forty-eight marriages).

The proper marriage starts with the boy asking his parents for financial support in order to marry a certain girl; or, in case he has no definite person in mind, by expressing his general desire to marry. In the latter instance, his parents may advise the boy concerning suitable individuals belonging to the sib with which one usually intermarries. Under these circumstances, the mother, who belongs to the specified sib, is of great help and may suggest some of her own distant relatives (of the younger generation) as prospectives spouses for her son. After the choice has been made and the son and parents are in agreement, the boy goes to the girl's family and asks for their consent. The discussion between the suitor and the maiden's brothers and parents concentrates almost always on the amount of the bride price. Other considerations, such as the welfare of the bride, may be hidden or couched in economic terms, and the girl's mother may safeguard her daughter from marrying a violent man by asking a forbiddingly high price. The outcome of the discussion depends mostly on the bride's mother and brothers. The father, on the other hand, is tabooed (in the Kamu Valley) from taking any part of the price. He serves more as a moderator than as a party in the process. After the price and date of payment have been agreed upon, the happy boy leaves with his sweetheart for his home where the couple live until the payment ritual, a period lasting from two to about forty days. There is no ceremony when the bride arrives at the groom's home, and the payment ritual is entirely a financial affair between the groom's and the bride's families. The bride has no part in it whatsoever.

The bride price is composed of two parts: *one*, a payment made by the groom or his creditors, and *kade*, which forms an accessory to the first and more important part. It is composed mainly of small gifts from numerous relatives and friends of the groom. While all contributions to *one* are considered loans and are repayable after the bride gives birth to a child, *kade* gifts are never asked back unless very generous. However, the recipient has an obligation to reciprocate in case any of the donors marries.

One, as the main payment, has to be paid in the form of the old, most precious Kapauku cowries and pigs. The groom and his close relatives, if they themselves do not possess sufficient funds, visit their friends and borrow shell money, which always has to be repaid. The gathered fortune may be given to the bride's relatives any time.

Unlike the payment of *one*, the low value cowrie shells introduced by the white man, the low-priced glass trade beads, and the *dedege* necklaces made of small species of cowrie shell constitute the *kade* part of the bride price. It is payable on a specified day called *"kade makii naago*, the day when *kade* is laid down." Iron axes and machetes, dancing nets, and occasionally bows and necklaces may be added to compensate for a deficiency in the cowrie currency, or to make the bride price even more attractive. The transfer of *kade* assumes a ceremonial form and, because it is the only ceremony in the process of concluding a marriage, it may be assigned the name wedding.

An average bride price, on the basis of twenty-four cases, is approximately 300 beads, 120 old Kapauku cowries, 120 white man's cowries, three *dedege* necklaces, and one large male pig. The amount of bride price varies with the wealth of the groom rather than with the variables on the bride's side. The latter factor, however, may be of importance in the remarriage of an older widow or in the marriage of a very ugly or promiscuous girl, in which cases a reduced price is asked.

After the date of the ceremony has been determined, the groom and his close relatives, such as his father, brothers, and parallel cousins, start to collect the *one*, the agreed-upon bride price. Having determined how much they can put together themselves, they visit more distant relatives and ask for help from them. The father's brothers can usually be counted on for considerable aid. During these visits the men invite many people to come to the "wedding" ceremony, thus assuring themselves of additional contributions. Unless the groom is a rich man, or a son of one, no matter how hard he and his brothers work, they usually collect somewhat less than the amount of the bride price which has been asked. It is then up to the *kade* contributors to make up or, preferably, surpass the difference. At about ten o'clock in the morning on the day when the *kade* is laid down, the ceremony is opened by the mother, father, or older brother of the groom, who places a rain mat of pandanus leaves on the ground in front of the groom's residence. The *one*, if it has not been given before, is placed upon the mat by the groom's mother or the men who loaned it. Here it is left for public inspection. Many people arrive from the neighboring villages to act as contributors or simply as spectators. The bride's relatives are already there and they squat near the mat to inspect the number and the quality of the shells. From the usually somber expressions on their faces, one can guess right away that the currency is not what they expected it to be. They silently rise, move away, and squat together in one group to exchange stern looks and a few derogatory remarks about the accumulated bride price.

Now is the time for the *kade* contributors to come forward and place their treasures on the mat. The women relatives put down their *dedege* shell necklaces and strings of trade beads. Now and then a friend of the groom rises from a squatting group and adds a few white man's shells to the collection. The looks of the bride's party remain stern and the headmen are worried about trouble which may arise any time. To prevent it, they start making requests to incite the generosity of the people. They appeal in long speeches to the friendship ties and emotional bonds which bind the onlookers to the poor groom who, if the wants and expectations of the price collectors are not satisfied, faces a possible loss of the bride. To make the appeal more dramatic the headman may start *"wainai, a mad dance,"* by stamping the ground with his feet while the left arm is stretched and the right one bent at the elbow, as if imitating the discharge of an imaginary arrow. While furiously hitting the soil with the soles of his feet in a fast rhythm, the dancer screams and shouts his requests to the bystanders. To make the scene even more impressive, the bride's brothers start to shout reproaches, threats to break up the deal, or even insults addressed not only at the groom and his close relatives, but especially at their friends and co-villagers in order to make them feel ashamed of not being generous enough.

No matter what the bystander thinks about the situation or the speakers, he finds himself suddenly squatting about the mat and pulling out precious shells from the most remote hideouts in the corners of his netted purse and putting them down upon the mat only to regret the deed after his head has cooled off again. As more and more people go through this ecstatic generosity experience, the angry voices of the bride's party lower and are finally replaced by faint smiles of satisfaction. Now the happy groom knows the deal is consummated, his tear-stained eyes dry, and a conceited smile dominates his face when he at last presents the promised one or two pigs to his new "in-laws." The whole process of payment has to be concluded by three o'clock in the afternoon, lest a taboo be violated and a disease be brought on the individual who might contribute later in the day.

For the average young man the whole ceremony is an ordeal involving success or failure in the acquisition of a bride. For the rich man, however, the occasion provides an opportunity to enhance his own prestige by paying not only the price asked but even surpassing it extensively. Thus he renders the marital ties strong, and also elevates his own political and legal position.

The payment of the bride price has many important functions in the social life of the Kapauku. It is collected by the brothers and the mother of the bride, the father acting only as an umpire who decides which son's turn it is to keep most of it. For the mother, the occasion means money to buy more meat or to make loans to her sons, husband, or brothers, and thus to gain their gratitude and dependence. From then on they have to respect her wishes, since otherwise she may ask the return of these sums. In this way, the bride price gives the mother an opportunity to elevate her status in the family. For the brother of the bride, the payment provides the means to buy himself a wife. For the creditors, it means an opportunity to take a mortgage on a bride price. They acquire the right to deduct the loaned sum, if not paid earlier, from the price paid in the future for the daughter of the woman they helped to buy. It brings them the highest gratitude of the groom who calls them "father" and feels obligated to support the creditors in all their arguments and troubles. The more wives one buys for men in one's community, the stronger one's political and legal influence becomes. The ceremony itself legally concludes the marriage and gives to it the necessary publicity. Nevertheless, the most important function of the payment is the stabilizing effect upon the marriage itself. The higher the price paid, the less is the chance that the wife will be supported in marital arguments by her male relatives and consequently granted a divorce. On the contrary, if she should escape with a lover into the bush, the girl's relatives themselves would try to recover her in order to avoid the obligation of paying back the large sum the rich man had paid for her.

A second method of marrying solves the wedding problem of a poor boy or of a suitor rejected by the girl's relatives. Elopement is the means by which a boy may get his loved one despite the protests of her kin. A girl may elope to turn her wishes into reality. She may also elope after she gets married, so as to force her husband to grant her a divorce and her relatives to repay the bride price and accept a payment from her new lover. Although the practice of elopement is rather frequent, it is believed to be not only immoral but also dangerous to the society as a whole. There is a very good reason for this condemnation. The two most frequent causes of war in the Kamu Valley are elopement and witchcraft, the first being by far the more frequent. The divorce situation is explosive because marriage, although defined in monetary terms, also involves an emotional bond, and a husband who loves his wife may not settle his loss even for a larger price than the original one. Moreover, the relatives of the woman may argue that because the husband is guilty of neglect or cruelty, he himself is primarily responsible for the failure of the marriage and is thus obligated to allow a reduction in the repayment, especially if the woman bore him a child. If the relatives side with the husband and try to catch the wife and force her back into the marriage, friends and relatives of the seducer may give their aid to the couple and thus possibly start a war. The divorce situation belongs in the sphere of law and will be dealt with more fully later.

Adulthood. By marrying, the boy and the girl become adults and are called *jame* and *jagamo*, man and woman. Even when they marry prior to the age recognized as suitable, the new status makes them "adults" if the difference between their actual age and the marriage age is small. If they are very young, the words *agaana* and *api*, meaning single boy and girl, have to be replaced by the word "*joka*, a child." A single man is called *agaana* until he is about twenty-two years old. If he is not married by then, he is called "*jedema*, an old bachelor with adult status."

There are two sets of values to which adults should conform. One concerns their roles as husband and wife and is determined by the opposite sex, and the other concerns them as members of Kapauku society. An ideal husband must be healthy, wealthy, sexually attractive, easygoing and not too emotional. He should not punish his wife physically—a reprimand should be his harshest treatment. He should be generous in spending money to buy meat for his wife. Although the society is polygynous, many of the women prefer a single man to one who is already married. An ideal wife should be sexually attractive, industrious, and obedient to her husband. Both sexes ought to procreate many children. A wife is considered not only a sexual partner and mother of the man's children, but by her work in the fields and her ability to raise pigs, she is also an important economic asset. If she earns a great deal of money through her skill and effort, she is supposed to lend it to her spouse whenever he needs it.

Faithfulness is expected only from the wife and is considered one of her most important virtues. Adultery on her part is regarded as a heinous crime and is punishable by beating or death administered by the husband. As to intelligence, the ideal standard for a wife is well summed up by the following quotation of Ijaaj Jokagaibo who had five wives and ought to know: "I prefer a stupid but good looking woman. This kind is always faithful and hardworking. A man gets a smart woman like Pigome Oumau of Obajbega and shortly he is not good enough for her. She does not work, she runs after other men, and after causing so much trouble she even bosses her husband. Do you white people like such women?" The above statement seems to substantiate cross-culturally the validity of the hearsay that women in general have three virtues: intelligence, beauty, and faithfulness, but the presence of any two of these precludes the third in any specific case. The husband may date unmarried girls and take them into his household as additional spouses. Concubinage and sexual hospitality are unknown among these people.

The society views its ideal man as a most generous individual, who through the distribution of his fortune satisfies the needs of many people. Generosity is the highest cultural value and an attribute necessary for acquiring followers in political and legal life. To be able to function with great generosity one has to be rich. Success in business coupled with the giving away of riches, eloquence, and knowledge of traditions bring one to the top of the social pyramid. An individual with these qualities is called "*maagodo tonowi*, a really rich man," and functions as political leader and arbiter in legal disputes. Bravery is also an important virtue but is not a necessary one for achieving the top honors in this society. The Kapauku recognize that courage in battle is hard to acquire when one has a placid personality. To fail to be generous is proof of immorality and of a bad personality, whereas a lack of bravery is regrettable but excusable.

From the society's point of view, a good woman is one who is industrious, fertile, submissive, and faithful. By the last attribute she saves the lives of the husband's people and thus she is most moral. "Ijaaj Auwejokaamoje's wife is really a nice woman. I would like to have such a woman for my wife. She resisted, though in vain, the rape by Damianuti and reported the assault promptly to her husband." This statement of Ijaaj Jokagaibo, the headman of Itoda, reveals that being untouched by another male is irrelevant to the evaluation of a Kapauku woman. Her resistance to the rape, even if not successful, and her attachment to her husband make her moral and desirable in the eyes of the society.

For the Kapauku man, being an adult means the peak of his life, of his independence, strength, and economic prosperity. If he builds his own house he emancipates himself finally from the bonds tying him to his father. Not only is he free but he starts to have dependents such as wives, children, young brothers, sisters, and other residents in his household. Even a son who lives with his father may become the most important man in the household, controlling all its members including his aging parents. He then becomes the leader of his small group and may or may not follow the decisions of the village headman. The latter's control, however, is much less intensive than that which his father had yielded.

The woman, on the contrary, comes under a control harsher than that of her parents after her wedding. Thereafter, she is not supposed to flirt or even to look at men who are not her or her husband's close relatives. She has to work, bear children, and obey. Thus her position is definitely lower than that of an unmarried girl. However, as time goes on and she gives birth to children and lends currency to her husband and sons, she starts to emancipate herself once again from the power of her spouse.

Although a husband may punish his wife even by wounding her or, for a serious offence such as adultery, by killing her, his position never approximates that of a tyrant, a Chinese husband, or "pater familias" of Old Rome. Should he be harsh, unjust, or too emotional, his wife can always leave him and get a divorce even without the support of her relatives. Thus there is a point, differing from one marriage to another, beyond which a husband does not dare to go in his control. As in our culture so among these Papuans, there are women who control their husbands. The poor dominated Kapauku male has not even the chance a woman is given by her culture. Having a weak personality, he can neither rule the woman nor chase her away, and there is no place to which he may escape. This situation presents also a very interesting legal problem. A married woman is responsible only to her husband and not even an enemy in wartime can molest her. Her male relatives have lost their jurisdiction over her by her marriage and the headman can only punish her husband but he cannot touch her. Thus when she dominates her spouse there is no male in the whole Kapauku society who can do anything to her and she stands beyond the scope of law. She therefore enjoys an uncontrollable status which a man can never achieve. No wonder then, that the society, being limited to beating her unfortunate spouse as the only way to affect her, makes use of religion and charges her with being a ghoul. However, even this does not affect the woman who was previously willing to ignore the ostracism of the society. The people say that the first task they are going to request of the Dutch police after they take control over the Kamu Valley will be to put these women into jail until they promise either to obey or to divorce their husbands.

Senescence. Life is a cycle determined by Ugatame, the creator. Its decline is marked by the appearance of gray hair which defines men as well as women as "*adama,* the old people." The body of the old man is wearing out in order to terminate its existence and release the soul into the world (Pl. 8, *top left*). The process of the decline of physical strength has a direct effect upon one's economy and wealth. An old man gradually abandons working his fields, does not raise pigs of his own, and starts to spend currency he has saved during his life. In order to be an economic asset to the household, the old man starts concentrating on net making and the production of arrows. He spends a lot of time watching his grandchildren and educating them in folklore and history. He may, at the same time, watch over small piglets left to graze around the house. The decline of physical powers brings about the disappearance of his wealth and this, in turn, undermines the influential position he may have held in the political and legal life of his village. He is no more an emotional and eloquent strong man and no one expects him to be.

The ideal old man should be generous as before, non-aggressive, kind, and quiet. He should know many legends, be fond of children, and play the role of moderator and pacifier in the household. Although he lost his authority in the house when his son became the head and he has ceased to be a village headman and arbiter in disputes, he retains his role as a consultant and advisor to the new authority and the function of being a key witness in field boundary disputes. Also, he ceases to be admired as a brave warrior. To compensate for this, he gains immunity from being killed or molested by the enemy during a war. Interestingly enough, his magical power is believed to go with the deterioration of his physical condition. A physically weak man can no longer frighten away evil spirits and the latter attack the *adama* until they kill him. The admiration by other people of one's strength, skill, wealth gives way to a respect for old age and to being sorry for the old man. A fear of his magical and bodily powers is exchanged for a fear of his soul which may soon leave the body forever and take revenge upon individuals who once harmed him. It is considered immoral to use harsh words against a man with gray hair, and physical violence against him is unthinkable. An individual violating these moral rules would be punished immediately, not only by the younger male relatives of the injured man, but also by other people who stand in no close relation to him. In summation, gray hair brings to a man an eclipse of his independent position, makes him a member of the son's household, and gradually decreases his status.

Senescence has an opposite influence on the status curve of the woman. The older she grows, the more she becomes emancipated from the powers of her husband. Because he respects her age, she is no longer beaten or scolded. Since a woman never holds political or legal positions and because her wealth is never crucial to her prestige, she has little to sacrifice in these respects, whereas her husband's loss in these fields is felt most strongly. Instead of losing, she actually gains, with the advancing years, the respect of the younger generation. Everyone tries to please her in order to make her soul kind and helpful after its departure. While the magical powers of the shaman and sorcerer decrease and finally disappear in old age, the danger from "*meenoo*, the female ghoul," not only persists, but with the approaching end of the "body's existence" and the prospect of the ghoul being freed again to settle in another woman, its perspectives grow even larger. With the onset of the menopause, all the eating taboos attached to her fertility are lifted and a woman in this respect is even equal to a man. Thus, the total status curves of the two sexes meet again after having been separated since the seventh year of each individual's life (Fig. 2).

The Kapauku do not like to grow old and to lose their physical and social powers. Since it has been determined by Ugatame, however, and nothing can be done about it, the people accept the inevitable with fatalistic resignation.

Death. Although as one becomes older the body deteriorates and grows weaker, death itself is never regarded as natural. There is always an evil spirit manifested by a disease which enters the body, expels the soul, and eats the vital substance, thus killing the individual. In case of a disease one calls in a shaman who, if the patient is still young, performs curative magic. *Peu adama*, the old man or woman who is so weak that he is forced to give up most activities, does not bother with magic anymore.

"Son, there will be no use for me to be treated by your doctor just as there will be no use for white magic. I know I am going to die in about two days and I want to die. I do not like only to sit in the house and be cared for and fed," said Ijaaj Kamutaka of Botukebo to the writer shortly before his death. His sons, nevertheless, came to the writer's house to get some pills to save the old man's life. That evening the sick man called his male relatives and held a long talk with them while the women listened from their quarters. He advised mutual help, assigned his garden plots to individuals and discussed the inheritance, stated his financial obligations and assigned the different amounts of currency to his sons. He was careful to be "just" and to give the largest portion to the oldest son so that his last will could not be invalidated on legal grounds. If a "testament" is just, a violator

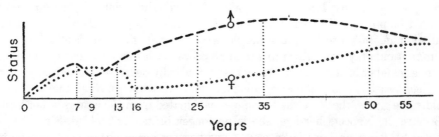

FIG. 2. Chart Showing Status Curves of the Sexes.

of it is believed to be punished by *"tene,* the departed shadow of the deceased."
For the following four days the old man did not talk, he just thought all the time
or slept. His sons stayed by and held him in their arms when his soul started to
yield its place to the evil spirit. As soon as this process was concluded, the sons
started to weep, eat ashes, and smear their faces with mud, yellow clay, and ashes.
Jii jii tai, a loud sing-song lamentation produced by the mourners, was carried by
the winds through the valley to announce the sad news to all the friends and relatives in other villages. The latter came rushing one by one or in groups to the
place of the death. The father's brother's daughter's husband of the deceased
came running into the house of the dead, his whole body plastered with yellow
mud. While wailing loudly he beat the hearth in the men's dormitory with a
long stick, thus punishing the spirit dwelling under it which is believed to consume
the corpse in the grave. Some of the relatives tore or burnt their carrying nets or
broke their penis sheaths to manifest their grief. As an expression of sorrow, one of
the sons decided to cut off the last joint of his left ring finger. Later, however, he refrained from doing it after the anguish had been partly assuaged by a generous gift
of shells presented by his best friend who arrived to mourn his classificatory father.
Moreover, as an additional gift he supplied a large pig, the pork to be distributed to
the mourners and friends of the dead during the funeral feast in the evening.

In the afternoon, the "in-laws" of the dead bound the corpse by its arms and
legs to a pole, and the husbands of the dead man's two sisters carried the cadaver to a
cliff overlooking the valley. There the sons built a tree house in which they deposited
the body of their father with his net, rain mat, and penis sheath. The window
structure was made in such a way that the dead man, bound in a squatting position,
could look down upon the house of his children. "We loved him very much. His
soul is going to come to our house and stay with us and help," declared one of the
undertakers. The sons climbed the tree and spent some time wailing while holding
the dead man's hand. When everyone was leaving the place, the eldest son stayed
behind squatting on the edge of the cliff, his eyes turned to the setting sun while he
talked silently with his father.

The funeral ceremony and the mourning described above may follow any of the different types of burials described in the first part of the monograph. The wailing is
continued for several nights and days. Especially during the first seven days after the
funeral, different relatives come to the grave to lament. The closest relative of the
dead man has the duty of remunerating everyone who expresses sorrow by a *"jii
jii tai,* lamentation," and he has to pay the "pall bearers" also, no matter how close
relatives they may be. After a lapse of seven days people stop visiting the grave—
one never knows what a *"tene,* the departed shadow" may do to one.

The widow, unless too old and sick, always remarries. To comply with mourning
custom, she has to wait for about ten days. During this time she is expected to be
sad and wail as much as she can, day or night. Should she remarry within three days
after the death of her husband, death by arrow shooting administered by sons of her
husband or by the latter's brother would be her punishment. If she remarries after

this period but prior to the required ten days of mourning, she is only considered immoral, gossiped about, and hated by the dead man's relatives.

The older children stay with their father's brother while babies live with their mother until they are old enough to return to "their home" in the paternal uncle's house. Most often, though, the final choice of a home depends on the will and emotional attachment of the orphan. This is usually respected by the mother as well as by the "legal foster father," the father's brother.

Conclusion. Kapauku are born, live, and die in the universe designed by Ugatame. Within it everything is natural, predestined, interrelated, and has an important function within the whole. Magic, spirits, dreams, souls, are as natural as men and animals. Their difference from the world of man or plants is comparable to that between the animate and inanimate world. Moreover, the latter difference may be even more profound to the Kapauku. The spirits move, behave, and live as men and animals do. They are heard at night, seen in visions and dreams, manifested by disease and death. There is nothing mysterious about this system when you think clearly about it. To Ijaaj Jokagaibo, for example, the nature of fire was more "supernatural" than any kind of spirit. You see the flames, you feel the heat, yet you cannot touch it. It is alive in the sense that it moves and is warm, yet it is dead in the sense that it is amorphous. Not the ghosts, but fire is supernatural and a mystery.

We have traced the life of the Kapauku in his natural universe from its beginning to its end. All the time our discussion focussed upon the individual within the world of Ugatame. Not losing sight of him and his philosophical outlook, we are going to shift our attention in the following part of the monograph to the social groups of which he, the Kapauku individual, is the constituent.

PART II: THE IJAAJ-PIGOME CONFEDERACY[3]

INTRODUCTION

IN THE following chapters an attempt is made to reconcile an analysis of the Kapauku cultural material with a description of different social units among which the community of Botukebo constitutes the main focus. It has been a tradition in current ethnographies to proceed from the least intricate and inclusive unit to the most comprehensive one, the assumption being that the latter is the most complex and is best explained by the units composing it. In Kapauku culture, however, it seems that the village, household and family involve an overwhelming majority of different relationship patterns, while the political confederacy is relatively a simple affair. Moreover, it is the household and the family which are the groups most important in the economy. Since the latter is the part of the culture which is most closely related to our problem of law, the writer considers it wise to bring economy and law into juxtaposition in this monograph and proceed in a reversed course, discussing first the most inclusive confederacy and then its division into sublineages, villages, households and families. The inquiry into law, which represents the content of the third part of the monograph, will thus closely follow the economic analysis. The different aspects of culture will be analyzed under traditional headings in the social unit to which they are most related: economics with family and household; political structure with confederacy, sublineage and village; war with confederacy only. Social structure, being pertinent to all groups, will be discussed at any time the need for it arises. Unlike that of the Pueblo Indians of North America, Kapauku religion is of minor importance compared to law. Because the practices and beliefs of religion are related principally to the individual, that aspect of culture has been treated at some length in the first part of the monograph. Nevertheless there will be a few references made to religion under the subject of war and also in the fourth part of the monograph where the author will try to lay down the boundaries between religion and related concepts of law.

"A long time ago Me Ibo (the great old man) came from Jugeibega, a village of the Mapia region, to the Kamu Valley. He married two women, settled down, slept and made fields in Botukebo, Aigii, Jagawaugii, Kojogeepa and Obajbegaa, thus laying the foundations of these five villages. He had many children and all the Ijaaj population of today (in the South Kamu Valley) are his progeny. Then came the Pigome people, who, being welcomed by Ijaaj, settled in Obajbegaa, where they have been given fields and married our women."

So runs the local legend about the origin of the confederacy. The Ijaaj people have the belief that they are all related to this common ancestor whose name has

---

[3] The presence of a hyphen in the name of a social group indicates that the group bears the name of its two constituent sub-groups. In such cases, the natives themselves use two terms to define the group.

been forgotten. Consequently they apply the appropriate kinship terms to each other.

A genealogy of six generations, involving about 2,000 individuals, dead and alive, has been assembled. Twenty-six major informants, whose statements have been substantiated by thirty-four other individuals, supplied the necessary data. The result of this effort has been the verification of the legend, a tree of progeny, growing from the "root" of the legendary Me Ibo, which includes all the Ijaaj people of the five villages. The question may arise as to whether this neat picture is not a product of a "Gleichschaltung," a streamlining produced by a cultural emphasis upon genealogies and common origin. The present author dismisses the idea for the following reasons:

1. There is no emphasis upon genealogies in this culture. An adult man would not know the name and relatives of his own grandfather if the latter happened to die prior to the birth of the informant. The present genealogy is a result of the author's activity, similar to assembling a mosaic. Each informant was able to contribute only a single glittering stone to the pattern. The location of each "stone" in the picture has been determined by the overlapping knowledge of various Papuans.

2. The members of four generations still living have been interviewed. This would leave only two generations as an opportunity for Gleichschaltung to result. Since the old people, during their youth, knew individuals from the sixth generation, and there is no reason why they should be distorting the truth, the genealogy that far is a historical fact.

3. Me Ibo himself, the only representative of the seventh generation, is claimed to have come from a specific village in the Mapia region. An investigation of the genealogies of that village revealed not only the relation to the Kamu Valley Ijaaj people but also the real name of the legendary Me Ibo. He was called Ijaaj Gepouja and lived in Jugeibega village. Thus, it seems that an investigation of genealogies revealed a Kamu legend to be history.

THE IJAAJ-PIGOME CONFEDERACY

GEOGRAPHY

About one hundred and twenty years ago, Ijaaj Gepouja started east from his native village and arrived in the South Kamu Valley (Fig. 3). The Kamu Valley is a drained lake bed, a swampy flat elevated fifteen hundred meters above sea level. It is surrounded by mountains which reach an elevation well over three thousand meters (Pl. 2, *top*). One of them, Mount Deijai to the north, is considered to be higher than any of its limestone brothers by at least seven hundred meters. Today the descendants of the original migrant occupy an area approximately six kilometers in length and two kilometers in width. The territory includes the valley bottom between the small mountains of Pouja and Jewei, which were originally islands in the center of old Kamu Lake, and the plain between the latter and Kemuge Mountain on the valley's edge. This land, although swampy and periodically flooded, is very fertile and lends itself in its more elevated sections to intensive cultivation

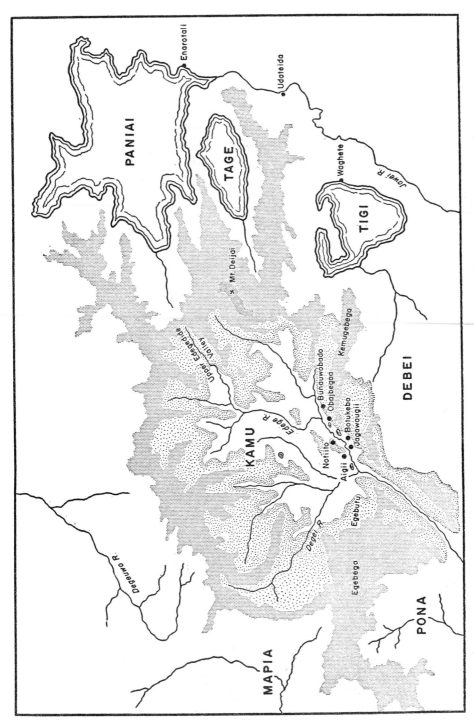

FIG. 3. The Kamu Valley and the Wissel Lakes.

during the dry season. This season lasts from October until May and differs from the rest of the year, or in other words from the rainy season, in that there is a little less rain. This slight difference is quite important in its effects on agriculture. Besides the cultivated fields of sweet potatoes and sugar cane, the valley is covered with grass and a growth of reeds two and a half meters high in which rats, muskrats, and several species of birds make their homes. This type of flat land is called by the Kapauku *geiga*, a word meaning "in the reeds." There are altogether about three square kilometers of this flat land owned by the confederacy. Edege River, the main stream which drains the valley and carries its rain waters to the south, divides this land from northeast to southwest into two irregular parts. It provides the people with a transportation route and with crayfish which constitute part of the protein supply of the population. It becomes a menace, however, when flooded and even under normal conditions two whirlpools in its large bend at Jewei serve as host to the treacherous Madou, a water spirit who tips over canoes and drowns people.

There are two small lakes, Kugumu and Tagepa, situated close to the river and connected with it by narrow outlets. In addition to crayfish, these lakes fill the nets of women and children with delicious dragon-fly larvae, tadpoles and water bugs, such as the backswimmer and water boatman.

To the east and three hundred meters above the bottom of the Kamu Valley lies the mountainous Debei Valley, the entrance to which is controlled by the confederacy. The valley's floor gives to the Ijaaj people an additional three-quarters of a square kilometer of fertile land which can be cultivated at any time irrespective of the season. In contrast to Kamu, there are no swamps in the Debei Valley and the uncultivated ground is covered by jungle with high standing hardwood trees suitable for canoe building.

The southern tip and the southeastern slope of Jewei Mountain, as well as the western half of Kemuge Mountain, together with the steep entrance to the Debei Valley, are under extensive cultivation. The sweet potato is the main crop. As in the Debei Valley, cultivation is successful all the year round and it is applied to an area of approximately three and a half square kilometers. The plots left fallow for some years are overgrown by young forest which provides important fuel for fires as well as wood for fencing in the gardens to protect them against pigs and wild boars.

The virgin forest on top of Kemuge Mountain, four square kilometers, belongs to the Ijaaj people. It is the home of boars. There rattan and the precious woods for canoe-making are to be found in abundance, and the boars, wallabies, rats, pythons, opossum and porcupines offer the Kapauku good hunting.

The five villages in this six kilometer long area are situated in a curved line extending from southwest to northeast in the following fashion: Aigii, Jagawaugii, Botukebo, Itoda-Kojogeepa and Obajbegaa. While the first four villages are built in the swampy *geiga*, the last is perched on the slope of Kemuge Mountain on a prominence called Obaaj from which it derives its name ("*Obaaj*, the name," "*bega*, the mountain"). To this union of five villages also belongs Notiito, a small place on Jewei Mountain populated by about twenty-five Ijaaj people of another lineage, and Bumauwobado, a village of the Dou sib, situated to the north of Obajbegaa. Both of these villages are only loosely connected with the confederacy. The latter one especially cannot always be counted on for help in occasions of hostilities.

POPULATION

The five main villages of the confederacy boast of a total population of four hundred and seventy-six individuals of which one hundred and twenty-three are adult men. Their ages range somewhere between sixteen and forty-five. Thus they are classified as warriors. There are one hundred and ninety-six children, one hundred of whom are males. The females of fertile age number one hundred and thirty-four. In the total population there are only eight males and fifteen females whose age is over fifty years. Notiito and Bunauwobado can supply forty-two more warriors. In addition to the above numbers, there are about thirty-five Ijaaj and Pigome males who, although residing outside the confederacy territory, can always be counted upon in case of war. Thus the total fighting force of the political unit consists of two hundred warriors (Table 1).

The sex ratio from five villages is 48.6:51.4 in favor of the women. The life expectancy of the population is very low and it is the writer's estimate that for males it does not exceed twenty-six years and for females about thirty-five. The difference between the two is caused by warfare in which the females are spared by the enemy but which eliminates a certain percentage of the males. During the writer's one year stay, seventeen births and thirty deaths occurred among the people of five villages. As far as the author could determine, all the cases of death were caused either by pneumonia—the normal killer of old people—or by bacillary dysentery, which destroys a high percentage of children under fourteen years of age.

Although the above data suggest a stable population, they give the picture for only a brief period and obscure the fact that the population in the southern part of the Kamu Valley has, according to informants, increased to a very considerable degree during the last hundred years. People are encroaching more and more on the

TABLE 1. DEMOGRAPHY OF THE FIVE FULL MEMBER VILLAGES OF THE IJAAJ-PIGOME CONFEDERACY

Village	Children		Adults		Old People		Total	
	M	F	M	F	M	F	M	F
Aigii	22	30	32	37	1	3	55	70
Jagawaugii	12	11	22	15	0	2	34	28
Kojogeepa	10	10	9	10	1	1	20	21
Botukebo	47	33	38	48	6	9	91	90
Obajbegaa	9	12	22	24	0	0	31	36
Total	100	96	123	134	8	15	231	245

Total Population: 476 Individuals. M = Males F = Females.

virgin forest which they cut down to provide additional fields for the growing population. Jewei Mountain has no virgin forest remaining and to reach the Kemuge Mountain forest one has to walk one hour from the nearest village, Obajbegaa, and over two hours from Aigii, whose inhabitants have their own forest on Kemuge Mountain. The Debei Valley has only a *gamouda* type of woods, a grove from which the precious canoe timber has already been cut and much of the rattan and wood suitable for plank-making has been harvested. With the retreat of the jungle, there was a parallel decline of larger game. The cassowary bird, once plentiful, is today exterminated in this part of the Kamu Valley. Ijaaj Awiitigaaj, when young, was still killing many wild boars right in the village of Botukebo and the people of Obajbegaa had to hunt this animal to protect their fields. Today, one has to go to Kemuge Mountain to find this species and even there luck must help the hunter. What has been said about the boar also applies to larger marsupials and rodents which became scarce even in the woods mentioned.

FOOD QUEST

The presence of agriculture and polished stone tools causes the Kapauku to be classified as neolithic people. Most of their food is grown in their fields. In the Kamu, these fields are usually square in shape with sides about thirty meters long. Such an individually owned area of nine hundred square meters, called by the natives *bugi peka*, is inherited from father to son. It is cultivated in slash and burn fashion approximately every eighth year for a period of ten months. The owner with his wives, first cuts and uproots the underbrush, leaving the cut material on the ground to dry. Formerly, men felled the trees with a polished stone ax, fastened by rattan and resin to a wood handle. Today they use an iron ax which arrived in the region from the southern coast prior to the white man's appearance. The native may also use an old iron machete blade hafted into a wooden handle by means of rattan lashing. While cutting the trees, the workman preserves all the forked branches and piles them in heaps. Strong sticks and stems are either cut in 170 centimeter lengths or, if nice and straight, are left in one piece. The cut poles, sticks and forked branches are used in the construction of a fence built around the field to protect the crop from destruction by domesticated pigs and wild boars which roam around the countryside looking for food. There are two types of fences built: *weedaa*, a simple structure in which vertical posts predominate, is used in the lowland where the soil is deep and permits posts to be stuck into the ground next to each other. The mountain slopes, with boulders and stone terraces, make it impossible to construct this type of fence and force the Kapauku farmer to turn to the more difficult and complex type of fence, *wageedaa*. In the latter type of fence, the horizontal poles, tied with rattan or vine to a few posts, cross the stony patches and form the essence of the contrivance. While it takes only forty-five minutes to complete two meters of the *weedaa* fence, the same length of the *wageedaa* type requires at least one hour for its construction.

A single worker spends about fourteen days, or one hundred and thirty-eight working hours, to prepare a field of *peka* size (900 square meters) for planting. Prior to planting, the dry slashings which litter the fenced-in area are burned, thus providing fertilizer for the future crop and destroying young weeds and grass which otherwise would soon overgrow the garden plot. At this point, the woman takes over and plants, by means of a long digging stick, shoots of sweet potatoes, placing five of them into one hole. Since the holes are one meter apart, an intercrop of *idaja*, a green resembling spinach, is often planted in between the sweet potatoes. The *idaja* seedlings mature and are harvested in about one month, thus not interfering with the growth of the tuberous plant. Most of the weeding and harvesting is the responsibility of the woman.

Although the production of the fields in the bottom land of the valley is much higher, the preparations which require more work than on the mountain slopes compensate for the advantage. One not only has to carry all the wood for the fences to these fields from the mountains but the farmer is also forced to dig ditches around the cultivated area to drain away the excess water which may cause his crop to rot (Pl. 4, *top*). This is hard work which is done by a man with a leaf-shaped wooden spade. The worker, standing in a ditch fifty centimeters wide and seventy-five centimeters deep, is able, by cutting and removing blocks of the black, muddy soil, to advance about one meter in fifteen minutes.

While extensive agriculture is practiced on the mountain slopes, the Kapauku farmer uses an intensive technique in the cultivation of the bottom lands of the valley. This practice is called *bedamai* and includes the placing of rotten leaves and green grass upon the surface of the ground and covering this layer of fertilizer with the soil dug out from shallower (25 centimeters deep) drainage ditches which cut the field into rectangular beds, each about five square meters in size. The harvest from such a field is double or triple that of the same area cultivated extensively on the mountain slopes.

Besides sweet potatoes and *idaja*, the two most important crops, several varieties of sugar cane are planted in the lowland and in the fields of the high Debei Valley. Except for the weeding, all the work is done by the man who considers sugar cane his plant. Taro is grown in the swampy lowlands as well as in the small depressions on the mountain slopes where rain water accumulates. Its tubers are eaten roasted and the leaves are steamed and eaten as a green with pork and other meat. Some maniok and "*apuu*, a vine with potato-like tubers," may be planted in the sweet potato fields to provide more variety in the diet. Besides *idaja*, the natives sometimes plant four other types of greens. "*Kagame*, a small plant belonging to the tomato group," is considered a delicacy and its green leaves can be eaten raw. "*Damuwe*, a parsley-like plant," "*dade*, a small shrub with edible leaves," and "*petai*, lettuce introduced by the white men," are cultivated for their leaves which, added to *idaja*, are steamed with meat in a cooking mound. Part of a field, with sugar cane as its main crop, may be reserved for *pego* cultivation. This is a reed about three meters high, the blossoms of which, while still in the bud, are roasted and taste like asparagus. Both types of cane are planted by sticking the tops of a harvested plant into the soil at a sharp angle. *Jatu*, a thick-stemmed grass with broad leaves, and *akakade*, a native version of beans, are grown on the bottom land of the valley, the former in long beds next to taro or sugar cane, the latter near a tree, rock, or fence which provides support for climbing vines. A few plants of "*wede*, ginger," may be found in a garden adjacent to a native house. Its roots are eaten raw in the way we eat an appetizer. The same field yields "*tuda*, a cucumber," "*nakapigu*, a squash," and "*bobe*, a gourd." These fruits are eaten roasted on embers and their leaves, used as vegetables, are steamed together with *idaja*. Besides having food value, the gourd supplies the natives with raw material for their penis sheaths, the only garment of the males. These long gourds are roasted for a short time. Then the inner part is cut out with a bamboo knife and the shell, after being cleaned and dried over a fire for several days, is ready to be worn. A few plants of introduced tobacco growing around a house give testimony of the male inhabitants' smoking habits. The leaves being cut, dried over a fire, crushed and put into a long, narrow, lengthwise folded pandanus leaf, are smoked in the form of a cigarette several feet long. Since the folded contrivance has an aperture all along one edge, the smoker can draw at any distance from the burning end.

The fifteen hundred meters elevation of the Kamu Valley allows cultivation of five different types of bananas. While three of these bear fruits which ripen and are eaten raw, two types with large fruits, *kugou* and *jigikago*, have to be stuck, green and unripe as they are, into hot ashes or roasted in a low burning fire to make them suitable for consumption. The last two types are considered delicacies by most of the men and are tabooed to women in their fertile period of life. Young banana plants, torn from the mother tree, are planted in the *geiga* grasslands of the Kamu Valley and in the villages next to the houses.

The Kapauku are devoted pig breeders. This animal not only constitutes their major source of protein but it also functions as an important part of the bride price, as a measure of one's wealth, as a source of an individual's prestige, political power and security, and it forms, together with the shell money, the basis of the economy. The mass slaughter of these animals has been institutionalized into the "*juwo*, pig feast" (Pl. 4, *bottom*) and the "*dedomai*, pig market," and it is present even in the "*tapa*, blood reward ceremony," discussed below under the heading of war. On the surface, the last ceremony resembles a pig market. Thus the sum of the roles a pig has in this culture attaches to this animal an importance comparable to that of the cattle of the Bantu cultures of East Africa.

The Kapauku pig is a dark skinned, long bristled, and snouted animal, which may reach, if properly fed, a weight of over two hundred kilograms. However, usually a pig is slaughtered when its weight ranges between eighty and one hundred and twenty kilograms. Approximately six weeks after its birth, the animal is taken from the mother sow and is fed and cared for from this time on by the wife of the owner. She chews cooked sweet potatoes for the small pig, keeps it overnight in her quarters, and takes it to the fields and swamps to teach it to eat tubers, roots, grubs, etc. Wherever she walks, the pig follows her and, when tired, it is carried in the arms or in the carrying net of its mistress. Thus the porker becomes attached to the woman to an extent which can be compared to the attachment of a dog to his master in Western culture. Leaving the little pig with the sow would make it wild, according to the opinion of the people, and, when adult, it would run away into the jungle.

At the age of five months, the pig starts to sleep under the elevated floor of the Kapauku house. Then it is fed four kilograms of sweet potatoes at six-thirty in the morning and six-thirty in the evening. During the day, the animal roams the swamp and forests looking for additional nourishment. To recognize one's property the pig is "branded" by cutting off its earlobes in a particular way. Meat for eating, tusks for the decoration of shoulder nets and the manufacture of nose plugs, bones for making needles, spoons and knives, remunerate the owner for his effort at the time of the slaughter of the animal.

Besides pigs, the chicken is the only domesticated animal of the people of the South Kamu Valley. The dog, so important in the adjacent Kapauku regions of Mapia and Pona, is, because of the scarcity of game and the resulting unimportance of hunting, absent in the region. The poultry, which has spread in the area after having been introduced by the Dutch Administration in the Tigi and Paniai region, is kept in the Kamu Valley for meat rather than eggs. The birds are fed broken pieces of sweet potatoes twice a day at the time of pig feeding.

Since it is not often that a Kapauku tastes pork or chicken, his protein supply has to come from other sources. Although hunting and trapping are important in the Mapia and Pona regions to the west and south, in the Kamu Valley which is void of extensive forests, they are considered sport rather than serious economic endeavors. Young boys and men make snares of rattan and set them on a path or in front of rat holes. To bag a rare, wild pig in the nearby forests of the Kemuge Mountain, they construct large snares or traps with spring spikes designed to tear the animal's abdomen. A large pit may also be dug on a boar's trail in the woods and the surface cleverly masked with branches. The pig, if caught in the pit, is shot by an arrow. An intentional break in the fence around a sweet potato garden may invite a boar to raid the growing crop. For the invader, there are many camouflaged bamboo spikes waiting on the other side of the fence to pierce the animal's body and leave it, too weak to climb back to freedom, bleeding to death in the garden. Snares may be also set on the edge of a lake to catch a duck or mud hen, led to its death by a V-shaped fence, the apex of which forms an opening for the trap.

Hunting is done with a bow and arrow. A wild boar may be stalked by a group of men, who follow its spoor, and is shot to death by a hunter who has circled ahead of the others and waited in ambush for the animal, which is chased toward him by the rest of the party. He would be kept informed about the movement of game by the advice yelled by his friends. A brave individual, such as Ijaaj Awiitigaaj of Botukebo, may catch a wild boar with his bare hands and shout for a man to come and club the beast to death.

Rats are shot on their trails with hardwood tipped arrows as they try to escape from a grassy area surrounded by men and stamped over by women. A moonlit night may give a hunter with barbed wood tipped arrows an opportunity to shoot giant rats or marsupials climbing the trees or crossing a path in the jungle. During such a night, the younger boys who are still afraid of evil spirits wait next to their houses with a *taka*, a large bird arrow with a four pronged point, to shoot a fruit bat feasting on banana or *ijade* fruit trees. A group of young men and boys may resort to an easy way of hunting rats. On a dry and windy day, early in the afternoon, they may start a huge grass fire and, while following the fireline, collect the roasted animals.

The large birds such as ducks, mud hens, hawks, cranes and cassowary birds are hunted with bamboo or hardwood tipped arrows. People try to approach the game and discharge their missiles from as close a range as possible. The smaller birds, which are plentiful everywhere, are shot with a *taka*, arrow with a reed shaft and several pronged points of hardwood or with a *"puguuto*, blunt end arrow." The hunter may stalk these birds or await their arrival in a hut made of reeds bent over and stuck into the swamp. For the same purpose, he may use a tree platform which is provided with a thatched roof to protect the hunter from the rain as well as from being detected by his prey. These small birds and rats, because of their abundance, supply the Papuans of the five villages with more proteins than the large game mentioned above.

The regular supply of proteins is derived from fishing. Women and children, equipped with large and small oval and circular nets mounted on frames of willow-like branches to which handles are attached, drag the bottom of the lakes and flooded swamps, fishing for crayfish, tadpoles, dragonfly larvae and water bugs. The catch is placed in bamboo containers which are tucked under the belts of the fishermen and plugged with stoppers made of crumbled grass. Except for the large crayfish, which are roasted on embers, the delicacies are stewed by simply sticking the bamboo container into the hot ashes. Fishing is done from a boat or by wading the shallows, or by building a dam of reeds or stones across a stream. In deep waters, women fish by sinking the large nets, weighted with stones and baited with pieces of water snakes, lizards or cooked sweet potato, in the depths and pulling them out after an hour or so by means of ropes (Pl. 2, *bottom*).

Besides the net, women may use a long, forked stick which they plunge into the weeds of the lake bed, rotating it in the hands and pulling it out with a bundle of water vegetation caught in the fork. By spreading the weeds over the edge of the canoe, they locate the prey which hides inside the bundle. Men may help their wives with the task of fishing by taking it up as a sport. Diving to the bottom and holding to roots and stones, they locate the crayfish and seize them by hand. At night, torches are used for the purpose of luring the prey, which is then speared from the canoe with a reed shaft eight feet long, tipped with a seven-pronged hardwood point.

A heavy rain in the upper Edegedide Valley, even if it lasts only two days, causes the Edege River to spill over its banks and, from what has once been a narrow valley with a small stream in its center, becomes a surging torrent of muddy liquid which, rushing all over the less elevated parts of the valley bottom, carries the high waters south to the Kamu Valley. There, the water level rises in the river until it spreads over its banks into the open grasslands and swamps, changing the landscape into a huge lake, thus reminding the inhabitants of the valley's character in the not distant past. If the reader thinks this inundation would be considered a calamity by the Papuans he is badly mistaken. On the contrary, this is the time for a holiday for all the population, an occurrence which repeats itself only about five times a year. The women especially welcome the change from the daily monotonous field work to the much more enjoyed activity of going by canoe all over the valley to collect the insects floating helplessly in the flooded grasslands. On higher grounds, where grass and reeds protrude considerably above the water, the women stamp down the vegetation to make the mole crickets, grasshoppers, and different species of stink bugs and cockroaches loose their support and leave the grass and try to swim for safety, thus becoming easy to catch. The insects are inserted into the familiar bamboo containers and in the evening they are steamed and eaten.

"I have not seen my wives for three days," complained an unhappy and starving husband. "I have to go myself and get some sweet potatoes. All they will bring from their expedition is a few bugs, which will not satisfy my hunger and, of course, heaps of mole crickets which we (men) do not eat." Although this complaint would suggest that the husbands and men in general suffer hardships during the time of a flood, the truth is that the occasion presents them with a unique opportunity to shoot, catch or club many of the flushed out rats, muskrats and birds and so feast on the delicious meat while their wives are absent and cannot claim their share.

Besides the extensive collecting activities during the flood, gathering on a small scale constitutes part of the daily activities of most of the Kapauku. Women and men stop on their way to their fields or to the neighboring village to look for grubs in rotting trees. They may inspect certain kinds of trees and shrubs looking for edible insects and occasionally pick up bird's eggs, lizards, and mushrooms, thus adding to their daily protein diet. During a dark night, two or three women may go with flaming torches into the swamp to collect frogs which they bring home the next day in big enough quantities to satisfy all the meat-hungry males of their households.

Collecting is not limited to animals only. *Uguubo*, a kind of green plant and various species of fern are gathered to be steamed with pork in the cooking mound. About seven different species of trees supply the people with their juicy fruits, while the plentiful large lemon and the small yellow lime add important vitamin C to the Kapauku diet. Although there are stingless honey bees living in the forest, it is only the wax that the Kapauku people care for. Honey, believed to be the excreta of bees, is considered inedible and a Kapauku would feel sick at the thought of eating it. "What rude kind of people are you to eat such disgusting things. Only the Kapauku of Mapia do that and you should be better than they," exclaimed the old headman of Botukebo after learning the white man's custom.

SOCIAL STRUCTURE

As the Edege River cut its bed deeper and deeper through the southern outlet from the Kamu Valley and more and more water was drained away, the swamp desiccated and some of the elevated ground became habitable and fit for cultivation. Then people from other regions moved in and occupied the new land. During this short migration, Ijaaj Gepouja arrived from the westward lying Mapia, married two women and claimed the land, today the property of the five villages. His sons and grandsons found most of their spouses among the members of the Pigome sib which, having come from the opposite direction and region of the large Paniai Lake, settled in the nearby Debei Valley.

Thus the core of the confederacy was formed by people from the two sibs. The Kapauku are patrilineal people grouped into totemistic sibs, twenty-eight of which are represented by their male members in the Kamu Valley. The people believe that the individual groups were created in the old days by Ugatame, the creator, and a special name given to each. All people of the same unit regard themselves as related through the father's line. The legend says further that the creator determined for all time special sib taboos on eating fruit and animals and on burning certain kinds of trees. The people have to obey these taboos lest they become deaf. The totemistic prohibition does not apply to the shooting of such animals or to the cutting of such trees. So, for example, Ijaaj people may kill and sell meat of a fruit bat but they are forbidden to eat its flesh. They may plant and harvest the "*kugou*, a non-ripening banana" but are forbidden to eat it. Similarly, the Goo sib, while allowed to cut, is prohibited from burning the following trees: *tekededege*, *ebijaaj* and *tagija*. In the South Kamu Valley, there is no belief in the origin of the sib's members from those species, neither is there any ceremony associated with this kind of simple totemism.

The sib arranges marriages, ideally making them exogamous. In all villages in the past, and in some of them still, male and female violators of the marriage rule may be killed by the relatives of the boy as well as those of the girl. Nevertheless, there is a change under way which tends to disrupt the exogamy regulations as well as those pertaining to the totemic taboos. The discussion of these changes will be taken up while dealing with the village of Botukebo and in the appropriate section on the law of incest. The unilineal, consanguineal group, which has been discussed, has no importance whatsoever in politics, war or economy.

The phratry. Certain sibs, usually two in a given case, are grouped loosely together and their members are believed to have belonged to a single sib. A myth presents a story about the origin of the junior member of this dual arrangement. The narrative in every instance tells about brothers of the senior sib—two, three or seven in number—the youngest of whom behaved in a strange way. The eldest brother gave him a name which reflected his peculiar activity and expelled him from the fold. Thus the youngest brother became a founder of a new sib which carried the name given by the eldest brother.

The myth of the origin of the Kotouki sib: At Egebega (in the southwestern part of the Kamu Valley), there lived two brothers among the Dimi people. Amoje, the younger of the siblings, used to build many bridges ("*koto*, the bridge") and did not relax for one single day working like an ant ("*uki*, the ant"). So the elder brother told him: "You do not relax, you are just building bridges, one after the other, and you are neglecting all other work. This is not correct. Now you are called Kotouki, you should go away." The youngest brother left for Pagoja in the Southern Kamu Valley, settled down, and his progeny are the Kotouki people.

Thus, members of both groups, the senior and junior sibs, consider themselves related. They not only share the story of the origin of the junior partner, and thus believe that they had a common ancestor, but they also have identical "*baita*, totemic taboos," as well as a common incest taboo with a third sib. Thus, the Tibaakoto sib "sprang off" from the Ijaaj sib and both of them are prohibited from eating the fruit bat, the *kugijaaj* bird, the *kugou* banana, and from marrying Pekej people. The informants reported also that once there existed a taboo on sexual intercourse between members of sibs linked in the same phratry. Today this taboo, if once really present, has disappeared. We may conclude by saying that the members of the two sibs, linked into a phratry, share totemic taboos and a common incest taboo with a third sib. They may have had a mutual incest prohibition in the past and believe themselves to be descendants of a common ancestor.

The subsib. Forty-five per cent of the sibs of the Kamu Valley are further subdivided into two groups which are identified by special names, always occupy separate settlements, do not cooperate at all, and are mutually very hostile. Thus, the Ijaaj sib is composed of Dege Ijaaj (light Ijaaj) and Buna Ijaaj (dark Ijaaj) which subsibs occupy different villages and belong to different, mutually hostile political confederacies. All Ijaaj people in the Ijaaj-Pigome confederacy are of the Buna Ijaaj subsib and their Pigome allies belong to the Umaagopa subsib.

The Pigome people of Demaago village in the Debei Valley, who are members of the Adaagopa Pigome subsib, constitute a part of another political unit which fought many battles against the Ijaaj-Pigome confederacy, the last taking place in the summer of 1954. The Tibaakoto sib, belonging to the same phratry as Ijaaj, is considered the worst enemy of the confederacy, partly because its founder is believed to have belonged originally to the opposite Dege Ijaaj subsib. While it is a deplorable crime to kill a man from the same subsib, although he even may have lived in another region than the killer, to shoot a Dege Ijaaj is for a Buna Ijaaj a regrettable, but sometimes politically necessary incident. Concluding this section, we may note that the "Ijaaj-Pigome confederacy" is actually not a proper term; the unit should be called the "Buna Ijaaj-Umaagopa Pigome confederacy." However, since the people apply only the names of their sibs to their confederacy, we shall make use of the same designation.

The lineage. Since the older people of the confederacy can actually trace their relationship through specific ancestors to the individual whom they call "Me Ibo," and whose actual name was Ijaaj Gepouja, and since they apply to each other kinship terms, irrespective of the fact that the ancestors of the other kinsmen are usually not remembered, we are justified in calling the aggregate of individuals inhabiting the five villages the Ijaaj Gepouja lineage. In a similar way, the Pigome people of Obajbegaa, who married into the Ijaaj Gepouja lineage, form another lineage which we shall call the Pigome Obaaj lineage. There are several important generalizations concerning this type of grouping to be pointed out:

1. Members of a lineage almost always occupy contiguous territory and belong to the same political unit.

2. The non-accidental killing of a member of the same lineage is always considered a heinous, deplorable deed, which threatens the unity and the welfare of the people and thus we are justified in assigning to it the name "murder."

3. All the individuals of the lineage consider themselves relatives, apply to themselves proper kinship terms, and exhibit affectionate tones in their mutual behavior. This behavior contrasts with that toward the outside world of non-relatives, irrespective of their sib membership. The statement has to be qualified by putting stress upon the word "all" and by specifying that any given individual would have relatives, such as "in-laws" and mother's relatives, outside his lineage unit, but they would not be considered related at all to other members of the consanguineal group. Thus, the lineage is the largest unit wherein all members are mutually related.

4. Since two whole lineages form the Ijaaj-Pigome confederacy, many statements about the behavior of the members of the confederacy will be true also for those of the lineage, unless specified otherwise.

POLITICAL STRUCTURE

The Ijaaj-Pigome confederacy is composed of two permanent members, the above-mentioned lineages and two more loose allies—a small Buna Ijaaj lineage of Notiito and a strong Pugaajkoto Dou lineage of Bunauwobado. According to informants, all five villages of the two permanent members were once the property of the Ijaaj lineage only. Pigome people married into the village of Obajbegaa and acquired their present possessions from Ijaaj. In this way, the foundations were laid for what is today considered one of the strongest and most aggressive political units in the valley and its vicinity. The Notiito, situated at the northeastern tip of Jewei Mountain, and thus exposed to attack from the Bobii people to the north, allied themselves with the Gepouja lineage in the sense that Notiito males participate in certain confederacy wars but not in all, thus forming a sixth star in the political constellation. The symbolic number of the Kapauku being seven, another ally has been added to complete the count. Bunauwobado, a large village of about one hundred and forty Pugaikoto Dou people, built at the northwest foot of Kemuge Mountain, became a strong ally of the Ijaaj-Pigome people. Nevertheless, this ally cannot be counted on in all the wars the confederacy has to fight. The Dou people themselves decide whether they will help in a given situation. Thus, their help does not amount to an automatic alliance such as exists in the five villages where a fight with one means an engagement with all. Ijaaj, Pigome and

Dou people of the confederacy's lineages, who went to live in other villages than their own, because of their kinship ties may be relied upon to come back and serve as warriors. However, because they made their homes in other localities, their participation ultimately depends upon their own decision.

Leadership. To continue the discussion of the political structure of the confederacy and its function, we must investigate the problem of Kapauku leadership. Since there is only one type of authority in the society which functions on the confederacy, sublineage, village and political faction levels, most of what we shall say here, unless specified otherwise, will also be valid for the leadership of the other political units. Furthermore, since this institution reflects other parts of the culture and not only politics, we have to refer here to values, economy, law and personality, as well as to social structure, a fuller description of which will appear later.

A European who spent some time in the Kapauku area informed the writer upon his arrival in New Guinea that there was a virtual absence of authority and leadership among these people. Another experienced man, whose opinion the writer values very highly, basically substantiated the first statement but with an important qualification, however: "There is a man who seems to have some influence upon the others. He is referred to by the name *tonowi*, which means 'the rich one.' Nevertheless, I would hesitate to call him a chief or a leader at all; *primus inter pares* (the first among equals) would be a more proper designation for him. If you find out about his attributes and function, please let me know. He is a mystery to me." In the following paragraphs the writer will try to give an answer.

The concept of freedom and independence. "The worst thing that can happen to a Kapauku is to be put into the white man's jail in Enarotali. We do not like to have even our enemies put there and we hate the police for this practice," stated a man from the Tigi Lake area. "What is wrong about a jail? Only bad men are placed there. In the old days you used to kill these people, but now they stay only a short time in jail and then can go home," the writer replied. "Jail is the worst thing. The man's vital substance deteriorates and the man dies. We used to kill only very bad people, but now one may get into prison simply for stealing or even fighting in a war. One dies if shot by an arrow, but in jail one has to suffer before death. One has to stay in one place and has to work when one does not like it. Jail is really the worst thing. Human beings should not act like that. It is most immoral."

The above quotation reflects one of the highest non-verbalized values of the Kapauku prior to the white man's arrival—the emphasis upon the physical freedom of an individual. There is no such thing in Kapauku society as locking one in a house, binding his hands, or forcing him by torture or physical harm, or by threat of these, to behave in a certain way. Moreover, there is no institution of war prisoners, slaves, nor anything that would even approximate the old dependence of European peasantry upon the landlords. A very bad criminal, or an enemy who could not manage to run away, would be killed but never tortured or deprived of his liberty. A culprit may be beaten or even wounded with an arrow, but he always has a chance to run away or fight back during the administration of the penalty.

If he does not, it indicates that he prefers to accept the punishment and live normally again with his people. Freedom of action is essential to life. When a body is
physically forced to remain in one place, such as prison, or to work, the soul, dis-
pleased with the state of affairs and especially with the impossibility of directing
the body's activity, leaves the body, thus causing death. "It is like in disease, you
cannot move and the soul leaves," was the opinion of Ijaaj Awiitigaaj of Botukebo.

Freedom of movement and of premeditated action is the basic condition for life.
Consequently, in a society with this kind of notion one cannot expect to find "enforcement of laws and of an authority's decisions." Inducement would be a more
suitable term for the agent of social control. A child, for example, may be slapped
for not having done something properly, but cannot be beaten into doing it better.
Sanction works as an inducement for better behavior in the future but not as an
enforcement of immediate behavior. Thus, one is independent in the sense that
all actions should follow one's own decisions rather than the mental process of
someone else. The latter case would be regarded as a cessation of the vital cooperation of soul and body, an equivalent to death.

It is natural that the pattern of Kapauku freedom and independence is reflected
in the sphere of economics. We may call this phenomenon "individualism" and in
many respects it exceeds even the famous American one.

"Two people cannot work together because they have two different minds" was
the reason given by informants in answer to a question about why there is always
only one owner of a thing. A house, boat, bow and arrows, field, crops, patches of
second growth forest, or even a meal shared by a family or household, is always
owned by one man. Individual ownership, contrary to the findings in the Paniai
region (de Bruijn, 1953) is so extensive in the Kamu Valley that we find the virgin
forests divided into tracts which belong to single individuals. A father and son,
brother and sister, two brothers, or a husband and wife would never hold a thing
in common ownership. As has been already pointed out, even an eleven year old
boy will own his field, his money, and play the roles of debtor and creditor as well.
There is no communal territory or corporations. The type of economy thus reflects
the basic cultural value placed upon personal independence in thinking and action.

"I do not like to be told when to make a field" would be another reason given
for individual ownership. "That is yours and here is my property and everyone
knows what belongs to him" is a common statement in the defense of the system
of private ownership. "If we were both owners, we would quarrel too much, we
would steal from each other in order to obtain most from the field. My children
and wives would probably go hungry—oh, it would be bad."

In this culture, there is also no institutional giving as we know it. *Jegeka motii*
—loosely translated by Europeans as "take it as a gift"—means exactly: "take it
without repayment in the immediate future." All "gifts" are actually loans, the
return of which can be asked any time. Since the people have money, the institution
of credit, interest, sales and capital, and because wealth is of paramount importance
in the individual's life, the writer feels justified in calling the economic system
primitive capitalism combined with individualism.

This individualism and independence, reflected in the different aspects of the Kapauku culture, as well as in the absence of "enforcement" and of the sequence "order—execution of order" gives an outsider the impression of a virtual absence of authority and leads him to the conclusion that all the people are *pares*—equals as to their importance, that there is no leader and no followers. Such an interpretation, however, leads one to the problem of how to account for the individual called *tonowi* and the fact that the people, although *pares*—equal and independent—seem to follow the "mysterious man" referred to by the Dutch. The easiest way to escape from this blind alley is to assume that "all people" move in a certain direction. The *tonowi* just happens to be the *primus inter pares*, first among equals, who does not actually lead but happens to be the first one moving toward the goal which would be achieved by the rest of the people even without the former's presence. This simple explanation, no matter how pleasing to some determinists, is based upon the Durkheimian myth of the possibility of separating society from the individual, and does not illuminate the reality at all.

"Tonowi, the authority." 1. Physical appearance. A man who is called *tonowi* is usually a healthy looking, middle-aged man in the prime of life.

2. Wealth. The Kapauku word *tonowi* literally means "a wealthy man," an individual who has much cowrie shell money, much credit, several wives, approximately twenty pigs, a reasonably large house, and who cultivates many fields. Wealth carries with it the highest prestige and is the main measure of one's status. With the accumulation of personal property, one climbs the Papuan social ladder, acquiring more respect until one reaches the status of a *tonowi*. This is the dream of every Kapauku youth, a goal toward which every man strives, a position achieved, however, by very few. Since the amount of riches a person assembles depends primarily upon his own work and skill, it is directly related to his physical condition. There are no *tonowi* who are feeble. With the coming of old age, a man's powers disappear and so do his fortune and prestige. The status of *tonowi* is lost by the old people and not yet achieved by the young who have not had time to accumulate a large fortune. Although many of the *tonowi* achieve this position by their own endeavors, a generous inheritance may accomplish the same result if received by a conscientious man. In the case of a lazy or inexperienced heir, the money can easily disappear within a few years and the people may mockingly recall, "He is one of those stupid fellows who did not know how to do business, who were once *tonowi* but wasted their money because of ignorance." In summary, the status of a *tonowi* depends on wealth, the increase and decrease of which produce parallel changes in the social standing of an individual and which is a condition *sine qua non* for political leadership.

3. Generosity. Although economic success is the basis for becoming a Papuan authority, not all *tonowi* have followers and pass weight carrying decisions. Only some of them achieve this. In other words, there are criteria other than sheer wealth which define a man as a leader.

It has been said that the Kapauku place a high value on individualism. However, it is not the rugged type of individual which is emphasized. To the natives, the amount of goods and money is not the only important thing. The way in which capital is acquired and how it is used makes a great difference, factors which distinguish from the number of rich candidates for a position of leadership those who comply with the requirement of being generous and honest. These two attributes are greatly valued in the culture. A man who steals from others, borrows without repaying, acquires money under false pretenses rather than through honest business deals, or a selfish individual who hoards money and does not lend it, never sees the time when his word will be taken seriously and his advice and decisions followed, no matter how rich he may become. The people believe that the only justification for becoming rich is to be able to redistribute the accumulated property among one's less fortunate fellows, a procedure which also gains their support. Thus, the emphasis upon capital and the acquisition of money is balanced by the highest value of the culture, *"ba epi*, generosity."* In the Kamu Valley, the rich men who fail to comply with this requirement are ostracised, reprimanded and thereby induced to become generous. In the Paniai Lake region, the people go so far as to kill a selfish rich man because of his "immorality." His own sons or brothers are induced by the rest of the members of the community to dispatch the first deadly arrow: *"Aki to tonowi beu, inii idikima enadani kodo to niitou* (you should not be the only rich man, we all should be the same, therefore you only stay equal with us)" was the reason given by the Paniai people for killing Mote Juwopija of Madi, a *tonowi* who was not generous enough. The people also resented the fact that his son who executed his "immoral" father was put into prison by the white man's police. It did not matter that he was sentenced for only three months.

Due to the fact that the highest status in the culture is achievable through the much publicized lending of money and that the hoarding of wealth for its own sake is considered unethical and is punishable by reprimands, ostracism and gossip, the people, although very willing to discuss their loans, are rather secretive about their cash. They are secretive so that no one can ask them for a loan or charge them with selfishness. A rich man in Kapauku society wears the same clothes as others, eats only a little better, and when he kills a pig he distributes all the meat without tasting a single piece. His house is large, but not because he would like to display his wealth; it is his many wives, children, "helping boys" and friends living in the *tonowi's* house who require for their own welfare a larger structure. Thus, contrary to Veblen's generalization, the rich Kapauku Papuan is conspicuous, not because of his consumption, but because of his generosity.

The *tonowi* who is generous and "moral" in the above-mentioned sense is sometimes called a *maagodo tonowi*, really rich man. Only such a man becomes an authority with followers, most of whom are his debtors. Thus, the economic institution of credit seems to play a basic role in the political as well as the legal structure.

4. Rhetoric and eloquence. Eloquence and the art of rhetoric are the last criteria of a Kapauku *tonowi*. Ijaaj Timaajjokainaago of Botukebo, although a very rich, generous and honest man, is not a leader of his community. He is afraid to talk at a gathering. He is too quiet a man to amount to anything in public. Seventy-five

per cent of the informants from his village think he would make a splendid leader and they would gladly follow his decisions "if only he would speak up." Unfortunately, he is pushed aside by a man who is less rich and less moral, but is brave and an excellent public speaker.

Thus we may conclude that wealth, generosity, and eloquence define an individual as an authority in the Kapauku society. There are some additional qualities which, although not indispensable, enhance the position of a headman. Bravery in war makes a man a *"jape uu me,* war leader." If this quality is present in the *maagodo tonowi's* personality his prestige is multiplied and his position is more secure. Skilled shamanism is highly valued by the natives and the practitioner occupies a status second only to the headman. If the *maagodo tonowi* happens to be also recognized as a shaman, his prestige reaches the highest peak achievable in Kapauku culture. This individual's power tends to transcend the limits of his community and to elevate him to the leadership of his lineage or even the political confederacy. As we shall see, this is the case of the Ijaaj-Pigome confederacy's leader.

Followers stand in various relations to the leader. Their obedience to the headman's decisions is caused by motivations which reflect their particular relations to the leader. Thus *"imee bagee,* the kinsmen," support and follow their rich relative because of their kinship ties which create between the individuals an emotional bond as well as a network of duties, rights and expectations of future favors. It is good for a Kapauku to have a headman as close relative because one can then depend upon his help in economic, political and legal matters. To follow such a man's advice and to fulfill his wishes always brings a reward. Individuals whom the rich man has helped support him out of thankfulness for his past generosity. However, the expectation of future favors and advantages should be regarded as the motivation responsible for the existence of most of the headman's followers. Strangers who know about the generosity of a headman try to please him and people from his own political unit attend to his expressed desires. Even individuals from neighboring confederations may yield to the wishes of a *tonowi* just in case the help of this man may be needed in some future situation. As it has been already pointed out, one is never forced into obedience and not a single one of the writer's one hundred and sixty informants admitted being afraid of the leader's physical punishment. Most of them, however, tried to avoid public reprimand administered by the leader as well as the consequent loss of face and ostracism by other people.

The debtors form one of the most dependable categories among the *tonowi's* adherents. Their fear of being asked to pay back money which has been loaned, coupled with gratefulness for the generosity of the credit allowed, makes them the stoutest supporters of the *tonowi.* They are always dependable supporters in war or in a legal suit. One may ask if the death of a *tonowi* would not be an advantage to the debtor by his being released from his obligation in this easy way. Nothing would be more erroneous than to assume such a thing. Debts and credits are inherited. Since one always has personal and, as a rule, cordial relations with the creditor, whereas one cannot depend on the "generosity" of the heir, the life and welfare of the *tonowi* are of vital concern to his debtors. Especially when a young man is buying a bride the emotional bond between the debtor and creditor is so intensified that the latter, out of gratefulness and reverence, is very often called "my father" by the young groom.

"*Ani jokaani,* my boys," form a very special group of the *tonowi's* partisans. They are not only very dependable and faithful to the cause of their master, but they are always at hand and ready to help whenever the need arises. They are the boys who come to live with a rich man to obtain from him a good education, especially in business administration, to secure his protection, to share his food and, finally, to be granted a substantial loan for buying a wife. In return, they offer their labor in the fields and around the house, their support in legal and other disputes, and their lives in case of a war. The boys may be from different sibs and confederacies, or they may be closer relatives of their tutor. The *tonowi's* house constitutes an educational and economic institution, as well as a unit important in politics, law and war. The "students" form a bodyguard for their *tonowi* and thus, by their physical presence alone, induce other people to respect the wishes of their leader. However, this contractual unity is quite loose. Both parties are free to terminate it at any time and the boy is never treated as an inferior by the rich man. He has the right to be fed, protected and granted a place to sleep. Moreover, the *tonowi* is morally obligated to buy a wife for "his boy" if the latter has fulfilled his own obligations of the contract. By moral obligation we mean that the headman cannot be legally induced to fulfill it although the requirement of generosity orders him to comply with this moral duty. A boy, cheated in this respect by his old master, becomes his enemy and spreads adverse propaganda to make other boys reluctant to join the "immoral" man.

The followers of a *maagodo tonowi* may constitute a political faction in a village, a sublineage whose members live in several villages, a lineage, or even a political confederacy numbering sometimes over a thousand individuals. In the role of the confederacy leader, he usually is the one who makes decisions about war and peace. His word induces the unit to support a man in a dispute and fight for his cause against other confederacies. His decision, on the other hand, may prevent a war when he admits the guilt of his followers and pledges to repair the damage. Authorities of lesser groups also have much to say in the above matters and they thus influence the decision of a confederacy leader. For some "justified reasons," they may withdraw the support of their constituents and thus sometimes induce others to oppose the decision of the headman. Since there are disputes between villages, sublineages and political factions which occur within the confederacy, the leaders of these units may, in an extreme situation, wage an inter-village battle with sticks against their fellow opponents.

All the *tonowi* function as authorities in disputes occurring among their followers. It is especially in this field of social control that the native leader's role as an authority, negotiator and trouble extinguisher is most important for the effective functioning of the group. His word also carries weight in economic and social matters. Thus, the pig feast, the communal dance expedition to other villages, the inducement of a man to become a feast's co-sponsor, the digging of a large drainage ditch, or the building and repairing of a bridge, demands the support of the pertinent *tonowi*. The multiple functions of these men will be discussed in connection with different groups as the need arises.

From what has been said, one would assume that a given group would have a single authority. Although this is the most usual case, it is by no means the only possibility. There are villages which are led by two *tonowi* who share their power over common followers. In most cases, their condominium is marked by full co-operation and respect for each other's decisions. Thus, within the Ijaaj-Pigome confederacy, the Dou village of Bunauwobado boasts of two brothers, both *tonowi*, who peacefully manage the political and legal affairs of their community. Dou Akoonewiijaaj of Bunauwobado, the older of the two brothers, seems to have slightly more prestige than his younger sibling, Dou Onetaka. Nevertheless, the latter's decisions are always upheld by Akoonewiijaaj, who respects them as definite. When one of the *tonowi* starts to argue in a dispute, the other keeps out of it and his comments and answers to questions about his own opinion of the case always conveys the notion: "You heard my brother, he spoke well." Thus the jurisdiction is simply determined by the first comment which identifies the authority in a given case. There are other villages in the Southern Kamu Valley, as for example, Egebutu, Degeipige, Bibigi and Pueta, where the cooperation of two authorities is as smooth as that mentioned above. However, not all personalities are compatible and thus not all Kapauku co-leaders tolerate each other or show mutual respect. Rivalry for leadership within the group may split it into two political factions, exhibiting mutual suspicion, intolerance and even hostility, thereby weakening the solidarity and consequently the power of the unit as a whole. This was the case in the Botukebo community, a full analysis of which has to be postponed to the section on the village itself.

The Ijaaj-Pigome confederacy is composed of the Ijaaj Gepouja lineage which occupies five villages, the Pigome Obaaj lineage of the Obajbegaa community, the small Ijaaj lineage of Notiito, and the looser member—the Dou Pugaikoto lineage of Bunauwobado. Each of the four lineages have a single *tonowi*, with the Dou lineage of Bunauwobado proving an exception by having two brothers as its leaders. Since the Notiito Ijaaj, the Obajbegaa Pigome and the Bunauwobado Dou each occupy only one village, their lineage authorities are identical with the village authorities, and there is no differentiation into sublineages in the last three groups. Since they have relatively small populations, it is apparent that the much stronger Ijaaj Gepouja lineage would be most likely to furnish a leader for the confederacy (Fig. 4).

An athletic man of about forty years of age whose name is Ijaaj Ekajewaijokaipouga, and whose large house (an area of sixty square meters) stands in the swamp of Aigii, the most western village of the confederacy, plays the role of headman of the whole political federation as well as that of the Ijaaj Gepouja lineage. In his person he accumulates several political functions and thus his position is a very complex one. He is the leader of the following units: his household, Aigii village, Ijaaj Jamaina sublineage, Ijaaj Gepouja lineage, and Ijaaj-Pigome confederacy. This accumulation is nothing exceptional. Actually it is a rule in this society that a man cannot control a more inclusive grouping unless he leads one of its constituent subgroups. The five different roles which converge in one individual manifest themselves in the decisions of the man which are necessarily of different natures, corresponding to their pertinent levels in the fivefold hierarchy. When deciding a dispute between the members of his household, no other *tonowi* can say anything. On the contrary, in dealing with a case involving members of different lineages, he has to listen to the arguments of the leaders of the other lineages and try to convince them of the correctness of his own decision. The leaders of the other four lineages, Ijaaj Anejaajtawii of Notiito, Pigome Pegabii of Obajbegaa, Dou Akoonewiijaaj, and Dou Onetaka of Bunauwobado, function always as consultants in matters that concern the whole political unit. Ekajewaijokaipouga is the richest man in the South Kamu Valley and one of the greatest *tonowi*. His fortune amounts to five wives, cash amounting to twenty-four hundred Kapauku cowries (representing a buying power of one hundred and twenty medium pigs, each of ninety kilograms weight), thirty-six hundred imported cowries (equivalent to eighteen medium pigs), thirty-three hundred beads (equivalent to five and a half medium pigs), ten *dedege* necklaces and ten *pagadau* necklaces (equivalent to one medium pig), five axes (equivalent to one medium pig).[4] In addition to the currency, he owns forty-two pigs. His credit is about as extensive as his cash. He bought wives for eleven people who have not yet returned the money. These loans total one thousand and forty Kapauku cowries (equivalent to fifty-two medium pigs), three hundred and sixty-five imported cowries (equivalent to two pigs of seventy kilograms of weight each) and four hundred and twenty beads (equivalent to a forty-five kilogram pig). He has a credit with twenty other individuals amounting to twelve hundred Kapauku cowries (equivalent to sixty medium pigs). His generosity is praised by all the people who know him. The large amount of cash mentioned above is not simply hoarded. Six hundred Kapauku cowries and the same number of imported cowries, as well as three thousand beads, were set aside for the sons as their inheritance. Since this headman imposed a taboo upon this money which prevents him from using it otherwise than for the inheritance mentioned, these savings are considered as most generous and give the man additional prestige. The rest of the cash is hidden and other people do not know about its existence.[5]

This headman is also an excellent speaker and one of the most powerful shamans in the region, as well as a brave warrior. He mocks the enemy in songs, never takes

[4] Index of values: one ninety kilogram pig equals twenty Kapauku cowries, equals two hundred introduced cowries, equals six hundred beads, equals twenty *dedege* necklaces, equals twenty *pagadau* necklaces.

[5] The writer, as the best friend of this man, has been told the exact amount of the headman's property.

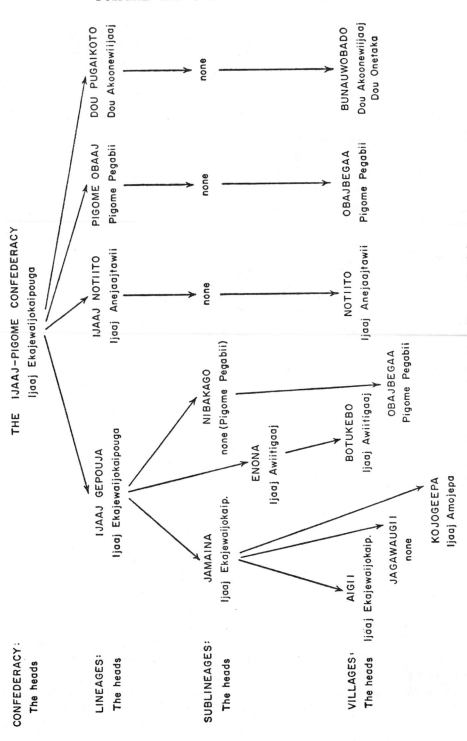

Fig. 4. Political Structure of the Ijaaj-Pigome Confederacy.

cover in the tall grass and dashes as close as thirty meters to the enemy's battle line to attack with no shield on his back. Several deep scars on his chest, back and limbs tell the story of his war exploits. At present (1955), he has five boys as apprentices who live in his house. About fourteen others already have married and left him. Nevertheless, their emotional bond with their master persists.

Ekajewaijokaipouga is a shrewd politician who lends money to important people outside of the confederacy, thus establishing a network of relationships all over the Kamu Valley. Because of this economic influence, his word is important beyond the boundaries of the Ijaaj-Pigome political unit and his wishes and decisions, given support by his various debtors, form the nucleus of a phenomenon which in nature and function recalls our international law. Since he is considered very moral and since his decisions incorporate the ideals of Kapauku culture, these verdicts and opinions are respected even by some traditional enemies of his confederacy. In this way, his judgments, supported by some other *tonowi*, resemble a decision of the international court in The Hague. In this inter-confederational function, Ekajewaijokaipouga utilizes his relations with his best friends as the pillars to hold up his whole network of influence. In order to understand his inter-confederational position and function we first have to learn some details about the "*maagodo noogei*, best friend," relationship.

The Best Friend Relationship

Two people, usually of the same sex, who have developed affection toward each other, may institutionalize their relationship by concluding a special friendship. The elder of the two presents his younger partner with a large gift which in value is relative to the donor's wealth. Thus a *tonowi* gives his younger friend a large pig or sixty to a hundred Kapauku cowries. At the time of the gift's transfer, the donor specifies the reason for the action and starts calling the recipient "my best friend." The beneficiary is neither obligated nor expected to reciprocate with a similar gift immediately. It is up to the recipient to choose the time for proving his affection to his older partner. Thus, a series of reciprocal gifts is initiated which stops only when one of the friends dies. Since in Kapauku culture there is no notion of an outright gift, the heir of a deceased friend claims—in case the balance is in favor of the deceased—a right to the unreciprocated gifts and the surviving friend has the duty of paying. In case the account is in favor of the surviving party, the heir is responsible and he must pay the debt. Since the latter, usually the son of the deceased, is often a young and not too wealthy boy, the best friend, being ethical, waits until the daughter of the deceased gets married. Then he collects the balance from the bride price paid for her. Besides the gifts, the friends have a mutual moral duty to help each other financially, to support each other in legal and political disputes, to arrange for the burial of the partner and to assist one another in warfare, dating and marriage arrangements.

Two women friends exchange a smaller amount of beads and edibles and help each other in cultivation, divorce proceedings and disputes. The writer has also observed the case of such a friendship concluded between a married woman and a married man. Their relation was affectionate but without any emphasis on sex. The couple acted as though they were of the same sex and the woman's husband tolerated their secret discussions, their walking and working together, acts for which, if they took place with another male, the woman would receive a severe beating and the male probably would be killed.

In Papuan culture, "best friends" are individuals who stand closer to each other than brothers. They freely discuss their troubles and problems and reassure or advise each other. They mutually reveal their most important secrets and spend hours in affectionate companionship. A special code of ethics and etiquette governs the affectionate relationship. Although in great need, a "best friend" would never ask his partner directly for help. The partner must know and give it without being told. "*Ani ego wedaba, noogei, kojoka te kateega* (I felt very ashamed, friend, therefore I did not ask you)" was the answer given by Ekajewaijokaipouga when questioned why he did not ask for a magazine which the writer discarded and a small boy took.

Especially during the various crises in one's life, it is the "best friend" who tries to alleviate the grief of the bereaved man. The death of a close relative, the loss of fortune, disease, the loss of a pig and divorce, are occasions for presenting the partner with a large gift in the form of a pig or a large amount of cowries. Once the writer was arguing ardently with some people of the southern clans about a divorce case of one of his "adopted sons." To accent his displeasure over his opponent's cheating of the boy, the writer started the Kapauku mad dance. The writer's best friend, Jokagaibo, who squatted nearby stood up quietly and left. In the evening of the same day, the writer received a small pig from him with the explanation: "I felt sorry for you because you became so emotional." It is a custom to present one's "best friend" with a gift when the latter becomes so emotional as to perform his first mad dance.

Friends visit each other, sit, eat and sleep together, and mutually extend kinship terminology to each other's primary and secondary relatives. The "best friend" does not monopolize his partner for himself. An individual may establish several relationships of this kind simultaneously and thus enjoy as many friends as he likes. A rich man may have five, ten and even more friends to count upon when the need arises. As a clever politician, he selects his friends from among important *tonowi* of other communities, thus acquiring the assurance of support from many individuals who happen to be followers of his "best friends" beyond his own direct political sphere. Ekajewaijokaipouga spread a cleverly designed network of friendship relations over the South Kamu Valley and even beyond this area. This intricate mechanism binds to him even the headman of Mogokotu, the leader of the traditional enemy of his own Ijaaj-Pigome confederacy. As a consequence, interestingly enough, while it is highly rewarding for a member of the Tibaakoto sib of Mogokotu to make vicious propaganda against his enemies, the Ijaaj people, at the same time it is dangerous for him to insult personally his enemy's leader, Ekajewaijokaipouga. The headman of the offender's own village would resent this and most probably punish the man by asking for an immediate payment of a debt or, if there are no financial ties between the offender and his headman, the latter may refuse financial or legal support in the future.

The friendship ties, coupled with extended credit, are a mighty weapon in the hand of the leader of the Ijaaj-Pigome confederacy which he uses not only for furthering his own personal goals but also as a channel for inter-confederational understanding and peace negotiations. In the network mentioned, the leader of the Ijaaj-Pigome confederacy stands as the only unifying link between his friends who need not be, and actually are not, friends among themselves. Thus personal enemies often have to get together to support their "best friend" whom they share in common. One can readily see what an important role this institution plays in counteracting inter-confederational antagonism.

In additional to the above function, the institution of "best friend" also buttresses the political structure of a confederacy. Thus, Ekajewaijokaipouga, by concluding friendship with the *tonowi* Pigome Pegabii of Obajbegaa and Ijaaj Anejaajtawii of Notiito, gained influential supporters in the two leaders of the confederacy's other lineages. Within his own lineage, he chose as best friends Ijaaj Buanainomuuma of Botukebo, an aggressive man of the opposite sublineage, and Ijaaj Amojepa, the leader of the community of Kojogeepa, and thus stabilized his lineage leadership.

We may observe that Kapauku politicians recognize clearly the advantage of befriending a few important men and thus gaining control over their followers, rather than trying to maneuver the multitude directly on the basis of too numerous interpersonal friendship ties.

War

The multiple functions of Ekajewaijokaipouga as leader of the Ijaaj-Pigome confederacy can be classified, according to their effect, in two categories: The first one includes those which foster the internal coherence of the unit, the second incorporates the effects of the leader's actions in his role as representative of the confederacy in the outside world.

Since the content of the first category implies his legal role, we shall postpone this discussion until we come to examine law. At present we shall occupy ourselves with the subject matter of the latter category, especially with its most conspicuous phenomenon, war.

Kapauku inter-confederational law, the mechanism of which relies upon the ties between "best friends" and the extending of credit, does not always succeed in solving problems in a peaceful way and thus forms no guarantee of settlement of disputes involving individuals from different political units. This situation stands in sharp contrast with the intraconfederacy affairs where war is prohibited and killing is conceived as murder. Thus war, the formalized and organized outlet of hostilities, based on the planned killing of as many opponents as possible, is strictly an inter-confederational affair. It is true that inhabitants of different villages of the same political unit may clash in a fight. However, they seldom fight with bows and arrows and the aim of the fight is not annihilation but rather a "settlement" of the affair. This type of fighting can be compared to a valve letting out surplus steam from an overheated boiler. It is an emotional rather than a premeditated outburst of violence which usually results in fighting only with sticks.

"War is bad and nobody likes it. Sweet potatoes disappear, pigs disappear, fields deteriorate and many relatives and friends get killed," explained Ijaaj Jokagaibo of Itoda. "But one cannot help it. A man starts a fight and no matter how much one despises him, one has to go and help because he is one's relative and one feels sorry for him." This talk is reminiscent of German soldiers insisting that they were anti-Nazi but had to fight for their Fatherland.

Divorce initiated by a woman is the most frequent cause of war in the Kamu Valley. Although witchcraft accounts for most of the hostilities in the neighboring Mapia region, it ranks second in the Kamu Valley. Out of eleven recent wars, two of which occurred during the writer's fieldwork, five had as their cause a divorce initiated by a wife or by her brother, two occurred because of killing by sorcery, one because of accidental killing and one started as a children's game of arrow shooting. Stealing and a breach of a monetary obligation accounted for the last two. A war may last only a few days or it may become a prolonged affair which disrupts the normal life of the Papuans for a period of several months. There may be only eighty people engaged in the fighting or over a thousand warriors may participate. The casualties depend primarily upon the duration of the hostilities. In eleven wars, no one died in three, although many people were wounded. In each of three others, the dead numbered less than ten, while in three more than fifty died. The last two surpassed the others in gravity by having at least eighty deaths in each. It was reported that about fifteen years ago there was a war in Egebutu and Degeipige, in the southwestern part of the Kamu Valley. The hostilities lasted over one year and the number of dead reached a total of more than two hundred and fifty, leaving the village of Degeipige practically without adult males.

The Ijaaj-Pigome confederacy is able to mobilize six hundred warriors, men ranging in age from fourteen to about fifty years (including "in-law" relatives, friends, and maternal relatives from villages of other confederacies). It is the *tonowi* who has the most influence in starting a war and he who, in case he considers it unjustified, may either prevent the war or stop it through legal channels. If he is not a brave man and a skilled warrior himself, his role is limited only to inducing his followers to fight or to conclude a peace.

If war begins, it is always because a man has been injured by an individual of another political unit. His wife may have been raped or induced to leave with her new lover. His relative may have died of sorcery. A pig may have been stolen or an economic obligation broken. To secure support from the rest of his community and confederacy, the aggrieved man pleads his case to the *tonowi* and demands action. If his case is "ethical," the authorities support him and call upon their adherents to go to war.

The injured man may disobey the advice of a *tonowi* and start the war on his own, thus forcing his community and even his confederacy into a conflict without an acceptable ethical reason and against the will of the headman, as well as that of the majority of the people. If he does this and is known to be a dishonest man and a confirmed criminal, he may risk capital punishment passed upon him in a secret sentence by the *tonowi*. Usually the culprit's paternal parallel cousins will be the executioners. They will kill him with arrows shot from ambush, not revealing their identity to the public. The authority either pretends that the man was killed by an enemy sniper or he may admit the execution, not disclosing the names of the killers. In either case the war is ended shortly.

An injured man in whose interest a war is fought is called "*jape ipuwe*, owner of the enemy." When his cause is a good one and he is fully supported by the community and confederacy leaders, a plan of attack is made in his house. Early in the morning on the following day the war party tries quietly to approach the enemy's village. Nevertheless, almost always there is someone who discovers the approaching danger and yodels: "*jape meete, jape meete*, the enemy comes, the enemy comes," in order to warn the threatened village. Men rush out from their houses and nearby fields and meet at an open place in the village. The approaching enemy yodels to them the reason for war. If the villagers consider the challengers unjust, which is the usual case, they perform the familiar *waita tai* dance. Then, led by the "*jape uu me*, war leader," they run to meet the enemy and thus to stop him short of the village. The *waita tai* dance, accompanied by singing, as well as the "yodeling telephones" tell other villages of the confederacy about the attack. Soon reinforcements start pouring into the battlefield from all directions. The enemy is usually stopped in an open grass area or in the fields. There, two parallel battle lines form which move back and forth as the fighting progresses (Pl. 6, *top*). The bravest Kapauku are usually also the *tonowi*. They do all the war planning, command other people, determine the strategy and, on the battle line, issue orders.

A Kapauku fights with a simple long bow made from dark hardwood with a rattan string. He uses reed-shaft arrows tipped with barbed or straight hardwood points, or with razor sharp bamboo blades. To protect themselves, the Kapauku carry small shields in their nets, suspended around their necks or from the top of their heads. These shields are actually cut planks which barely protect their trunks. While fighting, the Kapauku duck into the tall grass, ready an arrow and suddenly appear in order to discharge it into the body of the nearest enemy. To avoid the flying arrows, they jump from side to side, thus never providing the enemy with a static target. For the same purpose, a man also may hide in the grass or simply turn his back which is protected by a shield. A brave man has a different code of behavior. He never hides and, since he does not carry a shield, he never turns his back to the enemy. He may approach to within twenty meters and, jumping back and forth, discharge his own arrows. He seldom misses his target. As a sign of his leadership, he sometimes carries a long arrow with a huge, broad bamboo point. A man shot in his thigh with such a vicious projectile will have most of his muscles cut and thus be disabled for a long time.

Although the Kapauku have wood spears, they use them only for decorative purposes and never carry them to the battlefield. Since incessant shooting readily exhausts the supplies of ammunition and since the warriors find no time to collect stray arrows, it is the task of the women to collect the ammunition for their husbands. Thus they save time and make the war more interesting to the men. Their role as collectors is facilitated by a married woman's immunity from being punished, beaten or shot by anyone except her own husband. It is highly immoral for a man to shoot at a female during a battle and even an accidental injury to one may deprive a brave of all the prestige he possessed before. Even his own relatives would reproach such an unfortunate individual and ridicule him with the taunt: "all you can do is shoot a woman." Thus everyone is very careful not to make such a regrettable mistake. The women exploit this situation to the limit. Not only do they collect arrows behind, on and between the battle lines, as quietly as one would pick flowers or harvest cucumbers, but they even have the courage to climb a hill behind the enemy and shout advice concerning his movements. The only thing left for the poor enemy to do is to dispatch a few warriors to chase the women away from the height by beating them with bows or fists and pushing them down the slope. Leaving aside the derogatory and disgusting nature of such an occupation for a warrior, the success of the maneuver is sometimes dubious because of the long sticks wielded by the usually more numerous women. It is the men who sometimes get the pushing and beating. If it were not for the fact that men actually are killed, the scene would have the character of a farce.

From the description of the behavior of war leaders, one might get an impression of a gallantry similar to that of knighthood in Europe during the Middle Ages. Unfortunately, the reader has to be made familiar with other Kapauku customs which make the native war less attractive to the Western observer. Although married women escape any molestation, an unmarried girl is invariably raped if caught by the advancing enemy. Since it is taboo for the enemy to rape girls of the opposite camp, it is the friends and "in-law" relatives of the enemy who violate the girls.

"There is nothing to be sorry for," explained Ijaaj Jokagaibo of Itoda. "These girls like it anyway and some may even get caught willingly. During an attack on Degeipige, I raped a beautiful girl. She screamed and wept all right but this was only a pretence. After the cessation of hostilities she came after me to Aigii and asked me to marry her. She liked me so much." Even if we take the above statement with reservations and view it as extreme, we have to admit that an attitude toward rape is relative to the cultural milieu in which it happens.

A more serious problem is the practice of killing all males from the enemy's camp except a baby boy in the arms of his mother and a very old man. A boy of only two years of age may be killed. The young boy may even be the specific object of a raid by a brave man who penetrates deep into the enemy's territory. He is supported on his expedition by three to ten men. They steal quietly to the enemy's village during the day or night. At a certain distance from the destination, the brave man leaves his escort and proceeds alone. Any male he finds in the village serves as a target. Thus, even a little boy who has barely learned to walk fulfills the requirements of the "coup" and is mercilessly slain from ambush. The successful sniper proudly shouts "*wageega, wageega,* I killed, I killed," and performs an "*ukwaa wakiitai,* killer's dance." He runs in a small circle in counterclockwise fashion, holding his bow at the lower end in his right hand. He twists his hand back and forth at the wrist so that the bow turns around on its axis and he joyfully screams *wuii, wuii.* The dance, besides expressing the triumph of the warrior, functions on the battle line especially to identify the killer who thus earns prestige and a reward for killing an enemy. The reward is paid at the *tapa* ceremony which will be described below. The sniper, being surrounded by enemies, does not lose much time with the dance and disappears as fast as possible in the bush. He runs to the place where his companions await his return. All together they run back to their home territory to enter their village with the victorious yodeling which announces the success of the expedition.

To wait at night at the door of an enemy's house until the man has to leave the shelter to urinate is an enjoyable pastime. There is no better target than an erect, sleepy man standing in the door against the shimmering light of the fire inside the house.

In the evening on the day of the killing, the hero shoots one of his pigs and gives a feast called "*me nai,* to eat a man." Although the name may recall cannibalistic practices which might have been present in the remote past, the writer's data show no such evidence. The pork is cooked in the cooking mound and distributed to relatives and friends of the killer. People eat, gossip and talk about past war experiences and go late to bed. A shaman is called to perform magic with a Ti plant broom in order to protect the successful archer from the possible attack of the dead enemy's "*tene,* departed shadow." After the feast is over, some visitors go home, others stay overnight, sleeping in their friends' houses. One or two women may hide with sticks in the bush to protect their tired men during the night against a possible sniper.

The morning witnesses the people dancing *waita tai* and leaving once again for the battlefield. Women usually accompany the warriors, walking ahead, on the flanks and in the rear, acting as scouts to detect a possible enemy waiting in ambush. The enemy is already on the battlefield, ready to resume the fighting. Women take up their posts, men form the line, and arrows start whizzing again through the air. "In-law" relatives of the warriors may join the battle as active participants or they may only contribute to the military effort by supplying the fighters with fresh ammunition. Older men are left behind in the villages with the children, where they not only guard the latter but also work on new arrows. The responsibility for a steady food supply for the warriors and for arrow collecting rests with the older females and the children who have to harvest the necessary food. There may be a lull of several days during prolonged fighting to allow the males to work on new gardens. There is, of course, no armistice during this period and fighting may start at any time and anywhere. Therefore, every man, while working in his fields, has his bow and arrows ready just in case an enemy should appear. Usually several males work together to lessen the chance of a surprise attack.

It happens, sometimes, that one side starts winning, having succeeded in killing a few enemies and pushing the rest of them toward their village. The war leaders shout in order to stop the retreat. They scold and insult the panicky individuals but in vain. The retreat may be temporarily halted near the houses where barricades are made of short planks driven vertically into the earth. Soon the invading forces penetrate the village, looting and burning the houses, raping the unmarried girls, shooting pigs, cutting down banana trees and fences, and destroying the crop in the fields. After this is accomplished, the victors withdraw with their loot and leave the remnants of the village and crop to the beaten enemy. Land is never taken away from the defeated party.

The setting sun is a sign to stop the fighting. Both rival armies perform a *"waita tai*, a counterclockwise circular dance,"* and leave for their homes in the same fashion as they arrived at the battlefield—women in front, on the flanks and in the rear, and men in the middle. The wounded people are carried back to their villages on the shoulders of their fellow warriors. There, a skilled surgeon extracts the projectiles and makes an incision with a flint flake near the wound in order to let out the blood. This is also the time for the shaman to perform curative magic on wounded men and preventive magic for the healthy people. The dead are tied by their hands and feet to a pole and carried to the village where they are placed on a platform with the arrows left in their bodies. No war prisoners are taken. Instead, all the enemy are killed on the spot.

There are only a few taboos linked with war. Sexual intercourse is prohibited prior to and during the combat. *"Wainai*, the mad dance,"* and ditch digging are tabooed all the time during the hostilities. Since the breaking of these taboos would result in the death of other residents of the violator's village, the culprit is punished by beating and reprimand or sometimes even by death. On the contrary, painting oneself with red ochre or storing pork in one's house, both actions believed to cause the death of the violator alone, are not punished by the society.

Friends, "in-law" relatives and even blood relatives may meet on the battlefield as "enemies." To avoid killing one's own maternal uncle, wife's brother or best friend, one fights on the other end of the battlefield. Because of the institution of helping "in-law" relatives and friends in war, it may even happen that two brothers fight on opposite sides. They will go together to the battlefield and then split up, after making sure about each other's position on the battle line. Thus, a war is never a total one. Actually, it presents to the warrior as a target only those classificatory enemies who are neither tabooed to be killed nor constitute relatives or friends of the archer.

When both sides have an equal number of dead and are weary of the prolonged hostilities and the losses in lives and goods, the headman of one side may discuss the situation with other important men and dispatch a neutral "in-law" relative or friend as a go-between to negotiate peace. The enemy almost always agrees with the proposed peace, unless he has losses in lives in excess of those of the other side. If the dead are not matched in number, it is almost impossible to conclude peace unless one side is completely beaten or, in very rare cases, the other offers blood money to bring about the necessary balance. The official stamp is given to the peace at a pig feast. There, the former enemies dance together *waita tai* and *tuupe* dances and are addressed from the roof of the dance house by their leaders who declare the cessation of hostilities and exhort the people to mutual friendliness (Pl. 6, *bottom*).

Since a balanced number of dead is the basis for peace and because the subsequent death of an individual wounded during the war disrupts the matched numbers of the dead, peace is never regarded as a definite settlement. Its validity depends upon the balance which, if subsequently disturbed, has to be restored lest hostilities start over again. It is the main role of *"me mege,* blood money," to keep rather than create the important *uta-uta* balance.

The man who wounded an enemy in battle is responsible for the enemy's death if it occurs within a few years after the war. In order to keep peace he has to collect about one hundred and eighty Kapauku cowries and one hundred and eighty introduced cowries, as well as two pigs, from among his relatives and transfer this amount within three days after a request to the closest male relative of the deceased. Because of deep grief, the father of the dead person refuses to take any part of the payment. While the brother and son may each take a pig, the rest of the payment is distributed by the recipient among other relatives of the deceased. Relatives who receive larger sums are expected to distribute these, in turn, among their own close relatives. Thus most of the people related in any way to the man who has been killed get pacified by some sort of payment.

Another type of blood money is called *uwata*. It is a payment made by the *jape ipuwe*, the man for whom the hostilities were conducted, to the closest relative of a slain man who fought on the *jape ipuwe* side. The obligation must be fulfilled within three days or otherwise the *jape ipuwe* will risk a severe punishment. For refusal to comply with his duty, he may be bound to a pole by the enraged mourners and carried to the enemy who will inevitably kill him. Sometimes only his pig may be shot. In practice, the man almost always honors his obligation and pays one hundred and twenty Kapauku cowries and two pigs. This sum represents an average *uwata*.

The inhabitants of the Kamu Valley have a laudable institution of *dabe uwo*, a remuneration paid by a relative of a slain man to a warrior who avenges the death by killing an enemy. After the war is over, the successful archer asks a close relative of the man whose death he has avenged for the payment. The date for a *"tapa,* ceremony of the transfer of *dabe uwo,"* is set usually within a period of one hundred and eighty to three hundred and sixty days, counted from the day of the agreement. The relatives of the avenged man become the *"tapa ipuwe, tapa* owner." They announce the date to their relatives-in-law and maternal cross-cousins who are expected to contribute to the payment. The *tapa* ceremony takes place in the village of its "owners" and lasts only one day. However, prior to the ceremony, on any night when the moon is full and people feel like enjoying themselves, a dance takes place in the village. The celebration resembles that of a pig feast with the exception that there is no dance house and *tuupe* and *waita tai* are the only types of dances performed.

The *tapa* ceremony superficially resembles the pig feast. People come from all directions, kill pigs and sell the meat, trade manufactured goods, pay their debts, enjoy talking and cook and eat the meat which has been purchased. Nevertheless, the core of the celebration is different from that of a pig feast. The collection of the remuneration, which is the main reason for the occasion, is the focus of the event. "In-laws" and cross-cousins come from the various villages, those from each village or confederacy arriving in a group. They come running to the clearing in the village and dance *waita tai*. One of the dancers carries an arrow to which are attached strings with cowrie shell money. Later this money is given as payment to the avenger. After the dance, the money is laid on a rain mat.

The man to be remunerated is active, too. He performs *odija ugaa*, a dance consisting of tiny jumps with bent knees and with legs held together, accompanied by a song in which the donors are asked to be generous. The man may be helped by his wife or brother in this money raising effort. On the following day, a procession of people carries the cowrie shell and other contributions to the house of the man to be rewarded. The wealth collected may be considerable. Thus Jokagaibo of Itoda received for killing Jobee Ibo of Bauwo sixty axes and machetes (equal to nine medium pigs), sixty long strings of beads (equal to three medium pigs), three *dedege* necklaces, twenty-four hundred large trade beads (equal to four medium pigs), two hundred and forty Kapauku cowries (equal to twelve medium pigs) and six hundred introduced cowries (equal to three medium pigs). Unfortunately, the wealth cannot be used by the recipient, who must either lend it and collect the debts in the distant future or, if he wants to acquire great prestige, he may let the crowd take the whole amount. When the people hear the money is theirs, they throw themselves on the piled up fortune and grab what they can. Since, in this case, one cannot possibly identify the recipients of the money, there is no obligation to repay the acquired amounts. This kind of disposal of *dabe uwo*, being regarded in the Kapauku society as the greatest generosity, gives to the ambitious politician the highest prestige. Even many years afterwards people will remember the distribution and be willing, out of gratitude and affection, to help the generous man in his economic, political and legal affairs. However, not all people care for this kind of passing glory and non-material prestige. "They can have their praise and respect, I do not care for them," stated Ijaaj Awiitigaaj of Botukebo. "I prefer to collect and lend the money. This way one is rich and the debtors are dependent anyway. I am a headman, not because the people like me but because they owe me money and are afraid."

THE SUBLINEAGE

The progeny of Ijaaj Gepouja, who form the largest of the four lineages of the Ijaaj-Pigome confederacy, classify themselves into three sublineages, the members of which trace their descent from one of the three sons of Ijaaj Gepouja: Ijaaj Enona, Ijaaj Jamaina or Ijaaj Nibakago. Each sublineage is characterized by a very strong feeling of belongingness and a unity which surpasses in intensity that of the lineage. War is replaced by stick fighting within the lineage, but an organized

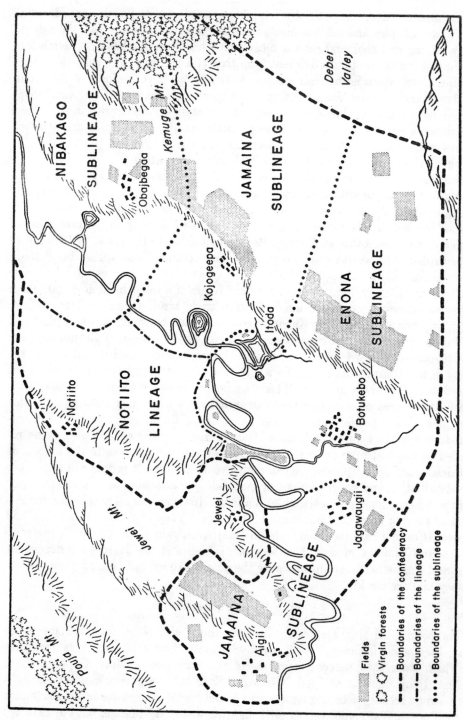

FIG. 5. Sublineages in the Southeastern Kamu Valley.

stick fight lasting more than one day is regarded as deplorable if it occurs between members of the same sublineage. It is the responsibility of the sublineage authority to settle disputes so that they will not disrupt unity and weaken the power of the group against outsiders. The extensive common responsibility for the delicts of all the relatives of the sublineage is reflected in disputes as well as in war. Thus, it is almost always a relative in the same sublineage for whose crimes one has to pay or suffer a forceful seizure of one's own property, such as confiscation of pigs, loans or cash. Moreover, in case of war, the enemy attacks any village of the sublineage, no matter in which one the man causing the war is residing.

The pattern of residence and land ownership illuminates an understanding of the sublineage. The lineage's territory is divided into sections belonging to the sublineages. In these sections, the sublineages' members have their fields and residences any place, irrespective of the existence of several villages in the same area. While the territory of one sublineage is separated from another by clear-cut boundaries, such as brooks, lakes, rivers and mountain ridges, there are no such demarcations within the sublineage irrespective of the number of villages involved.

While the Enona and Nibakago lineage members live in the communities of Botukebo and Obajbegaa respectively, the more numerous Jamaina offspring occupy the remaining three villages. The contiguous territory of the Gepouja lineage is divided into four sections, separated from each other by boundaries of brooks, rivers and ridges. Because the Enona sublineage of Botukebo occupies the central part of the lineage's territory, thus separating the Jamaina sublineage grounds into two blocks, one finds the area divided into four sections instead of three as would be expected (Fig. 5).

The resulting division of the land of the Jamaina sublineage has in no way reflected upon the social and legal organization of that group. People from Aigii and Jaga-waugii, villages of the western half of the sublineage territory, own gardens in the eastern half where Kojogeepa village is located. This village is separated from the western half by the enclave of Botukebo. A man from Aigii, who wishes to build a house on his land in any of the three villages may do so without anyone's permission. Thus, although geographically separated, the Jamaina territory and people form a socially indivisible unit. On the contrary, a man from Botukebo, since his sublineage occupies one village only, cannot freely move to any other place. He has to ask permission from the Jamaina people to be able to settle in one of their villages and must buy or rent some individual's lot for his new home.

Since in the next section we are going to investigate the Botukebo community, here our primary interest will focus on the Jamaina sublineage, the constituents of which live in the three villages: Aigii and Jagawaugii in the western half of the territory and Kojogeepa in the east. At the close of this section we shall discuss the Ijaaj Nibakago sublineage.

LAND OWNERSHIP

In order to clarify the various aspects of organization of the sublineage we must digress for a moment and describe Kapauku land ownership in general. At the outset, we should recall the Kapauku individualism and the fact that all productive land is individually owned. Also, the land is classified into several categories according to its use and quality.

1. *Mude* is a type of land which is under cultivation or once has been cultivated. Thus, the concept includes gardens, which are called *bugi* and fallow land, either overgrown with secondary forest and brush, called *gapuuga*, or areas which have reverted to grass and reed land, called *geiga*.

The concept of *bugi* has to be clarified further. Contrary to the finding of de Bruijn (1953) in the Paniai area, the Kamu Valley people do not conceive of *mude* and *bugi* as different land categories on the same level of classification. *Bugi* does not refer to the subsoil at all, but only to the result of work a man has spent on the surface of the land. *Mude* is not limited to the fallow land, but it includes *bugi* as well. This is apparent from the following: since a garden may be made on leased land, the "owners" of the "*bugi*, planted top soil," and of the "*mude*, subsoil," are in this case two different individuals. Thus, when asking who is owner of the *bugi*, one obtains the name of the lessee (the man with the present right of cultivation). On inquiring who is owner of the *mude* of the same lot, one receives the name of the landlord.

Individual lots of *mude* land are owned by persons who may sell, lease, or work them as a garden. The owners are not limited in their ownership except in the case of an old man with adult sons who has to ask his sons' permission to sell the land. Violation of this requirement makes the deal invalid after the old man's death. The landlord is also restricted in the transference of his land to a member of a hostile confederacy. In such a case, the authority may invalidate the agreement and prevent the new owner from taking possession of the fields.

There are no prohibitions against trespassing on fallow land. To walk in a garden of a man from another sublineage, however constitutes a breach of law punishable by reprimand or beating. The shooting of game on anyone's *mude* land is permissible except for rats, for which permission from the owner has to be sought. Trapping and the felling of trees of a secondary forest on *mude* land is the exclusive right of the owner and a violation of this right may be punished even by shooting. Old trees can be felled by anyone from the same sublineage, a regulation reflecting the fact that in the past, or prior to the appearance of the iron ax, it was quite different and difficult to cut an old tree with a stone ax or to fell it by burning. This seems to indicate a "legal lag" in which the law has not yet been adjusted to. the recent introduction of the iron ax.

The acquisition of *mude* land is realized mostly through inheritance and, less frequently, through testament, sale or gift. For details on these methods, the reader is referred to the appropriate sections in the third part of this work. Boundaries between individual plots of land are marked by *ude*, Ti plants, all of which are carefully removed from the inside of the area in order to prevent confusion.

2. *Gamouda*[6] is a type of land covered by forest in which most of the valuable

---

[6] The word is a compound of "*gaamai*, to split planks," and the suffix "*ida*, location." The word reflects the fact that the area was already exploited by cutting trees for making planks.

trees, the wood of which is used for canoe and plank making, have already been cut and the rattan vines harvested. There are no laws against trespassing and cutting the old, economically unimportant types of trees. However, the individual owner retains the exclusive right to the few remaining "plank and canoe trees" and to all second growth which he cuts for fence construction or firewood. The game regulations are the same as for the *mude* land with one exception: rats can be shot by any member of the landowner's sublineage.

3. *Buguwa* refers to a type of land covered with virgin forest which is still full of rattan and wood usable for making planks and canoes. Even this territory is not commonly owned by a group but consists, legally speaking, of individually owned segments, whose boundaries are marked by cliffs, depressions, streams, large trees and crevasses. The owner has an exclusive right to trap game in his section and to cut the precious *moane* tree for making canoes. Plank trees and the more inferior canoe wood and rattan are accessible to all members of the sublineage. The cutting of firewood, hunting and collecting are theoretically free to all. In practice, however, a traditional enemy would not dare to use this right for fear of being accused of trapping or of stealing from the traps.

4. *Bega dimi*, the unproductive wastelands on top of the rocky mountains—which are covered with short grass, stones and a few bushes—are considered property of the sublineage as a whole. Here the right to trap belongs to the sublineage, the members of other groups being excluded. Any other use of the land, such as for hunting, is free to all.

5. Waterways. Navigable rivers are international and are free for anyone to fish or navigate. Streams which are too small for canoes are the property of the sublineage if they cut their beds through its territory. In such a case, the sublineage has the exclusive right to fish. If the stream marks the boundary between any two units, it is considered their property in common. The drinking of water is permitted to all. Lakes in the Kamu Valley, on the contrary, no matter where they are located, are always the property of some lineage but accessible for fishing to all members of the whole confederacy.

A member of a sublineage enjoys many privileges in his group's territory which are denied to outsiders. His rights to the area, as a whole, are in conformance to and limited by the rights of owners of particular plots. Except for the hunting of animals other than rats, for collecting and for trespassing on uncultivated land, an outsider has no rights in the sublineage territory whatsoever. In contrast, all sublineage members may trespass any place, cut old trees on the *mude* land, trap on the mountain top wastelands, shoot rats, make planks and use inferior canoe wood in other men's *gamouda*, as well as collect rattan in the *buguwa* sections owned by other individuals of the same sublineage. While lakes belong to the lineage, all unnavigable streams are accessible as fishing grounds only to the members of the sublineage. Whereas an outsider is limited in using the land by the rights of individual owners and by the rights of the sublineage as a whole, a sublineage member, respecting only individual ownership rights, considers the whole territory as his home.

In the above sense, the Jamaina territory, although geographically divided represents a legal unity. Residents of Aigii and Jagawaugii have some of their fields in the Kojogeepa section and vice versa. Because there is no forest in the section of the first two villages, all the forest property of their inhabitants is found on Kemuge Mountain above the village of Kojogeepa. Brothers build their houses in different villages and in different sectors of the same sublineage territory. Consequently, they may reside even one hour's walk apart.

SOCIAL STRUCTURE

In the number of its members, the Jamaina sublineage is the largest of the three sublineages whose founders were sons of Ijaaj Gepouja. This fact assisted Ekajewaijokaipouga in achieving the position of lineage authority. Moreover, if we inspect the relative strength of the villages within the Jamaina sublineage, we find that Aigii, its largest settlement, is his residence. This situation suggests the hypothesis that in the Kapauku society, the most populous of the subgroups which compose a group of a higher level of inclusiveness tends to furnish the authority of the latter. This principle works in the Ijaaj-Pigome confederacy and the writer discovered its presence in a few additional confederacies.

Jamaina people consider themselves close relatives and try very hard to eliminate any controversies within the group. There are three important politicians in this unit: Ijaaj Ekajewaijokaipouga of Aigii, Ijaaj Jokagaibo of Itoda (the former's father's brother's son's son) and Ijaaj Amojepa of Kojogeepa (father's father's brother's son's son of Ekajewaijokaipouga). Jokagaibo is an ambitious young man who is already *tonowi* but who cannot assume leadership in any village because in his own village of Aigii Ekajewaijokaipouga already holds the position. The writer's arrival in the region unintentionally solved his problem. The writer built his house on the deserted site of an old village, called Itoda. This village was occupied for many years by an enclave of Moni Papuans. A long time ago these people were invited by the Ijaab sib to settle down on the land of the Ijaaj. They left Itoda for good during the Second World War. Since the writer built his house on the deserted place and thus created a new settlement on the old Itoda site, an opportunity was given to Jokagaibo to become a leader in his "own" community. He built his house next to the writer's and became *tonowi* of Itoda, finding followers in boys who came there to stay. The third man, Amojepa, an emotional speaker and an individual with a bad temper, is the headman of Kojogeepa community. Jokagaibo, being young, good natured and a close relative, is not considered a rival by Ekajewaijokaipouga. He follows the latter's suggestions without causing too many difficulties. With Amojepa, it is different. He is not of a younger generation and is a more distant relative from another village. Furthermore, he has his own constituency and followers. To eliminate a possible contest for power and thus prevent strife within the Jamaina sublineage, Ekajewaijokaipouga concluded a "best friend" relationship with the man, thus changing a possible rival into one of his stoutest supporters. Playing politics is not the monopoly of civilizations alone.

The people of the Jamaina sublineage, being consolidated into a strong unit by their skillful leader, have not experienced internal strife or division into political factions. A stick fight may last until Ekajewaijokaipouga appears. Then it stops and ways for peaceful settlement are always found.

The Nibakago sublineage of the village of Obajbegaa presents a special problem because the members have accepted people from another sib in the village. In the sublineage territory are living forty-five members of a single lineage of the Pigome sib who married into the group. The members of the new sib were given or bought their fields from the Ijaaj Nibakago people and became full owners of the land. As time went on their number increased and today they are more numerous than their Ijaaj hosts of the Obajbegaa village. Their legal position is a peculiar one. Although living in the Nibakago sublineage area they do not share the rights to the whole sublineage territory. Their own fields and woods form some sort of a legal enclave which they regard as their home. The territory in Obajbegaa which belongs to the Ijaaj sib members is not regarded by the Pigome men as their home and they behave in it as strangers. Correspondingly, the attitude of the Ijaaj Nibakago descendants toward the Pigome land in their own territory is changing from regarding it as their own home to respecting it as the territory of another sublineage. This change in the attitude of the Ijaaj hosts is still incipient. They still tend to regard the Pigome enclave as their home, thus making the legal position of the newcomers somewhat inferior. Nevertheless, people are fully aware of the historic reasons for this situation as well as for its changing character, so there is neither friction nor hard feelings about the "legal discrimination." It may be that a later generation of Ijaaj Gepouja people will see their lineage deprived of this village in the northeastern tip of their territory and the Nibakago descendents either resettled in other Ijaaj villages or absorbed by the more prolific Pigome.

THE VILLAGE OF BOTUKEBO

POPULATION

On the east bank (*kebo*) of the muddy Botu rivulet, which winds its way through the swampy bottomland of the southeastern Kamu Valley, lies the largest village of the confederacy, Botukebo (Fig. 6, Pl. 3, *top*). Its 181 inhabitants live in sixteen households which range in membership from five individuals, living in a smaller house, to eighteen people. The members of the large households are compressed into one main house of twenty-four square meters of floor space and two "*tone*, small houses for women," which occupy an additional area of eleven square meters. The population figure of the community, although equally divided between the sexes, favors adult women over adult men in a twenty-four to nineteen ratio and old females over old males in the rate of three to two. As can be seen from the Botukebo population chart (Table 2), the males in the lower age categories outnumber the opposite sex forty-seven to thirty-three, thus bringing the number of the sexes of the whole population into exact balance. This surplus of boys suggests either that

TABLE 2. DEMOGRAPHY OF THE VILLAGE OF BOTUKEBO

Household	Total		Children		Adolescents		Adults		Old People	
	M	F	M	F	M	F	M	F	M	F
1.	8	9	2	2	1	2	4	4	1	1
2.	7	11	2	2	1	3	3	4	1	2
3.	2	5	0	2	0	1	1	2	1	0
4.	6	7	3	2	0	0	3	5	0	0
5.	4	5	1	1	1	1	2	2	0	1
6.	8	8	5	2	0	0	3	6	0	0
7.	5	11	2	4	1	0	2	7	0	0
8.	4	2	0	1	0	0	3	0	1	1
9.	7	5	2	1	2	0	2	2	1	2
10.	4	1	2	0	1	0	1	1	0	0
11.	9	5	6	3	1	0	2	2	0	0
12.	8	7	5	2	0	1	3	4	0	0
13.	7	5	2	1	1	0	3	3	1	1
14.	6	3	1	0	2	0	3	2	0	1
15.	4	3	2	0	0	1	2	2	0	0
16.	2	3	1	1	0	0	1	2	0	0
Total	91	90	36	24	11	9	38	48	6	9

Total Population: 181 Individuals.   M = Males F = Females.

Botukebo had an increase of male births in the past fourteen years or that more female children died during that period. During the twelve months of fieldwork, the data on births and deaths show a reverse tendency. While there was not a single instance of the birth of a male, three female children were born; and whereas five boys died, only two deaths occurred among the girls. Since the time span of fourteen years is short, the excess of boys over girls may be regarded as a temporary phenomenon. The reversed sex ratio in the higher age categories can be explained by cultural and psychological factors. A Kapauku male is much more active than a female. His work period is shorter, but it exposes the body to greater strains. Hunting, fighting, running, felling trees, digging ditches, making planks, and hollowing out canoes are activities which, although not as time consuming as the women's planting, fishing, collecting and weeding, are more exhausting and consume great amounts of energy in a short span of time. Such male activities not only wear down the body, but they also expose an individual to risk of injury or even death in such enterprises as warfare, felling of trees, and hunting of wild boars. Moreover, a man is tense, aggressive, and most of the time in an emotional state, while the woman is relaxed, quieter, and always ready for fun.

SOCIAL STRUCTURE

The patrilineal Kapauku are, as a rule, patrilocal. However, a few individuals go *wakauwo* (spouse ridgepole)—to live with the wife's parents—if the latter have

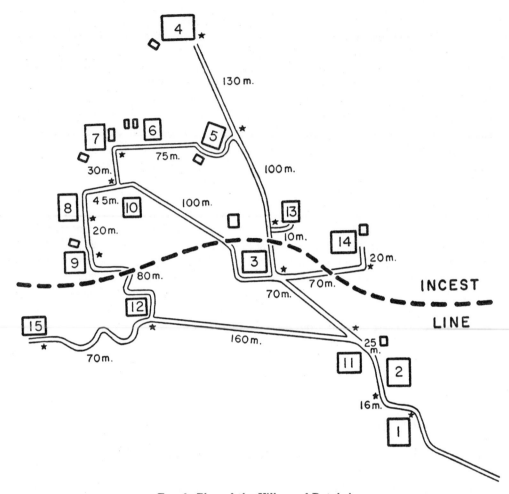

FIG. 6. Plan of the Village of Botukebo.

no male offspring, or they may stay with their maternal uncles, thus living in *ukwauwo* (mother ridgepole). Indeed, five such outsiders live in Botukebo. Three came to share the households of their fathers-in-law, while one preferred to live with a maternal uncle, and one was born in Botukebo where his father had come to live with his maternal uncle. The five men are of the following sibs: Dou, Pigome, Jobee, Adii. All the five men were given land by their in-law or maternal relatives. They share the village life, participate in dances, feasts, and wars as does any other villager. They are considered outsiders in several respects, however. They do not enjoy any of the rights which belong to the members of the sublineage. They have to ask permission for felling old trees, for shooting rats, and for felling plank and canoe trees in the forests. They do not share the ownership rights to the barren mountain land and waters with their Ijaaj co-villagers. Although they participate in wars of the community, they have the privilege of refraining from fighting when their own clan's members are the enemy.

Except for these five men, the inhabitants of Botukebo are all descendants of Ijaaj Enona, the eldest son of the founder of the sublineage. The women who marry into the village, although retaining their maiden sib names, are regarded as integral parts of the community and are referred to as "Botukebo *bagee*, the people of Botukebo." They participate in feasts and dances as do the other villagers and are considered legally equal to the unmarried Ijaaj girls. Consequently, they have the same rights with respect to fishing and gathering. The whole community acts as a unit in inter-village disputes and wars. The feeling of unity is so strong that an offence by an outsider against a member of a community is considered an insult by all of the population and compels all community members to act on behalf of the victim. Thus the writer feels justified in calling the population of Botukebo a village clan. However, it would be dangerous to generalize on the basis of this one instance about Kapauku society as a whole. In the discussion of the sublineage, we have indicated that several villages may form a unit analogous to the single village arrangement of the Botukebo people. Thus a Kapauku patri-clan can be defined as a compromise kin group of patrilocal and patrilineal blood relatives and their wives, the men tracing their descent from a common ancestor. They occupy a contiguous territory and reside in one or several villages. A whole lineage may constitute a single clan if its members are not too numerous and live in one village. The Pugaikoto Dou lineage of the Bunauwobado village is an example.

Economy

The Botukebo Ijaaj clan owns about two and a half square kilometers of the total property of the Ijaaj Gepouja lineage. On the west, its boundary is formed by a large drainage ditch, the Edege River, and a ridge on the Jewei Mountain, which separates Botukebo property from the fields of the Jamaina sublineage. On the south, the village territory borders on the land of the enemy, the Waine-Tibaakoto confederacy. The frontier runs from west to east, crosses the bottom of the flat valley, climbs the slope toward the entrance to the Debei Valley, and then continues eastward (see Fig. 5). After one-fourth of a kilometer the boundary turns in a right angle to the north, cutting across the Debei Valley along the property of the Debei Waine and Debei Pigome sibs, climbs Kemuge Mountain for a short distance only to be forced by the landholdings of the Ijaaj Jamaina sublineage to turn westward. The northern boundary descends the steep Kemuge Mountain slope into the Kamu Valley, continues along a creek and the northern bank of Kumugo Lake to close the area at Jewei Mountain, after having crossed the bottom of the Kamu Valley for the second time. Thus, the Botukebo lands are confined within an area shaped like a truncated triangle which points toward the east into the Debei Valley.

In April, 1955, there were about seventeen hectares (172,482 square meters) of

Botukebo land converted into gardens. There were two major types of cultivation: gardens with sweet potatoes and gardens with another type of crop. All the gardens on the mountain slopes of Kemuge Mountain (89,932 square meters) and Jewei Mountain (11,925 square meters) as well as all the gardens in the mountainous Debei Valley (38,313 square meters), totaling approximately fourteen hectares (140,170 square meters), were planted with the sweet potato as the main crop. As explained in the section on the food quest, agriculture on the mountainous slopes is of an extensive type with no drainage ditches and no fertilization practices involved. The productivity of these fields is only about half that of those in the lowlands. There the planting is not limited by the seasonal change of rainfall and does not involve nearly as much work as in the lowlands. As a secondary crop people may plant among the sweet potato shoots, the seedlings of the "*idaja*, spinach-like green," which ripens before the vines of the sweet potatoes claim the whole surface. In occasional depressions where rain water accumulates, a few taro plants, and in the Debei area, some bananas and sugar cane may be planted.

There is an additional one and a quarter hectares (12,800 square meters) of the valley floor used for the intensive cultivation of sweet potatoes. Large drainage ditches form the border of a field, the surface of which is divided by shallow ditches into small beds fertilized in the manner called *bedamai*, previously described.

The second type of gardening, which is applied to two hectares of the land (19,512 square meters), is limited to the floor of the valley. There, only a few sweet potatoes are grown or none at all. Their place is taken by taro, sugar cane, various kinds of greens, the *pego*, edible variety of reed, and a few banana trees. Gardens with this multi-variety of crops especially dominate the area of Botukebo village where not a single sweet potato field is located. This zoning of crops results not only because of the soil conditions but especially because of the relative value and possibility of preservation of the various crops. While sweet potatoes are still edible four days after their harvest, sugar cane and bananas must be consumed by the third day, and greens have to be eaten fresh. Moreover, a thief can easily pluck the leaf, stem, or fruit crops, and can even pull out a few taro plants, but it is more time consuming for him to dig sweet potatoes. The value of the potatoes is relatively lower than that of the former plants, however. Valuable crops such as gourds, squash, and tobacco are planted only in the garden near the owner's house.

In 1955, ten hectares (102,764 square meters) of the garden area of the Botukebo people were cultivated by the owners of the land. Gardens on an area of six hectares (57,918 square meters) were made by individuals who obtained the right to use the land free of charge from the landlords. Most of these permissions to plant were granted to people who were either close relatives or "best friends" of the land owners, or those who offered to the owners other land for cultivation in another place. The remaining one hectare of land (11,800 square meters) was leased for monetary remuneration to individuals who needed it.

Botukebo is almost exclusively an agricultural and pig breeding community. Gathering and fishing only supplement the garden produce. In 1955, an adult man of Botukebo had on the average of 2,704 square meters of gardens to supply him, his family, and his pigs with necessary food.

The residents of Botukebo raised thirty-one pigs in 1955. On the average, there was less than one pig per adult male (a total of thirty-eight adult males). Actually, the thirty-one animals were owned by only nineteen individuals. Thus, exactly fifty per cent of the men of Botukebo had no pigs and had to compensate for this lack by cultivating more fields.

Hunting and trapping are of negligible importance as a source of food and are practiced more as a sport. Fishing and gathering, on the contrary, supply the daily diet of the villagers with most of their proteins. Fishing for dragonfly larvae, tadpoles, and a variety of water bugs is an activity performed daily by about ten women who drag the bottom of the small Kugumo Lake with their nets. Edege River offers a moderate supply of crayfish. The gathering of bugs, bird eggs, caterpillars, beetles, grasshoppers, and grubs is practiced daily to a small extent. Frogs are gathered systematically at night with the use of torches. A flood, which sometimes forces the people to leave Botukebo and to make temporary shelters on the mountain slopes, presents an opportunity for the extensive gathering of insects. The village has no industry which might bring additional income from the outside.

A record of the volume of trade of the Botukebo people, kept for eight consecutive months during 1955, provides additional information on their economic activities. The residents of Botukebo bought during this period twenty-four pigs and paid 1,127 Kapauku cowries, 120 introduced cowries, 2,430 beads, two *pagadau* and six *dedege* necklaces. The total value is equivalent to approximately 4,912 pounds of pork. Among these animals there were fourteen sows bought for breeding purposes. During the same period, the people sold five pigs for a total of 133 Kapauku cowries, thirty introduced cowries, and 420 beads, which is equivalent to 600 pounds of pork. In this sale there were included two sows for breeding purposes. Thus in the eight months, the people of Botukebo imported nineteen pigs more than they exported and there was a deficit in the pig trade balance equal to 4,312 pounds of pork.

The balance of trade in pork was more even than that in pigs. One hundred and sixty-four pounds of pork were purchased for a total of twenty-nine Kapauku cowries, ten introduced cowries, 305 beads and, one *pagadau* necklace, the total being equivalent exactly to the customary price for 164 pounds of pork. Two pounds of pork were sold for two Kapauku cowries and thirty beads (an exorbitant price which usually buys five pounds of pork).

The only favorable balance came through trade in garden crops. During the period of eight months, nine sweet potato, two sugar cane, and one *idaja* garden were bought for ten Kapauku cowries, two *pagadau* necklaces, one *dedege* necklace, and thirty beads (altogether equivalent to fifty-six pounds of pork). During the same time, nineteen sweet potato gardens, three sugar cane gardens, one "*jatu*, edible grass" garden and one *idaja* garden were sold for a total of nineteen Kapauku cowries, one *pagadau* necklace, one *dedege* necklace, and thirty-five beads, altogether equivalent to eighty-eight pounds of pork. Thus, the Botukebo people made a profit worth thirty-two pounds of pork on deals with garden produce.

TABLE 3. FINANCIAL STATUS OF THE RESIDENTS OF BOTUKEBO

	Credit	Cash	Debt	Balance	Pork Equivalent
Kapauku cowries	4,129	688	2,250	2,547	10,188.0 pounds
Introduced cowries	1,499	1,044	1,466	1,077	430.8 pounds
Beads	4,400	1,947	2,920	3,427	456.9 pounds
Pagadau	63	313	3	373	1,492.0 pounds
Dedege	29	137	28	138	552.0 pounds
Pigs	18	31	7	42	3,400.0 pounds
Total					16,519.7 pounds

Since the items listed above constitute the major articles of production and sale, we may conclude that Botukebo had an unfavorable balance of trade for the eight month period in 1955. The total deficit amounted to 1,110 Kapauku cowries worth 4,439 pounds of pork. However, to make any long-term conclusions on the basis of these numbers would be quite erroneous. Since the Botukebo people planned a pig feast for 1957, they bought many pigs for breeding and feeding purposes during 1955. Moreover, there was a large pig feast in Botukebo in 1953 which left the livestock depleted, but filled the purses of the Botukebo people with money or increased credits. To secure a conclusive, long-term picture of the native economy, one would have to study the trade transactions for a period of four years at least.

The data in Table 3 show the total financial status (wealth) of the Botukebo residents.

The total favorable balance shows that the adult male population of Botukebo owns money and pigs worth a sum equivalent to 16,519.7 pounds of pork. Among the fifty-one males of Botukebo who handle their own finances (children are excluded), there were thirty-four whose money in cash and credits surpassed their debts. There were, however, seventeen individuals, the majority of whom were adolescents and young men, whose debts were larger than the sum totals of their cash and credits.

The Botukebo community impressed the writer by its size and political influence. Its economy, however, seemed to be mediocre. The writer made a similar analysis of the finances of the inhabitants of the village of Aigii. Since Aigii is known to be more prosperous, it did not surprise the writer that the assets of its residents surpassed by nine times those of the more numerous people of Botukebo. It is the impression of the writer, substantiated by the statements of several intelligent informants, that the Botukebo community is economically representative of an average village in the Kamu Valley.

POLITICAL STRUCTURE

Politically, the village is represented by the sublineage leader Ijaaj Awiitigaaj of Botukebo, a wealthy *tonowi* who married ten wives and in 1955 contemplated adding one more to his collection of feminine beauties.[7] Unusual bravery documented by fourteen deep scars scattered on his body, wealth, eloquence, and knowledge of the traditions make him a *tonowi*. His fortune consists of ten wives, two houses, four pigs, cash of sixty Kapauku cowries, 120 introduced cowries, 300 beads, and credits of 1,500 Kapauku cowries, 420 beads, twenty machetes, and twenty large bead necklaces. Nevertheless, people complained that he was not generous and easily gave way to his temper, a weakness which several times brought the village into an unnecessary war. However, his powers were not contested by anyone and most of the people followed his advice. The only person who opposed him was Ijaaj Bunaibomuuma, a notorious criminal. He had already been reprimanded several times. His last defiance nearly resulted in his execution. As a village and sublineage leader, Awiitigaaj functioned as a legal and political authority, a war leader who enjoyed a rather free hand in the fighting and whose advice was most influential on Ekajewaijokaipouga, the confederacy headman. When the people of the Enona sublineage of Botukebo became involved in an argument with the members of the Jamaina sublineage or with Dou or Pigome people of the same confederacy, Awiitigaaj became their supreme commander. Several times he was the master-mind behind stick fights which seldom settled a problem but always cooled off hot heads and thus facilitated negotiations by the confederacy headman. Since it is considered a crime to kill people from the same confederacy, there are some rules which must be observed in a stick fight. No arrows, axes, or machetes are used. The only weapon is a stick about two or three meters long. This is used as a device for beating rather than for stabbing. The objective of the fight is the adjustment of the state of affairs existing in a political unit, rather than vengeance or killing. A man who asks for mercy or promises to stop fighting is not molested further and is permitted to withdraw from the engagement. The writer has not heard of an individual being killed in these fights although a fractured forearm and bleeding wounds on the head and upper part of the body are considered normal casualties.

Awiitigaaj, unlike Ekajewaijokaipouga, is a rather selfish individual. He was charged by his followers with having failed to buy wives for his boys and with spending most of his money to satisfy his own sexual desires by purchasing many wives for himself. Bribery is another vice to which the man was susceptible. We may illustrate this weakness of Awiitigaaj by describing his behavior in the legal case of Ijaaj Dimiidakebo of Botukebo. Dimiidakebo owed a man from the Paniai region the large sum of 240 Kapauku cowries and three pigs, equivalent altogether to 1,200 pounds of pork. The creditor appeared once in Botukebo and asked for the payment of the loan. The debtor immediately called on Awiitigaaj and in a secret deal offered him thirty Kapauku cowries and a male pig of about fifty kilograms of

---

[7] Because all members of the Ijaaj Enona sublineage settled in Botukebo, the status of the headman of this group approximates that of a village headman. In a sublineage whose members live in several villages, however, all the sublineage headmen have jurisdiction over all the villages of that group. It is only because most of the disputes in a village are settled by the sublineage authority who resides locally that we may call him a village headman.

weight for help against the creditor. The headman readily accepted the offer. When the matter came up for public discussion, Awiitigaaj argued in favor of the debtor and exhorted the creditor to accept only sixty Kapauku cowries, sixty imported cowries of poor quality, and 320 beads. He threatened the poor Paniai man with violence should he insist on repayment of the full price. Being in a foreign territory, the creditor could not put up strong resistance. He had to accept the offered sum, thereby losing currency worth 640 pounds of pork. This was a loss of over fifty per cent of the original loan. Awiitigaaj obtained his bribe, but as nothing can be kept secret among the Kapauku, the people soon found out about the dishonest arrangement.

Awiitigaaj's lust for women drove him to break an incest taboo and to marry not only women from the same sib, but also two of his second paternal parallel cousins from his own village. His breaking of the incest taboos was accepted by his co-villagers and they followed his example. Although people in other villages and confederacies condemned this village endogamy, Awiitigaaj's personal power and headmanship proved strong enough to withstand the external pressure. To make his innovation more appealing, he drew a new incest line within the village, thus actually dividing it into two incipient moieties. Once the new practice had been started, other people followed the pattern and today there are ten incestuous marriages in the village and an additional one in the Jamaina sublineage. (We shall return to this case of change of incest taboos in the section on legal dynamics, where it will be analyzed more fully.)

Although today Botukebo presents the picture of a solid political unit under the uncontested leadership of Awiitigaaj, its affairs were different only two years ago when two people competed for primacy in the village. The internal strife was manifested by two political factions whose leaders were the present headman and Ijaaj Dimiidakebo of Botukebo. The latter was an eloquent and brave man. He was also very rich and had five wives. Rich and brave as he was, he could not match Awiitigaaj in eloquence and number of wives. Although he tried very hard to become a headman and was ready at any time to contest the right in a stick fight, he never succeeded in "unseating" his opponent. This was mainly because Dimiidakebo failed to comply with the basic moral requirement for the *maagodo tonowi's* position. He was not only more selfish than the present headman, but he delighted in embezzling money, in borrowing under false pretenses, and he very seldom returned in full what he had borrowed. Consequently, only twelve people offered him support in his disputes, while Awiitigaaj succeeded in rallying behind himself exactly twice the number of his opponent's helpers. Only close relatives helped Dimiidakebo, and even they did so only because of the kinship ties. All of them admitted that their late leader was a dishonest man and a troublemaker. "We had to help him in a stick fight. We knew he was wrong, but we felt sorry for the poor fellow who was left alone."

In the event of a stick fight, an impartial household sent half of its males to one side and half to the other. Consequently, Timaajokaimopaj and Timaajokaipouga, although identical twins, found themselves on opposite sides. "We never fought each other, of course. We just picked personal enemies who happened to be fighting for the other side and gave them a thorough thrashing." Thus, most of the fighting force had "combat motives" completely unrelated to the official cause of trouble. We may call this splitting up of households, which gives a fair chance to both sides, a Kapauku sense of sportsmanship.

In the long run, of course, Dimiidakebo suffered by distrust, ostracism, and a lack of people who would trust him or conclude business agreements with him. He sustained several public reprimands from Awiitigaaj, who was supported by Ekajewaijokaipouga and by headmen from the other sublineages and lineages of the confederacy. Practically all the headmen of the confederacy finally decided on Dimiidakebo's execution. To make the execution as simple as possible, all of the headmen tried black magic. Thus, throngs of helping evil spirits and *tene* were believed to be attacking the body of the bad man until finally they succeeded in expelling the soul. Dimiidakebo died of pneumonia during the summer of 1953. There were not many people who wept. On the contrary, the name of the dead man is recalled in a derogatory way in most of the public reprimands administered today by the headman of the Ijaaj-Pigome confederacy: "You are almost like Dimiidakebo. You had better change your ways or you will perish as he did." Strong is the magical power of the moral Ijaaj headmen!

Today, Awiitigaaj is the only leader in Botukebo whose advice is followed. This does not necessarily mean that he is liked by all the Botukebo residents. On the contrary, seventy per cent of the people complain about his lack of generosity and his quarrelsome nature. Why do they follow him? There is simply no other man to take his place. Sixty-five per cent would like to replace him with Ijaaj Timaajjokainaago of Botukebo, a rich man who has five wives, who is generous, popular, and kind. However, the trouble is that this man is too quiet and shy. He has no political ambitions whatsoever. He admitted quite frankly: "I am not brave. I am afraid of flying arrows and harsh words. I do not know how to speak well. People always ask me to speak up at a quarrel and settle the dispute, but I am afraid. I do not like to shout and argue. I leave all of this to Awiitigaaj. He loves it."

Thus, Botukebo and its Ijaaj Enona sublineage has to be contented with the present leader and hope that the younger generation will furnish a new, rich man as a leader. Will it be Pilkiiwode, Ogiibiijokaimopaj, Onebiiwode? "We do not know. It depends on them."

THE HOUSEHOLD

RESIDENCE

Should one be interested in the Kapauku concept of the aggregate of people who reside in one house, which in our culture is called the household, he would be confronted with a residential rather than consanguineal idea. The name "*uwougu*, ridgepole hearth," means to the Kapauku a group of people who share warmth and shelter, the inhabitants of the same building. These need not be close relatives.

Although it is common for brothers and their respective families to live together in one house (ten out of sixteen Botukebo households), there are distant relatives who also join their residence, if invited. Thus, we find in Botukebo a man named Pigome Naago who shares a house with the family of his dead wife's father's father's brother's son's son; Ijaaj Bunaibomuuma who accepted into his home Adii Gipemeide with his family, his father's father's sister's son's son; Epibiiwenekaipouga living with his father's brother's son's son; and Ijaaj Nakepajokaipouga who lives with his mother's father's brother's son's son's son. The *ani jokaani*, unmarried boys who live with a rich man, although sometimes barely related, are also counted as household members.

The material aspect of the household is the *"owa,* house" (Pl. 3, *bottom*). Its walls are made of at least two layers of planks which, after being sharpened at both ends, are driven vertically into the ground. On the inside of the wooden wall the *"tiba,* bark of a pandanus," forms a solid screen which prevents the wind from blowing into the structure and also functions as insulation against the low temperatures during the later part of the night. The wall is held in position by poles or additional, large, horizontal planks. The floor is elevated about seventy centimeters above the ground and consists of crosswise beams and more numerous, but thin, lengthwise poles which support the *tiba* which constitutes the Kapauku version of linoleum. Rattan vines, split with teeth, serve as binding material. The lengthwise ridgepole supports a sloping roof thatched with long pandanus leaves or with reeds or grass. Although the Kapauku in other regions make use of bark from a special tree as a house cover, the local shortage of these trees in the Kamu Valley precludes its use almost entirely.

A Kapauku dwelling is about six meters long, four and a half meters wide, and four meters high. The floor space is divided into halves by a partition of planks which separates the frontal *"emaage,* men's room," from the rear *"kugu,* women's quarters." The *kugu* is further partitioned to achieve the ideal of one room per wife. Since there are always more women than available space, one additional *kugu* compartment may be built on each side of the elevated and roofed-over gangway leading to the front door of the *emaage,* which is the main entrance of the house. Each *kugu* has a separate door to the outside and a small aperture, usually large enough only for children, which connects it with the men's dormitory. Every room within the house has its own fireplace. The fireplace has the form of an upside-down stone pyramid, which, with its truncated tip resting on the ground, offers its upturned base at the level of the elevated floor as a safe place for a fire. The stones are held in position by sticks bound together with rattan. Most of the day and during the whole night a low fire, started by means of a firesaw, serves to cook meals for the Papuans, as well as to keep them warm during the night. The smoke rises into the thatch and escapes through the apertures left in the walls near the roof. The elevated floor serves not only as good insulation against the damp and often flooded ground, but the space underneath provides quarters for pigs.

The residential pattern within the house is characterized by the common male dormitory and by small rooms, each of which is assigned to one adult woman who lives there with her unmarried daughter, small sons, and sometimes her old mother. Since there may be many women in a household whose numerous compartments would make the house clumsy, several one room houses (four square meters of floor space) are built, one for each adult woman at a distance of a few meters from the main edifice. The number of occupants of the households in Botukebo ranges from five individuals to seventeen. Since women can live in additional *tone* huts if they find themselves crowded in small quarters, it is always the male who suffers in the large household units. The number of men in relation to the size of the men's dormitory usually determines the splitting up of the residential unit.

Daily Life

The cold of the night condenses the vapors rising from the jungle and swamp into walls of fog. They envelop the higher reaches of the mountain slopes or hang over the flat surface of the valley, finally to descend, heavy with water, as rollers of steam down the rock cliffs. Thus, they transform themselves into dew, which the shimmering twilight lightens up into glittering gold and silver. It is six-thirty in the morning. The solemn quietness of nature dressed in spectacular pastel colors, pregnant with mystery, is disrupted suddenly by the brutal, worldly swearing of a Kapauku male whose bodily necessities drive him out from the warmth of the house into the cold of the dewy morning. A European, whose romantic and aesthetic feelings have been shocked by this "barbarian" behavior, may look with disfavor upon the savage individual of neolithic culture. "Inhuman" may be his evaluation of the deed. Yet the dark eyes of the Papuan would quietly counter his reproach: "You give me your clothes and I shall enjoy nature with you."

The ribbons of smoke rising from the roofs of the houses betray the woman's first activity of the day. She roasts sweet potatoes in the fire and hot ashes to supply her family with food not only for breakfast but also for lunch. Each male depending on her, such as her husband, son, or husband's father (if a widower), receives a net-bag full (three kilograms) of the roasted tubers to last him for the day. While the wife is well under way with her task, her husband, still sleepy, adds some sticks from a rack suspended under the roof to the smoldering fire in his quarters. He reaches into his "*agija*, net carrying bag," fishes out a few raw sweet potatoes, and starts to fix part of his breakfast himself. One by one the other males wake up and join in the roasting activity. At seven-thirty in the morning, breakfast is finished and the people, loudly discussing their program for the day, wade through the already dry grass on the way to work in their gardens. Since the Kapauku have a conception of balance, only every second day do they work. A work day is followed by a rest day in order to regain lost power and health. This monotonous fluctuation of leisure and work is made more appealing to the Kapauku by adding more prolonged holidays spent in dancing and visiting. Thus, we usually find only part of the people departing for the fields, the others staying behind either to loiter around the village or to rest at home. At eight-thirty in the morning, when the sun finally conquers the mountain peaks and spills radiant light over the gardens, it finds the Kapauku already at work.

At about eleven, a decent man takes lunch. He may kindle a fire and roast a few raw sweet potatoes, or he may just squat and enjoy the tubers cooked for him by his wife. While he is feasting in solitude, his wife has joined a congregation of women in another field. The lunch of the women is not only an affair of mastication of the food; it is an educational, social, and informative occasion to which only a male who does not grasp its essence and importance would refer as gossip. The exchange of information about qualities and behavior of female members of the same or a neighboring village who are not present, educational advice documented by experience as to how to cheat or control husbands, and aesthetic evaluations of various males are the important subjects which contribute to the formation of a well-rounded educational background of a female Kapauku. Individuals of the weaker sex, sophisticated in these subjects, derive prestige from their female colleagues. This is more important than the displeasure and deriding remarks of the men.

While men stop working at about two o'clock in the afternoon, the women stay in the gardens until about four or five o'clock in order to finish their field work, dig sweet potatoes for the next day, and collect some dry branches of firewood. While they are working, their husbands squat at the houses, exchange news of a political nature, or they may start cooking an *ano*. *Ano* is a ball of long reed leaves bound together with vines. It contains green leaves of *idaja* and taro, several kinds of fern, and young shoots of squash. The bundle is simply placed on the fire and when the surface leaves of reed turn into charcoal, the food is steamed and ready to be eaten with a few drops of native salt. The men must hurry with the eating, otherwise they would have to share the food with their returning and hungry wives. When the women appear, the men with carefully wiped mouths and eyes rolling in simulation of hunger, ask them to hurry with the evening meal. They surely will die, they assert, if the food does not come fast. "What was the smoke I noticed in the afternoon coming from our house?" would be a most impolite question asked by a suspicious and therefore unworthy wife. Thus, they force the poor men into lying. The dinner is ready at about six o'clock in the evening. Women give the males roasted sweet potatoes in exchange for sugar cane or sometimes pork, which the men steam together with greens in a "*dopo*, grass cooking mound," by application of preheated stones. If the wife has been fishing, she may add to the diet a few large crayfish roasted on the embers, or tadpoles, frogs, dragonfly larvae, and water bugs steamed in long bamboo segments stuck into the hot ashes. If nothing exciting is going on in the village, the men lie in the *emaage* and talk as they fall asleep one by one. At ten o'clock it is quiet in the village, the men sleeping in the closed rooms with their feet toward the low fire and their hands between their thighs. Usually the sleepers lie on one side with their legs bent at the knees. Women have an advantage in having their long "*jato*, net bag," as a cover when sleeping. The night is full of sounds made by frogs and various evil spirits which shriek from the jungle or make rattling noises in the nearby trees. A few women with torches lit spend the night away from the village collecting frogs at nearby Kumugo Lake.

Men spend a leisure day by devoting it to business administration or to sleeping. In the former case, the man makes monetary and economic deals or visits a man who feeds his pig in order to check on the animal's progress. He may also secretly count his shell money or enjoy the day in political talks with neighbors. If he happens to be a keen businessman, he may try to make some counterfeit cowries out of imported shells. These he exchanges for goods in the Moni country, whose people have not yet learned to distinguish the old shells from the counterfeits. Either a woman may visit her sister, a friend, a brother, or parents, or she may join a group of females and go fishing in the lake in order to cool off in the water, to gossip, and to have a good evening dish of meat.

Economy

Except for the construction of a bridge over a stream, the building of a feast house, or the digging of a large ditch to drain water from the gardens belonging to several residents of a community, there is little economic cooperation outside of a household. This group of people figures, together with the family with which it is often coincident, as the only unit of people who coordinate their individual efforts in pursuit of economic goals. Ownership and distribution of goods and capital is the sphere of the individual, while the organization of production and consumption pertains to the household as a whole. The interrelation of production, distribution, and consumption makes it imperative to discuss the economy systematically in this place, thus violating our organizational scheme by including the individual's economic role in a chapter on the household. The writer feels that this action is justified in the light of functional efficiency.

The house is always owned by an individual man and he, ideally, should serve as the authority. Although this is usually the case in the village of Botukebo, there are two households which are exceptions. In household number fifteen (see Table 2) the son took over the power from his aging father. Pigome Oumau of household number three, mother-in-law of the quiet and placid landlord Dou Enaago, rules in the house as the intelligent, energetic, and attractive wife of an aging husband. Although the mother-in-law actually determines policy, she always acts as if her decisions were those of the supposed authorities. "My son-in-law would never think to make a field in the Debei Valley now because we have small pigs and cannot walk so far. Is it not so?" cunningly and with a sweet voice, she asked her son-in-law. With an apologetic smile, he rejected an offer of help in making a garden by replying, "I guess so."

Aside from these exceptions to the rule, it is the landlord who makes the program for consuming goods. It is he who asks his co-residents to help with food preparation and for contributions to the food supply. He has the right to induce the residents of his house to work in his fields if it is needed. He coordinates the economic activities of various individuals and discusses plans for future fieldwork and business transactions. He also functions as a legislator who enforces his own laws in the household.

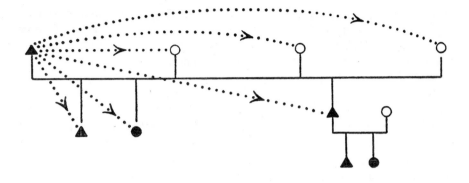

••••• Direct control relationship   •• > The direction of subordination

FIG. 7. Diagram Showing Social Control in the Family.

Conformance may be ultimately induced by threat of eviction from his house. His powers over the different members of the household vary in extent and application according to the mutual relationship involved. While a man directly controls all males, his own wives, and his close consanguineal female relatives, the females who have married other men in his household escape his direct influence (Fig. 7). The only way of controlling such women is through their husbands. In general, the male heads of the nuclear families which compose a household act with their landlord on behalf of their primary relatives.

Individualism. While analyzing the political authority of the confederacy, we inspected the conception of Kapauku freedom which is based upon individualism. This conception is most important for understanding the motivations, reasoning, and activities involved in the production, distribution and consumption of native goods. All one does in terms of work is executed primarily because one wants to do it for his own benefit. "*Ani beu kai peu,* I need," is the usual argument rather than a phrase referring to the common need of a group of people. Because it is "I" who needs, it is "I" who owns all the means for satisfaction.

Individualism penetrates the culture of the people so completely as to leave almost no room for common property. The exceptions seem to be the barren mountain tops and the larger streams "owned" by the sublineage and the small lakes owned by the lineage. Nevertheless, even these exceptions are rather illusory. Barren land unfit for cultivation and water by itself have no economic value. The insects, crayfish, frogs and rats which one secures from these areas are the actual objects of the rights. Since a man does not have a direct interest in their habitat but rather in the moving animals, the phrase "this lake is ours" would be more exact if expressed in terms of fishing rights. The animal becomes an individual's possession as soon as it is killed or caught. Water for drinking, rocks, and grass on the waste land are free to all. Thus, in the mind of the people, even these phenomena do not constitute an example of "common ownership."

Another documentation of individualistic thinking is the attitude of the people toward a community's main drainage ditch which has been constructed by the cooperative effort of all the people of the village. One would be mistaken if common ownership were postulated. The ditch, legally speaking, consists of many segments, each having a single owner whose right of ownership is determined by the boundaries of adjoining gardens. Similarly, a bridge, the product of a cooperative effort, would be loosely referred to as the property of the people of Botukebo in the same way as one points to a complex of individually owned fields. Actually, the bridge is a conglomerate of ownership rights of many men who consider the single poles, sticks, and rattan which compose the bridge and which they contributed as their personal property.

Accordingly, the Kapauku of the Paniai Lake area regard the District Officer as the owner of all the Netherlands Government property. The missionaries of the Franciscan Order are considered liars when they try to explain to the people that all the goods they manipulate are the property of the Order and that they had renounced all their rights to ownership. "They lied to us to make us sorry for them, and, therefore, they are no good. To whom belong all the things which they eat and wear and possess?" declared one of the native philosophers who, digusted with the whole idea of the absence of individual ownership, stood up and walked away.

All economic cooperation within the household has to be viewed in the perspective of individualism. Whenever the landlord asks for help with fieldwork, canoe or plank making, in tending pigs, or digging ditches, he is proposing a business contract. He always has to repay in goods, services, or money. Thus, a group of people working in one garden, on a canoe, or on a fence represents the execution of obligations stemming from business contracts. The result of such work is never the common property of the workers but always that of a single man. Wealth, as has been pointed out, is of paramount importance for an individual. It is the only way of acquiring political and legal importance, the main source of prestige, and a prerequisite for marriage and polygyny as well as for the acquisition of influential friends. Generosity, on which the highest value is placed, is made possible only through monetary resources. The Kapauku philosophy of life, discussed in the first section of this monograph, brought out the differentiation of realities of various orders. This emphasis on objectivity, on exactness, is manifested in the personality of a Kapauku by his quantitative, rather than qualitative evaluation of phenomena. Consequently, a tall man is valued; the weak or small one is *"peu,* bad." *Peujoka* means not only bad child, but actually a small child under seven years of age. Most of the things which are small are bad or at least not as good as large ones. A large number is more important and better than a small number. Their quantitative approach, suggested in the records of the Rorschach tests by an emphasis on a mosaic-like conceptualization of the inkblots, became quite apparent to the writer at the time he received a magazine from a Dutch friend. On the magazine cover was a picture of a beautiful, smiling girl. The writer showed it to several of the Kapauku. He expected an outburst of enthusiasm over the girl's appearance, and started to smile in expectation of some jokes of a sexual nature. The Kapauku reaction to the girl not only froze the smile on the writer's lips, but produced an expression on his face resembling that of a man witnessing the landing of a flying saucer or watching a brontosaur taking a sun bath on the roof of a house. The Kapauku counted her teeth!

And so it went with every picture. In the picture of downtown Los Angeles, they counted cars. A Navy carrier was considered magnificent because its deck was covered by numerous airplanes. A football match with crowds of spectators was the thrill of the day. Two of the Papuans almost started a fight over a discrepancy in the numbers of spectators counted. On the contrary, the grim look of Mr. Malenkov with nothing to count proved to be a complete failure. The editor of a magazine who would like to make good with the Kapauku is advised to present cover girls with as large mouths as possible in order to satisfy the people's delight in counting. Perhaps a centipede would make the best magazine cover for the Kapauku.

The emphasis on quantity manifests itself in elaborate numeration. A decimal system which stops at sixty and starts over again, having as higher units 600 and 3,600, is an excellent means for satisfying the Kapauku craving for counting and its presence is especially apparent in the field of economy. People count their wives, children, days, visitors at a feast, and especially their shell money. Hours are spent by people squatting over strings of shells and counting them. The writer adapted himself to this cultural pattern by rewarding his best informants and his best "adopted boys" by giving them permission to count thousands of his small trade beads. The honored and fortunate individual often squatted over the box of beads from six o'clock until ten in the evening. His departure was usually accompanied by a victorious smile and a statement such as: "You have 2,368 beads in this box. That is 261 less than when Akaawoogi counted them five days ago." Outside of the house, the less fortunate boys waited for the announcement of the result of the counting. Often even several hours later the writer heard comments on the counting and on his spendings. The writer had never had his finances in better order.

The Kapauku economy is a money economy. Cowries provide the standard currency and the imported white man's beads make the monetary system even more intricate. The shell money falls into two main categories: the new yellowish cowries imported by the white man and the old original cowries, well polished, with the dorsal part of the shell split away. Their age is documented by the luster of the surface as well as by the accumulation of dirt inside. The newer shells serve as material for counterfeiting. Their surfaces are polished with a soft stone to produce a resemblance of the old currency. The writer introduced cylindrical blue beads, six millimeters long. When discussing prices in this paper, the blue bead will be used as the unit for comparison with the different currencies.

As with European bank notes, the value of the old Kapauku cowrie, called *Kapauku mege*, differs according to shape and size.

Kawane, an elliptical cowrie shell, is worth two or three beads, depending on its size.

Bomoje, or *Wei mege*, are precious old cowrie shells which have an angular outline and are worth thirty beads each—these we shall symbolize in the future by the abbreviation "Km" (*Kapauku mege*).

Dege bomoje is a variety of the *bomoje* worth a little more than the Km shell (about thirty-five beads).

Buna bomoje is worth forty beads. It is larger than Km and bluish in appearance.

Epa mege is a large cowrie of angular shape worth about sixty beads.

Bodija is the most precious cowrie, worth, according to its size, over sixty beads and reaching a value of as much as 300 or 360 beads per piece.

"*Tuani mege*, the white man's cowries," which will be symbolized by Tm, are worth from two to eight beads, depending on their size. If they are elliptical instead of angular in shape, they have no value.

There are also some articles which are so often used in payments that they acquire, to some extent, the characteristics of currency. *Dedege* necklaces, made of tiny white shells, are worth thirty beads if they are as long as a man's arm. Their value increases with their length. Necklaces of small glass beads, called *pagadau*, have the same value as the *dedege* necklaces. With the increased supply, the value of iron axes used in some payments decreased from 10 Km, or 300 beads, to 5 Km or 150 beads each.

Production. Five or six hours of steady, intensive work characterize the labor efforts of a Kapauku man. We have already mentioned that leisure is enjoyed every second day. Consequently, the laborer is always well rested when he starts his fieldwork in the morning. During his short period of work, he is steady, thorough, and fast, rather than sloppy and slow in his performance. A woman, on the contrary, works at least two hours longer a day and is always slower than the male worker. Unlike the leisure time of men which is spent in talking and planning, her days of "rest" are dedicated to fishing, collecting, or paddling in her canoe. While her husband's time is divided into periods of intensive activity followed by complete physical rest, the woman is occupied with slow, unstrenuous work.

Because of the individualism previously mentioned, the work is mostly solitary, or when it is done by a group of people, one individual's accomplishments can be distinguished from those of another. Thus, teamwork such as in bridge and house building, the digging of a main ditch, or in carrying pigs or canoes, is a sporadic affair.

For the most part, the division of labor follows sex lines. Certain tasks are considered to be exclusively the domain of one of the sexes. Other tasks are only preferentially so. The rest of the work is shared equally by both sexes. The men consider war, hunting, trapping, felling of trees, digging of ditches, and the construction of fences, canoes, and houses as their work. Similarly, dealing in politics, dealing in legal affairs, trading with pigs, pork and salt, the butchering of animals, as well as the planting and harvesting of bananas and tobacco are men's prerogatives. Burning over the garden plot and planting and harvesting sugar cane and manioc, although done by both sexes, are regarded as preferentially a man's task. On the other hand, males are excluded from planting sweet potatoes and *jatu*, a type of grass, and from fishing with nets. These are women's occupations. The males may do some weeding, planting of taro, harvesting of sweet potatoes, and some collecting of insects and frogs, although these activities are primarily those of the women. Men and women equally share in harvesting taro, *idaja*, an edible green, *jatu*, *pego*, and in planting *idaja* and *pego* as well as clearing the land of underbrush. The art of magic is open to both sexes.

Since the Kapauku have a "capitalistic" economy, one can sell his labor to another individual. Women, however, do not take advantage of this opportunity to acquire wealth, and work only for their husbands and close relatives without pay. They are rewarded by reciprocal services only. The work of a Kapauku is not remunerated according to the time spent while working. Pay is related to the result of the work, rather than to the effort itself. Out of thirty-two cases which represent the total work for reward by Botukebo men for a period of eight months in 1955, only one man agreed to accept wages determined by the time spent on the work itself. The rest of the laborers received remuneration for a finished product. The usual work done for "pay" is that of making a piece of land ready for cultivation by cutting the brush and building a fence around the area. The usual fee is 2 Km for one *peka*, a square of approximately 900 square meters of cleared and fenced land.

A man almost always works for a relative or a co-villager. Twenty-one of the thirty-two labor contracts were between two individuals of Botukebo. Six people worked for residents of one of the other villages of the same confederacy. Only five cases involved employers from outside of the Ijaaj-Pigome political unit. However, all instances of the last category involved close relatives, such as a wife's brother, a mother's brother, a wife's father, or a mother's brother's son. During the period of eight months, the people of the Botukebo community made fields for eleven outsiders, while hiring only two workers for their own fields. There were only four men who, being rich, did not work for the others, and two or three poorer, notoriously lazy fellows who preferred loitering and poverty to physical effort and earnings.

In Western culture, we attach high value to hard work and we admire people who earn a living through their diligence and personal sacrifice. Among the Kapauku, little value is attached to the effort itself. Work has no value. Its effects do. In other words, a man is honored because he is wealthy but it makes little difference whether he acquired his wealth in business, through inheritance, or in hard physical endeavor. Besides, one does not become rich through working other people's gardens or by home industry. The way to a fortune is through the successful breeding and selling of pigs.

To be able to keep pigs, one has to start with a field of sweet potatoes. This is the only crop which, besides forming the most essential components of the menu, plays the role of capital. Because of this, all the rest of the plants, which have only consumption value and which number sixteen different species, occupy only 19,512 square meters of land, while sweet potatoes cover 152,970 square meters, or eight times as much area as that occupied by all the other sixteen crops together. The sweet potato grows in all types of soil and at all elevations in the South Kamu

Valley. Its yields vary, however, with the quality of soil and the type of cultivation. An average harvest from ten square meters amounts to about eleven kilograms of tubers. An area of 2,704 square meters of medium good soil could support a family of five and one medium-sized pig for a period of approximately ten months.

Sweet potatoes when used as capital are fed to the pigs. A young man strives to gather enough money to be able to buy a female piglet, to raise it, and later breed a grown sow. From the litter, he saves all the females for breeding purposes. Thus, one acquires more and more of these animals. The increased stock, however, requires more food. Since one is limited as to how much he can personally cultivate, one has to hire other people to clear new land in order to keep his economy expanding. Nevertheless, making another garden is not enough. The area has to be planted and constantly weeded, the crop harvested, and the pigs fed twice a day. The only economic solution to this problem is to buy an additional wife who can do the work. Thus, the basic economic cycle, the Kapauku magical ring of success, is completed. One marries a woman and she plants fields and harvests sweet potatoes. With the tubers, one feeds his pigs which are sold to provide money for buying additional wives who cultivate new land. The more fields one has, the more crops, pigs, and money one acquires for buying additional wives. Since a wife, though only a figure in our economic calculation, is still a woman, she, unlike the pigs, sweet potatoes, and fields, makes certain social demands on her husband. He, being only human, is unable to meet these increased personal duties indefinitely. There is a limit to the number of wives which a Kapauku can accumulate. This has been recognized even by Awiitigaaj of Botukebo who, having married ten wives, was contemplating an additional marriage. "This will be the last one. I simply cannot have any more," was his statement.

It must have been an old Kapauku "Adam Smith" who removed this curb on the accumulation of wealth by inventing an institution called *ekina munii*. We may label the device a "pig breeding contract." Since all the legal aspects of contracts are to be discussed fully in the section on law, we shall now outline only the major features of this one. A man agrees to care for a piglet for the owner until it reaches approximately ninety kilograms of weight. For this he is usually rewarded with 4 Km. When such payment is given, the fattened animal, ready for slaughtering, is turned over to the owner who either butchers it himself or sells it alive to another person. Should the breeder be allowed to kill it himself, as he usually prefers to do, he has the right to the pig's head, to all the entrails, and to two pieces of pork of approximately four kilograms in weight. All the rest of the meat is sold and the profit turned over to the owner. This old invention of the pig breeding contract made it possible for a man to own sixty pigs and, at the same time, to avoid a harem of about thirty wives. To appreciate fully the importance of this type of contract, the reader is reminded that a Kapauku wife comes much closer to an American woman in her freedom and influence than to a traditional inmate of a harem.

Although hunting is of major economic importance in the neighboring mountain valleys of the Pona and Mapia regions, in the forestless Kamu Valley this activity has no monetary importance. Only a few adults engage in it. The only occasion resembling a hunting season presents itself at the time of the floods which occur approximately five times a year. Then all the men get their bows and arrows and try to shoot rats swimming to safety or stranded on small islands in the inundated valley. Nevertheless, even this opportunity gives a successful hunter only two or three rats as a reward for the whole day's hunt. Were it not for the recreational aspect and a taste for the game, no one would be interested in this kind of "production."

In the Paniai, Tigi, and Tage Lake areas, fishing is an important economic activity which produces most of the daily supply of proteins. In the Kamu Valley, where crayfish are scarce because of the lack of a large lake, fishing for larvae and tadpoles and the gathering of insects and frogs provide the people with the bare minimum of proteins. While game in the Pona and Mapia regions is an important article of trade, the inhabitants of the Kamu Valley depend for trade almost entirely on their production of pork. This is demonstrated by the number of pigs kept. A *tonowi* in the Kamu Valley must have at least twenty pigs, while a man in Mapia who owns only five of these animals is already considered a rich man.

Industry in the South Kamu Valley suffers from the lack of suitable raw material. Unlike the situation in the Pona region, there are only a few trees left in the Kamu Valley whose inner bark is suitable for string making. Thus, there are only five individuals in the whole Ijaaj-Pigome confederacy who make nets for sale and are known as experts in this art. They have to acquire most of their raw material through trade with the Debei and Pona people, however. Of these five men, two live in Botukebo. Since there is almost no good bow wood available, one finds that Ijaaj Bunaibomuuma of Botukebo is the only known master of bow making who sells his produce.

There is no stone industry because limestone forms all the mountains in the area. Thirty years ago stone axes and stone machetes were still bought from "the Kajaa people."

In the Kamu Valley, the raising of pigs constitutes the only type of production which can result in an accumulation of wealth. Since prestige, social mobility, status achievement, political power, legal power, and polygyny are dependent on wealth, the pig and the activities connected with its breeding constitute the "focus" of Kapauku culture. This importance is also reflected in the value system of the people. The most honored occupation for a boy, girl, or woman is herding pigs; and for men it is to engage in buying, selling, and slaughtering the animals. All the other occupations which either contribute to animal husbandry or directly satisfy the basic needs of the people are not, to any important degree, a source of income.

Distribution. All articles of trade have a customary price from which the actual price may differ due to the factors given. A moral value is attached to the customary price. It is regarded as a fair price and the man demanding it is considered honest. There are seldom disputes after a customary price has been paid. To give the reader an idea about the Kapauku sales, we include a table with some of the customary prices.

1. One *peka* of land (equivalent to 900 square meters) is leased for 1 Km. A standing crop of sweet potatoes on the same area is sold for 5 Km.

2. One *"kado*, piece of pork,"* of about two kilograms is sold for 1 Km.

3. One iron ax costs 5 Km.

4. One iron machete costs 3 Km.

5. A pig of approximately ninety kilograms costs 20 Km. The price of pigs differs according to the weight. In general, a pig for slaughtering purposes is worth as many Kapauku cowries as the number of *kado* of pork that can be obtained from its carcass.

6. One chicken sells for 2 Km.

7. One *kemo* of salt (equivalent to two kilograms) costs 1 Km.

8. A good canoe costs 2 Km.

9. A large house costs 5 Km, a medium-sized one, 3 Km.

10. Seven *woda* (marsupial or larger rodents) costs 2 Km, five pieces cost one *epa mege* (equivalent to 40 beads).

11. Thirty rats are sold for 1 Km.

12. A net carrying bag of good quality costs 1 Km.

13. Ten penis sheaths of good quality cost 1 Km.

For the exchange rate of the different types of currency, the reader is referred to the previous discussion of money.

The actual price paid for a commodity may differ from the above list because of the following factors:

1. Supply and demand. As in our culture, so in the Kapauku economy, the rule that the larger the demand, the higher the price, is generally true. Ijaaj Dojaugi-jokaibo of Obajbegaa leased 900 square meters of land (one *peka*) for 2 Km (instead of 1 Km) to Ijaaj Degepaaj of Obajbegaa because the demand for fields in that section was high at that time. Similarly, at the pig feast in Tuguteke in 1951, Ijaaj Jokagaibo of Itoda had to pay 6 Km for two *kado* of pork instead of the customary 2 Km. "There was so little pork for sale that I had to pay Anou Wape-jaajtawii of Tuguteke this exorbitant price in order not to be meat-hungry." When the demand is small and the supply large, prices tend to be depressed below the customary level. Pigome Ipouga of Obajbegaa bought from Pigome Gaajabii of Obajbegaa two pieces of pork for only 1 Km, because there was too much pork at that time.

In general, however, the fluctuation of price because of temporary imbalance of the supply-demand level is rather infrequent. On the contrary, a steady increase of supply may bring about a steady decline of the actual price. The permanence of this state has an effect upon the customary price which tends to be identified with the actual payments. Thus, before 1945 when iron axes had to be brought from the coastal people, the customary price for an ax was 10 Km. The coming of the white man and the resulting increase and direct supply of axes, reduced the old price to half the former amount. The process is still going on and the actual price in 1955 tended to fall below the new customary price of 5 Km per ax.

2. The factor of kin and friendship ties between the parties tends to lower the price. Thus, Pigome Pegabii of Obajbegaa sold to his brother Pigome Ipouga of Obajbegaa two *kado* of pork for only 1 Km.

3. Competition between two sellers has a lowering effect on the price. Ijaaj Jokagaibo of Itoda wanted to buy a pig. People offered him pigs worth 15 Km for 16 Km, trying to make a good profit on the sale. However, the buyer was secretly offered a pig of the same weight for 14 Km by Ijaaj Amoje of Bukwaapa, who thus undersold his competitors.

4. A political leader, a *tonowi*, often is given a commodity for a lower price than normal because the seller expects future favors from such a man. Ijaaj Ekajewaijokaipouga, the headman of the Ijaaj-Pigome confederacy, bought several pigs from people of his own constituency and even from outsiders for a lower price.

The sale contract.—The exchange of a commodity for currency is the basic distributional device for the Kapauku. Although barter does occur, sale accounts for at least nine-tenths of the transfers of ownership. Since the buying of a wife and the sale of labor have already been discussed, and since they differ in some respects from ordinary sales, we are omitting them in the following discussion. It may be interesting to learn that the Kapauku reject the idea that a woman is bought like a pig, although both transactions are labeled by the same term, *edai*. The purchase of one's labor is never called *edai* and thus it is formally distinguished.

Here, we shall discuss only the formal and sociological aspects of the different transactions. The analysis of the various rights and duties of the parties, as well as their liabilities stemming from the contract, will be treated in the next part of the monograph which deals with law.

A Kapauku sale contract, unlike that in Roman law, is not considered closed by the mutual agreement of the parties. Not until the sold object is transferred and the full payment made does the object belong to the buyer. This fact has very important consequences in the fields of liability and annulling of the deal. Furthermore, in case of tacit underselling which consists of the acceptance of a low price for a commodity without explicitly agreeing to the finality of the deal, a sale may be invalidated by the seller or his heirs any time in the future. Under certain circumstances (see the third part of the monograph), sales of land may be declared invalid by the legal heirs. The legal irrelevance of an agreement and the frequent possibility of breaking a contract differ profoundly from the Romanistic notions of contracts.

Bargaining is acceptable in the sale of most commodities with the exception of pork. Because of the usual shortage of meat and the force of the customary price, the buyer of pork simply offers a shell and waits tacitly for approval by the seller. In other deals, the price and quality of the merchandise may be the subject of a long and fervent discussion.

Publicity is never required for any deal and the word of the party is trusted. Usually, there are witnesses to the deal so that the settlement of a possible dispute can be based on objective evidence.

The sale of land.—It is only the owner who can sell his land. Other persons such as his prospective heirs, headman, or agent cannot effect the sale of another man's land. The agreed upon payment of at least the customary price, which is set up at 5 Km for 900 square meters, fully transfers the ownership.

If, however, the seller is an old man with adult sons, their agreement is necessary in validating the contract. Although full ownership is transferred, the heirs of the seller always retain a preemptory right indefinitely, especially if the buyer is an outsider. This restriction enables the clans to preserve the integrity of their area. The new landlord also has to honor a *ususfructus* right of another person to the land on the terms of the original agreement between the man who subsequently sold his land and the individual who rented it.

The sale of crops.—When a garden crop is sold, the buyer acquires only the right to harvest it. After the harvest is completed, the land returns to the owner. The customary price for a sweet potato crop on one. *medeke*, which is an area of approximately 180 square meters (one-fifth of a *peka*), is 1 Km. Consequently, the crop from a whole *peka* of land costs 5 Km or, in other words, the same price as an uncultivated area of land of the same size. The seller has to protect the buyer legally from being disturbed in his harvest by other people. Since the seller has constructed the fence, he is liable if pigs invade the garden and destroy the crop. In such a case, he has to return the amount paid for the crops.

The sale of pigs.—There are two different types of pig sales. In one a pig destined for slaughtering is sold. In the other, a piglet for breeding purposes is the object of the contract.

The price for the pig bought for slaughter varies with its weight or with the possible number of *kado*, two kilogram pieces of pork, that can be cut from the pig. Consequently, an animal of about ninety kilograms costs 20 Km. The fifty kilograms unaccounted for in the price is the weight of the bodily juices, entrails, bones, and head. In this type of sale, the seller is not liable for any future accident to the pig because what he has actually sold was meat rather than some intrinsic or hidden properties of the animal.

For a small male pig purchased for fattening purposes, one may either pay the total price of 7 Km immediately or only 1 Km immediately and about 10 Km at the time of the pig's slaughter. The difference in the price in the second instance is to be accounted for by the delayed payment. Because the seller has the duty to reimburse the loss a buyer may suffer in case of an accidental and premature death of the small pig, the postponed completion of the payment gives the buyer security that the seller will comply with the rules of such transactions.

A down payment of 5 Km is required from the buyer of a small female pig acquired for breeding purposes. At the time of killing the sow and some of her male offspring, the seller has a right to an "*epaawa*, final payment," of 60 to 120 Km. The actual price reflects the profit the buyer made on the breeding of the animal. If the sow bore him, let us say, sixteen piglets, he would have to pay 120 Km. On the contrary, if the sow proved sterile, he would not be liable for more than about 30 Km, depending upon the weight of the slaughtered animal.

An alternative to the above contract is an immediate payment of 40 to 50 Km to be followed by a final payment, a female piglet born to the sow. As with the male pig, the seller bears the risk accompanying breeding and the price is reduced to compensate for the loss to the buyer in case the animal dies.

In the above contracts, we again find manifestations of the Kapauku idea of justice. The conviction that neither party should lose in a deal is part of the Kapauku concept of "*uta-uta*, equity," which we discussed in connection with peace negotiations. While justice was then viewed as a balanced number of dead on both sides, this time it is an equal profit or loss by both parties on the sale of a pig, equity being assured by the changeable price.

The sale of chickens.—An immediate payment of 1 Km is required for a chicken of either sex. An additional payment of 3 Km is made when chicks of a hen which has been sold are hatched. Should the fowl die while still small, the price is fully returned on receipt of the dead animal.

The sale of a dog.—There are no dogs in the southeastern part of the Kamu Valley. In Degeipige, situated to the west, the price varies from 2 Km to 4 Km, depending on how good the dog is at catching game. Only old dogs are sold and since they are not eaten, their hunting abilities determine the price.

The sale of a house.—Since the buyer always moves the house, it is the planks which are actually sold. A price of 5 Km is paid to the owner. The buyer, because he does not own the land on which the house is standing, is required to move the structure. The price fluctuates with the quality of the planks and the size of the house.

The sale of artifacts.—The prices for the various artifacts which appear above in the list of customary prices are paid at the time of the delivery of merchandise. An object may be ordered from the maker who delivers it for the agreed price. The buyer may refuse it or ask for a reduction if the object is of inferior quality.

Barter.—As compared with sale, barter is rather a rare contract. An equivalent of some commodity is offered for the desired goods. Thus, pork may be exchanged for sweet potatoes, salt for pork, and a bow or net for sweet potatoes. Pigs, planks, and canoes are never used in barter. The work of a future son-in-law in the house of his bride's father, done in order to obtain a reduction in the bride price, may be regarded as barter involving a bride.

Trade does not involve relations between only producer and consumer, although these are the most frequent ones. There are middlemen among the Kapauku who, although they are farmers, also specialize in trade. They concentrate their business efforts on intertribal and inter-regional trade, and sometimes upon a special commodity. Thus, we find "pig dealers" and "salt traders" who carry on trade between certain regions and tribes in addition to their regular farm work.

Intra-regional trade.—It is only the pig trade which attracts individuals to act as middlemen within a given region. In the Ijaaj-Pigome confederacy, Ijaaj Iibii of Aigii is a man who goes to a remote village of the Kamu Valley, buys a pig, and a few days later sells it on the other side of the valley for a large profit. Thus, in January, 1955, he bought a male pig from Dogomo Tajajtawii of Eboweja for 9 Km and sold it to a Dou man from Jotapuga, only a few days later, for 15 Km, making a phenomenal profit of sixty-six per cent. It should be stressed that a trade between a middleman and a consumer is a rather sporadic affair so that Ijaaj Iibii, who makes approximately two such deals in a year, has to engage, as do other traders, in the normal farming activities. Thus, all the "tradesmen" are only partly specialized.

Inter-regional trade.—This type of trade offers a much better opportunity to a business man. Because of the difference in physical environment, in resources, and in regional cultural emphasis on the production of a specific product, inter-regional trade involves a greater variety of goods.

The Kamu-Mapia inter-regional trade is conducted in net bags decorated with boar tusks and orchid wrappings, and pigs from the Kamu Valley. From Mapia come "*jape daagu*, charm stones," cassowary bird feathers, and long bones, as well as feathers of birds of paradise used for headdresses and hairpins. In the Ijaaj-Pigome confederacy, it is Botukebo village which specializes in business with Mapia.

In the Ijaaj-Pigome confederacy, the Kamu-Pona trade is carried on by traders from Aigii. In this trade, pigs and net bags decorated with boar tusks are exported from the Kamu Valley region. Imported are brightly colored feathers, cassowary bones, bundles of inner bark for string manufacture, resin and roasted carcasses of *woda*, marsupials and giant rats.

Goods from the Paniai Lake region are exchanged in the Ijaaj-Pigome confederacy especially by the people from Kojogeepa, Notiito, and Jagawaugii. Exported to this region are surplus articles obtained from Mapia and Pona, as well as pigs bred in the Kamu Valley. Since Paniai is a poor region without a special produce of its own, it offers in return only goods which it acquires through inter-tribal trade from the northern Moni, Ndani, and Uhunduni people (see below under inter-tribal trade).

Since the Tigi Lake and Debei Valley regions do not have local specialties, the only intensive trade with the Kamu Valley is the exchange of pigs. In addition to the pigs, a few bundles of inner bark are imported from the Debei Valley. All the five villages of the Ijaaj-Pigome confederacy engage in trade with this region to approximately the same degree.

In concluding the discussion on inter-regional trade, it should be noted that the "traders" who engage in this type of exchange of goods often act also as agents of inter-tribal trade.

Inter-tribal trade.—The Kamu Valley forms a segment in a chain of trade which starts in the Mimika coastal area to the south and ends some place in the interior of the mountainous valleys northeast of the Kapauku territory. The inter-tribal trade can be compared to a chain reaction. It starts at the coast and follows the route to the north and east. It involves many regions and tribes whose traders exchange commodities, carry them a relatively short distance, then trade them with their colleagues from the north, receiving goods which thus go in the reverse direction. *Woti*, a large species of shell, *dedege* necklaces of tiny shells, and iron axes and machetes move along the trade route by pulsation of the chain reaction from the coast into the interior. From the interior come red ochre, palm wood, and stone axes and knives. The stone stools are said to be produced in Kajaa country, located some place near the Baliem Valley. From the Moni country, the south-bound trade takes bundles of native salt and carries them as far as Pona and Mapia. Here, all the articles from the north are substituted for dogs and tobacco. These commodities reach the coast, thus concluding the cycle. The advent of the white man in the Paniai region furnished a new source of goods which, picked up by this trade, are carried south and northward. However, the new source of iron axes disrupted the import of metal tools from the coast.

To this inter-tribal exchange, the Kapauku of the Kamu Valley do not contribute any commodity except the counterfeit cowry shell money. They receive from the white man low valued uncut cowries. A specialist like Ijaaj Taajwiijokaipouga of Botukebo cuts the shell, and polishes it until it acquires the wonderful white luster of the true Kapauku cowry shell. To make it seem even more authentic, he puts some wax and dirt into the interior of the shell. To distinguish this product from a real old shell requires the eye of an expert and an amount of skill comparable to that needed to distinguish a cultivated pearl from a natural one. Since many of the "inexperienced Moni people" and the Ndani to the northeast are not aware of the counterfeiting, they are cheated by the Kapauku. The counterfeiting is regarded by the Kapauku as a national "top secret." Since some white missionaries and administrative officers are cheated in the same way as the Moni and Ndani, the clues for differentiation between a real shell and a faked one are supposed to be kept as a secret by all the Kapauku. The inter-tribal trade is carried on in the Kamu Valley usually by groups of about three people who travel northward to the Moni country. During the twelve months of the writer's research, there were three such expeditions, two from Aigii and one from Kojogeepa. To facilitate trading in a foreign country, the trader has a Moni business friend in one of the Moni villages with whom he stays overnight. The Moni friend gives the Kapauku trader food and halps him in his business deals with the other Moni people. The Kapauku reciprocates in the same way when his Moni friend comes visiting him in turn.

Ijaaj Jokagaibo of Itoda sold on his last expedition twelve *dedege* necklaces for 12 Km, two *woti* shells for 10 Km, and a large *bodija* type of a cowry shell for the exorbitant price of 30 Km and 10 Tm, making a profit of 15 Km on the sale of the *bodija* shell alone. Furthermore, he bought twelve large pieces of salt for 12 Km, which he sold in the Kamu Valley for 24 Km; two *boote* bows for 2 Tm, which he sold at home for 2 Km; and five pieces of ochre for 1 Km, which he sold later in the Kamu Valley for twice that amount. This expedition brought him a profit of 30 Km, or the value of two medium-size (forty kilograms) pigs. On another expedition, the same man made 9 Km profit through the sale of fake shell money alone.

Although this enterprise is very lucrative, the risks of going through many different territories as well as the difficulties of walking from seven to ten days one way permit few individuals to engage in such an activity.

A trader always cheats people. For this reason intra-regional trade is rather frowned upon while inter-tribal trade gives to the businessman prestige as well as profit. It should be added that inter-tribal trade is made possible by the universal acceptance of cowries as currency.

Besides being important in inter-tribal trade, the *woti* shell is the only medium of speculation on the domestic market. The demand and supply of the shell which is also used in the manufacture of necklaces varies remarkably from time to time. This permits the use of the shell as an article of speculation. Ijaaj Jokagaibo of Itoda bought three *woti* for two pieces of pork (equivalent to 2 Km) when the demand was low and the supply large. He deposited the shells in his cache and kept them there for five months. After this period of time, when the price went up again, he sold the shells at a pig feast in Obano for 3 Km, as well as a male pig worth 5 Km, thus making a net profit of 6 Km or three hundred per cent of the original price.

Most of the buying and selling is done on an occasion such as pig feast or the "*tapa*, blood reward ceremony." Nevertheless, since these ceremonies are not very frequent and are connected with elaborate preparations and formalities, the Kapauku businessmen invented an institution called a "*dedomai*, pig market." This is an occasion for business only, when no dancing takes place and no ceremonial structures are erected. One man functions as the "*ipuwe*, owner," of the market. He determines the day of the occasion and arranges for its publicity. All people, including the owner, who have pigs ready for market come to the *dedomai*, slaughter the pigs, and sell the meat. Traders with foreign commodities, as well as with domestic articles other than meat, are also welcome to transact business at that time. Although this day resembles a pig feast, its significance and functions are entirely economic, being limited to the informal redistribution of goods and shell money.

Sales of services.—There are a few other specialists, besides the traders, who sell their services to people. The shaman's and sorcerer's professions have already been discussed. In addition to these, there are expert surgeons who are skilled at taking out arrows from a wound and at making an incision with a flint knife, either in the wound or nearby, to let out the infected blood. If one survives, one pays only five beads for the best treatment. Since one's eventual death is believed never to be related to the surgeon's lack of skill but rather to an attack by an evil spirit, the surgeon charges the mourning heirs sixty beads instead of the normal small amount. The difference in price is paid because the doctor suffers by being sorry about the death of one he so eagerly tried to save. Dentists classify themselves in two categories: gum cutters, who save the teeth by incising the gum with a bamboo knife thus relieving the pressure, and extractionists. The writer watched an operation performed by a gum cutter on a patient who had suffered for seven days and whose pain could not be relieved by aspirin supplied by the writer. The patient became well in one day after a single incision. In more serious cases, the patient has to make an appointment with the extractionist. These specialists are rigorous in their business and are offended if one pleads with them to save the tooth. "You just go to Jikiiwiijaaj with this kind of work, I will not do it," was the angry reply by an extractionist from Aigii to a man who asked only to have his gum incised. An extractionist cuts open the gum with a bamboo knife and extracts the tooth with his fingers. Two helpers hold the patient's head while he is lying on his back during the operation. If it hurts severely, the dentist may give one "anesthesia" by kneeling on one's stomach. This miraculously distracts one's attention, holds down the body, stops the patient from hollering by forcing the air out of his lungs, opens his mouth, and permits the "doctor" to complete his task undisturbed. While for gum cutting the dentist does not charge at all, one has to pay five beads for an extraction. The fee may be doubled if one has bitten the practitioner.

Lease contracts.—An uncultivated patch of land overgrown with secondary forest may be leased for the period of time required for growing and harvesting one crop. For one *peka* (900 square meters) of land the owner charges 1 Km or he may enjoy in the future the same right to the land of the leasee. There is no responsibility on the part of the landlord if the crop is destroyed and the grower has to pay under all circumstances. To make a garden on another man's land is a quite common phenomenon. It occurred in fifty-five cases (involving a garden area of 69,718 square meters) out of a total of 134 gardens under cultivation in the Botukebo area (which occupy 172,482 square meters). The main reason for leasing land is not that one would not have enough of his own land. Instead one wants the advantage of making a garden next to one already in use, thus avoiding the necessity of building a fence on one or even two sides of the field by using the neighbor's fence as a protection for one's own garden. Also, the location of the various fields and the different quality of soil may induce people to lease.

The lease of a residential area.—In order to live a short distance from other houses, some people lease land for house building. For only a small lot they pay 1 Km for a period of approximately two years. If the house owner decides to move, the price paid is not returned, even if the property has been used for only a short time.

An ornamental net decorated with boar tusks, an ax, a machete, a bow and arrows, or a fishing net may be loaned. All these artifacts may be used without payment. The man who borrowed them has to take good care of them and return them any time he is asked to do so. However, an ax, stone ax, or machete, because they are tools which deteriorate through use, are often leased rather than loaned. The owner stipulates that the tool should be used only for making one garden. The fee is low, about one or two beads, so that everyone can afford to rent such tools. The worker is liable only for negligent and intentional loss or damage to the leased object.

Credit.—Credit is extended to people not because one expects to enrich oneself through interest, but because this is the proper expression of generosity and the safest way to acquire great prestige. The political and legal implications of credit have been already discussed with the concept of *tonowi*. In this place, it remains to point out the nature of the various contracts and their economic significance.

Unlike Western capitalism, the Kapauku economic system contains no legally enforced payment of interest. One can borrow shells and promise to pay a few more for the favor, but this promise, if not kept, does not constitute cause for legal action. It depends entirely on the debtor and on his desire for prestige whether he pays the agreed sum or not. However, to break one's promise is bad. It is a demonstration of one's lack of generosity, and one which may result in mistrust by other individuals. Thus, we may say that to pay interest is moral but not a legally enforceable duty.

There are several types of loans.

1. *Daba menii* is credit extended to a person who either did not specify the use to be made of the currency or who stated a use which did not identify the loan as one of the Kapauku special types of loans described below. Although interest is never enforceable, the loan has a disadvantage over our institution of credit. Its return may be required any time with full legal backing. The recipient of the loan may pay the borrowed sum in any type of currency.

2. *Waka jaedai*, to lend money for the *one* part of the bride price, is considered a very special contract. The return of the currency should not be requested until the wife has borne a child. It is legally enforceable, but utterly immoral to force the debtor to pay prior to this date.

3. *Kade jamakii*, contribution to the *kade* portion of the bride price, may be asked to be returned legally when the creditor himself gets married. At that time the former *kade* recipient is morally, as well as legally, expected to repay the debt and, according to the moral code, to give something even in excess of the sum originally received. This loan usually consists of only a few introduced cowries, beads, or a necklace.

4. *"Nogei menii*, a loan or gift to one's best friend,"* consists usually of a larger amount of currency which, according to the moral code, should never be asked to be returned during the life of the friend. The abstract legal rule, however, permits the creditor to violate the moral code and to request the return of the gift at any time. However, the proper way is to wait until the best friend reciprocates on his own. The Kapauku law gives the donor the right to ask the heirs of his best friend to repay the gift if adequate reciprocation had not occurred during the friend's lifetime. Such a procedure is moral as well as legal.

The above discussion again illustrates *"uta-uta*, equity,"* which is the key concept of Kapauku justice. It permits the donor, even against the canons of the moral code, to ask for repayment and thus re-establish the original balance, which had been upset by his gift.

The *"jegeka*, gift."*—One cannot forfeit, even by an explicit declaration, one's legal right to ask the return of something which has been given to another person without the latter's reciprocation. A gift gives an advantage to one side and thus creates an automatic obligation, on the recipient's part, to return the favor. Thus a gift, as we know it in our legal thinking, does not exist among the Kapauku. *Jegeka* can be most correctly translated as a donation to be repaid on request in the distant future. The request can be made by the donor or by his heirs, and the liable person, the recipient or his heirs, must comply. A large gift is usually asked to be returned when the obligated man happens to acquire a large sum of money. Such large sums may come from a pig feast given by the recipient of the gift who collects many shells for the meat sold by him, or at the occasion of his sister's or daughter's marriage when he receives the bride price. To ask the return of a gift at such an occasion is not only legal, but also moral.

Land can be a gift, but its return can always be asked for by the son of the donor. Ownership of land can be transferred only to one's heir or to one's daughter's husband, in case the donor has no sons. In such a case, the heir cannot take the land away from the son-in-law of the deceased man.

Investment. Since the Kapauku do not have legally collectable interest, credit cannot be considered an investment if by investment we mean a conversion of money into some commodity, activity, or security with the expectation of future monetary profit. The only economic investment a Kapauku can make is the conversion of currency into pigs or trade objects with the hope of selling the commodities for an increased price or of breeding the pigs and thus multiplying the original capital.

Surplus capital is not all invested in the above commodities. Accumulation of cash is an important institution which gives a Kapauku money whenever he needs it. Since there are no banks or legally collectable interest, the Papuan is content to deposit his shells in a cache among the rocks, or in some of the thousands of small caverns in the limestone cliffs of the Kamu Valley. A man's wife or mother can function as some sort of a bank by carrying her husband's or son's fortune in her net carrying bag. Ijaaj Jokagaibo of Itoda sold ten huge pigs at a feast and received 480 Km. From these he deposited 240 Km, an exact half, and the rest he spent on gifts, credit, and investments. While some of his savings were deposited with his mother and his first wife, the rest of them were hidden in a crevasse on the Jewei Mountain. They were to be used whenever the need should arise.

A special kind of savings is "*daa mege,* tabooed cowries." The owner of the capital imposes a taboo upon part of his savings and transfers these to the custody of his wife or mother. From the time of the imposition of the taboo, the owner is prohibited from using the money in his business transactions lest he become sick and his son die. The treasure is destined to be inherited after the man's death by his sons, in order to help them acquire wives and to give them a start on their way toward becoming *tonowi.*

Consumption. Since there are no clothes and few ornaments to buy, food constitutes the most important article of consumption. Except for pork and salt it is almost always produced by the household from different types of fields and through hunting, fishing, and gathering. Any harvested crop is always the property of a single individual. He brings it home and functions as a host to the rest of the household members. Everyone is expected to share his food with the rest of the co-residents. They, in turn, should share their supplies with him on the morrow. The owner of the sweet potatoes, meat, or vegetables has the right to distribute them himself and no one should touch the edibles prior to his consent. Since there is no way of preserving food, it is desirable that all crops be consumed on the same day they are gathered or on the following day. In order to coordinate the food providing activities of the household, and thus to assure a steady and adequate flow of edibles, the landlord acts as an informal authority who, through advice and consultations, apportions the duties and makes definite plans for the meals of each day. Since it is usually he who has several wives and many gardens, more of the supplies are expected to come from him. A woman never functions as host to the rest of the household. She must give food to her husband and sons, who, in turn, distribute it among the people. This, of course, does not prevent her from giving food to any other person she likes.

Since pork is quite an expensive food, the landlord, as the richest man of the group, is expected to supply most of it. The young and poorer members of the household repay with game which they occasionally trap or shoot. A rich man very seldom engages in hunting and, therefore, he appreciates a good meal of rats, opossum, wallabies, or fruit-bats provided for him by his son or another member of the household. Thus, although on the surface the sharing of food seems to be the consumption pattern of the Kapauku household, if analyzed, every situation is revealed to have a causal nexus relating a previous receipt of food with a present reciprocation.

THE FAMILY

The Nuclear Family

In fifteen out of sixteen Botukebo households, the nuclear family is incorporated into the extended family unit. Ijaaj Bunaibomuuma's household forms the only exception by being composed of two nuclear families and one polygynous family, none of which are closely related to each other. The absence of an extended family in this household is easily explained by the fact that Bunaibomuuma is a quarrelsome individual who, through embezzlement, fraud of various kinds, and even through outright stealing, antagonized many people including his brothers who, ashamed of their relative, left for another region of the Kapauku country.

Although the nuclear family is, as a rule, integrated within a larger kinship unit, there are some important functions left to it which set it off from the larger group. Especially its functions in education and social control classify the family as an autonomous unit. The father is the proper individual to punish and admonish his children, and the husband has exclusive authority over his wife. Consequently, the older of the two brothers who happens to be the head of the household has direct jurisdiction over his brother but never over his brother's wives and very seldom over the brother's offspring. If he punishes his nephews it is done only with his brother's consent. Indeed, from this aspect of social control the household looks like a mosaic picture composed of the individual stones of the nuclear families. The nuclear family is responsible for most of the educational functions, as we may recall from the discussion of the life cycle. Moreover, while financial help to a member of the household is considered a favor on the part of the donor, help to one's father, son, or brother when in need, is regarded as a moral duty. Inheritance also favors the nuclear family as the first unit from which heirs are recruited. Even in the field of food consumption, coherence of the smallest kin unit is felt. A man who shoots a wallaby or a giant rat usually feasts on it in the bush with his wife and his children. The latter are asked not to reveal the secret meal to the rest of the extended family.

In the following paragraphs we shall devote a few remarks to the relationships between specific members of the family.

1. Husband-wife relationship. The husband is the only authority to whom a married woman is subjected. No one else may harm her, unless she becomes involved in a fight with another woman. Individualism defines the property of the married couple as separate, and the husband has no right to take anything away from his wife. If he does so, the act always creates an obligation to repay in the future. The husband directs the wife's fieldwork and productive activity if he can. As has been stated already, in a few cases the reverse is true. In sexual matters the wife is required to be faithful to her husband while the latter is free as a butterfly to suck the nectar from any flower which is available. The wife sometimes helps her husband to acquire a new spouse. She acts as a go-between and even invites the girl to share her room.

2. Father-son relationship. The father functions as the authority, teacher, and the source of economic assistance in the form of gifts of fields and currency and of inheritance. With his son's maturation, the power of the father diminishes. In later years, when the son is an adult man, the old father is honored and serves as an advisor only. The emotional tie between the two is usually strong, although the writer saw several cases of the splitting up of households because the old men were unmanageable.

3. The father-daughter relationship. The relationship is characterized by a high degree of affection. The daughter performs minor services for her father, giving him presents in the form of food or money. The father in turn, protects a daughter against the punishing hand of her mother. This attachment is often interrupted at the time of the girl's marriage when the father tries to force her to follow his wishes. As time goes on, however, this spot on the otherwise clean record of a father's behavior is soon forgotten.

4. The mother-daughter relationship. This relationship parallels that of the father and son. The mother is the main educator in the family and she punishes her daughter in order to bring her up properly. However, during the crisis of the daughter's nuptials, the parents seem to exchange their roles. Then, it is the mother who protects and the father who punishes the daughter if she refuses to accept his choice of groom.

5. Mother-son relationship. This is analogous to that of the father and daughter with the exception that the affectionate relationship may be spoiled a little by brief beatings in infancy which are soon forgotten by the growing son. Very often the

mother protects her son from the father's punishment, and the surprised head of the household instead of the son may receive an unexpected beating. Thus among the Kapauku one hears the following notorious story: "And what happened after you ate all your father's pork?" "I watched my parents fight each other in order to decide whether I should be punished or not."

6. Older brother-younger brother relationship. When still small, the younger brother is often under considerable influence from his older sibling who may induce him to help in the household with the cooking, to work in the garden, and to accept advice on how to behave. If the age difference is considerable, the younger sibling may be reprimanded for disobedience. However, as soon as the boy reaches the age of fourteen, his brother tends to feel embarrassed if he orders the adolescent around. If the older brother happens to be the household authority, he exercises his influence upon the younger sibling through informal counseling which is usually well accepted. Common responsibility for delicts committed against outsiders forges a unity of interest which dictates automatic help in disputes and economic as well as financial assistance. However, a notorious criminal, such as Bunaibomuuma of Botukebo, is inevitably deserted by his brothers who, by terminating the common residence and association, declare their independence and in this way protect themselves against the retaliation of their brother's victims.

7. Older sister-younger sister relationship. Since there is no common responsibility of the female siblings, economic and legal bonds between the two are almost nonexistent. From childhood their finances are kept separate. They always have their own sections of garden to weed, and although fishing is done together, the catch is owned by each individual. The sororate being exceptional, marriage definitely separates the two sisters into different economic and residential units which, by belonging to different confederacies, may even be hostile toward each other. Nevertheless, sisters develop mutual bonds of emotion which urge them to frequent visiting after marriage and to mutual assistance in case of divorce or disease.

8. Brother-sister relationship. About this very affectionate relationship we may say that, except for the sexual role of a woman, a sister exhibits toward her unmarried brother a behavior pattern which is analogous to that of a wife. Like a spouse, she may weed her brother's gardens, plant sweet potatoes for him, and present the boy with a netful of sweet potatoes in the morning. She often functions as a go-between in the boy's love affairs and arranges dates for him with various girls. For such arrangements, if successful, she may be remunerated by thirty to forty beads or by a *dedege* necklace. The boy may reciprocate by imitating the husband's role and protecting his sister against outsiders. He makes gardens for her, helps her with weeding, buys pork for her, and proudly presents her with game he has bagged. At the time of a pig feast, he may let his sister wear his dog teeth or shell necklace, or even give it to her as a gift. Should his sister marry a man prior to the arrival of his own marriageable age, he usually feels jealous of the new husband who has interfered so suddenly with his emotional relationship. When Ijaaj Pilkiijebauwo, the daughter of Ijaaj Bunaibomuuma of Botukebo, was married to

Ijaaj Imopaj of Botukebo and resisted the change of residence, her nine year old brother, armed with a stick and crying loudly, attacked the husband as well as his own father who had consented to the marriage. If the sister is of marriageable age the affectionate relationship may be spoiled by the brother trying to force his sister into a profitable marriage. After what is usually a very short time of antagonism, the previous happy state of affection and respect is restored. The sister continues to lend money to her brother, to help him gain many wives, or even to work in her brother's garden. Her assistance to her brother is often accompanied by the protests of her husband. The brother's house is the place to which she would return in case of an unsuccessful marriage, and her brother is the man who would help her to break the unfortunate marital bond. Thus throughout life, the quasi-spouse roles of the siblings of the opposite sex interfere with marital duties, especially those of the female partner.

The Polygynous Family

The collected genealogies reveal approximately one third of all marriages to be polygynous, with an occasional man having as many as ten wives. Sororal polygyny, the sororate, and the levirate are permitted but are not preferential forms of mating. In 1955, out of the thirty-eight marriages in Botukebo, twelve, or thirty-one and a half per cent, were polygynous. Awiitigaaj held first place by having married ten women, and Timaajjokainaago, the beloved but cowardly *tonowi*, figures as second in this respect. However, the number of wives does not reflect only one's success in love. As we have seen, polygyny, fitting into the economic cycle of an individual's success in business, occupies a position of permanent importance with respect to the accumulation of wealth and consequently is indispensable for the acquisition of political and legal authority.

The organization of a polygynous family is characterized as follows. Every wife has her own room in the house. Her economy is independent of that of the co-wife and there is no sharing of property or pooling of wealth. Each wife, independently, supplies her husband with a netful of sweet potatoes twice a day. The sections of land that they cultivate are staked out with sticks in the gardens of their husbands. The yields of their areas belong to them, and they act as donors when they transfer the food to the men in their household. The husband, of course, has access to all the fields which are his, and whatever he harvests belongs to him. Cooperation between the co-wives is usually minimal. They refuse to help each other even in times of sickness. Thus, the only helper of the wife in a polygynous family is usually her mother or sister. In times of urgent need the husband may order some mutual assistance. However, this is seldom accomplished, and such an authoritarian decision usually results in a family crisis.

With few exceptions jealousy constitutes the main problem in the management of a polygynous family. The husband has to be very careful in assigning the garden plots to the care of his wives and in distributing meat, sugar cane, and other delicacies. He must avoid all favoritism and discrimination lest a fight between the co-wives result. In sexual matters, however, he is not required to rotate his attentions. The fact that almost all cohabitation takes place during the day in the fields makes it easy for the husband to gratify his momentary taste in selecting a partner. Nevertheless, long neglect of a wife makes the husband's cheating obvious to her and she can retaliate by beating the favorite co-wife or by destroying the husband's garden. Such rivalries may be the prelude to a divorce.

A special sort of hardship faces a husband who marries wives from two sibs between which intermarriage is prohibited. Although he is free to espouse females from either or both of the sibs, it is taboo for him to have sexual relations with one of the women less than seven days after doing so with the other. Should he violate the supernatural prohibition, he and his wives will die. "Believe me, this is hard to take," was a statement made in a convincing tone by Ijaaj Jokagaibo of Itoda who married Goo and Edowai girls. Although he has three other wives who can easily fill in the gap of seven days in his marital schedule, he still finds the taboo quite a problem.

All co-wives are equal to each other and no single one has a right to dominate another. The husband is the only authority and coordinating link in family activities.

Social control in the family is indicated in Figure 7.

The behavior, attitudes, and affection between half siblings can be defined as qualitatively the same as between full siblings, except for a diminished intensity caused by the natural priority of full brothers and sisters. The relation between the father's wife and her husband's children on the other hand, will always be influenced by the mutual attitudes and feelings of the co-wives. A range of relations, from almost maternal affection to ostracism, distrust, and hatred, is the reservoir of possibilities from which a group of these individuals may make a selection.

ADOPTION

The Kapauku institution of "*joka munii*, to bring up a child," presents a classificatory problem. In many cases, especially that of taking in an orphan, it approximates an adoption because of the man's acceptance of the child as his own. He gives it his own sib name and brings it up in the belief that the adoptive father is the real consanguineal parent. However, there are other, more important aspects, which classify the institution as a foster home, rather than one of adoption. Most of the "adoptees" are not taken into the new homes until they are four to seven years old. In this case, it is impossible for the man to pretend that his parenthood is real. Although the foster child is treated as a real son or daughter, it is always excluded from inheritance by the consanguineal heirs. As soon as the child grows to adulthood, he shakes off the sib name of the foster father and starts using his real one. The adolescent is made aware, if he or she does not know already, of his true sib and clan affiliation by some of his blood relatives and is urged to return to the village of his true parents. The foster father is remunerated for bringing up the child by *mune*, a reward of 5 Km payable at the time when the adolescent boy first becomes a co-sponsor of a *tapa*, blood reward ceremony. In the case of a girl, the foster parent receives the *mune* from the bride price paid by the girl's husband to her closest male blood relative. The relation of the foster child to the true children of the foster father is similar to the relations between half-siblings. The boys usually become "best friends." Although the whole affair of bringing up a foster child looks like a business deal, the emotional bond between the persons involved as well as their mutual support seems to be the most important aspect of this institution and the reason for its existence.

The Extended Family

A household is not necessarily identical with the extended family. Nevertheless, since the latter group is either coincident or fully integrated into the former, most of what has been said about social control, economy, and residential arrangements of the household is valid for both of the groups. In the following discussion we shall concentrate on the relationship patterns between the various relatives.

Kinship behavior. With regard to behavior toward Ego the consanguineal relatives fall into two broad categories. The first includes all male paternal relatives of Ego and their spouses with the exception of cross-cousins (*noone*), male Ego's sororal nephews (*naama*), and female Ego's fraternal nephews (*ani ooka*), and their spouses, e.g., paternal grandparents, male paternal parallel cousins with their wives, paternal uncles with their wives, and the reciprocal relatives of these. The second category comprises, in general, all remaining consanguineal relatives.

All relatives of the first category display behavior very similar to that of Ego's parents and siblings, naturally with diminishing intensity. The male relatives share in common with Ego legal responsibility toward any third person, duty for blood vengeance, and mutual liability for payment of the *dabe uwo*, reward for killing the assassin of one's relative. All of them also have the right to collect the *"me mege,* blood money,"* paid by the killer of one of the relatives. The members of this category (including the women) can be depended upon for help in buying a wife by contributing to the *kade* as well as to the *one* parts of the bride price. Visiting and helping with work in the fields for the customary payment is rather frequent. The individuals of the older generations function as coeducators of a boy or girl. They love them but do not hesitate to mete out occasional punishment. Toward the young girl, they behave affectionately. However, in case of her resistance to a marriage with a husband selected by her father, all these relatives support the father's choice, punish her, and try to induce her to accept the proposed husband. This category of relatives constitutes the more important source of one's financial support. There is no shame or embarrassment felt which would inhibit one from asking them for help.

The second category of blood relatives is residual to the first one. The relationships with these relatives are emotionally stronger than in the previous category. They are further characterized by the lack of common legal responsibility and by feelings of shame in asking for financial help. The duties of blood vengeance and sponsorship of the *tapa* are less intensive, and the right to collect blood money from the killer of one of these relatives is absent. The houses of these kinsmen function as asylums against parental wrath. However, the financial and judicial assistance is less than that obtained from members of the first category. The relatives, for example, do not contribute to the *one* part of the bride price at all.

Within this second category, the various relatives may be further subdivided into two groups according to some specific behavior patterns toward Ego. Maternal grandparents, all cross-cousins, maternal uncles, paternal aunts, and female paternal parallel cousins are more emotionally involved with the individual than are maternal parallel cousins and maternal aunts. While the affection of the former group results in indulgence, the other relatives are more objective. They criticize as well as punish by mild reprimands or, under very unusual circumstances, by spanking. The child or the adolescent obviously finds it more attractive to visit the relatives who never punish him. For this indulgence, the boy reciprocates through gifts of game. Most often this game consists of those species which are subjected to the totemic taboos of Ego's own sib but which are acceptable to some of these relatives as food. Particularly, the home of a mother's brother is considered a paradise. Although the amount of affection of the maternal uncle does not surpass that of the father's sister, as a male he is better able to resist anger and pressure from parents eager to punish their child. The parents may even wage a stick fight with the mother's brother to regain control over their misbehaving child. "I had such fun watching my father arguing or fighting with my mother's brother that I sometimes started trouble on purpose to enjoy it more often," confided Ijaaj Akaawoogi of Obajbegaa.

The relations with affinal relatives merit a few comments. In-law relatives may share the same household in case of exceptional matrilocal residence or at the time when the woman's old parents come to live with their married daughter. As in our culture, the mother-in-law and even the father-in-law are not people of whom one is expected to be particularly fond. Since especially the mother-in-law often visits and helps her daughter, as well as observes and criticizes her son-in-law's behavior, the development of the son-in-law's positive feelings is prevented. The relation of the man to his brother-in-law and that of the woman to her husband's sister, however, often develop into mutual respect and deep friendship. The young wife also quite often finds her mother-in-law a protector against the anger of her husband.

Ego's relations with his in-laws and with his consanguineal relatives of the second category exhibit some common features. In both cases we may observe the absence of common responsibility, the exclusion from the right to claim blood money paid by the relative's killer, as well as the duty of blood vengeance for the death of a relative of either category. The similarity is even more accentuated by the feeling of shame in asking for financial support, as well as by the willingness to become a co-sponsor of a "*tapa*, blood reward ceremony," given to honor the killer of the father-in-law's, brother-in-law's, or son-in-law's murderer. However, unlike the situation with the consanguineal relatives, one does not seek support from in-law relatives in case of marital troubles. Their house does not represent an asylum in any sense of the word; and the affectionate feelings, so characteristic of consanguineal relatives of the second category, are, if not sometimes entirely lacking, often rather weak. Since marriage can easily be terminated either by divorce or death, it is understandable that the potentially temporary bond does not equal the effect of permanent blood relationship.

To complete our discussion of kinship we shall give a brief outline of the Kapauku kinship terminology which is correlated with the patterns of behavior described above. It is of the Iroquois type.

Kinship terminology. Kapauku kinship terms may be divided into two categories: the first includes "absolute terms" which are applied to an individual irrespective of the speaker and thus may be used by anybody; the second category is made up of "relative terms" which define a relation between the speaker and the person spoken or referred to.

Absolute terms:

1. *Ibo, ibome:* oldest of male siblings born by a woman to a man. Thus there may be as many *ibo* sons of a man as there are wives. A given woman has sons called *ibo* as often as she remarries and bears a son.
2. *Ipouga, ipougame:* second oldest male sibling with the above specifications.
3. *Mabii, mabiime:* siblings of either sex between the second born and the last born of the same sex with the above specifications.
   a) *Degemabii:* The third born of the siblings of either sex with the above specifications.
   b) *Bunamabii:* the fourth born of the siblings of either sex with the above specifications.
   c) *Kepagamabii:* the fifth born of the siblings of either sex with the above specifications.
   Note: Terms 3a to 3c are used only if there are several persons called *mabii.* This is the case only if a woman bears five or more children of the same sex to the same husband.
4. *Amoje, amojeme:* the last born of the male siblings with specifications given under 1.
5. *Oumau, oumaume:* the first born of female siblings with specifications given under 1.
6. *Maga, magame:* the second born of female siblings with specifications given under 1.
7. *Amaadii, amaadiime:* the last born of female siblings with specifications given under 1.
8. *Enaago:* an individual of either sex with no siblings of the same sex.
9. *Epame:* the first wife.
10. *Jupikaame:* the second wife.
11. *Imoudame:* the last wife.

12. *-pa:* a suffix added to the above eleven terms connoting an offspring of either sex. Thus, *Ibopa* means a son or daughter of *Ibo*. In the cases of 9, 10, and 11, the suffix *-me* (man) is dropped and replaced by *-pa: Imoudapa.* In case of 9, to avoid immediate repetition of the same syllables (*epaapa*) *ko* (demonstrative feminine article) is inserted: *epakopa.*

13. *Aejoka:* a baby.

14. *Peujoka:* a child up to seven years.

15. *Bebej:* a male child between two and seven years.

16. *Ejaajta:* a child between seven and sixteen years.

17. *Api:* an unmarried girl with grown breasts.

18. *Agaana:* an adolescent male.

19. *Jame:* an adult male.

20. *Jagamo:* an adult woman.

21. *Jedema:* an old bachelor, unmarried, older than twenty-three years.

22. *Jokaago:* a man or woman who has children.

23. *Ejai takimijo wageta:* an individual with married children.

24. *Ibo bagee:* old people (with gray hair).

25. *Wakaago:* a married person.

26. *Adama:* an old individual of either sex (with gray hair).

Relative terms:

1. *Noone:* a child of a father's female bilateral consanguineal kinsman of his generation or of the mother's male bilateral consanguineal kinsman of her generation. E.g., FaSiCh, MoBrCh, FaFaSiDaCh, FaMoBrDaCh; but not, for example, FaFaSiSoCh, MoFaSiDaCh.

2. *Ani ijoka:* a child of a mother's female consanguineal kinsman of her generation. E.g., MoSiCh, MoFaBrDaCh, MoFaSiDaCh, MoMoBrDaCh; but not, for example, MoFaBrSoCh, MoMoSiSoCh, MoMoBrSoCh.

3. *Ani paneka:* a consanguineal kinsman of the opposite sex who is a child of the father or of his male bilateral consanguineal kinsman of his generation. E.g., male speaking: Si, FaFaBrSoDa, FaMoBrSoDa; female speaking: Br, FaBrSo, FaFaSiSoSo, FaMoBrSoSo; but not, for example, female speaking: FaMoBrDaSo; male speaking: FaFaBrDaDa.

4. *Ani weneka:* a younger consanguineal kinsman of the same sex and generation who is a child of Ego's father or of Ego's father's male bilateral consanguineal kinsman. E.g., male speaking: yBr, yFaBrSo, yFaFaBrSoSo, yFaFaSiSoSo; female speaking: ySi, yFaBrDa, yFaFaSiSoDa; but not, for example, male speaking: yFaFaSiDaSo.

5. *Nauwa:* for a male Ego, an older member of the same sex and generation who is a child of Ego's father or of Ego's father's male bilateral kinsman. E.g., male speaking: oBr, oFaBrSo, oFaMoBrSoSo; but not, for example, male speaking: oFaFaBrDaSo, oFaMoBrDaSo.

6. *Anibai:* for a female Ego, an older member of the same sex and generation who is a child of Ego's father or of Ego's father's male bilateral consan-

guineal kinsman. E.g., female speaking: oSi, oFaBrDa, oFaFaSiSoDa; but not, for example, female speaking: oFaFaSiDaDa, oFaFaBrDaDa.

7. *Anepa:* a member of the same sex and generation who is a child of Ego's father's male bilateral consanguineal kinsman. E.g., male speaking: FaBrSo, FaFaBrSoSo; female speaking: FaBrDa, FaFaSiSoDa; but not, for example, FaMoBrDaCh.

8. *Naitai:* father.

9. *Niikai:* mother.

10. *Naita:* a father's male bilateral consanguineal kinsman of the father's generation. E.g., FaBr, FaFaBrSo, FaFaSiSo, FaMoSiSo.

11. *Niika:* a mother's female bilateral consanguineal kinswoman of her generation. E.g., MoSi, MoMoSiDa, MoMoBrDa, MoFaSiDa, MoFaBrDa. This term is also used for step-mother in a polygynous or monogamous family.

12. *Naama:* a) a mother's male bilateral consanguineal kinsman of her generation. E.g., MoBr, MoFaBrSo, MoFaSiSo, MoMoSiSo, MoMoBrSo.

   b) For a male Ego, a child of a female bilateral consanguineal kinswoman of Ego's generation. E.g., male speaking: SiCh, FaBrDaCh, MoSiDaCh, FaSiDaCh.

13. *Ani ooka:* a) a father's female bilateral consanguineal kinswoman of his generation. E.g., FaSi, FaFaBrDa, FaFaSiDa, FaMoSiDa.

   b) For a female Ego, a child of a male bilateral consanguineal kinsman of Ego's generation. E.g., female speaking: BrCh, FaBrSoCh, MoBrSoCh, MoSiSoCh, FaSiSoCh.

   c) Loosely extended to female consanguineal relatives of the second ascending generation who are also called *ani muuma.* E.g., FaMo, MoMo, FaMoMoSiDa.

   d) Loosely extended to the wives of male consanguineal relatives of the second ascending generation who are also called *ani muuma.* E.g., FaFaBrWi, MoFaBrWi.

   e) Loosely extended to the wives of Ego's spouse's male consanguineal relatives of the second ascending generation who are also called *ani muuma.* E.g., WiFaFaBrWi, HuMoFaBrWi.

   f) Loosely extended by a female Ego to the reciprocals of the kin-types of 13c, 13d, 13e. E.g., female speaking: SoCh, DaCh, BrDaCh; HuBrSoCh, HuBrDaCh; HuBrSoDaHu, HuBrDaSoWi.

14. *Ani joka:* the child of Ego or of a bilateral consanguineal kinsman of the same sex and generation. E.g., male speaking: Ch, BrCh, FaBrSoCh, FaSiSoCh, FaFaBrSoSoCh, MoBrSoCh; female speaking: Ch, SiCh, FaBrDaCh, FaSiDaCh, FaFaBrSoDaCh, MoBrDaCh; but not, for example, male speaking: SiCh, FaSiCh.

15. *Ani muuma:* a) a bilateral consanguineal kinsman of the second ascending or descending generations. E.g., FaFa, FaMo, MoMo, MoFa, FaFaFaBrSo, MoMoMoSiDa, SoSo.

   b) A spouse of a bilateral consanguineal kinsman of the second ascending

generation. E.g., FaFaBrWi, FaMoSiHu, MoMoBrWi, MoMoSiHu, Mo-
FaBrWi, MoFaSiHu.

c) A spouse's bilateral consanguineal kinsman of the second descending
generation. E.g., HuBrSoSo, WiSiSoDa.

d) Extended as an alternative term (in place of *ani baaka*) to a spouse's
bilateral consanguineal kinsman of the second ascending generation, and
to his spouse. E.g., HuFaFa, HuFaFaBrWi, HuMoMo, HuMoFa, Hu-
FaMo, HuMoFaBrWi.

e) Extended as an alternative term (in place of *ani baaka*) to a spouse of a
bilateral consanguineal kinsman of the second descending generation, and
to a spouse of the spouse's bilateral consanguineal kinsman of the second
descending generation. E.g., SoSoWi, DaDaHu, DaSoWi, SoDaHu;
HuBrSoSoWi, WiSiSoDaHu.

16. *Ani aija:* A bilateral kinsman of Ego or of Ego's spouse, of the third ascending or descending generation, or his respective spouse, analogous to the
kin-types called *ani muuma*.

17. *Ani pigoka:* A bilateral kinsman of Ego or of Ego's spouse, of the fourth
ascending or descending generation, or his respective spouse, analogous to
the kin-types called *ani muuma*.

18. *Ani baaka:* a) a spouse of a bilateral consanguineal kinsman of the same
generation and of the opposite sex. E.g., male speaking: SiHu, FaBrDaHu,
MoSiDaHu.

b) A spouse's bilateral consanguineal kinsman of the same generation and
opposite sex. E.g., WiBr, HuSi, WiMoBrSo, HuFaBrDa, WiFaBrSo.

c) A spouse of a bilateral consanguineal kinsman of any of the descending
generations. E.g., DaHu, SoWi, SoSoWi, FaBrDaSoWi, MoBrSoSoWi.

d) A spouse's bilateral consanguineal kinsman of any of the ascending generations. E.g., WiFa, WiMo, HuFa, HuMo, WiMoBr, HuFaFaBrSo,
WiFaFa, HuFaMo, HuMoFa, HuFaMoBr.

e) A spouse of the spouse's bilateral consanguineal kinsman of any of the
ascending generations. E.g., WiMoBrWi, HuFaFaBrSoWi, WiMoMoBr-
DaHu, HuFaFaBrWi.

f) A spouse of the spouse's bilateral consanguineal kinsman of any of the
descending generations. E.g., WiBrSoWi, WiBrDaHu, HuBrSoWi.

19. *Ani geeka:* a) a spouse of a bilateral consanguineal kinsman of Ego's generation and sex. E.g., male speaking: BrWi, MoBrSoWi, MoSiSoWi; female
speaking: SiHu, MoBrDaHu.

b) A spouse's bilateral consanguineal kinsman of the same generation and
sex (as the spouse). E.g., HuBr, WiSi, WiFaBrDa, HuFaSiSo, WiFaSiDa.

20. *Ani wape:* a) a spouse of a female bilateral consanguineal kinsman of the
first ascending generation. E.g., FaSiHu, FaFaBrDaHu, FaFaSiDaHu,
FaMoBrDaHu, MoSiHu, MoMoSiDaHu.

b) A wife's bilateral consanguineal kinsman of the first descending generation. E.g., WiSiCh, WiBrCh, WiFaBrDaCh, WiMoBrSoCh.

21. *Naamai:* a) a spouse of a male bilateral consanguineal kinsman of the first ascending generation. E.g., FaBrWi, FaFaBrSoWi, FaFaSiSoWi, FaMo-BrSoWi, MoBrWi, MoMoBrSoWi, MoFaSiSoWi.

b) A husband's bilateral consanguineal kinsman of the first descending generation. E.g., HuSiCh, HuBrCh, HuFaBrSoCh.

22. *Ani waka:* the spouse.

23. *Ani geeto:* a spouse of the spouse's bilateral consanguineal kinsman of the same generation. E.g., WiBrWi, HuSiHu, WiSiHu, HuBrWi, WiFaBr-DaHu, HuFaBrSoWi.

PART III: RULES AND DISPUTES IN THE KAPAUKU SOCIETY

THE title of this monograph, *Kapauku Papuans and their Law*, refers to one of the traditional concepts of Western society which has not been generally utilized in anthropological studies. The most important reason for this is that law has not been defined in a way that is satisfactory to most ethnographers.

There are many theories, some of them contradictory, that define law by differentiating it from custom. W. G. Sumner (1938: 911), for example, claims that laws are positive, while mores are undefined and unformulated. Giorgio del Vecchio (1938: 931) is of the contrary opinion and says that laws have their concrete existence in customs. Even if an ethnographer were to select one of the existing theories of law, the differentiation of law from other social phenomena is usually so unprecise and vague as to militate against the use of the concept as a tool for analysis. Many theories provide no objective criteria to guide the ethnographer, and as a result he completely omits the category of law from his monograph.

If we turn for help from the confused situation in our literature to the Kapauku, we find that they themselves have not surpassed our writers on law in solving the problem of conceiving of a workable category of phenomena which could be called law. "*Kou dani te tija, kou dani daa*, one does not act like this, this is prohibited," is a common phrase one hears in various disputes coming from the lips of important *tonowi*. However, if we were to think of the word "*daa*, prohibited," as associated only with matters under dispute, we would be far from comprehending its meaning. It does not, by any means, confine itself to prohibitions made by the native authorities, or to those embodied in customary regulations of the relations between man and man. A nonpunishable breach of etiquette, a prohibition sanctioned by the supernatural as well as by the society, a purely religious taboo which defines a relation between an individual and the supernatural and the violation of which does not concern anybody else except the actor, and, finally, a moral but not enforced creed, all these various phenomena are assigned the same name.

Since this part of the monograph should furnish us with material for the analysis of the Kapauku legal system and thus provide us with data against which the author's theory of law may be checked, any arbitrary selection made on the part of the author might be suspected of preconception. Thus it seems advisable to make a compromise and, while including in the following investigation examples from every aspect of the Kapauku concept of *daa*, to concentrate upon those prohibitions the violations of which give rise to disputes among living people. Unlike *daa*, the phrase "*mana koto*, the dispute," is a clearly defined behavioral concept which always involves the party making an accusation and the accused.

In the following description of the violations of prohibitions, we shall in every instance state first the ideal rule, *daa*, and afterwards list the concrete *mana koto*, cases pertaining to it. Thus, in the introductory abstract statement about a type of relation, we shall present the ideal rule for behavior and the following cases will constitute the actual counterpart to the rule. In other words, the ideal "what should be done" in case of a violation of a prohibition will be juxtaposed to what actually is done.

The material on most of the 176 cases of disputes and all the 121 abstract rules has been obtained from informants. During the sessions with these informants there were always several, sometimes as many as twenty, individuals present who would check the narrator on his accuracy and who would fill in the gaps in his memory. An additional verification has usually been obtained from other people at a later date, in the absence of the original informants. There are also several cases which were witnessed by the author himself, which fact will always be indicated by an asterisk. Since the author does not see any reason for being secretive about the identity of the persons involved in the disputes, actual but abbreviated names of all the participants, together with the places and approximate dates will be made available to the reader.[8] Because it would have involved unnecessary repetition, inclusion of impertinent data, and a way of expression not understandable to the reader who is not familiar with the Kapauku language and culture, both the rules and the cases are not presented in the original wording. If, for various reasons, it seems necessary to introduce the original version, the translation is marked by quotations.

All the disputes have been grouped into categories which have been assigned names by the author. This classification, based upon the content of the prohibition rather than on such things as function, problems of justice, and nature of authority, has been arrived at through the author's conceptualisation. Relying primarily upon the native classification manifested by the few legal concepts present in the Kapauku language, and secondarily upon his legal background, the author, through long discussions with informants and work with the material, organized the legal cases in the following manner. Since the classificatory headings and the groupings of the types of cases according to their content are only for the benefit of the reader and bear little relation to the analytic part which concludes this monograph, the use of impression as a criterion of organization may be considered justified.

The rules and cases of disputes are presented in five main categories: offences against persons, against rights in things, against contractual agreement, against and by authority, and against society. Every category will be further subdivided according to the subject, and the cases arranged, as far as the knowledge of the dates permits, in chronological order. Comments on some aspects significant for our later discussion will be attached to individual cases.

OFFENCES AGAINST PERSONS

The cases described in this chapter all have in common the feeling of the Kapauku that the particular offence has been directed toward a specific person, injuring the

---

[8] In the third part of the monograph all native names have been abbreviated to the first two letters of the sib name, to the first three letters of the given name, and to the first four letters of the name of the person's village; for example: Ijaaj Ekajewaijokaipouga of Aigii has been reduced to Ij Eka of Aigi.

integrity of the latter without being mediated through loss of goods, breach of an agreement, or insubordination to the injured person's authority. Contrary to the expectation of a lawyer, our traditional criminal delicts, such as murder or rape, are classified together with sorcery and breaking of taboos, as well as with purely "civil cases," such as divorce, disputes over bride price payment, and those associated with matchmaking. Killing by sorcery, by an arrow, or by violation of an eating taboo constitutes an identical crime according to the Kapauku. Paying a low bride price for a man's daughter or sister is equivalent to a verbal insult or an attack with a stick, although on the surface. the marital cases may give an impression of a business deal. One never becomes violent while bargaining for a pig, but it is very common to have a fight instead of a wedding.

MURDER

For the classical Western concept of intentional killing of a man without resorting to supernatural means, there is no special term in the Kapauku language. The expression *"me wagimakai*, to kill a man," refers primarily to the result of the action rather than to the motivation or deliberateness of the action. However, since intention and premeditation, which are causally connected with being sentenced to death, carry a legal importance, the author feels justified in introducing this category.

Rule 1: a) Premeditated killing of a member of one's own sib is punished by execution with an arrow, administered by close relatives of the culprit; usually his own brother discharges the first arrow.

b) Premeditated killing of a member of one's own political confederacy, who belongs to a different sib, is punished after extradition by the members of the killer's sib. The execution is administered in the manner described above by close sib relatives of the killed man.

c) Killing outside of the political unit is not punishable (a war usually results).

Case 1.

  Place: Kojo.

  Date: ca. 1938.

  Parties:

    a) *Defendant:* Ij Tid of Kojo.

    b) *Murdered man:* Ij Ina of Obaj.

    c) *Authority:* Ij Uga of Kojo (now dead, father of the present *tonowi*, Amo).

Facts: The Ij-Pi confederacy was at war with the Goo people from the south. For no other apparent reason than self-aggrandizement, the defendant ambushed Ina, shot him, and delivered the string of his bow to the enemy, for which he collected *dabe uwo*, the reward.

Aggravating circumstances: The defendant was known to have stolen garden crops and pigs. The murder occurred during a war, and the payment of a reward by the enemy brought shame upon the confederacy.

Outcome: The authority wanted to execute the criminal but commuted the sentence—after a plea for leniency submitted by the brothers of the defendant—to public reprimand and flogging, which lasted several days. The punishment was executed by the authority and the brothers of the defendant. The latter accepted the beating with remorse. The son of the dead man wanted to shoot the culprit but was prevented from doing so by the authority.

The culprit was not asked to pay blood money to the close relatives of the victim.

Comment: Request for leniency and the remorse of the culprit seem to have effected a lighter sentence. The man is today a respectable member of the confederacy. He lives in Kojo and has ceased to be a notorious criminal.

Case 2.
  Place: Kego (South Kamu).
  Date: ca. 1948
  Parties:
      a) *Defendant:* Ed Tun of Dege.
      b) *Murdered man:* Iw Gek of Kego.
      c) *Authority:* Ed Pai of Dege.
      d) *Executioner:* younger brother of the killed man.
      e) *Man executed:* Ed Tod of Dege (FaBrSo of the murderer).

Facts: Someone had destroyed the traps of Gek. He charged the defendant with the crime and a stickfight resulted. A few days later the defendant murdered Gek by shooting him from ambush.

Outcome: Although the murdered man belonged to a different political unit, the authority, in order to prevent war, extradited the defendant to the Iw people for punishment. Since the culprit escaped into the jungle and could not be found for approximately ten months, the brother of the murdered man lost his patience and killed the FaBrSo of the refugee. Thus the dead on both sides were matched and peace restored.

The murderer, however, had to pay blood money to the older brother of the victim of the enemy's revenge. He paid: 60 Km, 60 Tm, one small female pig, and one large male pig worth 12 Km.

Comment: Contrary to the rule, the killer of a man from another confederacy was extradited to the enemy. This case exemplifies also the common responsibility of parallel cousins for delicts against outsiders.

Case 3.
  Place: Dogi, Debei Valley.
  Date: ca. 1953.
  Parties:
      a) *Defendant:* An Dek of Dogi.
      b) *Victim:* Ed Tid of Dogi.
      c) *Authority:* An Pot of Dogi.
      d) *Executioner:* An Mou of Dogi, SiSo of victim.

Facts: People were arguing in the bush near the home of the defendant. He became angry and shot into the group of men, wounding Tid. The victim died four days later.

Outcome: The victim's sister's son, later on the day of the shooting, entered the culprit's house and shot the latter to death. The authority called the case closed and urged relatives on both sides to make peace.

Comment: The decision of the authority confirmed the revenge as righteous.

Case 4.
  Place: Mogo, South Kamu Valley.
  Date: June or July, 1954.
  Parties:
   a) *Defendant:* Ti Jaj of Mogo.
   b) *Murdered man:* Pi Meb of Obaa (Debei).
   c) *Authority:* Ti Mab of Mogo.

Facts: The defendant and Pi Meb had gone into the woods together. In the evening, the defendant returned alone and announced that the other man had fallen from a tree and died. However, he refused to lead people to the place of the accident. About twenty people combed the forests and finally found the corpse bearing a deep wound in the face, apparently inflicted by a stick. Since the defendant was reluctant to bring the search party to the place, and because the body lay in a very soft terrain full of rotten leaves and moss, which could not account for the deep wound, the defendant was charged with murder.

Outcome: The defendant and the murdered man were from two different political units. To prevent war, the authority ordered blood money to be paid to the Pi people of Obaa. Close relatives of the defendant delivered 180 Km and 240 Tm to the brothers of the victim. The defendant was reprimanded for several days, but he escaped any bodily injury.

Case 5.
  Place: Mogo, South Kamu Valley.
  Date: ca. 1954.
  Parties:
   a) *Defendant:* Ko Pud of Mogo.
   b) *Murdered men:*
       Ko Ipo of Moga, older brother of the defendant.
       Ko Puj of Moga, younger brother of the defendant.
   c) *Authority:* Ko Mab of Moga.

Facts: Pud became insane when about seven years of age. He talked about lots of things people could not understand, he laughed when he was not supposed to, and was angry when everybody enjoyed himself. However, he did not bother anybody, worked on his fields, and lived with his brothers and mother in Moga. In

1954, unprovoked, he killed his older brother with a bamboo-tipped arrow while the latter was asleep. He escaped into the woods where he remained hidden for thirty days. Then he appeared again and ambushed his younger brother on a path to the fields. He shot him to death and tried to run away from the scene of the murder. This time, however, he was shot three times in his chest and abdomen by the people who were working in the near-by fields. Badly wounded, he succeeded in eluding his pursuers and disappeared in the jungle. Nobody heard from him for about two months. Suddenly he appeared again in the village, completely recovered from the wounds which all the people had considered lethal.

Outcome: The people were of the opinion that only an evil spirit could have helped him survive. Because of his recovery from the attempted execution and because of the Dutch administration's plea against violence, the authority asked that his life be spared. In consequence, the man was allowed to go on living in his house with his old mother.

Comment: Insanity does not excuse a man for having committed murder. Unsuccessful execution, however, tends to preclude further punishment for the past crime.

ATTEMPTED MURDER

Rule 2: A man is responsible only for the result of his actions. Thus for injuring somebody in murderous assault, the man should be injured to the same extent.

Case 6.
  Place: Aigi.
  Date: ca. 1950.
  Parties:
    a) *Defendant:* Ij Utu of Aigi.
    b) *Wounded man:* Ij Deg of Aigi, brother of the defendant.
    c) *Executioner:* Ij Amo of Aigi, younger brother of the defendant.
    d) *Authority:* Ij Eka of Aigi.

Facts: The two brothers quarreled about the boundaries between their fields. Utu, enraged, shot his older brother in the abdomen and escaped. The victim, however, survived.

Outcome: Eka declared the deed a crime and urged the younger brother of the culprit to shoot the latter, but not to kill him. Amo found the defendant in the woods and wounded him with his arrow in the leg. The case was regarded as closed, because of the matched injuries.

Comment: If a crime happens within a family or a community, the closest kin (brother or parallel paternal cousin) are the executioners. The case again illustrates the matching of injury on both sides, the Kapauku balance of justice.

MANSLAUGHTER BY ACCIDENT

Rule 3: Killing of an individual from the same sib or political unit, if done by accident, is not punishable by execution. The reason for this leniency is that the defendant has not intended to kill. However, the defendant is required to pay blood money to the nearest kin of the dead man.

Killing an individual from another political unit is equivalent to murdering him.

Comment: The rule clearly indicates the importance of intention. In this respect, Kapauku reasoning parallels Western legal thinking. Killing, however, also brings an economic loss to the household and close relatives and has to be compensated for by payment of blood money.

The rule also shows the irrelevance of intention outside the political unit, where a legal process would be replaced either by war or payment.

Case 7.
  Place: Tugu, South Kamu Valley.
  Date: ca. 1953.
  Parties:
    a) *Defendant:* Ij Aba of Tugu.
    b) *Victims:*
        Pi Uwo of Kebo (married woman).
        Pi Ama of Kebo (maiden).
        Pi Amo of Kebo (small boy).
    c) *Surviving passenger:* Pi Mab of Kebo.
    d) *Authority:* Go Ota of Tugu.

Facts: The defendant was fishing in the Edege River. The Pi people wanted to cross the stream and called for transportation. When they were crossing the river, the canoe tipped over in the middle of the stream and three of the passengers drowned. The relatives of the dead people came to the village of the defendant's husband and asked for blood money. One of them was dressed in a white man's trousers and pretended to have a friend in the Dutch police force. Thus, he hoped to induce the defendant to pay blood money.

Outcome: The village authority asked the husband of the defendant to pay the indemnity. However, the authority did not feel that justice had been done. He wanted only to avoid trouble and potential war by the advice he gave. "Since they (passengers) asked for transportation, Aba was not responsible for the accident. However, we wanted to avoid war and, therefore, her (defendant's) spouse paid 60 Km and 60 Tm as blood money," said the authority.

Comment: The case is an example of a diplomatic settlement between two political units. The decision of the authority, however, may be considered as legal as far as it resulted in the payment made by the resident of the authority's village.

Case 8.
  Place: Aigi.
  Date: ca. 1950.

Parties:
   a) *Defendant:* Go Mab of Aigi.
   b) *Victim:* Ij Dou of Obaj.
   c) *Authority:* Ij Eka of Aigi.
      Ij Jok of Itod.
   d) *Executioner:* Go Deg of Tugu (older brother of defendant).
   e) *Collector of indemnity:* Ij Deg of Obaj (brother of the victim).

Facts: Adolescents were playing around a fire at night, and the defendant unintentionally pushed a girl into the fire. She succumbed to burns the next day.

Outcome: The boy was punished by a mild beating administered by Jok and his older brother. However, all the authorities helped him to pay the indemnity of 120 Km, 180 Tm, one ax, and one long *dedege* necklace.

Comment: The boy, though from another sib, was punished as well as helped by authorities from the place of his own residence. Thus, residence rather than sib affiliation determined the jurisdiction.

Case 9.
   Place: Moma, North Kamu Valley.
   Date: ca. 1948.
   Parties:
   a) *Defendant:* Go Ipo of Moma.
   b) *Killer:* Bo Boo of Okog.
   c) *Victim:* Bo Ama of Okog (sister of killer and lover of defendant).
   d) *Authority:* Bo Ipo of Okog.

Facts: At a pig feast in North Kamu, Go Ipo, who was disliked by Boo, courted the latter's sister. She returned his affection. Her brother became so enraged by her disobedience that he shot her in the thigh, without intending to hurt her seriously. However, the arrow severed an artery and the girl bled to death. The grief stricken brother tried unsuccessfully to kill other women to relieve his grief.

Outcome: Public opinion condemned the brutal act of the brother. However, the authority, complying with law, sentenced the courting boy to pay 120 Km, one pig, one *dedege* necklace, and some beads to the brother. The latter's right to control the courting of his sister, her disobedience, as well as the lover's interference over the protests of the brother were the reasons behind the decision.

Comment: The responsibility for consequences of an illegal action which figures as *causa sine qua non* is demonstrated in this case. The lover, though his action did not directly cause the accident, was held responsible for the death because it would not have occurred were it not for his illegal interference with the brother's authority.

Rule 4: Death by neglect should be punished by beating and reprimand. When a beating is administered, no payment is made.

Case 10.

Place: Botu.

Date: ca. 1900.

Parties:

    a) *Defendant:* Ij Ipo of Aigi.

    b) *Victim:* Ij Ibo of Botu.

    c) *Authority:* Ij Don of Botu.

Facts: Adolescents and adults were playing *kimutii*, a game simulating war, with blunt arrows. The defendant mistakenly discharged a war arrow which penetrated through the eye socket into the brain of the victim. The killer, frightened by his deed, escaped to the Tigi area.

Outcome: The defendant chose lifelong banishment rather than to endure the beating, shame, and public reprimand, and thereafter made his home in Kadi, Tigi area.

Comment: Self-imposed banishment is considered an adequate punishment for the crime, and people refrain from further molestation of the defendant.

Case 11.

Place: Kojo.

Date: ca. 1953.

Parties:

    a) *Defendant:* Wa Pak of Kege.

    b) *Passengers who survived:* Wa Mab of Kojo.

       Ti Oum of Mogo (daughter of Mab).

    c) *Victim:* Ti Ama of Mogo (daughter of Mab).

    d) *Authority:* Ij Eke of Aigi.

    e) *Executioners:* Ij Peu of Aigi (father of the victim).

       Brothers of the culprit (live in Kojo).

Facts: The defendant transported three passengers across the Edege River. During the crossing, she played and jerked the canoe until it tipped over. Ama drowned and the culprit escaped into the woods, where she remained in hiding for ten months. During this time her husband died. Finally, she was captured and brought to Kojo where her brothers lived. Since she was then a widow, this was her home and her brothers regained power over her.

Outcome: The authority recommended flogging and reprimand which lasted ten days. The father of the victim and the brothers of the defendant administered the flogging.

Comments: The case shows again that residence determines jurisdiction and that corporal punishment precludes financial responsibility.

BATTERY

Rule 5: Battery is punishable by beating and reprimand, or by a payment proportionate to the delict.

Case 12.

    Place: Kojo.

    Date: ca. 1952.

    Parties:

        a) *Defendant:* Ij Amo of Kojo.

        b) *Victim:* Ij Iib of Aigi.

        c) *Authority:* Ij Eka of Aigi.

Facts: Amo had lost three arrows and thought that Iib had stolen them. He struck Iib several times over the head with a stick, producing two deep, bleeding wounds.

Outcome: The authority decided to beat the culprit, but the latter offered a large *woti* shell, which was accepted.

Comments: The defendant avoided punishment by the payment. Since he himself was an authority and the plaintiff was from another village, Eka, the head of the lineage, functioned as proper authority.

Case 13.

    Place: Kojo.

    Date: 1954.

    Parties:

        a) *Defendant:* Ij Amo of Kojo.

        b) *Victim:* Ij Ema of Kojo (younger brother of defendant).

        c) *Authorities:* Ij Eka of Aigi.

               Ij Awi of Botu.

               Ij Jok of Itod.

               Pi Peg of Obaj.

Facts: Amo was known as an emotional individual and a troublemaker. In the summer of 1954, he wanted to buy a quarter of a pig from his brother for a ridiculous price of 5 Km. The owner of the pork refused to sell. Amo started a stickfight in which his brother suffered lacerations on the head.

Outcome: The authorities decided on public reprimand which lasted one day.

Comments: This case represents the absence of indemnity payment when other punishment is administered. Because Amo himself is an authority, the headmen from all the villages of the lineage participated in the trial. As the leader of the lineage and confederacy, Eka's word, however, carried most weight.

ATTEMPTED SUICIDE

Suicides are usually committed only by women. Drowning is their most frequent technique. The act is considered immoral and a personal offense to the "owner of the woman," the individual who paid her bride price or who is entitled to it when she gets married.

Rule 6: Attempted suicide is punishable by a beating administered by the "woman's owner."

Case 14.

  Place: Bibi.

  Date: ca. 1953.

  Parties:

  a) *Defendant:* Go Ama of Bibi.

  b) *Man whom she was forced to marry:* Ti Eto of Mogo.

  c) *Authorities:* Her brother and father.

  d) *Man whom she finally married:* Ij Jok of Ito.

Facts: The girl was being forced to marry a man she did not like. She attempted suicide several times in order to prevent the marriage. She was always saved from the river or captured on its bank.

Outcome: Every time she attempted a suicide, she was beaten severely afterwards. Since she did not stop, her brother and father consented to her marriage with Jok whom she loved.

Sorcery

Killing by witchcraft constitutes the most common medium for revenge used against a personal enemy who belongs to another political unit. In the Mapia area, most wars start because of sorcery; while in Kamu, divorce and adultery prove to be more important in this respect. Nevertheless, even in this area sorcery accounts for about thirty per cent of the conflicts. Sorcery is very seldom used against a person from the same village or political unit. The case given below is the only one the writer could collect from all his informants. The second case is just an illustration from many notes on sorcery occurring between individuals of two political units. Since war belongs to politics rather than to the legal sphere, one example should be sufficient for illustration.

Case 15.

  Place: Ekau, North Kamu Valley.

  Date: ca. 1934.

  Parties

  a) *Defendant:* Ka Ibo of Mauw.

  b) *Victim:* Ga Gej of Ekau.

  c) *Executioner:* Ga Ged of Ekau (older brother of the victim).

  d) *Authority:* Man from the same village, name forgotten.

Facts: Gej married a girl the sorcerer loved. The successful suitor died shortly after the wedding, and his death was attributed to the revenge of Ka Ibo. The leader in the village was of the same opinion and recommended capital punishment. The older brother of the victim shot the sorcerer.

Outcome: The relatives of Ka Ibo refrained from any revenge and the case was considered closed.

Comment: Death following a quarrel is enough evidence of sorcery if the defendant is known as an expert in this art.

Case 16.

   Place: Tuge, Kamu Valley.
   Date: ca. 1935.
   Parties:
      a) *Defendant:* An Mou of Tuge.
      b) *Victim:* Du Oka of Mauw, North Kamu Valley.

   Facts: Oka stole a pig from Mou. A short time afterwards the thief died. Since -the two men were from different political units, and Mou was a reputed sorcerer, the crime of sorcery was regarded as proven.

   Outcome: War resulted in which eight sibs participated and seventy people were killed.

   Comment: This case is clearly outside the scope of law because of the war and the interpolitical unit quality of the case.

TABOO

Unlike the people of Polynesia, the Kapauku do not regard taboos or the prohibitions vested with supernatural sanctions which rest upon a mystic power, as a significant category deserving a special concept. Since spirits, which manifest themselves in disease, and the soul are all conceived by the Kapauku as being as natural as are men, stones, animals, and plants, the natives do not need to separate the punishments administered by any of such phenomena from those of men. Though the name *daa* has been translated by some missionaries as taboo, the present writer has found that it is applied in South Kamu also to breaches of etiquette, to misdemeanors, as well as to "crimes," none of which have any relation to the category we call supernatural. Thus, this separate section has been devised by the present writer to reorganize the material.

   The following category includes all prohibitions which are provided with a sanction based partially or entirely upon the action of an imaginary agent. There are two types of these agents: the evil spirits and an unreal causal relation between a violation and an event objectively unrelated to the breaking of a taboo.

   An evil spirit punishes a violator of a personal taboo which is a prohibition imposed by a shaman upon specific individuals during their lives. The shaman while curing a man from attack by an evil spirit advises the patient to avoid eating a specific food, or to refrain from behaving in a specific way for a certain period of time or for the rest of his life. By obeying these prohibitions, the patient is supposed to be safe and protected against further molestation by the evil spirit.

   The second type, the general taboos, which involve imaginary causal relations between phenomena, are believed to have been determined in the old days by Ugatame. These prohibitions apply to all individuals who are defined in the taboo by group attributes, such as by being a member of a sib or being a married woman. The sanction is conceived as a natural consequence of the violation, a consequence initiated by the will of Ugatame and which has nothing to do with evil spirits. Thus, the two categories of taboos differ as to their origin and agent of punishment, as well as in the definition of the scope of their subjects.

Personal Taboos.

Rule 7: The individuals who violate a prohibition imposed upon them by a shaman who has cured them from an attack of an evil spirit will henceforth be entirely unprotected and susceptible to an attack by that specific agent.

Case 17.
  Place: Obaj.
  Date: Summer, 1955.
  Parties:
   a) *Violator:* Ij Ito of Obaj.
   b) *Authority:* Ij Uma of Botu.

Facts: Ito became very sick. The shaman was called in. He determined that Madou had attacked the patient. He performed white magic and imposed upon Ito a lifelong prohibition against eating *teto*, the deep red variety of sugar cane. After about three years, Ito violated the taboo and fell sick three days afterwards.
  Outcome: He called on the shaman, who, after the patient had promised to keep the taboo, cured him again.

Case 18.
  Place: Buna.
  Date: Summer, 1955.
  Parties:
   a) *Subjected to the taboo:* people of Buna.
   b) *Authority:* Do Ibo of Buna, the shaman.

Facts: The Go people made black magic against Buna. All pig owners of that village were destined to die. The shaman performed a magical rite in which he destroyed the black magic and chased away the evil spirits who helped the enemy. He imposed upon all the residents of Buna a taboo which prohibited them from drinking water and doing field work for seven days. Should anyone violate the rule, sickness and death would be his penalty.

General taboos.

Rule 8: A woman in her childbearing age (between the first menstruation and the onset of the menopause) is forbidden to eat *apuu*, a potato-like fruit of a vine; *teto*, the red variety of sugar cane; *kugou* and *jigikago*, the two varieties of nonripening bananas; *wiijaj* and *pugaago*, two species of parrots; and the *agou*, a marsupial. Violation of this rule would cause the death of the woman's husband, for which she should be punished by death. Should her husband discover the violation, he should beat the culprit.
  Should a young girl eat too much of the above fruit prior to her first menstruation, her breasts would stop growing.

Case 19.

   Place: Aigi.

   Date: ca. 1940.

     a) *Defendant:* Do Mag of Jota.

     b) *Victim:* Ij Kag of Aigi, husband of the defendant.

     c) *Executioner:* Ij Tid of Kojo (son of the victim).

     d) *Authority:* Ij Eka of Aigi.

Facts: The wife ate fruit of *apuu* and her husband died within a few days. The son of the dead man and of a co-wife heard about the delict from other people who saw the woman eating the forbidden fruit. He reported it to the authority.

Outcome: Eka, being convinced of the crime, suggested an execution. The son shot the woman while she worked on her field. Other people erected a platform *keage* and abandoned the corpse on it.

Comment: Breaking of the taboo had been sanctioned supernaturally as well as socially.

Rule 9: It is forbidden to fell the *kugai* palm and the *kuja* tree. If they are felled, the violator will die.

   No case reported.

Rule 10: It is forbidden to fell trees planted or consecrated during a magic ceremony. If a tree which has been used in magic given for a person is felled, the violator will get sick and die. If a tree which has been used in magical rites affecting a whole group is felled, the offender will be beaten by the people and later die because of the violation.

   No case reported.

Rule 11: Men are tabooed to eat *betu*, a small species of crayfish. The violator will get sick and die.

   No case reported.

Rule 12: An individual is tabooed to burn or eat totemic plants and animals of his own sib, of his mother's sib, and also of the sib of his wife. The violator will become deaf.

Case 20.

   Place: Aigi.

   Date: November, 1954.

   Party:

     a) *Violator:* Ij Deg of Aigi.

Facts: Ij Deg ate his totemic animal, the fruit bat. He declared he was old, he liked the meat, and did not mind becoming deaf. Nobody objected to his eating, and the deafness did not appear either.

Comment: No social sanction.

Rule 13: A pancreas should always be eaten by the breeder of the pig and never be distributed. If this taboo is violated, all pigs of the owner will die. If a pancreas is distributed by the wife, she will be beaten.

No case reported.

Rule 14: A nightmare seen by a woman during her first two menstruations should be reported to her husband. Nonreporting would cause her husband to die. Violator should be beaten by the husband; and in case he dies, she should be executed by her husband's closest relative.

Case 21.
   Place: Itod.
   Date: June, 1955.
   Parties:
     a) *Defendants:* Three wives of the victim.
     b) *Victim:* Ij Jok of Itod.
     c) *Authority:* Ij Uma of Botu, shaman.

Facts: Jok became sick. The shaman's diagnosis stated that three of his five wives had violated the prohibition and had not reported nightmares during their menstrual periods.

Outcome: Since the shaman was not sure about their identity, Jok did not punish anybody but issued a few general threats directed at his wives and made complaints to other people.

Comment: Only sufficient proof can be a basis for legal action.

Rule 15: An individual whose father, mother, wife, husband, or brother dies, or who has been involved in magic against Tege, a spirit, is forbidden for seven days to make a new field. A man violating the mourning taboo would cause all the fields of the village to be destroyed by rain. For this, he should be punished by a beating with a stick. A man who violated the prohibition associated with the magic would get sick and die.

No case reported.

Comment: No social sanction in case of the magic violation.

Rule 16: A widow should not remarry until ten days have passed after the death of her husband. Should she remarry within three days, she should be executed. However, if unpunished, she would die anyway from a disease. Should she remarry later, but within the tabooed ten-day period, she would become sick and die.

No case reported.

Comment: Remarriage within three days is considered a grave insult to the relatives of the husband.

Rule 17: A man will die in war if he paints his face red or if he has sexual intercourse in the morning prior to going to war.

No case reported.

Rule 18: Performance of *"wainai,* the mad dance," during war causes many co-villagers of the dancer to die. The violator should be put to death. Digging ditches during hostilities brings death to the brothers and father of the offender. Execution should be his penalty.

No case reported.

Rule 19: A man who kills a member of a sib which stands to his own sib in the special war taboo relation (discussed under the heading of war), such as, for example, the relation of Ijaaj and Pekej sibs, would become sick and die.

No case reported.

LYING

Kapauku distinguish two types of lying. One is directed against other people with the intention of harming them, and the other, used usually in self-defence, does not have a negative affect upon other people's affairs. The second, although considered immoral, never constitutes reason for punishment, while the former, because of the damage done to other individuals, always causes disputes and is punishable.

Rule 20: Lying, if it injures other people, is punishable by a stick-beating administered by the offended person.

Case 22.
   Place: Boob, South Kamu Valley.
   Date: ca. 1950.
   Parties:
     a) *Defendant:* Ko Imo of Boob.
     b) *Plantiff:* Ko Peg of Boob.
     c) *Authority:* Ko Ija of Boob.

Facts: The defendant accused the plaintiff of having raped his wife. The latter denied it, and so did the accused woman. There was no other proof of the alleged rape. Since the whole story sounded very vague and unreal, and the accuser could not produce any details of the crime and was known for frequent lying, the authority decided against the accuser.

Outcome: The defendant, however, did not stop his charges and Peg became so enraged that a duel with bows and arrows resulted. Though several arrows were discharged, no one was hurt. The authority asked other people to refrain from interference, and after the duel was over he scolded the defendant slightly.

Comment: The start of the duel by the plaintiff precluded any punishment of the defendant which might otherwise have been administered. Here, a duel was an alternative to punishment procedure.

*Case 23.
  Place: Itod.
  Date: January 5th, 1955.
  Parties:
    a) *Defendant:* Go Ama of Tugu, married in Botu.
    b) *Plaintiffs:* Ten boys of Botu.
    c) *Authorities:*
      Ij Tig of Botu, husband of the defendant.
      Ij Awi of Botu, village headman.
      Ij Jok of Itod, village headman.

Facts: On January 5th, 1955, the defendant spread news in Botu that she had been approached by an Itod boy and asked for sexual intercourse. This was supposed to have happened on the evening of January 4th. The boys charged the woman with lying and asked for a public trial. The husband of the defendant gave his approval to the proceedings and told the people they could punish her, if she were found guilty. Awi, the headman of Botu, agreed to this procedure and thus the woman was brought to Itod. A great gathering of people watched the event. Jok, the authority of Itod, asked the woman to present her case. She told her story in vague terms and could not identify the seducer. Her talk was interrupted on several occasions by the boys shouting, "Lie, lies, she is lying. We are all here, why does she not say which of us asked her for the intercourse?" The authority, however, always stopped them saying: "Let's hear what she has to say, then it will be your turn to speak." When the boys were allowed to present their points of view they charged her with lying. "We all were here last night and you know it because you gave all of us pork and we ate and danced with you. Her lie is obvious because she cannot identify anyone." The authority agreed with the boys, ridiculed, and cross-examined the woman, and finally charged her with lying and gave the boys permission to punish her. Every one of them struck the woman about three times with a stick or his fist. When the writer tried to stop the punishment, he was told that every offended individual had the right to beat her and should be permitted to do so.

Comment: The woman could stand trial only after the husband's extradition. Because Jok is the Itod headman and the defendant belongs to the Botu authority's jurisdiction, the latter had to give his consent to the trial in Itod.

Case 24.
  Place: Itod.
  Date: June, 1955.
  Parties:
    a) *Man who gossiped:* Ed Tig of Dege, southwestern Kamu Valley.

    b) *Victim:* Ij Jok of Itod.

    c) *The disputed girl:* Iw Ama of Kego.

Facts: Tig wished to marry Ama. She, however, preferred Jok. To take a revenge on his rival, the rejected suitor spread gossip which charged Jok with not paying back borrowed money.

Outcome: The people did not believe the gossip because they realized the rivalry between the two men and knew Jok as an honest man. The latter was very angry and threatened to beat the liar.

Comment: No authority was available who could decide the case because of its inter-confederational nature.

RELATIONS BETWEEN THE SEXES

Intersex relations are subsumed under the category "Offences against Persons" because the violations of them result in delicts against persons, no matter how much they may be couched in phrases emphasizing their monetary aspect.

Below, we will examine rules and cases pertaining to the courting pattern, incest, adultery, rape, and divorce. Since a husband constitutes an authority in his family, the cases involving punishment and disputes between him and his wives, though actually involving relations between the sexes, will be taken up in the section on delicts against the authority. The justification for this arrangement lies in the fact that the most basic character of those cases is the identification of the plaintiff with the authority. Since that aspect is common to cases in the last of our categories but foreign in the present one, it seems only appropriate to make the present arrangement.

Rule 21: A man who grasps the breasts of an unmarried girl against "her owner's" will should pay 2 Km as indemnity.

Case 25.

    Place: Egeb, southwestern corner of Kamu Valley.

    Date: ca. 1953.

    Parties:

        a) *Defendant:* Go Mab of Aigi.

        b) *Victim:* Di Imo of Egeb, a young girl.

        c) *Father of the girl:* Di Wat of Egeb.

        d) *Authority:* Ij Jok of Itod.

Facts: The defendant, a boy of about seventeen years of age, saw the victim fetching water from a river. He chased her and finally caught her and held her by her breasts, trying to seduce her into intercourse. The girl screamed and beat the culprit. He was afraid and let her go. The girl's father came to Aigi and asked for indemnity.

Outcome: The authority found the boy guilty, but the whole incident was so ridiculous to him that he could not help laughing. He, himself, paid the 2 Km for the boy because the latter did not have his own money. He laughed again, ridiculed the boy for clumsiness, and advised him on the art of seduction.

Comment: The behavior of the authority diametrically opposes the abstract rule. Since the boy was not punished at all, and actually encouraged to molest other girls, the authority's action is not just.

Rule 22: A man can date and marry a girl only with the consent of "her owner." Otherwise, he is liable and can be punished by beating.

Case 26.
   Place: Magi.
   Date: Spring, 1954.
   Parties:
      a) *Defendant:* Ij Dim of Botu, wealthy man.
      b) *His rival:* Ij Imo of Magi, his half brother.
      c) *Disputed girl:* Au Oum of Maat.
      d) *Authority:* Ij Ded of Magi.

Facts: Dim, a rich but dangerous man of Botu, disputed rights to a girl with Imo. Though the latter had the girl's love and her brother's consent, because of the rage and power of the rival it was dangerous for him to marry her.

Outcome: The authority's argument was as follows: Imo has the girl's love and consent of her family, but Dim is a powerful and rich man of Botu who can start a fight. Therefore, it is my opinion that in order to avoid all these troubles, the girl should be married to a third person. Her parents and brother complied with the authority's request.

Comment: An example of a political decision overriding an established legal rule of the society.

Case 27.
   Place: Puet, south from Botu.
   Date: February 15th, 1955.
   Parties:
      a) *Defendant:* Wa Ipo of Puet.
      b) *Brother of the girl:* Au Ena of Maat.
      c) *The girl:* Au Mud of Maat.

Facts: The defendant was dating a girl against the will of her brother. One day the brother came to the house of the paternal parallel cousin of the defendant and found the latter sitting there by the fire.

Outcome: An argument developed and the infuriated brother twice struck the culprit over his head with a stick, took from him 3 Km as indemnity, and left the house. After the girl was married, the brother returned the three cowries to the boy. However, he did not pay a requested indemnity of 2 Km for the beating.

Comment: Since the brother beat the boy, he had no right to take any money from him. A physical punishment precludes payment of indemnity.

Rule 23: Bride price should be paid to and determined by the girl's brothers and father or, in their absence, by the girl's first paternal parallel cousin. If not paid, the man to whom the bride price is due can take back the girl or force the indebted party to pay. If they resist, he can beat and wound the couple with arrows shot through their thighs and arms.

Case 28:
   Place: Jaga.
   Date: ca. 1953.
   Parties:
     a) *Defendant:* Ko Ija of Pago, mother's brother of the girls.
     b) *Plaintiff:* Ij Tek of Jaga, brother of the girls.
     d) *The girls:*
        Ij Map of Jaga.
        Ij Goo of Jaga.
        Ij Kan of Jaga.

Facts: A mother's brother collected bride price for three of his nieces whom he brought up in his house. A brother of the girls asked for the money collected by his maternal uncle. Though the collector was entitled only to *mune*, the payment for the upbringing of the girls, the rightful owner's request was rejected. An argument developed which finally evolved into a stickfight in which the Ij-Pig confederacy fought their Ko in-laws and maternal relatives for several days.

Outcome: As far as is known, the brother still has not received the shells.

Comment: The case illustrates absence of an authority who could decide the dispute between the two political units.

Case 29.
   Place: Jaga.
   Date: February 7th, 1955.
   Parties:
     a) *Defendants:*
        Ij Pig of Jaga.
        Ij Ene of Jaga, half brother of the woman.
     b) *Woman:* Ij Imo of Jaga.
     c) *Plantiff:* Ij Kaa of Jaga, brother of (b).
     d) *Authority:* Ij Eka of Aigi, sublineage headman.

Facts: The two defendants collected bride price consisting of 120 Km, 60 Tm, and one pig. The owner of the price, the full brother of the bride, consented to the action because Ene wanted to use the money for buying himself a wife. In February,

Kaa asked for an installment but was refused with the explanation that the price belonged to the half brother.

Outcome: In the dispute which followed, the authority decided upon the right of Kaa to the price and asked the defendants to pay back at least part of the price. The defendants complied with the decision and paid a first installment of 5 Km.

Comment: The case belongs here because its essence is bride price adjudication, rather than back payment of the debt.

Case 30.

   Place: Buna.

   Date: July, 1955.

   Parties:

    a) *Woman:* Pa Jeg of Muji (northern Kamu Valley).

    b) *Her lover:* Ag Iid of Boma (central Kamu Valley).

    c) *Brother of the woman:* Pa Ket of Muji.

Facts: A couple eloped without payment and against the will of the girl's brother. In Buna, Ket met the couple at a pig feast and demanded the bride price. The lover did not have the shells with him.

Outcome: Though Iid promised to pay in the future, the enraged brother started discharging arrows into the couple, wounding his sister in the abdomen, thigh, and neck, and her lover in the knee.

Comment: Since the payment after the shooting will most probably be refused, Kamu Valley may witness another war in the near future. The action of Ket was considered unjustified by most of the people.

INCEST

Rule 24: A man is prohibited from marrying anyone in his own sib under the penalty of death, administered by his brothers, sons, and father.

Case 31.

   Place: Jiib (Pona region).

   Date: ca. 1947.

   Parties:

    a) *Defendant:* Bo Wog of Jiib.

    b) *Executioner:* Bo Deg of Jiib, half brother of the defendant.

    c) *Authority:* Bo Gek of Jiib.

Facts: The culprit was known as a notorious thief who stole many garden products and food from other people. He raped many women, including the wife of his half brother. Finally, he seduced his second parallel paternal cousin.

Outcome: All the people were upset by this outrage and the half brother of the defendant volunteered, after the decision of the authority, to execute the criminal. He killed him with a bamboo-tipped arrow shot from ambush.

Case 32.

Place: Dege, South Kamu Valley.

Date: ca. 1948.

Parties:

a) *Defendant:* Ed Ged of Dege.

b) *Victim:* Ed Amo of Dege (FaBrDa of a).

c) *Authority:* Ed Pei of Dege.

Facts: Ged liked his pretty cousin. Once on her way home from the fields, he ambushed and raped her. She wept, went home, and told the story to her father.

Outcome: Without discussing the horrible deed with anyone, the father of the raped girl took bow and arrows and went after his incestuous nephew. In the fight, he shot the criminal in the chest and left him lying on the battlefield to die. The authority and all the people decided that this was a just punishment for the culprit.

Case 33.

Place: Botu.

Date: ca. 1940.

Parties:

a) *Defendant:* Ij Awi of Botu, headman of Enona sublineage.

b) *Woman:* Ij Ena of Kojo.

c) *Father of the woman:* Ij Uga of Kojo, village headman of Jamaina sublineage.

Facts: About fifteen years ago, Ij Awi fell in love with Ij Ena of Kojo (his FaFa-FaBrSoSoDa). At that time he already was a wealthy man and authority of Botu. His love being incestuous, he feared punishment from his own as well as the girl's relatives. To avoid this, he eloped with the girl and hid in the bush. His tactic was based upon the assumption that the girl's father, realizing the futility of trying to catch him, after a while would be anxious at least to get payment for his daughter. As soon as he would ask for the bride price—and this would have to be given eventually to prevent a rift within the political unit—the marriage would be formally concluded and Ij Awi would not have to fear execution. Although he was the first in his sib, as well as in the South Kamu Valley, to conclude such an incestuous marriage, he knew that in Pona area, south from the Kamu, some Ko people had been successful in concluding such marriages and that they had been granted pardon by the society. At the start, affairs seemed to develop contrary to the plans of the young social reformer. His relatives and those of the girl combed the woods for days trying to catch them.

Outcome: After a while, however, Uga, the father of the girl and headman of Kojo, became tired of the futile hunt and asked Awi's relatives for bride price. These people refused to pay and insisted on punishing the couple. Uga, who came to be more interested in getting the money then in seeing his daughter executed, managed to secure the support of the whole Jamaina sublineage; with the help of its numerous members, he fought a stick battle against the Enona sublineage of

Botu. By this action, the whole Jamaina sublineage actually accepted the incestuous marriage as rightful. Otherwise, there would have been no reason to fight for the bride price. Moreover, by fighting the stick battle they absolved the Botu people from payment of the bride price. This, in turn, induced the relatives of Awi, who were the latter's followers anyway, to accept the inevitable and recognize the incestuous marriage. The happy groom, however, paid the bride price later.

Thus, Awi, headman of Botu, through his cunning, courage, influence, and awareness of the rules, started an important change in law and social structure which tends to transform the Botu community into an endogamous village with incipient moieties already present.

Comment: Awi continued violating incestuous taboos and married two of his second paternal parallel cousins of Botu. Many other people followed his example and caused the law of incest to change. This subject will be taken up later in the discussion of legal change. Here we may note that authority changed a basic law of incest and that this change, although present in a primitive culture, is of a revolutionary rather than an evolutionary nature.

Rule 25: Marriage between all paternal blood relatives is tabooed except between those who are of different sibs, are of the same generation, and are at least of second degree of collaterality (i.e., marriage of first paternal cross-cousins is tabooed, while a second cross-cousin is a potential spouse of ego). Violation of this taboo should be punished by execution of both defendants. In case of leniency, the defendants as well as their relatives are expected to die of supernatural causes.

No case reported.

Comment: It should be recalled that the statement is an abstraction made by the informants, rather than an actual case. The rule has never been strictly enforced and marriage between first cross-cousins, though no case was reported, would probably not result in execution. The sanction would also diminish in its severity according to the relative degree of relationship until it disappeared altogether.

Rule 26: Marriage to any maternal blood relative is tabooed unless one is of the same generation and at least of the second degree of collaterality. Thus, first cross-cousins are prohibited from marrying. The sanction is the same as above.

No case reported.

Comment: As above.

Rule 27: It is taboo to take widows of blood relatives as spouses unless they are of the same generation as ego. Violators should be punished by execution if they marry widows who have been wives of relatives less distant from ego than two connecting links. Otherwise, stick beating is the punishment.

No case reported.

Comment: As above.

Rule 28: Marriage to all relatives of one's wife is tabooed if they belong to a generation older than that of the wife. All other relatives are acceptable as spouses. Sanction as above.

No case reported.

Comment: As above.

Rule 29: Marriage to all widows of one's wife's male relatives is tabooed. Sanction as above.

No case reported.

Comment: As above.

Rule 30: All wives who have deserted any kind of a relative are acceptable as spouses.

No case reported.

Comment: It is, however, immoral to marry a wife who has deserted one's own relative.

Rule 31: To marry one's best friend's relatives is nonpunishable, but it is immoral.

No case reported.

Rule 32: Intermarriage between Moni and Kapauku tribes is tabooed and in case of such an act, both offenders should be put to death.

No case known.

Rule 33: It is not punishable to marry a person from a tabooed sib (such as the relation between Ijaaj and Pekej). However, the person is expected to die of a disease.

No case reported.

ADULTERY

A Kapauku woman is considered to be dependent entirely upon her husband. He alone has the power in the society to punish her for any offense that she may commit, even those directed against third persons. The husband, therefore, is responsible for the offences of his wife. Since she is inaccessible to the authorities, it is he who suffers punishment, however, unless he punishes his wife with a penalty imposed upon her by the authority.

The husband also has the exclusive right to sexual relations with his spouse. Since marriage, as a result of the bride price, is an economic as well as a social matter, and since most wars start because of violations of the husband's exclusive sexual rights, the delict of adultery, as well as the rape of a married woman, is considered the most heinous of crimes. The penalty for it is execution. The latter may be avoided by payment of a large indemnity to the husband who may or may not accept it. Because of this uncertainty, most of the culprits do not make an offer, thus precipitating an execution or, if from another political unit than the husband, a war. Since intent is obvious on the man's part in both adultery and rape, there is no difference in punishment for the two offences. On the other hand, a woman, while often executed like her adulterous partner, may escape with a beating even if she has willingly submitted to sexual intercourse. Because intent, rather than the effect, is of importance, she is safe and not punished if raped. She has, though, the duty to report it immediately to her husband.

Rule 34: If a married woman submits voluntarily to sexual intercourse with another man, the couple should be punished by death. The husband, however, may take pity on his spouse and only beat her. Sufficient indemnity, if voluntarily offered by the male offender, may be substituted for his execution.

Case 34.

   Place: Botu.

   Date: ca. 1950.

   Parties:

     a) *Defendant:* Ij Maw of Botu.

     b) *Woman:* Pi Mag of Obaj.

     c) *Her husband:* Ij Ida of Botu.

     d) *Father of the woman:* Pi Idi of Obaj.

     e) *Authorities*:

        Ij Awi of Botu, Enona sublineage headman.

        Ij Eka of Aigi, lineage and confederacy's headman.

Facts: The defendant had sexual intercourse with the woman several times. Finally, one of the wives of his landlord reported the relations to the husband of the adulterous woman. The latter became furious, took his bow and arrows and went to the culprit's residence. Since it was noon, and all the people were in the fields, he found the house deserted. Blind with emotion, he burnt down the house which belonged to the first paternal parallel cousin of the defendant. Then he shot a sow of his enemy, took it to his home, cut it up, cooked the meat, and distributed it to all the people who came to the feast. The adulterous wife was meanwhile taken to her father's village by her parents, who feared she might be executed. When the owner of the house returned and found his home burnt down, he rushed to the feasting party of Ida and started a stick fight. The residents of the village fought each other for three days with sticks, with most of the people, including the village authority, fighting on the side of the offended husband.

Outcome: Since the village headman participated in the fight, and thus allied himself with one party, he could not decide the case. The confederacy's leader, accompanied by headmen from all the villages, appeared on the scene and urged a peaceful settlement. The fighting stopped and Eka decided that the sides were then even. The culprit had committed adultery, but he and his relatives were sufficiently punished by the loss of the house and the confiscation of the sow. Nevertheless, the authority reprimanded the defendant for one day to emphasize the gravity of his offence. The adulterous woman, on the pleading of her father, was granted a divorce by the offended husband but with the stipulation that she would never marry the culprit. This having been promised, full bride price was returned and the woman married a man from another village.

Comments: Here we have an example where the authority, by becoming involved in the fight, forfeited his right of adjudicating the case. Since he was the village headman and the head of the Enona sublineage, the jurisdiction went to the authority of the whole confederacy who, supported by all the headmen, settled the case. The taking of the sow and the burning of the house took the place of other indemnity and precluded capital punishment. Moreover, leniency was shown to the wife.

Case 35.

  Place: Botu.

  Date: ca. 1951.

  Parties:

  a) *Defendant:* Ij Nak of Botu.

  b) *Married woman:* Ij Gek of Botu.

  c) *Her husband:* Pi Ena of Botu.

  d) *Authorities:*

  Ij Eka of Aigi, confederacy's leader.

  Pi Peg of Obaj, headman of the Pi Obaj lineage.

Facts: The defendant fell in love with a married woman and they committed adultery. Fearing the reaction of the husband, they escaped into the woods. The enraged husband searched the country trying to bring the culprits to justice.

Outcome: Since each party to the dispute belonged to one of the two sibs of the same confederacy, the problem, involving political considerations, was very delicate. One of the authorities, functioning also as the confederacy's leader, appeared on the scene and asked for restraint and avoidance of violence. It was decided that the case should be settled peacefully, and the adulterer was sentenced to payment of the full bride price and to a severe reprimand lasting several days. The offended husband accepted the payment and granted a divorce to his wife. The people do not consider this settlement as either just or moral. However, they recognize its political necessity.

Comment: Political considerations overrode, in this case, morals and the abstract rule.

*Case 36.

  Place: Itod.

  Date: January 1st, 1955.

  Parties:

  a) *Defendants:*

  Ti Tib of Mogo, the male party.

  Go Ama of Bibi, wife of Ij Jok of Itod, the female party.

b) *Authority:* Ij Jok of Itod, husband of the woman and headman of Itod.

Facts: On January 1st, 1955, the last wife of Ij Jok escaped into the woods with Tib. They stayed there together and committed adultery. Not until January 3rd was the wife caught by an expedition of the men of the Ij-Pi confederacy. The woman was beaten by her husband and several of his relatives. Bleeding, with bound hands (acculturation to white man's way), and with a swollen and bruised face, she was brought to Itod where about two hundred people gathered. The woman had to stand in the center of a semicircle while all the headmen, and especially her husband, reprimanded her publicly and beat her with sticks. During a period of cross-examination she claimed that she had been kidnapped and raped. No one believed her, however, and she received a further beating from her husband. The husband's mother took the side of the woman and pleaded with her son for leniency. Finally, Jok gave in, untied the hands of his wife and took her home. The next day a war party was organized and the confederacy went south to Mogo where they determined either to kill the adulterer or to start a war if resistance were met. The Ti people, however, met the party outside of the village and presented the husband with a huge pig. Jok accepted this indemnity and returned happily to Itod, where, in the evening, he killed the pig and distributed the meat to all the people who had helped him in the affair.

Case 37.
   Place: Jaga.
   Date: March 6th, 1955.
   Parties:
      a) *Defendants:*
         Man: Pi Oub of Jaga.
         Woman: Di Ena of Egeb.
      b) *Woman's husband:* An Teu of Odee.

Facts: The wife escaped into the woods where she remained in hiding for many days. During this period she committed adultery with her young lover. The husband, with a number of his friends, combed the forests and finally caught the woman. Since, however, he had not paid a bride price for the woman but had only given 40 Km to her father's brother, he was not regarded as her legal husband. The paternal uncle demanded that the wife should be given to her lover and furthermore proposed to repay the 40 Km. The public agreed with the proposal and considered it a just solution. Teu, however, afraid of losing his wife, took her to Enarotali (the Dutch Administration post) and there, through misrepresentations, tried to secure help from the Dutch officials.

Outcome: The district officer enquired into the matter and found out the cause of the trouble. Since he did not formally control Kamu, he suggested a peaceful settlement by which the lover should go unpunished and the wife should stay with her husband, but the latter pay the bride price in full. This solution, considered just, was accepted by both sides and the case closed.

Rule 35: If a married woman is forced into sexual intercourse and reports the event to her husband, the male offender should be put to death. Sufficient indemnity, if voluntarily offered by the culprit to the husband, may be substituted for his execution.

Case 38.

   Place: Kojo.
   Date: ca. 1951.
   Parties:
      a) *Defendant:* Ij Mud of Noti.
      b) *Victim:* Pi Bug of Obaj.
      c) *Her husband:* Ij Wig of Kojo.
      d) *Authority:* Ij Ane of Noti.

Facts: When the woman went to her fields, she was raped by the man from Noti. She wept, went home, and reported the case to her husband. He tried to kill the offender, but the latter remained in hiding for five months in the jungle.

Outcome: The husband, not being able to take revenge, divorced his wife and was paid back the full amount of bride price. Then he promised the authority at Noti not to harm the culprit. Thus the case was closed.

Comment: The settlement of the case does not comply with the rule. It also represents the redirection of the aggression of the husband from the culprit to the raped wife, likewise manifested by the divorce.

*Case 39.

   Place: Botu.
   Date: July 26, 1955.
   Parties:
      a) *Defendant:* Ad Wen of Igoo.
      b) *Victim:* Ko Ama of Boob.
      c) *Husband of the victim:* Ij Bun of Botu.
      d) *Authorities:*
            Ij Eka of Aigi, head of confederacy.
            Ij Jok of Itod, village headman.
            Ij Awi of Botu, sublineage headman.
            Pi Peg of Obaj, Pi Obaj lineage headman.

Facts: The defendant was an old suitor of the woman. However, she did not return his love and gave preference to Bun whom she finally married. The rejected lover met her later on a path and asked her to marry him. When she refused he grabbed her by the bark wrap near the pubic region, but she managed to beat him off with a stick. All the Ij-Pi confederacy's authorities asked the Ko people for indemnity. They replied by extraditing the culprit who appeared in front of a gathering of the confederacy's leaders.

Outcome: All of the authorities except Peg scolded him; but because the attempted rape was not carried out, and because the man was the first, though rejected, lover of the woman, no indemnity was asked for.

Comment: Note that the defendant's love for the woman and his first courting was taken as an alleviating circumstance.

Rule 36: If an unmarried girl is forced into sexual intercourse, 6 Km should be paid by the culprit to her brother or parents.

Case 40.
  Place: Boga, north of Buna.
  Date: ca. 1950.
  Parties:
    a) *Defendant:* Pi Edu of Boga.
    b) *Victim:* Ij Ega of Obaj.

Facts: While returning in the night from a pig feast, a group of girls was attacked by several boys and men. One of the girls was caught by the culprit in the bush and raped.

Outcome: A peaceful settlement was precluded by an attack of about sixty Ij-Pi people who entered the village of Boga and took twenty-two bows and a great deal of salt as indemnity for the rape. During the raid, they fought only with sticks and did not burn down any houses "because they were not at war." The case was thus closed.

Comment: The village of Boga has friendly relations with the Ij-Pi confederacy. Therefore, no war resulted from the incident.

Case 41.
  Place: Boga.
  Date: ca. 1951.
  Parties:
    a) *Defendant:* Do Amo of Boga.
    b) *Victim:* Do Epa of Boga.
    c) *Authority:* Do One of Boga.

Facts: A man approached the girl on the path when she was returning with a small boy from a dance. He declared that he would rape her and ordered the boy to leave. He took her into the bush and raped her twice.

Outcome: The authority decided the culprit was guilty and established indemnity as 7 Km. The father of the girl, however, asked for 10 Km. The defendant not only paid the higher indemnity which the father demanded, but he added 4 Tm to the sum in order to restore good relations with the girl's family.

Comment: The indemnity paid in this case was higher than the rule asks for. While case 40 illustrates an intervillage dispute, this case presents a delict which involves individuals from the same village.

DIVORCE

Kapauku marriage is not necessarily a permanent union. A man can divorce his wife without any reason whatsoever, everything depending ultimately upon his will. If, however, he does not have reasons recognized by the society as a justification for dissolving the marital union, he has to sacrifice part or all of the bride price, the return of which may be refused by the wife's relatives. Since a man can marry several women, and every woman is at least an economic asset, the divorce proceedings started by the husband usually do have a justification recognized by the society.

Since it is the woman who is paid for, she is not as free in the matter of divorce as is her spouse. Her way of securing dissolution of the marriage takes the form of an elopement with another man, or of hiding for a considerable time in the woods while her relatives try to negotiate a settlement with her husband. Thus, she is always dependent upon another person in dissolving the bond with her husband.

Rule 37: A woman should be granted a divorce if her spouse is cruel without reason, and if he does not feed and provide adequate shelter for her and her children.

*Case 42.
   Place: Jaga
   Date: January, 1955.
   Parties:
      a) *Wife:* Go Pet of Tugu.
      b) *Her husband:* Ij Aik of Jaga.
      c) *Authority:* Ij Auw of Jaga, a contributor to the bride price paid for the wife.

Facts: The wife declared to Auw that she would leave her husband because the latter did not give enough food to her two children from her first marriage. Since Auw helped to buy the woman, he became alarmed by the statement and questioned the husband who denied the charge.

Outcome: They both reprimanded the woman for lying and she promised not to leave.

Comment: The authority, who had paid part of the bride price which the husband still owed him, in case of a divorce resulting from the husband's guilt, would have lost that part of his money which the woman's relatives might refuse to return.

Case 43.
   Place: Kega, south of the Kamu Valley.
   Date: ca. 1937.
   Parties:
      a) *Defendant:* Ad Deb of Kega.
      b) *His wife:* Pi Geg of Botu.
      c) *Authority:* Ad Epe of Kega.

Facts: The marriage of this couple had not been a happy one. The husband was very emotional and cruel. He used to beat his wife for no apparent reason, did not give her enough pork, and once even shot her in the leg with an arrow. She asked her brother for help in divorce proceedings.

Outcome: The brother agreed on the necessity of a divorce and offered to pay back the full price. However, the husband refused to give his consent and insisted upon the continuation of the unhappy union. The authority stepped in and demanded a divorce for the woman, charging the man with cruelty. The husband finally surrendered to the pressure and accepted the returned bride price.

Rule 38: If a wife deserts her husband, who is not guilty of cruelty or nonsupport, she should be captured (preferably with the help of her male relatives), punished by stick beating, and brought back to her husband.

Case 44.
   Place: Obaj.
   Date: ca. 1949.
   Parties:
      a) *Wife:* Pi Ija of Obaj.
      b) *Husband:* Do Ako of Buna, headman of village.
      c) *Authority:* Pi Ija of Obaj, father of the wife.

Facts: The wife did not like her husband, although he was a kind and generous man. She escaped from his house and hid in the jungle. She was caught, after a few days, by her father and brothers.

Outcome: They beat her with a stick, bound her to a pole by her hands and feet like a pig, and carried her back to her home. After several days she escaped again, but this time with a man of the Do sib whose relatives offered to repay fully the bride price to her husband. He accepted the payment and released his wife from the marital bond.

*Case 45.
   Place: Botu.
   Date: August 20th, 1955.
   Parties:
      a) *Wife:* Ij Pik of Botu.
      b) *Husband:* Ij Ogi of Botu.
      c) *Her father:* Ij Bun of Botu.
      d) *Her mother:* Ij Gan of Botu.

Facts: Pik was married when she was fourteen years old. Although her husband, a young man of Botu, was very kind and paid a large bride price for her, she did not like him. Her mother tried to exploit the situation and asked the husband for additional money as an amendment to the bride price. First he refused to comply with this extortion practice, but after his wife had escaped into the bush and was supported there by her mother who supplied her with food, he consented and gave an additional pig and a few beads to the unethical mother-in-law. However, she still asked for more. At this point, the husband brought the affair to the attention of Ij Awi, the headman of Botu, and Jok, the headman of Itod.

Outcome: Both authorities supported his cause and urged the wife's parents to restore her to the husband. The girl's father, together with the husband, caught the young wife and dragged her, over the protests and lamentations of her mother, to the husband's house. Since the authorities charged the girl's mother with disturbing the marriage and urged her punishment, the girl's father complied with the request and beat her with a stick.

Comment: In the punishment of the bad mother-in-law, the authorities depended upon her spouse's action.

Rule 39: Sterility of the husband is grounds for divorce. A wife's sterility, however, does not give the husband the right to terminate the marriage.

No case reported.

Comment: The Kapauku reason that a woman's sterility, because of the practice of polygyny, does not deprive a man of the opportunity to become a father. In the reverse case, the wife, since she has just one spouse, may be deprived of her motherhood through her husband's sterility and should therefore be allowed, through divorce and remarriage, to achieve that status.

Rule 40: A husband has the right to divorce his wife under any circumstance. If, however, there is no guilt on the wife's side and the latter bore children, the man should not recover the whole bride price when a divorce is granted.

Case 46.
    Place: Aigi.
    Date: ca. 1953.
    Parties:
        a) *Wife:* Pi Ama of Obaj.
        b) *Husband:* Ij Eka of Aigi, confederacy's headman.
        c) *Relig. authority:* Ij Mab of Aigi.

Facts: The husband became very sick. The shaman identified the cause of the illness as the coincidence of the date of the patient's wife's first menstruation with that of the payment of the bride price. He saw divorce as the only way to save Eka's life.

Outcome: The heartbroken husband complied with the shaman's order. Since there were no children in the marriage, the whole bride price was repaid.

Case 47.
    Place: Mogo.
    Date: ca. 1953.
    Parties:
        a) *Wife:* Wa Ena of Puet.
        b) *Husband:* Ti Web of Mogo.
        c) *Authority:* The husband is headman in Mogo.

Facts: The husband was the headman of the village of Mogo. He did not like his wife for some unknown reason and chased her away.

Outcome: Although his deed was considered immoral, he was paid back the whole bride price since there were no children.

OFFENCES AGAINST RIGHTS IN THINGS

Our second division of rules and disputes deals with violations of the rights of a person to an object. Although infringement on ownership rights will form the content of most of the cases, it will by no means constitute the sole subject under discussion. Other rights, such as *usus*, the right to use a thing; *superficies*, a long standing right to the surface of an area; *ususfructus*, a right to use a thing and collect its produce; and a right to inherit a specific property, have necessarily to be included in this section.

Although the first division represents the author's reflection on a tendency of the Kapauku to classify in a single category phenomena, such as marriage, murder, and the breaking of a taboo—which appear incongruous to a European lawyer—this category compensates for that difference between Kapauku and Western legal thinking and presents an organization which recalls that of the Old Roman Law.

Agijo widii tai, to dispute a thing, is an expression used for all the disputes classified in this division. Moreover, unlike the next division on contracts in which two people must discuss their mutual agreement, the argumentation in the procedure of solving the present cases focuses always upon the relation between a person and an object. There is also a difference in the method of finding the evidence. It is much easier for an owner of a thing, or holder of a *ususfructus*, to prove his right than it is to demonstrate the content of an unwritten contract between two parties, concluded sometimes without any witness whatsoever.

Thus, the present division is based upon the conviction of the writer that the above combination of linguistic, legalistic, and procedural impressions from the Kapauku culture reflects a feeling of unity on the part of the natives.

Though there is much evidence that in the field of magic there exists a more clearly formulated conceptualization of rights to intangible property, such as a specific sequence of tasks in the practice of curing magic or the wording of a magical spell, the Kapauku never conceive of these as a subject of litigation or dispute. This is because of the belief that the effectiveness of these phenomena depends upon their association with the proper individual, thus making the "theft" of them impossible.

All of our cases, therefore, consist of such materialistic topics as land and boundary disputes, stealing of movables, destruction of property by intent, negligence, or accident, and violations of the *ususfructus*, *superficies*, and rights of inheritance.

Ownership of Land

To get away from the traditional Roman concept of ownership, which formulates too narrow a definition to be useful cross-culturally, the present writer conceives of the concept as a jural relation of men with regard to some subject matter, which is typified by the tendency of an automatic increase of rights on the part of the owner at times when those rights cease to be exercised by other individuals. Thus, for example, the owner of the land is identified by an automatic gain of the right to cultivate a plot of land when the individual who made a garden on it ceases to use it. An owner of a house would be a man who gains, automatically, the right to use it exclusively after his brother, who had the right of residence, moves away.

We have already discussed the individual ownership of land in the second part of the monograph. In this place it should be stated again that it is always one single individual who owns a piece of land. Since the Kapauku do not know of the acquisition of property by detention, the title to land is limited to inheritance, to sale, and, in a very few cases, to gift. Most disputes thus arise from doubt about the legality of these titles. Since sale and gift are contracts, and the dispute is directed toward the agreement between the contractees rather than toward the relation between the field and the owner, we shall discuss such disputes in the next chapter.

The bulk of our material concerns boundary disputes and claims made by several persons upon the same piece of land. Such claims are commonly based upon different titles obtained through inheritance.

Rule 41: Boundaries should be respected. Should doubt arise about their demarcation the *ude*, Ti plants planted as property markers on the field's peripheries, and the old people's testimony are decisive. Violations are subjected to *restitutio in integrum*, the restitution of land to such a state as it was prior to the violator's act.

Case 48.
   Place: Kojo.
   Date: ca. 1948.
   Parties:
      a) *Defendant:* Ij Uga of Kojo.
      b) *Plaintiff:* Ij Aik of Jaga.
      c) *Authority:* Ij Eke of Aigi, confederacy's headman.

Facts: Uga, headman of Kojo, made a garden on the slope of Kemugebega. Aik found out that part of his land had been included in the new garden of Uga who had fenced it in as if it were his property. Aik became angry and went to another garden of his enemy which lay on the bank of the Edege River and started chopping down the tall sugar cane which grew on it. Uga, having heard about the vandalism, rushed to the scene and started a stick fight. Next day he went to Jaga and challenged Aik to a duel with sticks. However, a stick battle developed in which most of the confederacy's men participated, as well as many of the maternal relatives of the participants who offered a helping hand. The fight lasted three days. On the fourth day, the Botu people who were helping started discharging war arrows. The situation became very serious because it was feared that the confederacy might be destroyed by an internal rift. Eke, the confederacy's authority, appeared on the scene and sent the headmen of Botu and Itod to their respective opponents to argue for peace.

Outcome: The mission was successful. Eke could pass his judgment and declare the right of Aik to regain the disputed strip of land.

Case 49.
   Place: Botu.
   Date: ca. 1949.
   Parties:
      a) *Defendant:* Ij Jik of Botu.
      b) *Plaintiff:* Ij Mak of Botu.
      c) *Authority:* Ij Awi of Botu, headman of Botu.

Facts: Jik made a garden on the slope of Kemugebega. Mak appeared on the scene and charged the working man with stealing a strip of land on their field boundary. A fight took place between the two in which most of the people of Botu ultimately participated. Jik suffered a deep wound on his head and Mak's forearm was broken by a blow of a machete. The authority, who fought on the side of Jik, urged peace.

Outcome: The opposite side gave in and the authority decided in favor of the maker of the garden who retained his possession.

Comment: Although the authority took part in the fighting, he was still able to decide the case.

Case 50.
   Place: Botu.
   Date: ca. 1952.
   Parties:
      a) *Disputants:*
         Ij Uma of Botu.
         Ij Taj of Botu.
      b) *Authorities:*
         Ij Awi, headman of Botu.
         Ij Eka of Aigi, confederacy's head.

Facts: The parties to the dispute owned neighboring lands. The boundary line disappeared in the jungle overgrowth and the old people who had known its location were all dead so that no one in the village could exactly determine the demarcation. Both parties claimed lines which gave them territorial advantages. The pugnacious headman of Botu again started a fight which was stopped by the arrival of Eka, the leader of the confederacy.

Outcome: Since there was no way to find out the true boundary, he established a new demarcation line lying halfway between the lines claimed by both parties. His decision was regarded as very wise and was accepted as a final settlement.

Comment: An excellent example of jurisprudence based upon a compromise. In its reasoning it is close to case 26.

*Case 51.
   Place: Kojo.
   Date: May 3rd, 1955.

Parties:
- a) *Owner of garden:* Ij Jok of Itod, headman.
- b) *Challenger:* Ij Amo, headman of Kojo.
- c) *Worker:* Ad Gip of Botu.
- d) *Authority:* Ij Eka of Aigi, headman of the Jamaina sublineage and of confederacy.

Facts: The hired worker was clearing a new garden plot on the Kemugebega mountain. Amo, who owned the neighboring plot, which was overgrown by jungle, came by and argued that the worker had cut part of his forest. The latter, therefore, stopped and waited for the arrival of his employer. The shouting of Amo lured many people to the scene and finally Jok, the owner of the field, appeared and an argument started. Jok claimed that all the field was his, including the disputed strip. He based his argument upon the evidence of the *ude* Ti plant markers. Amo's claim to the strip rested upon the evidence of the difference in growth of trees on the two neighboring properties. The trees on the disputed strip resembled, in their height and age, those on his own plot. He also stated that his father had worked the disputed land. There were many witnesses for both sides, among them the mother of Amo who testified that she planted sweet potatoes on the strip some fifteen years before. Jok admitted it but claimed that the father of Amo had cheated his father in the old days. Now, he argued, he, himself, had grown up and wanted the land which belonged to him. Eka, the head of the confederacy, was sitting in the crowd listening to the testimonies. When the argument became too emotional, he admonished the parties by talking to them individually. In the evening, the members of the opposing camps went home, promising each other a fight the next day.

Outcome: Eka decided in favor of Jok. The next day he went to Amo and persuaded him to give in. Amo complied with the decision.

Comment: The decision was given informally and separately to each party, and the authority's personal persuasion achieved the acceptance of the verdict.

*Case 52.
    Place: Kojo.
    Date: August 8th, 1955.
    Parties:
- a) *Married woman:* Ij Wou of Botu.
- b) *Wife of the neighbor:* Go Mab of Bibi, wife of Ij Amo of Kojo.
- c) *Advisor:* Pi Geg of Botu.

Facts: The married woman was supposed to clear underbrush in the jungle to provide an area for a new field. She was not sure about the boundary and so she yodeled down the mountain for help. The neighbor's wife and an older man came to help her.

Outcome: Pi found an *ude* Ti plant marker in the thick growth of forest, and thus the problem was solved without a dispute and to the satisfaction of both neighbors.

Rule 42: Land is always owned by a single individual. No one should make a field on another man's property without the owner's consent, lest the fruit of his work belong to the owner. The ownership is established by sale, gift, or inheritance. If an owner dies intestate and the heir is not clear, the land belongs to the person who undisputedly worked it last.

Case 53.
  Place: Kojo.
  Date: ca. 1951.
  Parties:
    a) *Defendant:* Ij Amo of Kojo, village headman.
    b) *Plaintiff:* Ij Utu of Aigi (FaBrSo of Amo).
    c) *Authority:* Ij Eka of Aigi, the head of the confederacy.

Facts: Amo worked a piece of land inherited by his paternal parallel cousin, Utu. When the latter claimed the field, Amo insisted that it was his because he worked it prior to and after the death of Utu's father. The legal heir, enraged over the skillful twisting of customary rules (no. 42), destroyed twenty sections of his opponent's fence. A stick fight started in which four other close relatives joined the contestants. The second day Eka stopped the fight by dancing the *wainai* dance and speaking against violence. Two people were wounded on each side.

Outcome: The authority recognized the ownership of Utu and induced his rival to accept it as a just claim.

Comment: The title to the land claimed by Amo represents a skillful misinterpretation of the rule. He lost the case because inheritance rules define sons as exclusive heirs to all land property. Thus, inheritance is inconclusive only in case of a dispute between sons or between parallel nephews of the decreased, but never in the case of a son and a nephew.

Case 54.
  Place: Obaj.
  Date: Summer, 1954.
  Parties:
    a) *Older half brother:* Pi Wed of Obaj (So of 1st Wi).
    b) *Younger half brother:* Pi Imo of Obaj (So of 2nd Wi).
    c) *Authority:* Pi Peg of Obaj, village headman.

Facts: The two brothers inherited property from their father. Wed, the older brother and son of the first wife, started clearing an area in the woods near Obaj but his right to the plot was challenged by his younger half brother. The dispute soon developed into a stick fight in which the authority participated on the older brother's side. However, Imo's more numerous party prevailed, so that the authority himself shouted for peace.

Outcome: The authority conceded the land ownership to the young victor, although he had opposed him previously.

Comment: The authority's decision had been reversed as a result of losing the fight.

Rule 43: All second growth trees belong to the owner of the land. A violator should return any wood taken or pay indemnity.

Comment: Trees are considered part of the land.

Case 55.

    Place: Kojo.

    Date: ca. 1953.

    Parties:

      a) *Defendant:* Ij Amo of Kojo, village headman.

      b) *Plaintiff:* Ij Aik of Kojo.

      c) *Authority:* Ij Eka of Aigi, the head of the confederacy.

Facts: Amo, the authority in Kojo, felled young trees on the land of the plaintiff. The latter tried to stop him, but a fight resulted in which people of all the villages of the confederacy participated.

Outcome: The authority stopped the fight and decided that Amo should stop cutting wood and pay for the damages. The defendant complied with the decision and gave the owner of the land 1 Tm.

Rule 44: Very old trees, unsuitable for canoe or plank making, no matter on what type of land they grow, are free to be cut by any member of the sublineage of the land owner. Others are violators and should return any wood taken or pay indemnity.

*Case 56.

    Place: Itod.

    Date: February 5th, 1955.

    Parties:

      a) *Defendant:* Ij Imo of Botu.

      b) *Authority:* Ij Jok of Itod, headman of Itod.

Facts: Imo, a member of the Enona sublineage of Botu, took wood from an old felled *uwaa* tree which grew on the territory of Jamaina sublineage. He was stopped by Jok and asked to lay down the wood he was carrying. Since he did not obey, the authority knocked the whole pack of wood from his shoulder. A violent argument started which threatened to evolve into a fight. However, the culprit quieted down and left the wood in Itod.

Rule 45: Moane trees of the virgin forest, which provide the most suitable raw material for canoe making, belong to the land owner. Though other trees may be felled in the virgin forest by people of the same sublineage as the landlord without permission of the latter, the *moane* tree constitutes an exception. The violator should give up the tree or pay indemnity.

Case 57.

   Place: Obaj.

   Date: 1954.

   Parties:

      a) *Defendant:* Pi Amo of Obaj.

      b) *Plaintiff:* Pi Gaa of Obaj, older brother of Amo.

      c) *Authority:* Pi Peg of Obaj, village headman.

Facts: Amo asked his older brother for permission to fell a *moane* tree in the latter's forest. Gaa, however, refused to comply with the request. An argument ending in a stick fight started between the two brothers.

Outcome: The authority stopped the fight and decided that since Gaa was the owner, he had the right to refuse. Peg urged Amo to be quiet and to look for canoe wood some place else.

Comment: Though Gaa's action was in conformity with the rule, his refusal was considered unethical by most of the people of his village.

TRAPPING AND HUNTING LAWS

Rats, which the Kapauku consider to be attached to a specific plot of land, belong to the landlord if the area is a garden or a second growth forest. All other animals, such as birds, wild boars, reptiles, bats, and marsupials, because they are thought of as roaming over wide areas, may be hunted by all the sublineage members over the territory of their unit irrespective of the individual ownership. Virgin forest is a free hunting ground for everyone, without any restrictions. Trapping, since it is connected with changes in the land itself (pits, snares in houses of mud, etc.), is always the exclusive prerogative of the owner of the land no matter on what type of land it occurs.

Rule 46: Rats are the exclusive property of the owner of the *mude* type of land. Their trapping and shooting without the owner's permission should be punished by payment of an indemnity.

Case 58.

   Place: Aigi.

   Date: ca. 1953.

   Parties:

      a) *Defendant:* Ij Mot of Jaga.

      b) *Plaintiff:* Ij Deb of Aigi.

      c) *Authority:* Ij Jok of Itod.

Facts: The defendant hunted rats in a grassy area which belonged to Deb. He succeeded in killing about ten rats. The owner of the land learned about the activity and challenged the right of the hunter to shoot "his animals." A stick fight between the two accompanied by shouting and screaming brought Jok to the scene.

Outcome: Although the latter is a headman in another village, he acted as the authority and decided this case in favor of the land owner. The hunter accepted the decision and gave to Deb part of his prey as indemnity.

Comment: Ij Jok, although head of Itod, decided a case in Aigi village because Eka, its headman, was not present.

Rule 47: When two hunters hit a wild boar and it dies, the man who scores the first hit is the owner of the animal. He keeps the tusks, tail, and jaw as trophies. Violators should pay indemnity and return the meat.

Case 59.
   Place: Botu.
   Date: ca. 1953.
   Parties:
      a) *Hunters from Botu:*
         Ij Awi, headman of the village.
         Ij Kam.
         Ij Kek.
      b) *Killer of the boar:* Pi Amo of Jaga.
      c) *Authority:* Ij Eka of Aigi, headman of the confederacy.

Facts: The three hunters of Botu wounded a wild sow which was killed later in the day by Pi. The latter took the game to the Kojo village and divided the meat among the people of the Jamaina sublineage. The three men who wounded the sow, one of whom had the full ownership right, were not given anything. A stick fight resulted.

Outcome: The confederacy's authority pacified the two parties and decided that the whole affair should be considered closed and no payment made because of the fight.

Comment: The decision contradicts rule 47. This case represents a flagrant injustice committed against the Botu people of the Enona sublineage.

Case 60.
   Place: Obaj.
   Date: Spring, 1954.
   Parties:
      a) *Man who hit first:* Pi Ama of Obaj.
      b) *Killer:* Pi Peg of Obaj.

Facts: Ama first hit the wild boar, but the arrow just wounded the animal. The second hunter killed it.

Outcome: Ama kept ears, tusks, and tail as trophies. The meat, however, was divided between the two hunters equally.

Comment: This peaceful settlement is again contradicting the rule. The first man who wounded the animal should have been the owner of the whole carcass.

Rule 48: Trapping is the exclusive privilege of the land owner. A violator of this right should give up his catch or pay indemnity.

No case reported.

OWNERSHIP OF MOVABLES

Like land, all movable property is owned by a single individual. Since robbery, or taking things by force, is unknown to the Kapauku, offences against one's property comprise theft, destruction, and damage. The institution of ownership, however, does not involve only rights. It becomes a source of duties at those times when ownership hampers the rights of other people. In such cases, the European lawyers speak about liability and associate the latter primarily with the responsibility of an individual rather than with the object itself. Thus we speak about accident, negligence, criminal negligence, and intent, adjusting the punishment of the liable person according to the degree of his guilt. The payment of damage, on the other hand, the European lawyers consider as a civil aspect of the case and determine its amount according to the loss suffered by the plaintiff.

Among the Kapauku, liability for an object or animal has little to do with the intention or action of the owner. What is decisive is the fact of ownership and the damage inflicted on another person. Much less important are the facts about the owner and the object itself. Thus the difference between a trap set on a path and one constructed in one's garden would have little effect upon the liability of the trapper for damage done to other people. While we look for negligence, intent, and the nature of the object, the Kapauku use the simple fact of ownership as the main factor in determining liability and the amount of the damage as a measure for indemnity.

Theft. "*Oma motii,* to take by theft," applies to an act of taking an object or an animal from the owner without his knowledge and with the intention of not returning it. Since the pig plays such an important role in the Kapauku economy, the rules concerning its theft should resemble in their harshness those which dealt with cattle rustling and horse stealing on the American western frontier. Because of the cultural emphasis on the pig and the expected differential treatment of the thief, all cases pertaining to pig stealing are put into a separate subdivision at the end of this section.

Rule 49: Stealing of food and crops should be punished by beating if the stolen goods are not voluntarily returned.

Case 61.
 Place: Kojo.
 Date: ca. 1951.

Parties:
  a) *Owner of the field:* Ij Mab of Kojo.
  b) *His wife:* Ko Oum of Boob.
  c) *Denouncer:* Ij Nak of Kojo.
  d) *Falsely accused:* Pi Ama of Kebo, wife of Ij Tid of Kojo, younger brother of
      the accuser.
  e) *Real culprit:* Ij Tim of Botu, wife of Pi Peg.

Facts: Someone stole sweet potatoes from the garden of Mab. His wife discovered the deed and started wailing in her garden on the mountain so that all the people could learn about the crime. Nak, an older man from Kojo, came to the screaming woman and told her that Pi Ama, who lives in his village, was responsible for the delict. The offended woman immediately went to Pi Ama's home and asked her about the theft. The accused denied the charge and claimed it was a lie. Under these circumstances, Oum told her the name of the denouncer and they both went to see the man about the details. Seeing the two women approaching his house, he fled, thus indicating that he had probably lied.

Not until three months later was another clue to the identity of the thief found. This time the wife of the headman of Obaj was accused by another person. When asked about the theft, she kept quiet, thus giving the evidence of her guilt.

Outcome: Peg, her husband, paid ten beads as indemnity for his wife's crime and beat the latter with a stick.

Case 62.
  Place: Aigi.
  Date: ca. 1953.
  Parties:
    a) *Defendant:* Go Mag of Tugu.
    b) *Her husband:* Ij Kag of Aigi.
    c) *Plaintiff:* Ij Eka of Aigi, headman of the village and confederacy.

Facts: Many large taros had been stolen from the field of the headman of Ij-Pi confederacy. Since the theft occurred in the morning when the soil was still wet, the owner and his helpers followed the tracks of the culprit until they reached the quarters of the defendant. There, under a pile of wood, the taro tubers were found. The woman was charged with theft. By keeping silent, she confessed to the crime.

Outcome: Her ashamed husband paid 1 Km and thirty beads as indemnity and returned the stolen food. Then he beat his wife with a stick.

Comment: The indemnity, coupled with the returned tubers, make the sanction quite harsh.

Case 63.
  Place: Obaj.
  Date: 1954.
  Parties:
    a) *Victim:* Pi Mad of Obaj.

Facts: Someone had stolen *pego*, reed blossoms which taste like asparagus, from the garden of Mad. A man carrying a bundle of such plants had been seen walking on the path between Kojo and Obaj in the evening of the day during which the theft occurred. It was already dark and the people who saw the man from a distance could not identify him. Since it was impossible to detect the culprit, the owner of the stolen crop resorted to the technique of shaming the unknown thief. He took an armful of cut *pego* stems from his garden and planted them on the muddy path where the mysterious man had been seen.

Outcome: The guilty individual has never been detected. However, he has been punished morally by the bunch of reeds stuck into the path. The growing reed remind the people of the shameful story of the theft. To avoid destruction of the monument, a new path has been made around it. My informants claimed that each time the culprit walked on the path, he was reminded of his crime. The close members of his family, who must have shared the stolen food and know about the deed, also feel ashamed for him.

Comments: There is no magical significance attached to the act of shaming described above.

Case 64.
  Place: Kojo.
  Date: Summer, 1954.
  Parties:
    a) *Defendant:* Jo Mab of Botu.
    b) *His father:* Jo Ibo of Botu.
    c) *Plaintiff:* Ij Mab of Kojo.

Facts: Mab, a twelve year old boy of Botu, was caught stealing sugar cane in the garden of Ij Mab.

Outcome: The owner lightly spanked the boy and, feeling sorry for him, let him go. He did not even tell the father of the young delinquent about the incident. The boy's parents heard about the incident from other people and the father severely scolded the culprit.

*Case 65.
  Place: Kojo.
  Date: May 29th, 1955.
  Parties:
    a) *Defendant:* Ij Ame of Kojo.
    b) *Authority:* Ij Amo of Kojo, older brother of defendant and headman of the
       village.
    c) *Outside authority:* Ij Jok of Itod, village headman.

Facts: It is customary for a man to cut some sugar cane for his immediate consumption from the field of his brother without asking permission. Ame was hungry and went with his friend to the garden of his older brother, Amo, and helped himself to four sticks of cane. In the evening, however, Amo, offended by the action of his younger brother, shouted in anger in Kojo so that the boys who slept in a house in Itod could hear it. Ame, becoming frightened, collected twenty beads from his friends and went to his brother to pay for the food he had taken. The angry man refused to accept the money and continued to shout and scold the boy. The latter became enraged over this injustice, rose, and declared he was leaving. He struck the shouting Amo with a stick and threw the beads on the floor of the house.

Outcome: The angry man grabbed a heavy piece of firewood from the rack and dealt the boy two heavy blows on the head, inflicting a deep, bleeding wound across his scalp. The screaming boy, with blood all over his face, neck, and chest, fled to Itod. Many people gathered around the weeping victim. Finally, Amo appeared and offered two precious Kapauku shells to his brother as indemnity. The wounded boy refused them, and Ij Jok, headman of Itod, publicly reprimanded the cruel man, charging him with being notoriously cruel and quarrelsome.

Comment: Amo, though himself an authority in Kojo, had to take a reprimand from the headman of Itod.

Case 66.

    Place: Obaj.

    Date: July 5th, 1955.

    Parties:

        a) *First wife:* Te Mag of Dune.

        b) *Second wife:* Pi Oum of Kebo.

        c) *Husband:* Ij Adi of Obaj.

Facts: The first wife of Adi received some pork ribs and a pork leg from her husband. She left the leg at home and went to the home of her son by her first marriage and gave him the ribs as a present. Upon her return, she discovered that somebody had stolen her pork leg while she was gone. She shouted, charging her husband and his second wife with the theft, and she partially destroyed the house. Adi merely stood by helplessly watching her destructive activity and protested verbally. The infuriated wife was not satisfied with destroying the house, but she went to the garden and uprooted many sweet potatoes, gourds, and wrecked part of the fence. Then she left for her son's home, where she stayed for three days.

Outcome: The husband did not punish her for the destruction because he had taken and eaten the meat while his first wife was absent.

Comment: This family had been disrupted by the continuous strife between the two wives. This case forms part of a long story of jealousy and rivalry illustrated by case 66 and continued in case 67.

Case 67.

    Place: Obaj.

    Date: July 12th, 1955.

    Parties:

        a) *First wife:* Te Mag of Dune.

        b) *Second wife:* Pi Oum of Kebo.

        c) *Husband:* Ij Adi of Obaj.

Facts: The first wife stole sweet potatoes from a field where the right of *ususfructus* belonged to the second wife. The latter, in retaliation, destroyed many sweet potatoes in the first wife's field, scolded her, and left, offended, for the village of Kojo to spend a few days with her son by her first marriage.

Outcome: The husband decided the first wife was guilty and punished her by reprimand.

Comment: Case 67 constitutes a further example of the rivalry pattern in case 66.

Rule 50: Stealing of money should be punished by beating if the stolen goods are not voluntarily returned.

Case 68.

  Place: Kego.

  Date: Spring, 1954.

  Parties:

   a) *Defendant:* Iw Mau of Dege, a ten year old boy.

   b) *Plaintiff:* Iw Mak of Kego.

   c) *Authority:* Iw Tit of Dege, father of the boy.

Facts: The defendant, a boy of ten years age, came to the house of Mak at noon when nobody was around. He entered the house which was closed with a piece of bark and found a net full of money under the floor. He stole 10 Km and one hundred and twenty beads; the rest he left behind. Then he departed, hoping that the theft would not be discovered. However, a neighbor's child saw the juvenile burglar and reported the case to the owner of the house. The latter went to Dege and complained to the father of the boy.

Outcome: After the boy admitted the deed, the father thrashed him with a stick. Under the impact of this persuasion, the boy returned the stolen things.

Case 69.

  Place: Botu.

  Date: June 7th, 1955.

  Parties:

   a) *Defendants:* Three men of the Debei Valley, their leader: Da Tod of Waag.

   b) *Plaintiff:* Ij Taa of Botu.

   c) *Authority:* Wa Dek of Kege.

Facts: One night three men from the Debei Valley came to Botu. They circled the village and approached a few houses looking for loot. One of the men found a cache with ten large imported cowries which he took. Then, still at night, they left by way of Puet village for Debei. The next morning their fresh tracks were discovered, and people, suspecting them of evil intentions, set out to capture the three men. Nothing was known about the theft. Since the tracks led them to Puet, the Botu people thought that the people of this village, a traditional enemy of their confederacy, were involved. However, the tracks led away from the houses and ascended the slope toward the Debei Valley. A few Puet people, trying to show good will, joined in the hunt. The way led to Keg village.

Outcome: To their surprise, the party was suddenly met by the headman of the village they were approaching who was carrying the stolen shells and who declared that he had confiscated the loot from the thief who had stopped at his house. He said also that he had scolded him. The owner of the cowries, who had not even discovered the plundering of his cache, thanked the honest headman.

Comment: The case shows an interesting cooperation of three confederacies whose members, though traditional enemies, joined to rectify a crime.

Rule 51: A stolen object should be returned. If this is impossible, indemnity should be paid. Refusal to return the object should be punished by beating.

Case 70.
   Place: Jaga.
   Date: ca. 1953.
   Parties:
     a) *Defendant:* Pi Imo of Jaga.
     b) *Plaintiff:* Go Ipo of Tukw, Tigi region.
     c) *Authorities:*
        Ij Eka of Aigi, headman of the confederacy.
        Ij Jok of Itod, headman of Itod.

Facts: Pi Imo went on business to the Tigi region. There, in the Tukw village, he entered a closed house and stole an ax, a bow, and a carrying net and went back with the loot to his village. A man who knew him and saw the theft reported it to the owner of the stolen things. The latter went to Jaga to claim his property.

Outcome: The two authorities listened to his complaint and decided on the guilt of the burglar. However, the latter refused to return the stolen goods and kept denying the whole thing. Since the authorities did not press the case, the owner had to leave empty-handed.

Comment: The pertinent rule was not enforced in this case.

Case 71.
   Place: Kojo.
   Date: February, 1955.
   Parties:
     a) *Defendant:* Ij Epa of Kojo.
     b) *Plaintiff:* Ij Mab of Kojo (FaFaBrSoSo of a).
     c) *Authority:* Ij Amo of Kojo, older brother of the defendant.

Facts: Epa, a fifteen year old boy, stole a machete from Mab. He refused to return it and kept denying the theft, although there were several witnesses to the incident.

Mab became weary of the denials and reported the case to Amo, the headman of Kojo and older half brother of the defendant.

Outcome: Amo beat the boy severely and asked him to return the machete. The delinquent, however, refused and escaped to a mission school in the north, where he remained.

Comment: The white man's arrival gave the chance of escape to many native criminals.

Case 72:

   Place: Botu.

   Date: August 3rd, 1955.

   Parties:

     a) *Defendant:* Ij Oum of Botu, wife of the older brother.

     b) *Plaintiff:* Ad Oum of Maab, wife of the younger brother.

     c) *Older brother and authority:* Ij Kem of Botu.

     d) *Younger brother:* Ij Kem of Botu.

Facts: Ad Oum and Ij Oum were wives of two brothers who lived together in one household. Ad had hidden a large bundle of inner bark for string making in a cave. Someone had found out about it and had stolen it. A few days later the victim noticed that the wife of her brother-in-law was making lots of string. She asked her about the source of the raw material, but the worker refused to tell. This denial furnished sufficient proof of her guilt. Ad started scolding her and asked for the return of her property. The shouting of the two women brought their husbands, who continued the dispute of their spouses.

Outcome: The older brother denied the guilt of his wife and refused to pay. Since he was the owner of the house, the younger brother could not put up much resistance. He had to sacrifice the property of his wife, and his only revenge consisted of ignoring his brother.

Comment: The older brother, as an authority in the household, exploited his position by covering up the crime of his wife.

Rule 51: One who steals chickens or game should restore the stolen goods or pay an adequate indemnity. In case of refusal to meet these demands, the culprit should be punished by a stick beating.

Case 73.

   Place: Obaj.

   Date: ca. 1953.

   Parties:

     a) *Defendant:* Pi Gaa of Obaj.

     b) *Plaintiff:* Pi Mab of Obaj, FaBrSo of the culprit.

     c) *Authority:* Pi Peg of Obaj.

     d) *Executioner:* Pi Gaa of Obaj, brother of the defendant.

Facts: The defendant stole five cooked marsupials from the house of his first parallel cousin. Since the meat was prepared for a birth ceremony, the offence was considered especially grave. The children of the offender told about the deed of their father to other children who reported the theft to the owner.

Outcome: The village headman decided to have the guilty man punished by stick beating. The latter's older brother was persuaded to be the executioner. In addition to the corporal punishment, the thief was exposed for three days to public reprimand.

Comment: If the stolen meat is intended for a ceremony, the offence is considered especially grave.

Case 74.

   Place: Botu.

   Date: June 10th, 1955.

   Parties:

     a) *Defendant:* Ij Bag of Botu.

     b) *Plaintiff:* Pi Ama of Obaj.

     c) *Authorities:*

        Ij Awi of Botu, village headman.

        Ij Tim of Botu, wealthy man.

     d) *Helper of the plaintiff:* Ij Beg of Jewe.

     e) *People who paid indemnity:*

        Ij Nak of Botu, older brother of defendant.

        Ij One of Botu, half brother of defendant.

        Pi Geg of Botu, MoBrSo of defendant (lives in the same household).

        Do Ena of Botu, BrWiBr of defendant.

Facts: During the night, Bag came to the house of Ama and stole a hen from the chicken house. In the morning, Beg discovered the partial destruction of the chicken house. With the owner of the stolen hen, he followed the fresh footprints which led them to the defendant's house. This house stood on the bank of the Edege River, about a twenty minute walk from Botu. Finding the house deserted, they entered and looked around for some evidence. They found a few charred bones and feathers in the fireplace. The two investigators began shouting and telling the Botu people about the crime committed by a Botu man against a man from Obaj. The commotion soon caused most of the men from both villages to assemble.

Outcome: Tim and Awi, the two important rich men of Botu, decided on the guilt of the defendant. Since the thief escaped into the woods, his brothers and close relatives were asked to contribute to a collection which would pay for the stolen bird. They gave sixty beads to the plaintiff and provided him with another chicken, thus satisfying his demands. The culprit, however, remained in hiding in the bush because he feared his relatives would beat him. They destroyed his house and threatened corporal punishment.

Comment: Because the headman of the culprit's village arranged for compliance with the request of the plaintiff, the matter was not brought to the attention of the head of the Ij-Pi confederacy.

Theft of a pig. Because a pig represents a highly valued property which cannot be hidden but is quite easily accessible and because pieces of pork, unlike many other things, are hard to identify, pigs and pork constitute ideal objects to steal. At the same time, the realization of most economic as well as political aspirations of a Kapauku depends upon the successful breeding of his pig. Because of these reasons, we would expect that ownership would be protected by rules harsh enough to deter potential criminals. With surprise, however, we find that our hypothesis is not borne out by abstract rules among the Kapauku. It is mainly the frequency of the theft of pigs and the emotional involvement of their owners which justify our special category.

Rule 53: If a pig is stolen, an adequate indemnity should be paid. If this is denied, a pig which is owned by the thief or by one of his relatives may be taken as re-imbursement. Should this be impossible, the culprit should be beaten with sticks.

Case 75.
  Place: Botu.
  Date: ca. 1940.
  Parties:
    a) *Defendant:* Ij Geg of Botu.
    b) *Plaintiff:* Bo Kaw of Tada.
    c) *Authority:* Ij Eka of Aigi, headman of the confederacy.

Facts: The defendant stole a pig in the Debei Valley, brought it to Botu and there secretly cut it up and distributed or sold the meat to several people. The next day the Debe people appeared in force on the mountain slope over Botu and demanded justice. They were assured that the matter would be attended to if they would return the next day.

Outcome: Eka, the confederacy's leader, after hearing several testimonies, found the culprit guilty. The latter had to pay for the stolen animal in cowries and was reprimanded for three days.

Comment: This case involved parties from two different regions.

Case 76.
  Place: Botu.
  Date: ca. 1950.
  Parties:
    a) *Defendant:* Go Ken of Tugu.
    b) *Plaintiff:* Ij Awi of Botu, a village headman.

Facts: Awi's pig disappeared. After two days, a man from Tugu reported the culprit to the pig's owner. The Botu people took weapons and went to Tugu.

Outcome: The inhabitants of that village refused to pay indemnity. The expedition party caught a pig that belonged to the first paternal parallel cousin of the culprit, bound it, and carried it away. The Goo people started a fight with sticks but were chased away. Awi, after having killed the pig, distributed some meat to his helpers and sold other pieces for cowry shells. The pig taken in the exchange was much heavier than the stolen one.

Case 77.
   Place: Botu.
   Date: ca. 1951.
   Parties:
      a) *Defendant:* Go Teg Pit of Tugu.
      b) *Plaintiff:* Ij Jik of Botu.
      c) *Thief's younger brother:* Go Ken of Tugu.
      d) *Denouncer:* Go Teg of Tugu, FaBrSo of the thief.

Facts: Pit stole a pig in Botu, brought it to his village in the other confederacy's territory, killed it there, and ate the meat with his family. His first paternal parallel cousin, being angry with the culprit for other reasons, denounced him for a reward of one Kapauku cowry and forty beads from the pig's owner.

Outcome: The Botu people organized an expedition to Tugu, where they stealthily captured a pig belonging to the youngest brother of the thief and carried it away as indemnity.

Case 78.
   Place: Botu.
   Date: ca. 1952.
   Parties:
      a) *Defendant:* Ij Taa of Botu.
      b) *Plaintiff:* Ij Dan of Botu.
      c) *Falsely accused man:* Wa Eba of Puet.
      d) *Wounded man:* Wa Jam of Puet, FaBrSo of the falsely accused man.
      e) *Denouncer:* Pi Oum of Kebo.
      f) *Possible authorities:*
         Ij Awi of Botu, village headman.
         Ij Jok of Itod, village headman.
         Ij Eka of Aigi, headman of the confederacy.

Facts: Taj of Botu stole and killed a pig belonging to his neighbor. In order to cover up his deed, he falsely accused a man from Puet, a village of the enemy, the Wa-Ti confederacy. The pig owner went to the enemy and, in a dispute, shot Jam in the abdomen. A war which resulted from this false accusation lasted three days. Since there were no dead, and both sides lacked enthusiasm as well as a strong cause, peace was easily concluded.

However, during the war a woman who knew about the theft by Taj and who was angry because she had not received enough meat, denounced the culprit to the offended man. The latter decided to shoot the thief and deliver his rattan bowstring to the enemy in order to stop the warfare and receive a remuneration.

Outcome: The early end of the war prevented the realization of the plan.

Comment: Ij Jok, leader in Itod and the writer's informant on this case, asserted that had the thief been killed, he would have considered it proper and just.

Case 79.
   Place: Aigi.
   Date: ca. 1953.
   Parties:
     a) *Defendant:* Iw Eto of Dege.
     b) *Plaintiff:* Ij Iib of Aigi.
     c) *Authorities:*
        Ed Pei of Dege, village headman.
        Iw Tik of Dege, village headman.
     d) *Denouncer:* Ed Ena of Dege.

Facts: A large sow disappeared and the people of Aigi searched the woods and grasslands, but in vain. After one month, on the bank of the Degei River they found bones which could have belonged to the lost animal. A woman from Dege, a village near the place where the bones were found, pointed out the killer of the animal. The search party approached the man, showed him the bones, and asked him: "What do you know about this?" He kept quiet and thus admitted his guilt.

Outcome: Because the authorities from his village called him guilty and urged him to repair the damage, he asked the Aigi people to come on the next day. On that day he presented them with a huge sow as indemnity and the party, satisfied, left for home.

Case 80.
   Place: Botu.
   Date: ca. 1953.
   Parties:
     a) *Defendant:* Pi Ama of Obaj.
     b) *Plaintiff:* Pi Geg of Botu.
     c) *Authority:* Ij Jok of Itod, village headman.
     d) *Denouncer:* Ij Jik of Botu.
     e) *Authorities helping with the case:*
        Ij Amo of Kojo, village headman.
        Pi Peg of Obaj, lineage headman.

Facts: Jik was known to have lied on several occasions. Once he claimed he had deposited 300 Km with his wife, but she proved he lied by showing the contents of her net to her brother.

When the pig of Geg became lost, Jik secretly accused Ama of the theft. Because the latter convincingly denied the deed, the pig owner disclosed the identity of the accuser. When confronted with the accused man, the denouncer kept quiet.

Outcome: The authority reprimanded Jik for lying and urged the people to look for the lost pig. It was found two months later in the woods near Puet village.

Comment: The past record of the accused made his testimony untrustworthy.

Case 81.
  Place: Aigi.
  Date: ca. 1953.
  Parties:
    a) *Defendant:* Do Ako of Buna, village headman.
    b) *Plaintiff:* Ij Eka of Aigi, headman of the confederacy.
    c) *Denouncer:* Pi Jun of Obaj.

Facts: Do Ako, one of the two headmen of Buna, a village united by a bond of allegiance with the plaintiff's confederacy, was accused of stealing a pig from the authority of the confederacy. He kept denying it for twenty days. To convince other people, he tore his net carrying bag, broke his penis sheath, and smeared his face with ashes. The authority tried to be diplomatic and told the man who denied the theft: "If you confess to us, you will have to pay only cowries. Tell us and we will not fight with sticks or start a war." However, all the efforts were in vain.

Outcome: Because the denials and the accusations were so convincing and there was inadequate evidence, the case remained unsolved: "*ewo gaajake jaikai,* because of ignorance we left (the case)."

Case 82.
  Place: Buna.
  Date: 1954.
  Parties:
    a) *Defendant:* Do Deg of Buna.
    b) *Plaintiff:* Ag Pod of Mado.
    c) *Authority:* Do Ako of Buna, village headman.
    d) *BrSo of defendant:* Do Deg of Buna.

Facts: Deg stole a pig from Ag. The latter, uncertain about the possible outcome of an argument with the thief, resorted to self help. In turn, he stole a pig from the culprit's brother's son. The young man, using the same technique, took a pig from his guilty father's brother.

Outcome: Authority upheld the actions of both men and found it proper to deprive the thief of his own pig. Deg accepted the verdict.

Comment: This case is actually composed of two separate legal actions: one between the offended man and the nephew who suffered a loss because of his uncle's crime; and the second between the nephew and the uncle by which an equilibrium upset by the theft was re-established.

Case 83.

  Place: Kego.

  Date: June, 1954.

  Parties:

    a) *Defendant:* Ed Mab of Dege.

    b) *Accomplice:* Ij Ima of Dege.

    c) *Plaintiff:* Ij Jok of Itod, village headman.

    d) *Denouncer:* Iw Deg of Kego.

    e) *Authority:* Ed Pej of Dege.

Facts: Two men from Dege stole a pig from Jok, the leader of Itod. After a few days, a woman approached Jok and offered to disclose the identity of the criminals for sixty beads. The anxious pig owner paid the price. After having heard the names, he led an expedition of Ij-Pi people to Dege and there they demanded justice. The two defendants denied the deed and a fight almost started. However, the authority of Dege sided with Jok and urged the culprits to pay an indemnity: "Ij is a really rich man, and has many wives. Therefore, I am very much ashamed (because of you). You repay him with a pig, or I shall feel embarrassed even to look at him."

Outcome: The culprits complied with the request and gave a pig which was worth 12 Km.

Concluding remark: All except two of the above cases of pig theft involved parties from two different confederacies. In the two which did occur within the confederacy, no punishment was administered to the culprits. None of the punishments were heavier than those for other types of theft, while some of them were even lighter and most of them involved no corporal punishment whatsoever. Therefore, we are justified in concluding that though pigs are the basis of the economy, the source of fortune, and the most precious possession of a Kapauku, the stealing of a pig does not elicit a punishment comparable to the animal's importance.

DESTRUCTION OF PROPERTY

Rule 54: Those who destroy another man's property should pay an adequate indemnity to the owner. For refusing to pay, one may be beaten or his property taken as compensation.

Case 84.

  Place: Obaj.

  Date: ca. 1951.

  Parties:

    a) *Defendant:* Te Mag of Dune.

    b) *Plaintiff:* Ij Doj of Obaj.

c) *Authority:* Pi Peg of Obaj, village headman.

d) *Husband of the defendant:* Ij Adi of Obaj.

Facts: Doj of Obaj told Adi he would like to buy the crop in his garden. While the two men were negotiating, Adi's wife went to her husband's garden and dug a large amount of sweet potatoes. After hearing about the digging, the prospective buyer withdrew his proposition. The infuriated Mag waited for a time when the village was deserted, and then she burnt the house of the plaintiff. The wife of the latter, in turn, burnt the house of Adi.

Outcome: The authority prevented a fight and decided that since each side lost a house and both sides violated the customary rules of a sales contract, the relation of the parties to the dispute was *uta-uta*; in other words, the damages on both sides were matched.

LIABILITY FOR PROPERTY

The right of ownership carries a liability for damage caused to other people by the property. If the owner is willing to compensate for the damage by an adequate payment, it almost never happens that emotions cause either of the parties to commit a violent act. Unlike theft, rape, lying, and killing, this type of a misdeed does not attach to the defendant an attribute of immorality and no rule carries a provision for corporal punishment.

Rule 55: The owner of a trap is responsible for the device. If it wounds or kills a man or a pig, the owner should pay indemnity.

Case 85.

  Place: Obaj.

  Date: ca. 1951.

  Parties:

  a) *Defendant:* Pi Amo of Obaj.

  b) *Plaintiff:* Pi Wed of Obaj.

  c) *Authority:* Pi Peg of Obaj.

Facts: The defendant made a boar trap in his garden. He left an opening in his fence and in front of it he camouflaged several bamboo spikes. Wed's pig entered the garden and after it had eaten some sweet potatoes, it pierced its abdomen with one of the hidden spikes and bled to death. In a dispute, the pig owner asked for 20 Km as indemnity, but the trapper charged 20 Km for the destroyed garden.

Outcome: The authority decided that one-quarter of the pig pierced with the spike of the trap should be given to the trapper and he, in turn, should pay 10 Km indemnity to the pig's owner. Both parties complied with the decision.

Comment: Though the outcome is different from the rule, the informants claimed that this solution is customary.

General principle: Damage caused by animals should be paid for by their owners if the damage is not a consequence of an illegal act of the injured person.

Rule 56: Should a pig destroy the crop in a garden, the owner of that crop is allowed to shoot the pig if it is caught in the action. The carcass should be kept by the pig's owner, except for the quarter pierced by the arrow. This quarter should be given to the killer. If the marauding animal is not shot, an adequate indemnity should be paid by the animal's owner to the owner of the garden. In case of refusal, a commensurate amount of property belonging to the liable person may be confiscated.

Case 86.
   Place: Botu.
   Date: ca. 1953.
   Parties:
      a) *Defendant:* Ij Nak of Botu, owner of the house.
      b) *Plaintiff:* Ij One of Botu, half brother of Ij Nak.

Facts: One's field was invaded by a pig belonging to his half brother. After the latter had refused to pay indemnity, the enraged owner of the garden started a stick fight. Since they were half brothers and lived in the same house, other people were asked by the authority not to participate in the dispute. Both men suffered deep wounds on their heads.

Outcome: No indemnity was paid because the fight settled the affair.

Case 87.
   Place: Aigi.
   Date: ca. 1953.
   Parties:
      a) *Defendant:* Ij Iib of Aigi.
      b) *Plaintiff:* Ij Jok of Aigi.
      c) *Authority:* Ij Eka of Aigi.

Facts: Jok's sow, worth 30 Km, entered the garden of Iib through a dilapidated fence. The latter discovered the pig eating his sweet potatoes. Although the sow did not do much damage, he shot it with an arrow.

Outcome: The authority decided that since the sow had done scarcely any damage and the fence was in a very poor shape, Iib should repay part of the value of the animal to Jok. The latter received 16 Km and 5 Tm. He gave a quarter of the carcass with the wound from the arrow to the killer.

Case 88.
   Place: Obaj.
   Date: June 24th, 1955.
   Parties:
      a) *Defendant:* Pi Dim of Obaj, now living in Buna.
      b) *Plaintiff:* Pi Ama of Obaj.
      c) *Authority:* Pi Peg of Obaj.

Facts: Ama's garden was partially destroyed by a pig belonging to a Pi man who lived in Buna. The angry man followed the spoor of the animal and shot it. The arrow merely wounded the animal. The owner of the pig, hearing by the yodeling system about the shooting of his pig, grabbed a stick and rushed to Ama's village. The two men met in front of Ama's house. The argument was on the verge of becoming a fight when the authority arrived.

Outcome: He pacified the parties and decided that the case should be considered closed. Ama had no right to shoot the pig outside of his garden. However, the animal had not died and therefore neither party owed the other anything.

Case 89.

   Place: Obaj.

   Date: July 6th, 1955.

   Parties:

   a) *Defendant:* Pi Eka of Obaj.

   b) *Plaintiff:* Pi Gaa of Obaj.

   c) *Authority:* Pi Peg of Obaj, village headman.

   d) *Plaintiff's wife:* Ij Oti of Giiw.

Facts: The wife of Gaa discovered a pig eating sweet potatoes in her garden. She identified the animal and shouted the bad news to her husband who was in the village. He rushed to the scene, surveyed the damage, and advised his wife to go to the pig's owner and ask for beads and shells as indemnity. This she did. The liable person refused to pay, however. He claimed he was not responsible for the damage because the fence was in bad repair.

Outcome: The authority upheld the defence of the pig owner and decided the latter was not liable.

Case 90.

   Place: Obaj.

   Date: July 12th, 1955.

   Parties:

   a) *Defendants:*

      Pi Teb of Obaj.

      Pi Tod of Deem, Debei Valley.

   b) *Plaintiff:* Ij Ket of Obaj.

Facts: During the absence of Peg, the village headman, five pigs destroyed the whole crop of sweet potatoes of Ket. He saw the animals in action and shot each of them with a bird arrow hoping only to scare them away. On asking the pig owners to pay damages, he was offered only two beads. He asked for at least sixty. After his price was not met, he destroyed the fences of the defendants and cut their sugar cane. Tod, the owner of three of the pigs, went to retaliate by destroying Ket's sweet potato field. The latter, armed with a stick, stopped Tod who, though without a weapon, challenged the angry man: "Just beat me if you want; go ahead!" However, Ket refrained from a corporal assault and attempted instead to burn down the houses of the pig owners.

Outcome: Since the village headman was not present, all the people of Obaj stopped Ket short of burning the houses and prevented further violence.

Comment: The case exemplifies an emergency situation in which the whole community, in the absence of the authority, stopped the parties to the dispute from further destructive activities.

USUSFRUCTUS

In the Kapauku economy, there are two types of the right of *ususfructus*. One type arises from a contract by which a garden is leased for a period necessary for growing one crop. Because there are no cases in which the right has been violated by a third person and because disputes between contractees belong to the section of contracts, there will be no disputes of this type discussed below.

The second type involves the economic relationship between wife and husband. While the latter is the owner of the land and garden as a whole, the wife has a right to a section of it. Here she plants and weeds from time to time, considering the crop her own property. Her husband has a right to all the crop he may harvest, a right which he sporadically exercises. Because his wife has the duty to feed his pig with her sweet potatoes, she expects to be repaid at the time the animal is slaughtered.

Rule 57. Garden space should be divided equally among a man's wives. Repetitive disregard of this rule provides grounds for divorce. Infringement upon her right by a person other than her husband should be punished by collecting an adequate indemnity.

Case 91.
   Place: Jaga.
   Date: June 29th, 1955.
   Parties:
      a) *Defendant:* Ij Auw of Jaga.
      b) *Plaintiff:* Jo Ena of Dodo, wife of defendant.

      c) *Authority.* Same as defendant.
Facts: In dividing his field, Amo favored his second wife. His first wife felt offended and asked for justice. An argument developed during which the husband slapped his complaining wife. The latter left the house and went back to her brother's home, thus suggesting the opening of divorce procedure.

Outcome: Her husband went after her, apologized, and promised to review his partitioning of the field. The wife, satisfied, returned home.

Case 92:
   Place: Kojo.
   Date: Summer, 1955.

Parties:
  a) *Defendant:* Ko Oum of Pago, 1st wife.
  b) *Plaintiff:* Ad Oum of Ijom, 2nd wife.
  c) *Authority:* Ij Mab of Kojo, husband.

Facts: The first wife received a larger piece of land than the second one. The latter, in the absence of the first wife, pulled out the sticks which marked the boundary between their plots and made a new demarcation line which she considered just. The first wife retaliated in the same way. After the second wife changed the line for the second time, the first wife beat her with a stick. Weeping, the beaten woman went to complain to her husband.

Outcome: He refused to take any measures and told his weeping spouse: "You did move the boundary line which I set up, and you received a beating. Now you women are even."

Intestate Inheritance

In intestate inheritance, the Kapauku recognize three different situations which are relevant to the allocation of the property of a deceased in the absence of a testament. Two of these situations are defined by the sex of the deceased. Thus, different rules apply to the inheritance of property left by a man as against that left by a woman. The third type of situation involves children under eight years of age. This we may call "inheritance by a minor."

Intestate inheritance from a male. There are three categories of property to which different rules of inheritance apply. These do not differ in allocating specific property to different heirs. Indeed, in all of them the eldest son is the main heir. The difference lies rather in the degree of inclusiveness of the siblings of the main heir in the sharing of the estate.

Rule 58: The eldest son of the deceased possesses an exclusive right of inheritance to the following items from the estate: bows and arrows, net carrying bags, necklaces, charm stones, house, "*tone,* the woman's house," dogs, chickens, all cowries and beads used in trading, and all pigs. In case of deficiency of sons, the eldest living brother is the heir. In the absence of the latter, the eldest son of the eldest brother inherits. In the absence of first fraternal nephews, the father inherits. In case the father has died, the eldest father's brother inherits. If all paternal uncles have died, the eldest son of the eldest father's brother becomes the exclusive heir, etc.

Comment: Though the rule gives to the eldest son, brother, nephew, uncle, or cousin an exclusive right to all pigs, the moral code of the Kapauku asks the heir to surrender some of the animals to the heir's full siblings.

No case reported.

Rule 59: "*Daa mege,* tabooed cowries," tabooed beads, tabooed small beads of *pagadau* type, and tabooed *dedege* necklaces become the property of the eldest son who has a duty (legal) to distribute some portion of them among his siblings. If the tabooed beads and necklaces (but not cowries) have been kept during the life of the deceased by his wives, the sons of every wife are entitled to the share kept by their mother. In the absence of sons, under conditions analogous to those described above, the inheritance goes to brothers; in their deficiency, to sons of the oldest brother; in deficiency of nephews, to the father; in his absence, to the father's brothers; in their absence, to sons of the oldest father's brother, etc.

Comment: The tabooed cowries, tabooed beads, tabooed small beads, and tabooed necklaces represent a man's savings and are deposited in a cache or with his wives. These valuables are destined for inheritance and are tabooed from use by the depositor. The taboo is self-imposed, carries a supernatural sanction of death to the violator, and gives the depositor high prestige.

Case 93.

  Place: Aigi.

  Date: ca. 1940.

  Parties:

   a) *Defendant:* Ij Ato of Aigi, eldest son of the dead man.

   b) *Plaintiffs:* The younger brothers of Ij Ato.

   c) *Dead man:* Ij Kag of Aigi.

Facts: After the death of the wealthy man of Aigi, his eldest son took possession of the entire amount of 300 tabooed Km and refused to give any portion to his half brothers.

Outcome: In the dispute, he argued that he had the right to keep all of the tabooed cowries because his mother was dead and therefore all his father's beads and necklaces which were kept by his father's spouses went to his half siblings. People from the village and finally his co-heirs agreed.

Case 94.

  Place: Botu.

  Date: ca. 1943.

  Parties:

   a) *Dead man:* Ij Tij of Botu.

   b) *Defendant:* Ij Tim of Botu.

   c) *Plaintiffs:*

       Ij Imo of Botu.

       Ij Ipo of Botu.

       Ij Amo of Botu.

   d) *Authorities:*

       Ij Awi of Botu, village headman.

       Ij Eka of Aigi, headman of the confederacy.

Facts: Tim, a rich man from Botu, died leaving ten pigs and 360 Km with his first wife and 360 Km with his second wife. His eldest son by the first wife took all ten pigs and the 360 Km deposited with his mother. When the second wife left her net carrying bag lying in her room, he took the other 360 Km from it. During an argument with his cheated half brothers, the village authority suggested that he should give the other 360 Km to his half siblings. Tim's refusal precipitated a fight with his half siblings, during which the outnumbered eldest brother escaped into the bush with the fortune. There he remained in hiding for a while.

Outcome: The authority decided that Tim, although owner of the cowries, should give those taken from the second wife to his half brothers. The defendant promised to do this and the brothers continued to live together in one house.

Rule 60: All land, stone and iron axes, knives, machetes, and salt should be divided among all sons of the deceased man on the basis of mutual agreement. If a son worked a piece of land during his father's life, this piece upon the death of the owner becomes his.

No dispute reported.

Intestate inheritance from a woman.

Rule 61: A woman's eldest son inherits her *ako* necklace and her net carrying bag. Should there be no sons, the husband inherits everything.

No dispute reported.

Rule 62: All the beads of a dead woman—small beads and *dedege* necklaces— become the property of her eldest son, who has the duty to give a portion (usually thirty per cent) to his full brothers. He should also give some to his full sisters. In the absence of sons, the husband inherits all of these things.

No disputes reported.

Rule 63: A dead woman's iron machete, stone machete, and stone knives should be distributed among her sons on the basis of common agreement. In the absence of sons, the husband inherits all of this property.

No disputes reported.

Rule 64: The eldest daughter inherits her mother's fishing net and "*jato*, the large carrying net." If there is no such daughter, the articles become the property of the woman's eldest sister. If no such sister exists, the oldest daughter of the oldest sister inherits both nets.

No dispute reported.

Intestate inheritance by a minor. When the father of a boy dies, the father's brother becomes a trustee of the inheritance and a guardian of the minor. The orphan has a right to stay in his uncle's home, to be fed and brought up. Under such circumstances, the uncle takes over completely the role of the father. A boy, however, may choose to stay with other persons, such as his mother and her new husband or his mother's brother. In such a case, this relative functions as a foster parent. No matter where the boy makes his residence, his father's brother has the duty of helping him to buy a wife at the time he comes of age. The boy has to pay *mune*, a fee for having been brought up, to any guardian other than his father's brother.

Rule 65: If a minor is an heir, his father's brother may cultivate the heir's fields but has to return all of them when the boy reaches adolescence (about fifteen years of age). In case there are no father's brothers, an adult paternal parallel cousin may take the trustee's position.
No dispute reported.

Rule 66: The trustee of an inheritance is required to guard and return all the tabooed currency to the boy upon his adolescence. The use of this type of currency by the trustee is tabooed.
No dispute reported.

Rule 67: The trustee is permitted to use non-tabooed currency from the inheritance and is required to return to the adolescent heir only part of the inherited sum, but not necessarily the same specimens.
No dispute reported.

Rule 68: All pigs become the property of the trustee, who should return at least a few at the boy's adolescence.
No dispute reported.

Rule 69: The guardian of the inheritance takes all stone and iron axes, stone and iron knives, stone and iron machetes, all necklaces, and nets. He has a duty to return a few of these only if he has received a large amount of them.
No dispute reported.

Inheritance of bride price.

Rule 70: The right to collect bride price for a girl at the time she marries belongs to her brothers and mother. The eldest brother takes the bride price of the first sister. The younger brother should be given the price collected for the second sister. Thus, each brother has his turn. In the absence of brothers and of the father, the girl's first parallel cousins, sons of the father's oldest brother, inherit the right to collect.
No dispute reported.

Concluding remark on intestate inheritance. The intestate inheritance may be called patrilineal with a strong emphasis upon primogeniture, which makes its appearance

also in the case of inheritance by daughters (see rule 63). The patrilineal primogeniture is absolute. Thus, the eldest son of the deceased inherits, irrespective of
whether his mother was first, second, or third wife of his deceased father.

A daughter inherits just the two articles listed in rule 63 and she should be given
a few beads and necklaces according to rule 61. A widow never inherits anything.
Unless she is too old, she always remarries.

TESTAMENT

The verbal form of testament was discussed in the first part of the monograph.
It may be stated here, as an introduction to the rules, that to make a testament is
considered an ethical duty of the dying man. Most testaments simply restate rules
of intestate inheritance. Though they may not differ in their content from rules of
intestacy, testaments eliminate possible uncertainties and troubles in dividing parts
of inheritance, such as land, currency, etc. However, there are occasions when
disinheritance takes place. When done for legal reasons, disinheritance is enforced
by members of the family as well as by political authorities. If the testament is unjust, it can be overruled. In addition to providing for the disposition of goods, a
testament includes instructions about the type of burial, the burial place, and
general advice for conduct.

Rule 71: No sons, brothers, father, or nephews, can be deprived of their share of
land under any circumstance. Statements contrary to this rule should not be respected after the death of the testator. Contrary to rule, however, one can will a
ususfructus right on a field until the first crop is harvested.

Case 95.

  Place: Botu.

  Date: June 16th, 1955.

  Parties:

  a) *Defendant:* Jo Ibo of Botu.

  b) *Plaintiff:* Ij Ogi of Botu.

  c) *Authorities:*

  Ij Awi of Botu, village headman.

  Ij Amo of Kojo, village headman.

  Ij Jok of Itod, village headman.

  d) *Dead man:* Ij Ajo of Botu, FaBr of plaintiff and SiHu of the defendant.

Facts: Jo Ibo started to make a garden in a plot, the *ususfructus* of which the
dying Ajo had willed to him. Ajo's heir, the eldest son of his brother, objected to
the right of Jo. To prevent him from continuing his work, Ogi started to work on
the same plot at the other end. The enraged heir of the *ususfructus* right destroyed
the fence of another garden of his rival. On the morning of June 16th, loud shouting
near Botu announced to the people of South Kamu that a dispute was in progress.
Many people gathered in the swampy foothills of the Kemugebega Mountain, while
on its slope Ajo with his supporters was working in the disputed garden. Ogi,

standing on the foothill, shouted charges up the slope: "I am the owner of the land; I have inherited it. You have not asked me for permission to make a garden. I have a right to cultivate my own land, and your destruction of my fence is a crime. I urge you to repair it. Your whole behavior is an act of ingratitude considering that I bought a wife for your son. Have you already forgotten that?" Many other reproaches were hurled up the mountain. Down came the following definition of the situation as seen by Jo Ibo: "The dead man was my sister's husband. He stated in his testament that I should work this field and, therefore, I do. I have no land in this village, but you have lots of it and you do not use it at all. Since the dying man gave me the right to use this field, I had no need to ask for your permission. I destroyed your fence only because you disregarded the testament and you tried to stop me. I am grateful for your help to my son, but that has nothing to do with this land."

Awi, the headman of Botu, who was listening to the charges and defense stood up and started shouting his decision, urging Ogi to let Jo make the field and asking Jo to repair the fence. He said he recognized Jo's right to the cultivation of the garden because of the testament and because Jo lacked fields, while the plaintiff had many and did not cultivate them. Jok was in full agreement with Awi's decision. Amo, the headman of Kojo, was of the same opinion, except that he did not see any reason why Jo should repair the fence.

Outcome: The parties to the dispute complied with their village authorities' decision except that they agreed that the plaintiff would harvest the crop he had planted on the plot, leaving the rest to Jo to cultivate. The latter promised to repair the fence.

Rule 72: No currency or pigs can be willed to individuals other than sons. However, a son may be disinherited for socially recognized reasons such as beating the testator, abusing him without reason, or neglecting him in disease or old age. In an absence of sons, the above restriction applies to brothers; in their absence, to fathers, etc.

Case 96.

    Place: Pona (region just south of Kamu).

    Date: ca. 1942.

    Parties:

        a) *Defendant:* Wo Nip of Pona.

        b) *Plaintiff:* Three nephews, sons of younger brother of the defendant.

        c) *Authority:* Wo Mee of Pona, village headman.

        d) *Dead man:* Wo Nip of Pona, testator and older brother's son of the defendant.

Facts: A boy of fifteen years of age who had recently inherited 240 Km, six hundred beads, and one ax was dying. His intestate heir was the younger brother of his father. Since he did not like his uncle for unknown reasons, he willed the whole of his fortune to his three first paternal parallel cousins, sons of a dead uncle. As soon as the boy died, his cousins took possession of the fortune, over the protests of the intestate heir. One evening when only one of the cousins was at home, the disinherited uncle came near the house and hid in the jungle. He waited until the young man left the house to urinate in the bush, then rushed in, took the net bag of his nephew containing the money, and fled home. The next day the disputants started a fight, making use of war arrows. The authority pleaded, talked, shouted, and finally succeeded in stopping the violence. The three nephews charged that their uncle stole from them, in addition to the inheritance, three hundred beads of their own which happened to be in the net bag.

Outcome: The authority decided that the three hundred beads should be returned. However, he argued that the whole inheritance should be kept by the uncle because he was the intestate heir and that the testamental disinheritance, because of the lack of any socially recognized reason, was invalid. The parties to the dispute complied with this decision.

Case 97.
> *Place:* Aigi.
> *Date:* ca. 1945.
> *Parties:*
>> a) *Defendant:* Ij Eki of Aigi.
>> b) *Plaintiff:* Ij Eka of Aigi.
>> c) *Authority:* Plaintiff is the headman of the confederacy.

Facts: Eka, the headman of the Ij-Pi confederacy, was disinherited by his father because of neglect and for beating the testator. The whole fortune went to Eki, a half brother of the plaintiff. Eka, dissatisfied with the testament, asked for a share.

Outcome: Eki, frightened because of Eka's influence and power, gave him twenty-two of the largest cowries of the most precious *bodija* type. This satisfied the complaining man.

Comment: The outcome of the case is contrary to the wording of the rule. Eki gave the shells because of the influential position of his brother.

Rule 73: The male testator is free to will to anybody the following items from his property: bow and arrows, net bags, and dancing net. The female testator is free to will to anybody her net bags, necklaces, and fishing nets. No charge opposing the disposition of these items is admissible.

No dispute reported.

Rule 74: If a father's brother is the intestate heir, the land may be willed directly to his sons and to the sons of an older but dead father's brother. The paternal uncle has no right to disregard such a disposition.

No dispute reported.

Rule 75: No man can be deprived by a testament of the inheritance of his sister's bride price. If the girl has no brothers, her first paternal parallel cousins, if heirs, may be deprived of the bride price for recognized reasons (rule 72) but only in favor of other first paternal parallel cousins. In the absence of these relatives, the testator may choose his beneficiary from the persons whose relation to the testator is of the same degree as that of the potential heir.

Case 98.
  Place: Botu.
  Date: ca. 1950.
  Parties:
    a) *Testator:* Ij Awi of Botu.
    b) *Beneficiary:* Ij Uma of Botu, FaFaBrSoSo of the testator.

Facts: Awi, having no sons and no first parallel nephews, bequeathed the bride price of his daughter to Uma, his second paternal parallel cousin. Though there were several second paternal parallel cousins older than the beneficiary, there was no dispute.

CONTRACT

Among the business-minded Kapauku, contractual relations which assume a few well-defined forms constitute causes for surprisingly numerous disputes. The cultural emphasis on the accumulation of wealth, achieved mainly through selling contracts, and the stress on its counterbalance, generosity which takes the form of money lending, and also the uncertainty in the mutual agreements and the difficulty of supplying evidence for the business transactions account for the high incidence of contractual controversies. To provide publicity for a contract and thus to achieve some security for the parties, close relatives often serve as witnesses. Some deals are made at public gatherings such as pig feasts. In deals contracted in the presence of only two individuals, the agreement is reported later to other people. A demonstration to other people of an absence or presence of some commodity or of money serves as additional evidence.

A Kapauku contract, unlike a Western one, is not considered to be concluded at the time of the mutual agreement. Not until both sides receive the remuneration expected from the agreement is the contract closed. Thus, when a man buys a small pig and it dies while still young, the man may return the dead animal to the seller and ask for the return of the money he paid. The risks arising from raising pigs rest with the seller until the slaughter of the animals.

Although custom defines reasons which are considered righteous for breaking a contract, a party to the contract may frequently and for any reason back out of a sales contract providing he returns what he received from the other party. The contract for lending money also substantiates the above statement. The creditor has a right to request the return of sums loaned at any time, even on the same day. This is not because the Kapauku think in terms of such short term credit.

The creditor simply changes his mind and backs out of the agreement which normally would have had at least four months duration.

SALES CONTRACT

Edai, the word for purchase, is applied by the Kapauku to all exchange of property, no matter whether the wanted commodity is acquired for money or by barter. Although barter and sale are thus classified together, the Kapauku make a difference between the two transactions. While anything can be purchased with money or beads, barter is limited to a few types of goods. Valuable commodities such as pigs, canoes, and houses are never acquired through barter. Pieces of pork, on the other hand, are often traded for a crop of sweet potatoes or a small garden of sugar cane. While a bow and some net bags may be used to purchase a field, they are, strangely enough, unacceptable for pork. Since the other Kapauku possessions that are eligible for barter, such as necklaces, have either too little value to be important in distribution or are considered improper to be used in such transactions, the volume of barter is negligible when compared to sales.

Because rules differ according to the commodities handled in a sale, the following organization of the rules and cases will be used to reflect this factor.

Sale of land.

Rule 76: The buyer is required to pay fully for land. The price should be at least as high as that determined by custom (nine hundred square meters for 5 Km). If underpaid, the seller or his heirs can always ask for additional money or take possession of the field.

Case 99.
  Place: Aigi.
  Date: ca. 1945.
  Parties:
    a) *Defendant:* Ij Epu of Botu, the buyer.
    b) *The seller:* Ij Eke of Aigi.
    c) *Plaintiff:* Ij Eka of Aigi, headman of the confederacy.
    d) *Moderators:*
        Ij Jok of Itod.
        Ij Iib of Aigi.

Facts: Epu bought fifteen *peka* (15 × 900 square meters) of land for the ridiculously low price of 10 Km. The customary price for this land would have been several times higher than the amount paid. After Eke, the seller of the land, died, his son and heir, Eka the present headman of the Ij-Pi confederacy, asked for additional payment. Because the buyer refused to pay, the headman wanted to lead an expedition to the village of Botu. This might have resulted in a fight between the two sublineages. Jok and Iib of Aigi talked their leader out of the plan.

Outcome: Epu, who became frightened by the rumors about violence, paid an additional 60 Km, thus bringing the price actually paid for the land close to its customary amount.

Rule 77: An old man cannot sell any part of his land without the consent of his adolescent sons. If the land is sold without such consent, the sons have the right to repossess it but they must return the amount of money paid for the property.
No dispute reported.

Rule 78: The vendor is not responsible for any damage to the land occurring after the acceptance of the money and after the transfer of the land.

Case 100.
  Place: Aigi.
  Date: ca. 1953.
  Parties:
    a) *Defendant:* Ij Deb of Aigi, the seller.
    b) *Plaintiff:* Ij Deg of Aigi, the buyer.

Facts: One *peka* of land had been bought for one machete, two *dedege* necklaces, 1 Km, and 1 Tm. After the money had been paid, a pig entered the garden and completely ruined the crop. The new owner of the land did not ask for return of the price because the pig belonged to his son.
  Outcome: Since the land itself, and not the crop, was the object of sale, such damage was irrelevant to the contract.

Sale of crops.

Rule 73: A growing crop of sweet potatoes, sugar cane, *idaja*, or taro may be sold without transferring the right of cultivation to the buyer. The latter should return the field to the landlord after completing the harvest. The landlord should protect the buyer and thus enable him to harvest all the crop. If he fails, the contract can be canceled and the price has to be repaid.

Case 101.
  Place: Botu.
  Date: July 1st, 1955.
  Parties:
    a) *Defendant:* Pi Oum of Kebo, married in Botu.
    b) *Plaintiff:* Ko Mab of Mogo, married in Botu, HuMo of the defendant.
    c) *Authority:* None.

Facts: The accused dug sweet potatoes in the garden which she had sold to her husband's mother for one piece of salt. She was caught in the action, and the infuriated buyer asked for the return of the salt.

Outcome: Because the offender promised not to do it any more, the case was settled by a few reproaches and a little shouting.

Rule 80: The vendor is responsible for the destruction of the crop if done by an invading pig or by the weather. In such a case, the price returned should be in proportion to the damage. The buyer has the right to cancel the contract.

Case 102.
  Place: Aigi.
  Date: ca. 1953.
  Parties:
    a) *Defendant:* Ij Iib of Aigi, seller of the crop.
    b) *Plaintiff:* Ij Jok of Itod, the buyer.
    c) *Authority:* Ij Eka of Aigi, headman of the confederacy.
Facts: The defendant sold a crop of sweet potatoes to the plaintiff. Shortly afterwards, pigs invaded the garden and completely destroyed the crop which had been purchased for 3 Km.
Outcome: The authority decided on the return of the price. The buyer, however, was satisfied with just 2 Km and left 1 Km to the seller because he felt sorry for the man's loss.

Case 103.
  Place: Aigi.
  Date: March 15th, 1955.
  Parties:
    a) *Seller:* Ij Utu of Aigi.
    b) *Buyer:* Ij Eka of Aigi, headman of the confederacy.
Facts: Pigs destroyed a crop of sweet potatoes which had been sold.
Outcome: The seller had to return only 3 Km of the 5 Km originally paid because the plaintiff felt sorry for the vendor.

Sale of pigs.

Rule 81: A female pig may be sold for a down payment of 5 Km and for *epaawa*, a large payment agreed upon by the parties, payable at the time of the killing of the sow with her offspring (customary *epaawa*, 60–120 Km). The buyer has the duty to pay the amount agreed upon and the seller has to transfer the animal upon the payment of the first part of the price. Violation invalidates the contract, and the price and the animal must be returned.
  See case 142.

Rule 82: A female pig may be sold for payment of the whole price at the time of the animal's transfer. The seller has a right to one of the offspring of the sow.

Violation invalidates the contract, and return of the animal and the payment should take place.

No dispute reported.

Rule 83: A male pig may be bought by full payment (6–7 Km is the customary price for a male piglet) or by a down payment of 1 Km and an agreed upon final payment (about 10 Km) at the time of its slaughter. The seller should transfer the pig, and the buyer should pay as agreed. Violation invalidates the contract, and return of the animal and the price should take place.

Case 104.
    Place: Jaga.
    Date: June 17th, 1955.
    Parties:
        a) *Defendant:* Pi Imo of Jaga, seller of the pig.
        b) *Plaintiff:* Pi Ene of Jaga, buyer, and son of the defendant.

Facts: A father sold his son a male piglet for 7 Km. After a lapse of time when the new owner wanted to execute his right of ownership, the father argued that the pig was his.

Outcome: A fight resulted in which the son suffered a deep wound on his head. The father's injustice precipitated a split within the household. The son built himself a new house and moved away from his father.

Comment: It is noteworthy that no authority from outside the household decided the dispute.

Case 105.
    Place: Botu.
    Date: ca. 1953.
    Parties:
        a) *Defendant:* Ij Dim of Botu, seller of the pig, a rich man.
        b) *Plaintiff:* Ij Teb of Botu, buyer.
        c) *Authority:* Ij Awi of Botu, village headman.

Facts: Dim, a rich man of Botu, sold a male piglet to a young boy. The latter paid him 5 Km, but the rich man failed to deliver the pig. When the boy asked for his money, it was refused. A stick fight developed in which the village authority fought Dim and his followers.

Outcome: Since the authority could not enforce his decision, Dim went unpunished. Because of this, the death of Dim which occurred shortly thereafter was ascribed by the people to punishment by evil spirits.

Rule 84: The seller of a pig should be held responsible for the premature death of the animal, irrespective of his actual guilt. If the sold animal becomes sick or dies, its seller should in case of installment payment refrain from asking final payment, or, in case of payment in full, he should return the price he received after the animal's body has been given to him.

Case 106.

  Place: Itod.

  Date: ca. 1951.

  Parties:

  a) *Buyer:* Ij Jok of Itod, village headman.

  b) *Seller:* Do Uno of Jota.

Facts: Jok's pig, worth 8 Km, died. Since he had paid 15 Km for it, he asked the seller for the return of the price. The latter refused to take back the dead animal and claimed he had spent all the shells he received.

Outcome: Jok felt sorry for the man and let the case go, losing 7 Km on the deal.

Case 107.

  Place: Bibi, South Kamu Valley.

  Date: ca. 1952.

  Parties:

  a) *Defendant:* Go Edo of Bibi, the seller of the pig.

  b) *Plaintiff:* Go Beg of Bibi, buyer of the pig.

  c) *Authority:* Ij Jok of Itod, village headman, SiSo of the defendant, and DaHu of the plaintiff.

Facts: A pig whose meat was worth 20 Km became sick. The plaintiff wanted to return it and collect the 50 Tm which he had paid for the piglet. The defendant refused to comply with the request and a quarrel followed.

Outcome: The authority, brought to the place of the dispute by the loud voices, decided that because it was dubious whether the pig was sick at the time of the sale, each of the disputants should keep half of the pig and the defendant should pay 20 Km because of his liability. The parties to the dispute accepted the solution.

Comment: Jok, although a rich man and headman of Itod, had no power in Bibi, a village of the Go-Bo confederacy. He was able to decide this argument because the defendant was his mother's brother and the plaintiff was his wife's father.

Case 108.

  Place: Itod.

  Date: ca. 1953.

  Parties:

  a) *Defendant:* Ed Ena of Kego, the buyer of the pig.

  b) *Plaintiff:* Ij Jok of Itod, seller of the pig and SiHu of the defendant.

Facts: A sow worth 30 Km which had already had two litters of pigs was sold for 1 Km paid immediately, and an *epaawa* of 120 Km and a female piglet payable in the future. The sow became sick and it seemed obvious that she had to be slaughtered. The buyer asked the seller to inspect her. The latter suggested that the animal be killed.

Outcome: The buyer kept all the meat and paid 40 Km and one female piglet to the plaintiff at the time of the killing. He also promised to pay an additional 80 Km in the future.

Comment: The payment of the full price for the pig was given only because the buyer wished to keep the slaughtered animal.

Case 109.
   Place: Itod.
   Date: ca. 1953.
   Parties:
     a) *Owner of pig:* Do Dod of Buna.
     b) *Breeder:* Ij Jok of Itod.

Facts: Jok bought a female piglet for 40 Tm and promised to pay 60 Km more at the time of the slaughter of the animal. The sow's weight increased, and indicated that she was worth 8 Km; then, she suddenly became sick and died.

Outcome: The seller asked for the dead animal; then he returned 20 Tm to Jok and absolved the breeder from payment of the promised 60 Km.

Comment: Jok's loss of 20 Tm on the pig deal was not consistent with rule 83.

Case 110.
   Place: Botu.
   Date: ca. 1954.
   Parties:
     a) *Buyer of the pig:* Ij Uma of Botu.
     b) *Seller of the pig:* Ij Jup of Aigi.

Facts: Uma of Botu bought a medium-sized male pig for 12 Km. The animal failed to eat sweet potatoes and showed signs of sickness.

Outcome: The buyer took it back to the original owner and received his 12 Km back.

Sale of chickens and dogs.

Rule 85: A hen may be sold for 1 Km and an additional, agreed upon payment, payable when the chickens hatch from the bird's eggs (which usually amounts to 3 Km). Should the hen become sick and die, the buyer has a right to refuse to pay the additional price. If he returns the dead bird to the vendor, he should be given back the 1 Km.

No dispute reported.

Rule 86: A cock may be sold for 1 Km. If it dies while still small, the buyer should have his money returned on presentation of the bird's body.

No dispute reported.

Rule 87: Because dogs are sold when they are mature and trained, there is no restitution at the time they die.

No dispute reported.

Sale of houses.

Rule 88: A house should be paid for at the time of its transfer. The contract is thus definite and cannot be broken.

No dispute reported.

Sale of movables.

Rule 89: A buyer of an object such as a net bag or a bow may cancel this contract on the same day or the next one. After that time, the deal is considered definite.

No dispute reported.

Agency in the sales contract.

The Kapauku use the members of their households as agents in the buying of house planks, pigs, or game (marsupials, rodents).

Rule 90: The buyer may return the commodity bought by his agent and the vendor is required to return the price.

Case 111.
   Place: Aigi.
   Date: ca. 1952.
   Parties:
       a) *Buyer:* Ij Eka of Aigi, headman of the confederacy.
       b) *Seller:* Do Ana of Puta.
       c) *Agent:* Ij Atu of Aigi.

Facts: A boy who lived in the household of Eka, the headman of the confederacy, was sent to the Pona region to buy a pig for 16 Km. He brought back an animal which the buyer did not like. He sent the boy back to Pona with the pig and commissioned him to request the return of the shell money. The vendor became offended by the canceling of the contract, took the animal as well as the shell currency, and went himself to Aigi. There, after having returned the shell money, he killed the pig and presented it as a gift to the buyer with the intention of shaming him in public.

Outcome: The leader of the confederacy could not neglect such a challenge to his prestige. He returned the 16 Km to the vendor, saying: "Because I am not a boy any more, I do not accept your gift. I am rich enough and I wish to pay."

Comment: Shaming, in terms of a challenge to a man's generosity, is a very effective means of inducing an opponent to accept the challenger's conditions in a contract. This method, of course, works only with "moral Kapauku," the individuals who try to acquire political and legal leadership by being generous.

Rule 91: The agent is entitled to a small reward by the buyer. He has no right to the entrusted money. Violations should be punished as theft.

Case 112.
   Place: Bibi.
   Date: Spring, 1954.
   Parties:
      a) *Defendant:* Ij Uno of Gino.
      b) *Plaintiff:* Go Epa of Bibi.
      c) *Authority:* Ij Kug of Gino.
      d) *Seller of the pig:* Ij Uno of Taba (Mapia region).

Facts: The plaintiff gave 40 Km to the agent and asked him to buy a pig in the Mapia Valley. The boy returned with a small animal and claimed he had paid all the 40 Km for it. The buyer became suspicious, inquired of the seller in Mapia, and found out that the boy had paid only 25 Km. After the boy was presented with the facts, he kept quiet. The authority of the defendant's village also kept quiet, thus delivering the dishonest agent into the power of the buyer.

Outcome: The boy became afraid and returned the 15 Km. The buyer, however, took pity on the young thief and gave him 5 Km from the sum returned. *"Okai juwii tou to,* he just listened and did not deny the charges," was the buyer's explanation for his generous deed.

Rule 92: The seller or buyer, if guilty of gross negligence or intention to harm the opposite side in the sale, will forfeit the rights from the rules given above.

Comment: Thus, a man who intentionally kills a pig (by starvation, for example) in order to be able to ask the return of the price will lose his right to do so.

No dispute reported.

BARTER

Since barter is considered equivalent to sale, rules regulating the sale of land or crops would apply to the barter of these commodities; and, similarly, rules regulating the sale of movables would relate to their barter as well.

Rule 93: The contractees of a barter may cancel the agreement within the first two days. After this time, the deal is considered closed.

Case 113.

> *Place:* Botu.
> *Date:* January 1st, 1955.
> *Parties:*
>> a) *Contractees:*
>>> Ij Epa of Kojo, seven year old boy.
>>> Ij Amo of Obaj.
>> b) *Authority:* Ij Jok of Itod, village headman.

Facts: A small boy seven years of age bartered his shorts (acquired from the writer) for a piece of pork. After three days, he asked Amo for the garment. Amo, however, rejected the request and pointed out that it was too late to ask after a lapse of three days and that the boy had already consumed the pork. The boy cried and insisted on recovering the pants.

Outcome: Although all the other boys and adults, as well as Jok, the village headman, kept telling the boy that he was wrong, he continued begging and crying. Amo finally agreed to return the shorts for 1 Km. He was moved to do so because of the boy's youth and also because he felt that he had cheated the young fellow in the barter.

PIG BREEDING CONTRACT

A contract to breed a pig for another person enables the breeder of the animal to earn money and obtain some pork. It also facilitates the keeping of many pigs by a rich man, for without the existence of this type of a contract, he could not care for so many.

Rule 94: The breeder of a pig is entitled to a remuneration consisting of shell money (5–20 Km) in case the pig owner does the killing. If the pig breeder himself does the slaughtering, he receives six kilograms of pork and the head with entrails. Payment is due at the time of the slaughter. It is up to the owner to determine the time. In case of violation, indemnity equaling the damage should be paid.

Case 114.

> *Place:* Puet.
> *Date:* August 16th, 1955.
> *Parties:*
>> a) *Pig breeder:* Wa Pig of Puet.
>> b) *Pig owner:* Ti Kin of Puet.
>> c) *Authority:* Ti Wek of Puet.
>> d) *MoBrSo of breeder:* Ti Oka of Puet.

Facts: A small female pig was sick, and the breeder killed it without notifying the owner. The latter became enraged about the action as well as the loss of a sow and consequently set the house of the breeder on fire. The sleepy residents of the structure barely escaped injury. At noon the next day, the pig owner repeated his crime and burnt down the house of a first maternal cross-cousin of the pig breeder, who happened to live in the same village. The total fire damage amounted to 45 Km.

Outcome: The village authority ignored the whole case. The house owner threatened the "firebug" with violence and asked for indemnity. The arsonist pig owner paid the 60 beads (equal to 2 Km) and 3 Km. He also let the injured people keep the dead pig and promised additional cowries in the future.

Rule 95: The breeder is liable for conscious mistreatment of an animal or for gross negligence concerning it. The owner has a right to inspect the pig at any time and should be notified about any problems. The owner may take the animal away any time he sees fit. In case of violation, adequate indemnity should be paid. The breeder is, however, not liable for accidents.

Case 115.
    Place: Maab.
    Date: ca. 1953.
    Parties:
        a) *Defendant:* Ad Mag of Maab.
        b) *Plaintiff:* Ij Mab of Kojo.
        c) *Authority:* Ad Dob of Maab, village headman.

Facts: Mag was a neglectful pig breeder. He did not feed the animal entrusted to him, and thus it ran away into the jungle. Mab, having heard about the mistreatment of the animal by Mag and the resulting incident, went to Maab to look for the pig.

Outcome: He severely reprimanded the culprit. Though the village authority recognized the culprit's liability, he urged a peaceful solution and did not support the plaintiff.

Rule 96: The breeder is entitled to the following parts of the pig if the latter is killed in his home: intestines, head, two large pieces of pork (six kilograms of meat), heart, lungs, liver, backbone, spleen, kidneys, and the parts of the legs below the ankles.

No dispute reported.

LAND LEASE

This type of contract helps individuals who do not own enough land of their own or who, for various reasons, prefer to cultivate a specific plot of land. Although payment is received in about forty per cent of the deals of this type, the majority of the land is leased as a favor and for no payment whatsoever.

Rule 97: The man entitled to cultivate leased land should use it for the growing of one crop only. He has a duty to pay the agreed upon fee for cultivation. The landlord has no right to change his mind after the cultivation has started. The crop serves as a guarantee for the payment of the sum agreed upon.

Case 116.
  Place: Kojo.
  Date: June 19th, 1955.
  Parties:
    a) *Defendant:* Ij Jok of Itod, village headman.
    b) *Plaintiff:* Ij Tid of Kojo, land owner.

Facts: Jok cultivated a small stony patch of land leased from Tid and located on the slope of Kemugebega. When the crop was about to be harvested, the land owner came and asked for the agreed upon fifteen beads. Jok told him he must wait. Enraged, Tid threatened to harvest all the sweet potatoes.

Outcome: Jok paid on the next day.

Rule 98: If a house is built on another man's land, the owner of the structure should pay an agreed upon sum (usually 1 Km). Unless a new agreement is reached, the tenant should have the land for approximately two years. The land owner should provide for undisturbed use of the land for the period stated; otherwise, he should return the rent received.

No dispute reported.

CREDIT

The Kapauku distinguish four types of currency loans. One is called *"daba menii, poor give him,"* a category which comprises all the cases not subsumable under the three following divisions. This category is the broadest one. The Papuan expression can be paraphrased as "giving without a specific reason." The second category, *waka jaedai,* includes cases of buying a wife for somebody else by providing some of the money for the first part of the bride price. *Kade jamakii,* contributions to the *kade* part of the bride price, forms the third division. Since credit extended to a friend, *nogei jegeka jamenii,* forms a transition between gift and credit, regulated by different rules, we have to treat it as a fourth division and thus differentiate it from normal credit as well as from gift.

Daba loans.

Rule 99: The recipient of a loan has to pay in kind at any time the creditor asks for payment. Failure to comply with the rule gives the creditor the right to seize the property of the debtor or that of his close blood relatives of the same sib. Should a fight result, this right is forfeited.

Case 117.

  Place: Aigi.

  Date: ca. 1952.

  Parties:

  a) *Defendant:* Pe Ipo of Odee, young man.

  b) *Plaintiff and authority:* Ij Eka of Aigi, headman of the confederacy.

Facts: The boy, Pe, lived in the house of the headman of the Ij-Pi confederacy. The latter loaned the boy 40 Km. Once, when the boy disobeyed the orders of the headman, he was asked to return the loan. The boy refused and fled to his home village in another political unit.

Outcome: The angered headman gathered his followers and led an expedition to Odee, the debtor's home. The boy's frightened relatives paid the money which was owed.

Comment: The case demonstrates the role of credit in the field of social control.

Case 118.

  Place: Botu.

  Date: ca. 1952.

  Parties:

  a) *Defendant:* Ij Bun of Botu.

  b) *Plaintiff:* Ij Mab of Botu, FaBrSo of the defendant.

  c) *Authorities:*

      Ij Awi of Botu, village headman.

      Ij Eka of Aigi, headman of the confederacy.

Facts: Bun of Botu owed his cousin 60 Km. The creditor, needing the money for a bride price payment, asked Bun to return the loan. The latter, however, refused and a duel resulted in which the combatants used sticks. The fight lasted, including intermissions, for two days.

Outcome: Though the authorities scolded the debtor and asked him to pay, he refused. "I need not pay any more because we fought," the debtor replied.

Comment: The decision of the authorities was contrary to rule 98.

Case 119.

  Place: Botu.

  Date: ca. 1953.

  Parties:

  a) *Defendant:* Ij Dim of Botu, a rich man.

  b) *Plaintiff:* Ij Ida of Botu, the creditor.

  c) *Authorities:*

      Ij Awi of Botu, village headman.

      Ij Eka of Aigi, headman of the confederacy.

Facts: Dim, a rich but dishonest man of Botu, borrowed 120 Km, 120 Tm, 20 *pagadau* bead necklaces, 420 beads, 20 machetes, and 30 axes from Ida, who had received these articles as part of *dabe uwo*, the reward for killing an enemy. After approximately two years, the creditor asked for the payment of the debt, but the rich man turned down his request stating that he had no money on hand. This was an obvious lie. The dispute which followed resulted in a stick fight in which many people participated. There were many injuries on both sides, and the creditor suffered a broken forearm. The village authority, helped by the headman of the confederacy, succeeded in stopping the fight.

Outcome: Because the debtor started the violence, the decision required his paying the debt. After long arguments with the headman, Dim paid 60 Km, 5 *pagadau* bead necklaces, and 120 beads. He promised to pay the rest of the cost in the future. The headman, while reprimanding the culprit, cursed him and predicted an early death. A few months later Dim became sick and died. Thus, the people believe, he was punished for his frauds by the headman's black magic.

Case 120.
   Place: Tugu.
   Date: ca. 1953.
   Parties:
   a) *Defendant:* Go Wit of Tugu.
   b) *Plaintiffs:*
      Go Den of Tugu.
      Go Ota of Tugu, half brother of the defendant.
   c) *Authority:* As above.
   d) *Executioners:*
      Go Ota of Tugu, half brother of (a).
      Go Pig of Tugu, FaBrSo of defendant.

Facts: The defendant was a notorious criminal. He borrowed money from many people but he never paid it back. He was suspected of having stolen two pigs and some sweet potatoes. Once, after he had again refused to pay his debts, the authorities decided to punish him, thus hoping to reform the defendant.

Outcome: Since the culprit had no pigs and no other property to be confiscated, the village headman decided to have the man beaten by his close relatives. The first paternal parallel cousin and the half brother were selected as executioners. Though they thoroughly beat the culprit with a stick, the punishment did not improve the character of the defendant.

Comment. A man's criminal record is an aggravating factor.

Case 121.
   Place: Jaga.
   Date: 1954.
   Parties:
   a) *Defendant:* Pi Idi of Jaga.
   b) *Authorities:*
      Ij Jok of Itod, village headman.
      Ij Eka of Aigi, headman of the confederacy.

c) *Plaintiffs:*
Ko Naw of Pega.
Uk Bag of Tigi.
Ij Jok of Itod, the authority.
Pi Ene of Jaga, BrSo of defendant.
Ij Eka of Aigi, the authority.

Facts: Idi was a petty criminal. He borrowed small sums totaling 26 Km from the plaintiffs and refused to pay his debts.

Outcome: The authorities finally decided on punishment. Since the defendant had not taken much, they asked the plaintiffs to refrain from beating the man. Instead, they reprimanded him for four consecutive days.

*Case 122.
Place: Itod.
Date: January 8th, 1955.
Parties:
a) *Defendant:* Ij Ame of Jaga, residing in Itod.
b) *Plaintiffs:* The authorities below.
c) *Authorities:*
Ij Amo of Kojo, village headman.
Ij Jok of Itod, village headman.

Facts: Ame is a man who does not work much and tried to get an easy income by borrowing money without paying his debts.

Outcome: Once when he became involved in obtaining some money from a man of Dege, the authorities came to his house in Itod and reprimanded him publicly. "You have no cowries, no beads. You do not work in your gardens and, consequently, you have neither sweet potatoes nor pigs. You are forced to go around and beg food and money from people. You have borrowed money which you have never repaid. Now you had better pay your debts and start making some gardens." While pointing their fingers at him and dancing the *"wainai,* mad dance," they shouted the accusations at the defendant. Ashamed, he returned the last loan and promised to improve his behavior.

Case 123.
Place: Gino.
Date: June, 1955.
Parties:
a) *Defendant:* Ko Wed of Gino.
b) *Plaintiff:* Pe Bun of Waug.
c) *Authority:* Ij Kug of Gino.

Facts: The defendant frequently borrowed quantities of currency and failed to pay his debts. Also, he killed a male pig and promised to pay 15 Km for it. When the creditor came to collect the debt, however, Bun tried again to avoid payment by making promises. This time the creditor insisted on immediate payment. To avoid intervillage disputes, Kug, the village authority, paid the debt.

Outcome: To stop this irresponsible behavior of the culprit, Kug decided to use a public reprimand and beating as a means of correction. The first paternal parallel cousins of the defendant became the executioners of the corporal punishment and beat Bun with sticks for three days. During this period the authority helped with the public reprimand.

Case 124.

Place: Botu.

Date: July 14th, 1955.

Parties:

   a) *Defendant:* Ij Bun of Botu.

   b) *Plaintiff:* Ba Amo of Tuwo, Tigi region.

   c) *Authorities:* Ij Eka of Aigi, headman of the confederacy.

      Ij Awi of Botu, village headman.

      Ij Jok of Itod, village headman.

      Ij Amo of Jaga, village headman.

      Pi Peg of Obaj, lineage headman.

Facts: Bun of Botu was known in South Kamu for his several frauds and his quarrelsome temperament. He did not work in his fields, neither did he breed pigs. Traveling, buying and selling of pigs, and especially borrowing shell money seemed to be his chief enterprises. From the fact that he had been able through these activities to feed his three wives and a half a dozen children, it was apparent that his business transactions were profitable. All the people from the Kamu Valley would agree with a statement that characterizes most of his deals as frauds or outright thefts. Residents of his own village had long been weary of the incessant complaints of creditors and of the constant fear of losing their own pigs or other property during a raid by the cheated men as a consequence of their common responsibility toward the outsiders for the crimes of Bun.

In March of 1955, Bun was traveling through the Tigi region. In Tuwo village he found a trusting individual who, after Bun had promised three large pigs, loaned him 2880 beads, 20 Km, and 30 Tm. Four months later, the Tigi people came to Botu to collect the pigs. To their surprise, they found that the culprit had none. Moreover, their money having been spent a long time ago, they realized that the only way to recover their property would be through a forceful seizure of pigs of the culprit's cousins or those of his other co-villagers. They threatened to take such action and collect the debt in a few days. The people of Botu, however, pleaded with them and declared that they should rather take revenge on the defendant who at this time was visiting some friends in the northern part of the Kamu Valley. A member of the defendant's household was dispatched to the north to fetch the culprit. The latter, however, refused to return. At a large gathering of Botu's important men, long speeches were made in which many of them asked for the death of the culprit.

On the 29th of July, the creditors returned to Botu. This time they were accompanied by many armed people from the Debei Valley. Long negotiations started between the war party and the people of Botu. Since Bun had returned to the village, he was brought to the scene and there he promised to collect the money and repay the debt within three days. After assurances from the culprit's relatives, as well as from the village headman, the Debei people left.

The departure of the creditors marked the start of a trial of the defendant. For about a week, all the authorities of the confederacy kept publicly reprimanding the culprit who was squatting at his house and looking at the ground. Jik, an old man of Botu, who had injured his leg while escaping from the village with his pigs to save them from confiscation, beat the culprit with a stick. Long accusations and demands for the man's execution were presented by many of the speakers. The authorities performed the mad dance and held a council in which the death sentence was discussed at length. The various speakers, in order to give accent to their oratory, not only danced, gesticulated, and shouted, but they also wept skillfully at important moments of their speeches.

Outcome: Most of the younger members of the council, such as Jok, the Itod headman, and Eka, the headman of the confederacy, opposed an execution and asked for leniency in the hope that the man might become better. Finally, they decided to make a collection among the relatives to pay the debt of the defendant and to give the man a last warning. Awi, the headman of the culprit's village, delivered the following concluding reprimand:

"You are a great thief. You will get into the white man's jail for this; they would shoot you through the neck and cut your throat with a machete, and it would serve you right. You simply travel and think how to steal something. You have forgotten how to make gardens, and how to make houses. You simply exploit all of us by eating from our shelves. You raise no pigs, you make no garden, you have no cowries, no beads, no houses. The creditors will take our pigs away and burn our houses. You are really a burden to us all, a bad man in our community. If the creditors take our pigs or burn our houses, we are going to kill you with *pogo* arrows. If Jik had sons, they would have beaten you or shot you to death because Jik injured himself so badly while escaping with his pigs for fear of your creditors.

"If you wish to get easy money, work your fields and raise pigs. If you go on stealing like this you will end up like Dimi who was stealing from people and raping other men's wives. [He died of a disease, probably pneumonia. People believe he was punished by spirits.] It will serve you right."

Rule 100: It depends upon the will of the debtor whether interest will be paid. Although immoral, nonpayment of promised interest is not punishable.

Case 125.
   Place: Aigi.
   Date: ca. 1953.
   Parties:
      a) *Defendant:* Ti Abe of Puet.
      b) *Plaintiff:* Ij Eka of Aigi, headman of the confederacy.
      c) *Authority:* Wa Imo of Puet, village headman and best friend of the plaintiff.

Facts: The defendant belonged to the Wa-Ti confederacy, which is a traditional enemy of the political unit of which the creditor, Eka, is the headman. The defendant borrowed 20 Km and promised to pay 60 Km in the future. Later on, however, he refused to pay anything. The plaintiff having the headman of Puet as his best friend asked him to intervene.

Outcome: Imo reprimanded and even beat the culprit with a stick. The latter gave a large pig to the plaintiff as reimbursement for the debt. The case was closed.

Comment: Since the pig was worth about 27 Km, part of the interest was paid.

Case 126.
   Place: Maab, South Kamu Valley.
   Date: ca. 1953.
   Parties:
      a) *Defendant:* Ad Gap of Maab.
      b) *Plaintiff:* Ko Wej of Gino, creditor.
      c) *Authority:* Ad Dob of Maab.
      d) *Second plaintiff:* Ad Toj of Maab, FaBrSo of the defendant.

Facts: The culprit borrowed 20 Tm, 20 Km, three *dedege* necklaces, and promised to pay 60 Km in the future. When after five months the creditor asked for payment, the defendant refused to comply with the request. The enraged creditor came to the defendant's village and killed and carried away a pig which belonged to the first paternal parallel cousin of the culprit. A fight resulted between the cousin and the defendant.

Outcome: The authority decided that the defendant should pay the indemnity to his cousin. The defendant complied with the decision and reimbursed his relative with a medium-sized male pig and 5 Km.

Comment: The creditor collected 40 Km for the meat of the confiscated pig, thus having part of his interest paid.

Case 127.
   Place: Aigi.
   Date: Summer, 1953.
   Parties:
      a) *Defendant:* Pi Geg of Aigi.
      b) *Plaintiff:* Ba Ked of Maki, Debei Valley.
      c) *Authority:* Ij Eka of Aigi, MoBrSo of the debtor.

Facts: The defendant borrowed 40 Km and 25 Tm from a man of the Debei region. He promised to pay 60 Km, but he never fulfilled his obligation. The creditor came several times to Aigi and asked for the money, but a dispute was the only result.

Outcome: Although the authority urged the debtor to repay the money, the case still had to be closed.

Case 128.
    Place: Tugu.
    Date: Spring, 1954.
    Parties:
        a) *Defendant:* Go Imo of Tugu.
        b) *Plaintiff:* Ad Naa of Taka.
        c) *Authority:* Go Ota of Tugu.

Facts: Sixty Km had been promised by the defendant for a loan of six hundred beads. At the time the defendant killed a pig and sold the meat, the creditor came to collect. He was denied the money, however, and went home weeping.

Outcome: The authority asked the culprit to repay. The latter promised to do so at the time of a pig feast in Tugu.

Case 129.
    Place: Jota, North Kamu Valley.
    Date: Summer, 1954.
    Parties:
        a) *Defendant:* Do Tot of Jota.
        b) *Plaintiff:* Ij Nak of Aigi.
        c) *Authority:* Do Uno of Jota.

Facts: Tot borrowed 30 Km and promised to return 35 Km. Although he later paid 34 Km, the creditor was not satisfied and started a dispute while visiting the defendant's village.

Outcome: The authority sided with the creditor and condemned the debtor for lying. He reprimanded him publicly.

Comment: The decision of the authority is contrary to rule 99 which explicitly states that the payment of interest should be voluntary and a refusal is not punishable.

Waka jaedai loans.

Rule 101: Loans extended for the purpose of buying a wife are payable any time the creditor decides to collect. It is, however, immoral to ask for payment before the woman gives birth to a child.

Case 130.

Place: Aigi.

Date: ca. 1953.

Parties:

a) *Defendant:* Ij Iib of Aigi, the creditor.

b) *Plaintiff:* Do Ipo of Neeg, lives in Aigi, the debtor.

c) *Authority:* Ij Eka of Aigi, confederacy's headman.

Facts: Do Ipo wanted to get married. Since he had not enough shell money, he borrowed 60 Km from Iib. Three months after the wedding, the creditor asked for his money back. All the people in Aigi, including the headman, pleaded with Iib and argued that the request was immoral and very hard on the young man who had not been given enough time to save for the debt. Iib ignored all the talks and insisted on collecting.

Outcome: Although the authority condemned Iib as acting immorally, he advised the debtor to pay because "the shell money is his [Iib's]."

Comment: Since the reprimand by authority is a punishment used in cases of other delicts, the case contradicts the rule.

Case 131.

Place: Itod.

Date: March 9th, 1955.

Parties:

a) *Defendant:* Ij Jok of Otod, headman of Itod.

b) *Plaintiff:* Iw Mab of Kego.

c) *Authority:* None.

Facts: Mab's father loaned Jok, his daughter's husband, money for buying an additional wife. After the woman had born two children, Mab, because he wanted to get married, came to Jok's house to ask for payment. The debtor explained that he had no money on hand and promised to pay in the future. The infuriated young man, who needed the money badly within seven days, shouted reproaches and threats and grabbed his own net bag and tore it to demonstrate his anger and the seriousness of the situation. He left with an ultimatum which gave the debtor only three days' time to gather the necessary currency. Jok, though a brave warrior and a courageous man who had killed many enemies, strangely enough was scared by the threats of a boy who belonged to a confederacy too weak to fight the political unit of the debtor.

Outcome: Jok collected the necessary shell money and repaid in due time.

Comment: The concern of the debtor can be interpreted as fear of losing face in public because of his violation of the rule.

Rule 102: The creditor who loaned money for *one*, the first part of the bride price payment, has a hypothecary right in the bride price paid for daughters of the purchased woman. No one should collect from the bride price until this debtor is satisfied.

No disputes reported.

Kadee jamakii loans.

Rule 103: The creditor has a right to ask for the payment at the time he, himself, gets married. At any other time his request may be denied by the debtor.

No dispute reported.

Nogei jegeka menii loans.

Rule 104: It is highly immoral to ask one's best friend for the return of a gift (loan). After his death, however, if the mutual gifts are not balanced, the surviving friend has a right to ask for any difference in his favor from the heir of the deceased friend.

Case 132.

   Place: Botu.

   Date: December 23rd, 1954.

   Parties:

     a) *Defendant:* Di Tat of Egeb, son of the deceased friend.

     b) *Plaintiff:* Ij Bun of Botu, surviving friend.

     c) *Man who objected to payment:* Ij Kug of Gino, maternal parallel cousin of the deceased friend.

     d) *Deceased friend:* Di Tat of Egeb.

Facts: Bun gave his friend Tat 40 Km on the occasion of the death of the friend's wife. He never received a gift which would balance this sum. After the death of the man, he went to the friend's son and sister asking for repayment of the debt. Kug, the maternal parallel cousin of the dead man, urged the son not to pay. Bun became angry and pierced his hand with a wooden hairpin. He left after having prophesied violence unless the debt were paid within three days.

Outcome: The frightened heir complied with the request.

LOAN OF MOVABLES

Rule 105: Net bags, bows, axes, fishing nets, and canoes, if loaned, may be requested to be returned at any time. If a charge for using the object has been agreed upon, it should be paid at the time of the return of the object. If the latter has been destroyed through gross negligence or through an intentional act of the borrower, he should repay its value in currency.

No dispute reported.

LABOR CONTRACT

The Kapauku do not pay for the time spent in work. The hired worker is paid for his actual accomplishment. Most people are hired as gardeners.

Rule 106: Unless the employer has not specified the reward prior to the start of the work, the employee has a right to the customary price (in 1954: 2 Km for turning 900 square meters of forest into garden land).

Case 133.

    Place: Obaj.
    Date: 1954.
    Parties:
        a) *Defendant:* Ij Deg of Gino, lives in Obaj.
        b) *Plaintiff:* Pi Ipo of Obaj.
        c) *Authority:* Pi Peg of Obaj, village headman and brother of plaintiff.

Facts: Ipo was hired to make a garden one *peka* in size. The employer paid him only 1 Km. Since he did not specify the price prior to the start of the work, Ipo demanded one more shell.

Outcome: Peg, the headman of Obaj, upheld the request and Deg paid the additional shell.

Case 134.

    Place: Kojo.
    Date: ca. 1954.
    Parties:
        a) *Defendant:* Ij Tid of Kojo.
        b) *Plaintiff:* Ij Deg of Kojo, the worker.
        c) *Authority:* Ij Amo of Kojo, village headman.

Facts: Deg made a garden one *peka* in size. As wages, he received only thirty beads (equivalent to 1 Km). The worker, dissatisfied with the low pay, asked for thirty more beads. During a dispute between the contractees which followed the request, the authority, because of political reasons, did not take action.

Outcome: The employer finally gave in and paid the additional amount of beads.

GIFTS

Except for few instances of the gift of land, the Kapauku do not have the institution of gift as we know it. All the movables given as *jegeka*, the Kapauku version of gift, have to be repaid some time in the future. *Jegeka motii* can be understood as giving some commodity without expectation of an early reciprocation.

Gift of land.

Rule 107: The giving of land transfers the full ownership only if the beneficiary is the heir of an intestate donor or husband of a sonless donor's daughter. In all other cases, the beneficiary has the duty to pay for the land upon the request of the donor or the heir.

No dispute reported.

Rule 108: A man who receives land from his wife's father cannot sell or give it to anyone. His heir may alienate it with the limitation of having to comply with a preemptory right of the heir of the donor.

No dispute reported.

Gift of movables.

Rule 109: All commodities given as gifts have to be repaid upon the donor's request.

See case 132.

FORCIBLE SEIZURE OF PROPERTY

The rejection of a request to fulfill one's obligation arising from a contract or a delict entitles the plaintiff to a forcible seizure of property. Pigs are the most suitable objects for the execution of this right. In a few cases, however, shell money may serve the same purpose. The institution of seizure of property against the will of the owner is important especially in interconfederacy disputes where enforcement of the rule, because of the absence of political integration, is mostly lacking.

Rule 110: Property should be seized by force if a man refuses to meet his obligations which have their origin in contract or in an act causing damage to other people. The act of seizure precludes any further obligation on the part of the defendant, irrespective of the possible low value of the property seized.

Case 135.
   Place: Itod.
   Date: ca. 1952.
   Parties:
      a) *Defendant:* Do Bob of Jota.
      b) *Plaintiff:* Ij Jok of Itod, village headman and wife's brother of the defendant.

Facts: Bob paid 120 Km, 120 Tm, and 240 beads for his wife. Jok, the brother of the wife, thought the bride price was too small. He believed that his brother-in-law should have paid at least 180 Km more. In order to obtain what he thought was his property, he proposed to buy a pig from his sister's husband. The latter agreed and sold him a small female pig. Jok stipulated that he would pay 120 Km at the time of the slaughter of the animal. After sixteen months of breeding the sow, it proved to be sterile and worth only 30 Km. Jok slaughtered her secretly and collected the shell money. When his brother-in-law asked for an explanation of this behavior, the man stated his right to an adequate bride price and confessed to the act of seizure.

Outcome: Bob agreed to the action and the case was closed.

Comment: Seizure occurred without a request for payment of a higher bride price, thus making the action contrary to the wording of the rule.

Case 136.

    Place: Botu.

    Date: ca. 1953.

    Parties:

        a) *Defendant:* Pi Geg of Botu.

        b) *Plaintiff:* Ij Eka of Aigi.

        c) *Authority:* Ij Eka of Aigi.

Facts: Geg owed the plaintiff 25 Km. When asked to pay the debt, he excused himself and promised to pay at some time in the distant future. The creditor, thereafter, secretly took from the defendant an iron ax worth 5 Km.

Outcome: The debtor agreed with the action, and thus the case was closed. The creditor lost 20 Km on the deal.

Case 137.

    Place: Tugu.

    Date: ca. 1953.

    Parties:

        a) *Defendant:* Go Wet of Tugu.

        b) *Plaintiff:* Ij Jok of Itod.

        c) *Authority:* Go Den of Tugu.

Facts: The defendant borrowed 40 Km from the plaintiff and promised to repay 70 Km in the future. Later on he refused to pay and denied the whole deal. The angered creditor gathered people from his confederacy and made an expedition to Tugu.

Outcome: At Tugu the party presented the case to the village authority who agreed to forceful seizure of the culprit's property. The Ij-Pi men caught two of the defendant's pigs and left the village without any resistance on the part of the Go people.

Case 138.

    Place: Puet.

    Date: June 6th, 1955.

    Parties:

        a) *Defendant:* Au Jug of Maat, lives in Puet.

        b) *Plaintiff:* Te Ibo of Wagh, the creditor.

        c) *Owner of the burnt house:* Wa Imo of Puet.

        d) *Authority:* Wa Eba of Puet.

Facts: The defendant borrowed 20 Km from Te Ibo of Tigi region. When asked to pay his debt, he refused. The creditor came with a party to Puet and there secretly killed a pig worth 10 Km. This pig belonged to Imo, a Puet resident unrelated to the defendant. The owner of the animal discovered the deed and pursued the creditor's party. He caught up with them in the Debei Valley and asked for an explanation. Te told him about the debt and his responsibility as a resident of the village of the culprit. He advised him to collect the money from the defendant. Imo went home and asked Jug for payment for the pig. On being refused, he threatened to kill the defendant. To induce the defendant to pay him, he set his own house on fire thus showing his fury.

Outcome: The defendant, overcome by the threats of Imo as well as by the authority's unfavorable verdict, paid 20 Km to Imo. Since the sow was worth 10 Km and the burnt house 4 Km, Imo made a profit of 6 Km. On the contrary, the creditor lost 10 Km on the deal. However, it was better for him to lose this small amount than everything.

OFFENCES AGAINST AND BY AN AUTHORITY

The presence of an authority as the offended or offending party whose power is responsible for his violation of the customary code of proper behavior or whose position constitutes an object against which an offence has been directed, serves as a criterion of this category. The cases listed below will comprise delicts against the authority as a person with power to pass decisions which should be followed, as well as the authority's delicts against customary rules, committed through exploitation of his special power. Thus, offences against the authority as a private individual, which were not directed against his power to pass decisions, and those committed by the authority himself without relying on the mentioned power in the resulting disputes are necessarily excluded. They have been discussed in the three previous divisions.

DELICTS BY AN AUTHORITY WHICH EXPLOIT HIS POWER TO PASS DECISIONS

See Rule 99.

Case 139.
   Place: Botu.
   Date: ca. 1950.
   Parties:
     a) *Defendant:* Ij Awi of Botu, village headman.
     b) *Plaintiff:* Mo Tuu of Bago, Jawei region, the creditor.

Facts: Awi, the village headman of Botu, borrowed 40 Km from Mo Tuu. The creditor came several times to collect his loan but the defendant always refused to pay, using his followers as a deterrent to more forceful action on the part of the plaintiff.

Outcome: Although several village headman from Awi's confederacy urged the defendant to pay, he continued to withhold the payment.

Case 140.

   Place: Botu.

   Date: ca. 1951.

   Parties:

      a) *Defendant:* Ij Awi of Botu, village headman, the debtor.

      b) *Plaintiff:* Te Uwo of Dama, the creditor.

   Facts: The defendant borrowed 30 Km. He used his position of village headman to repel the creditor.

   Outcome: He never paid the debt.

Case 141.

   Place: Botu.

   Date: ca. 1951.

   Parties:

      a) *Defendant:* Ij Awi of Botu, village headman and debtor.

      b) *Plaintiff:* Mo Deg of Bago.

      c) *Authorities:*

         Ij Eka of Aigi, headman of the confederacy.

         Ij Jok of Itod, village headman.

   Facts: The village headman of Botu borrowed 70 Km from the plaintiff. Always, when Deg came to collect, Awi gathered his followers and refused to pay.

   Outcome: Although authorities from other villages and the confederacy's headman reprimanded the defendant, the debt continued unpaid.

   See Rule 81.

Case 142.

   Place: Botu.

   Date: ca. 1952.

   Parties:

      a) *Defendant:* Ij Awi of Botu, village headman, the debtor.

      b) *Plaintiff:* Ij Mab of Kojo, the creditor.

      c) *Helper of the defendant:* Ij Dim of Botu, a rich man.

   Facts: Awi received a large pig from Mab and promised to pay 60 Km for it. After having paid 180 beads (equivalent to 6 Km), he denied the right of the creditor to the rest of the price. In order to get support from Dim, a rich man from Botu, he bribed him with one-fourth of the large pig. Dim with his followers supported the dishonest village headman in this dispute.

   Outcome: Mab, powerless against so many people, surrendered his claim.

   Comment: Should Mab have gone to an extreme, he could have secured the support of his whole Jamaina sublineage and started a fight with Botu.

   See Rule 53.

Case 143.

   Place: Botu.

   Date: ca. 1953.

   Parties:

     a) *Defendant:* Ij Awi of Botu, village authority.

     b) *Plaintiff:* Ij Obi of Botu.

Facts: Awi, the headman of Botu, secretly killed a large sow belonging to the plaintiff. Some witnesses reported the deed to Obi who charged the headman with theft.

Outcome: Being an old man, Obi did not press the case hard enough and the defendant, relying upon his many followers, denied the crime and refused to pay.

Delicts Against the Power of an Authority

All cases of non-subordination to the authority of any group will be listed below. Although the disobedience will be associated with various delicts, the fact of failure to follow a decision will be the primary reason for punishment in each case.

Rule 111: People should follow decisions and the advice of an influential and rich man (of their group). Failure to do so should be punished in accordance with the authority's opinion.

Case 144.

   Place: Aigi.

   Date: ca. 1953.

   Parties:

     a) *Defendant:* Ij Maa of Aigi.

     b) *Authorities:*

         Ij Eke of Aigi, confederacy's authority.

         Ij Kag of Aigi, village authority, father of the defendant.

Facts: Maa, son of the rich man Kag, was on trial for disobedience in a battle. During the questioning he became enraged and shouted at the village and confederacy's headman: "*ba*, feces."

Outcome: Both authorities beat the culprit with sticks so that he suffered two deep wounds on his head.

Comment: The punishment for the insult was severe because of the gravity of the delict for which the defendant was on trial.

Case 145.

   Place: Aigi.

   Date: ca. 1953.

   Parties:

     a) *Defendant:* Ij Nak of Aigi.

     b) *Authority:* Ij Eka of Aigi, confederacy's headman.

     c) *Authority's helper:* Ij Jok of Aigi.

Facts: The defendant fought intermittently for several days with Iib, his own brother. The authority wished to terminate the violence and asked the quarreling brothers to stop. Nak, in angry words, refused to comply with the request.

Outcome: The authority punished the man for disobedience by asking for the return of 120 Km which Nak owed him. Ij Jok of Aigi joined the authority in the act of punishment by asking for the return of his own loan of 10 Km. The defendant wept and pleaded to be excused. The authority insisted on his punishment, and the defendant had to kill two pigs to satisfy the creditors with the money received for the sold pork.

Case 146.
  Place: Botu.
  Date: ca. 1953.
  Parties:
   a) *Defendants:*
      Three sons of Ij Nek of Botu.
      Ij Kam of Botu.
   b) *Authority:*
      Ij Eka of Aigi, headman of the confederacy.
      Ij Jok of Itod, village headman.

Facts: Three sons of Nek of Botu and also a man named Kam refused to help to build a drainage ditch which would carry away the flood water from the area between Botu and Jaga as well as from their own fields. They counted on profiting from the ditch which other people helped to construct. The residents of Jaga protested against the refusal of help by the four Botu men. An order to help from the headman of the confederacy was also ignored.

Outcome: The authority sponsored the building of a dam in the existing ditch on the land of the Jaga village, which stopped the rain water and flooded the gardens of the defendants. Thus, they were induced to help. Awi, the headman of Botu, did not participate in the dispute because men from his village were involved as defendants, and he could not argue against them lest he lose his influence.

Case 147.
  Place: Aigi.
  Date: 1954.
  Parties:
   a) *Defendant:* Go Mab of Tugu, lives in Aigi.
   b) *Authority:* Ij Eka of Aigi, headman of the confederacy.
   c) *Authority of the defendant's native village:* Go Ota of Tugu.

Facts: Mab lived in Eka's house. He did not help in the gardens nor did he work in the house. Once when he refused to carry a pig for the authority, the latter punished him by asking for the return of a loan of 120 Km which had been used to buy a wife for Mab.

Outcome: The defendant wept and asked for pardon. He was not forgiven and had to go home to collect the money and pay his debt. The headman of his native village sided with Eka and thus contributed to the compliance of the defendant with the verdict.

Case 148.

   Place: Aigi.

   Date: Spring, 1954.

   Parties:

     a) *Defendant:* Go Mab of Aigi.

     b) *Authority:* Ij Eka of Aigi, headman of the confederacy.

     c) *Executioners:*

        Ij Nak of Aigi, lived in the authority's household.

        Ti Kop of Aigi, lived in the authority's household.

        Go Ipo of Aigi, brother of the defendant, lived in the authority's household.

Facts: Mab was a boy who lived in the household of the confederacy's headman. Once when he refused to bring sugar cane, he was slapped for disobedience. Enraged, he shouted at the authority: "You are a pig, you are a dog."

Outcome: The authority asked the other boys of his household to beat the culprit. They complied and thoroughly beat the young delinquent.

Case 149.

   Place: Aigi.

   Date: Summer, 1954.

   Parties:

     a) *Defendant:* Go Paj of Aigi.

     b) *Authority:* Ij Jok of Itod, village authority.

Facts: Paj was a very lazy boy who lived with Jok. He refused to work and simply hung around the house.

Outcome: Several times Jok gave him a good talking to, but he never beat the boy as he was sorry for him.

Rule 112: Disobedience of the orders of an authority during a war campaign should be punished by public reprimand.

Case 150.

   Place: Aigi.

   Date: ca. 1935.

   Parties:

     a) *Defendant:* Ij Maa of Aigi.

     b) *Authorities:*

        Ij Kag of Aigi, rich man and village headman.

        Ij Eke of Aigi, headman of the confederacy.

Facts: The Dou people of Buna fought the Pi-Ag-Ja confederacy of the North Kamu Valley. The Ij-Pi confederacy joined their Dou allies in this war under the leadership of their *tonowi*, Kag and Eke. During the fighting, Maa did not listen to the orders of the authorities, made his own plans, and failed to coordinate his actions with the rest of his group. As a result, he was wounded four times during the battle.

Outcome: After the day of fighting was over, the authorities without taking pity on the wounded man reprimanded him intermittently for three days and slapped him several times. They kept telling him: "You did not listen and therefore you are wounded. It serves you right."

Comment: Being wounded does not constitute an alleviating circumstance.

Case 151.

   Place: Dege.

   Date: ca. 1948.

   Parties:

     a) *Defendant:* Iw Gob of Dege.

     b) *Authority:* Iw Tit of Dege.

Facts: During the war between the Iw and the Di sibs, the authority had a bad dream. He therefore decided to stop the fighting for a day. The defendant, eager to avenge his killed relative, disobeyed the decision and went to the battlefield located between the two villages. The rest of his relatives, because they felt sorry, followed him. In the battle the defendant was shot in his eye and lost it.

Outcome: In the evening after the party had returned from the battleground, the authority reprimanded the disobedient man and struck him over the head with a log three times, thus causing bleeding wounds. He beat him because he was sorry that the defendant had lost his eye. Since the authority really felt sorry for the wounded man, he presented him with a small male pig the next day. The animal was used in a white magic ceremony performed in order to cure the defendant.

Comment: Punishment is definitely considered a corrective measure. Being wounded does not exempt one from punishment.

Case 152.

   Place: Jaga.

   Date: May, 1954.

   Parties:

     a) *Defendant:* Pi Ene of Jaga.

     b) *Authority:* Ij Eka of Aigi, confederacy's headman.

Facts: Ene twice disobeyed the authority during the war between the Wa-Ti and the Ij-Pi confederacies. Once he did not follow an order to move to the right flank of his sublineage's fighting unit; the second time he continued to fight although he heard the order for an armistice, and he knew that the authorities were negotiating peace. By his disobedience, which caused other people to follow him into battle, he prolonged the hostilities by one day.

Outcome: The authority reprimanded the defendant and wanted to beat him. Since the culprit was apologetic and humble, the authority felt sorry for him and refrained from corporal punishment.

Comment: The beating was a part of the decision. It was not administered because of alleviating circumstances.

Rule 113: Wives and children owe obedience to their husbands and fathers or substitute fathers in the matters of field work, cooking, etiquette, and other household activities. Violations should be punished according to the opinion of the husband or father. However, his sanctions should not be too harsh and should not involve punishment by shooting or stick beating which would cause deep wounds.

Case 153.
  Place: Obaj.
  Date: ca. 1953.
  Parties:
   a) *Defendant:* Ij Aka of Obaj.
   b) *Authority:* Pi Peg of Obaj.
   c) *Father of authority:* Pi Ibo of Obaj.

Facts: The defendant, while eating with his foster father and other people, spoke to his friend about sexual intercourse.

Outcome: The foster father beat him twice with a stick over the head, causing two bleeding wounds.

Case 154.
  Place: Obaj.
  Date: ca. 1953.
  Parties:
   a) *Defendant:* Ij Aka of Obaj.
   b) *Authority:* Pi Peg of Obaj, foster father of the defendant.
   c) *Father of authority:* Pi Ibo of Obaj.

Facts: The boy spilled drinking water on the floor by accident.

Outcome: The father of his foster father hit him under the right eye with a stick, inflicting a deep wound. The foster father became enraged, and, in turn, slapped his own father for being too harsh with the boy.

Comment: Ibo had no right to punish his son's foster child.

Case 155.
  Place: Itod.
  Date: 1954.

Parties:

   a) *Defendant:* Iw Ama of Kego.

   b) *Authority:* Ij Jok of Itod, her husband.

Facts: The defendant was asked by her husband to keep his savings for him. She wanted to avoid the troubles of safeguarding the money and therefore she entrusted it to the custody of her mother. The husband heard about the arrangement and asked his wife in an angry voice to fetch his savings immediately.

Outcome: Because she hesitated, he beat her with a stick. She went weeping to execute his orders.

Comment: Resistance to authority during a dispute is an aggravating circumstance.

*Case 156.

   Place: Itod.

   Date: December 21st, 1954.

   Parties:

      a) *Defendant:* Iw Ama of Kego.

      b) *Authority:* Ko Ipo of Wagh, Tigi region, husband of the defendant.

Facts: Ipo was sick and impatient. He ordered his wife around so much that the latter was quite upset. When he was cooking, he shouted at his wife again. Annoyed, she threw a stick into the fire, thus unintentionally scattering some ashes over the meal.

Outcome: The husband beat her with a stick. She wanted to leave him and go back to her village, but later she changed her mind and stayed.

*Case 157.

   Place: Botu.

   Date: January 17th, 1955.

   Parties:

      a) *Defendant:* Ko Ama of Egeb.

      b) *Authority:* Ij Pil of Botu, husband of the defendant.

Facts: Ama went to Ege to visit her parents. Although her husband had reminded her to leave him enough sweet potatoes at home, she had forgotten about it in the excitement.

Outcome: After she returned, she was slapped twice by her husband.

Case 158.

   Place: Itod.

   Date: February 17th, 1955.

   Parties:

      a) *Defendants:* Go Ama of Bibi.

         Ij Mag of Botu.

         Iw Agi of Kego.

      b) *Authority:* Ij Jok of Itod, husband of all the defendants.

Facts: Jok forbade his three wives to go to a pig feast. The wives were very angry, but they complied with the decision. Upon his return, the husband was not given any food by his wives. All of them went on strike for two days in revenge for his injustice.

Outcome: Other people took pity on the poor man and gave him food. He regarded the action of his wives as a big joke.

Comment: For the same offence, the wife in case 157 was slapped.

Case 159.

   Place: Botu.

   Date: July 12th, 1955.

   Parties:

      a) *Defendant:* Pi Ama of Obaj.

      b) *Authority:* Ij Mab of Botu, husband of the defendant.

Facts: Ama did not obey her husband and cut unripe sugar cane. She tried to sell it but could not.

Outcome: Upon her arrival home with the unripe cane, the husband struck her twice with a stick. Because she started to cry, he felt sorry for his wife and stopped beating her.

Case 160.

   Place: Kojo.

   Date: August 8th, 1955.

   Parties:

      a) *Defendant:* Pi Ena of Kebo.

      b) *Authority:* Ij Deg of Kojo, husband of the defendant.

      c) *Visitor:* Ij Aka of Obaj, brother of authority.

Facts: Aka visited his older brother. Although it was about noon, he felt hungry and asked his brother for some sweet potatoes. Ij Deg, in turn, asked his wife to give some food to his younger brother. She refused because custom prescribes giving sweet potatoes to one's husband only twice a day, in the morning and in the evening.

Outcome: The husband, considering the refusal an offence, beat his wife with a stick and took her sweet potatoes by force. She, in turn, went to her husband's garden and cut down some sugar cane and gourd plants. Her husband beat her again with a stick. She retaliated by cutting two banana trees and destroying some sweet potatoes in the field. The husband refrained from further punishment in order to save his property.

Comment: The wife resisted and became violent because the punishment was unjust.

Case 161.

   Place: Obaa, Debei Valley.

   Date: August 10th, 1955.

Parties:
- a) *Defendant:* Pi Ama of Obaa.
- b) *Authority:* Bo Ibo of Obaa, husband of the defendant.

Facts: Bo Ibo failed to give pork to his wife. When he asked her later in the day for sweet potatoes she was angry about the meat and lied, stating that she had no potatoes.

Outcome: Her husband beat her with a stick and she, while weeping, surrendered the requested food. His deed was considered by others to be immoral.

Case 162.

Place: Kojo.

Date: August 13, 1955.

Parties:
- a) *Defendant:* Do Oum of Daid.
- b) *Authority:* Do Deg of Buna, husband of the defendant.
- c) *Seller of the garden:* Ij Deg of Kojo, FaSiSo of the authority.

Facts: The Do couple came to Kojo to plant sweet potatoes in a garden bought from the husband's cross-cousin. They planted the first day. The next morning, the wife refused to plant and said she would continue in the afternoon.

Outcome: The husband became angry and beat her with a stick. She then destroyed part of the new fence around the garden. After he beat her again, she pulled out some vines of sweet potatoes and returned home. The husband refrained from further punishment and let her go, finally asking his cross-cousin's wife to plant the crop for him.

Rule 114: A husband divides his affection among his co-wives according to his preference. A jealous wife should be punished for her insults and assaults against a co-wife or husband according to the gravity of her delict. A wife, however, has a right to a share of food, garden plot, and money equal to those of other co-wives. Gross neglect in this respect on the part of the husband constitutes a reason for divorce.

Case 163.

Place: Botu.

Date: 1954.

Parties:
- a) *Defendant:* Ad Oum of Ipuw, 6th wife of authority.
- b) *Plaintiff:* Ij Uga of Kojo, 5th wife of authority.
- c) *Authority:* Ij Awi of Botu, village headman.

Facts: Ad Oum was jealous of the 5th wife because their husband had more affection for her than for any of the other wives. She quarreled often with her rival and once started a stick fight.

Outcome: Awi scolded Oum for her aggression and threatened to beat her, should she repeat her assault on his favorite spouse.

Case 164.

    Place: Kojo.

    Date: July 4th, 1955, evening.

    Parties:

      a) *Defendant:* Pi Ena of Obaj, second wife of authority.

      b) *Authority:* Ij Amo of Kojo, village headman.

      c) *First wife:* Go Mab of Tugu.

Facts: The husband killed three rats and tried to eat them with his first wife alone. Ena discovered the plot and started lamentations which were so intensive that the husband surrendered one rat and gave it to the weeping woman. However, he was wrong in assuming that this would stop her crying. She continued shouting reproaches and insults.

Outcome: Amo, who could not stand the nuisance any longer, beat his second wife with a stick. She retaliated by breaking some sugar cane near the house. Then she took her youngest son and left for her old home in the Debei Valley. After three days she returned to her husband.

Case 165.

    Place: Obaj.

    Date: August 19th, 1955.

    Parties:

      a) *Defendant:* Te Mag of Dune, first wife of authority.

      b) *Plaintiff:* Pi Oum of Kebo, second wife of authority.

      c) *Authority:* Ij Adi of Obaj.

Facts: Adi secretly ate some pork with his second wife. The first wife found out and started quarreling with her rival.

Outcome: The annoyed husband beat his first wife with a stick. After she had destroyed some sweet potatoes and part of the fence in her husband's garden, she left for five days to live with her married son from her first marriage. Upon her return, the husband acted as if nothing had happened.

Comment: The informant called this case an example of injustice on the part of the husband.

Case 166.

    Place: Obaj.

    Date: August 21st, 1955.

    Parties:

      a) *Defendant:* Te Mag of Dune, first wife of authority.

      b) *Plaintiff:* Pi Oum of Kebo, second wife of authority.

      c) *Authority:* Ij Adi of Obaj.

Facts: Upon her return home, the first wife started quarreling again with Oum. In her rage, she destroyed some of her rival's sweet potatoes. A stick fight between the two women resulted. After the second wife had destroyed a fishing net of Mag, the latter announced she would leave for good.

Outcome: Her husband did not feel sorry for her at all. Indeed, he reprimanded her and told her to go. She left, but after a few days she returned, acting as if nothing had happened.

Case 167.
   Place: Obaj.
   Date: September, 1955.
   Parties:
      a) *Defendant:* Te Mag of Dune, first wife of authority.
      b) *Authority:* Ij Adi of Obaj.

Facts: Adi bought one-fourth of a whole pig and distributed the meat among the members of his household. The first wife, who received a leg bone with some meat, thought that she was cheated. She became angry and shouted insults at her husband.

Outcome: Adi struck her three times with a stick and ordered her to be quiet. Instead, she threw the piece of pork into the corner of the house. Adi picked it up and ate it, not giving anything to the defendant.

Rule 115: All the wives of one man are equal. A husband should punish the wife who tries to dominate other co-wives.

Case 168.
   Place: Kojo.
   Date: July 14th, 1955.
   Parties:
      a) *First wife of authority:* Ko Oum of Boob.
      b) *Second wife of authority:* Ad Oum of Ijom.
      c) *Authority:* Ij Mab of Kojo.

Facts: The first wife brought home some firewood and asked the second wife to fetch some more wood for the evening. The second wife refused to obey and a quarrel resulted.

Outcome: The husband ignored the whole affair. After some time the women stopped their shouting. The younger wife, however, did not fetch any firewood.

DELICTS AGAINST SOCIETY

The following cases constitute delicts which the Kapauku feel to be directed against a political unit as a whole, rather than against a specific individual. They can be committed by anybody, no matter whether the delinquent is an authority or simply a follower of one. Thus ungenerosity combined with excessive wealth is an offence by an authority as well as by a politically unimportant man. Such offences are punished in the Kamu Valley by ostracism, malevolent gossip, and nonsupport. In the Painai area, execution is the punishment and it is administered by a close relative of the culprit.

Rule 116: Lack of generosity on the part of a wealthy man is an offence against members of the community. Ostracism and boycott should be the punishment.

Case 169.
   Place: Botu.
   Date: 1954–1955.
   Parties:
     a) *Defendant:* Ij Awi of Botu, village headman.
     b) *Leaders of opposition:*
        Ij Taa of Botu, a medium wealthy man.
        Ij Nak of Botu, a medium wealthy man.
        Ij Bun of Botu, an aggressive, poorer man.

Facts: Awi, the village headman of Botu, was considered a greedy man. He failed on many occasions to buy wives for some close relatives and friends. He used all his money to buy wives for himself. Although he already had ten wives, he contemplated marrying for the eleventh time.

Outcome: Since he was a courageous and a wise man, people followed his decisions which dealt with other people's problems. However, they refrained from complying with wishes which might give personal advantage to the defendant. Gossips urged people not to contribute to the bride price to be paid for the eleventh wife. When the defendant decided to have a pig feast, no one volunteered to join him in the sponsorship; and no one, not even his own sons, cut planks for his dancing house.

Comment: Three important men of Botu sponsored the action and influenced the public.

Rule 117 (Paniai region): An ungenerous wealthy man should be executed, preferably by his son, brother, or paternal parallel cousin.

Case 170.
   Place: Madi, Paniai region.
   Date: August 3rd, 1955.
   Parties:
     a) *Defendant:* Mo Juw of Madi, Paniai region, a wealthy man and village
        headman.
     b) *Killers:*
        Mo Jow of Madi, the defendant's eldest son.
        Two FaBrSons of the defendant and two unrelated men.

Facts: Juw was a very wealthy man but he failed to lend out his property in proportion to his fortune. People of his village, dissatisfied with the state of affairs, spoke to the paternal parallel cousins of the man and persuaded them to kill the culprit. They, in turn, talked to the man's eldest son who agreed to join them in the execution of his own father. He was promised a pig and 20 Km for his participation.

Outcome: When the rich man was working in his garden, five men approached him and started to discharge their bamboo-tipped arrows into his body. His son was the first who shot him. Then his two paternal parallel cousins shot and finally two other men followed with their arrows. The executioners built a scaffold for the dead man and smeared their faces with ashes and soot, thus expressing grief over the necessary action. To avoid the vengeance of the dead man's "*tene*, the departed shadow," they slept for two nights in the bush. On the third day they came back to the village where they killed a pig of the dead man and distributed the meat to all people who came. The killers divided the dead man's property among themselves (see also p. 80).

Rule 117: If a man causes war by a crime, and if there is much of loss of life among the home people, the culprit should be killed.

Case 171.
    Place: Ekau, southwestern Kamu Valley.
    Date: ca. 1948.
    Parties:
      a) *Defendant:* Jo Amo of Ekau.
      b) *Authority:* Jo Pog of Ekau.
      c) *Murdered man:* Jo Tab of Ekau.

Facts: The defendant was known as a notorious criminal. He loaned 10 Km to a man from another sublineage of his own sib. When he came to collect the money and was told to wait for twenty days, he killed his debtor with an arrow. A war followed in which the two sublineages with their allies fought each other. There were about twenty dead people on each side when the authority decided to punish the defendant and thus end the conflict.

Outcome: The authority held secret meetings with other people during which he persuaded the majority of the villagers of the necessity of executing the criminal. One evening, the defendant was asked to attend a war planning session in the house of authority. On his way to the place, he was ambushed and killed, probably by his paternal parallel cousins. His death was described as an exploit of an enemy sniper. The war was ended soon afterwards.

Rule 119: A man who deserts his village in order to avoid participation in a war should be publicly reprimanded.

Case 172.
    Place: Boga, part of Buna.
    Date: ca. 1935.

Parties:
   a) *Defendant:* Do Duu of Boga.
   b) *Authority:* Do Ako of Buna, village headman.

Facts: To avoid war, the defendant went to the region of Dege to the northwest of Kamu Valley. He returned home after he had heard that peace was concluded.

Outcome: The authority reprimanded him publicly for one day.

Rule 120: If a man allies himself during a war with the enemy, he should be killed in the hostilities as an enemy. In peacetime, only his property in his native village should be taken by his heirs.

If a man from the enemy's confederacy pledges alliance to another political unit, he should be accepted there as an equal, given fields to cultivate (*ususfructus* right), and protected as a regular member of the group.

Case 173.
   Place: Dege.
   Date: ca. 1949.
   Parties:
      a) *Defendant:* Ed Tun of Dege.
      b) *Authority:* Ed Ipo of Dege.
      c) *Killed man:* Ed Mou of Dege.

Facts: During the war between Dege and Egeb, Tun deserted his village and joined the enemy. He was accepted as one of their own people and he fought in the war, killing his own second parallel cousin.

Outcome: People of his own village tried to kill him during the hostilities, but in vain. When peace was concluded, the culprit's property was taken by his heirs. The people of his native village still ostracize and hate this traitor.

Case 174.
   Place: Mogo.
   Date: ca. 1951.
   Party:
      a) *Defendant:* Ti Ipo of Mogo.

Facts: Ipo married a woman of the Pi clan. Because of his own family's disapproval of his marriage, he went to live with his wife in Jaga, a village belonging to the Ij-Pi confederacy. This political unit is a traditional enemy of his village. There he was given land to cultivate and he was accepted as an equal. When war occurred between the two political units, he fought on the side of the relatives of his wife.

Outcome: Because of this treason, he lost all of his property in his native village, his land and his house being inherited by his heir.

Comment: A male traitor is treated as if dead.

Rule 121: If a woman commits espionage against the people of the political unit of her husband, she should be beaten by her spouse. If he refuses to punish her, he should be beaten.

Case 175.
 Place: Botu.
 Date: Spring, 1954.
 Parties:
  a) *Defendant:* Ad Mag of Dogi.
  b) *Authority:* Ij Tim of Botu, husband of the defendant.

Facts: Mag's three brothers lived in Puet, a village of the Wa-Ti confederacy, an alliance hostile to the political unit of her husband. During the war between these political units, the defendant overheard war plans made by her husband's relatives for the next day's fighting. She reported her findings to her brothers and allegedly asked them to come to her home and kill her husband from ambush. Her treason was reported to her husband by another woman.

Outcome: Tim beat his wife severely with a stick so that she bled heavily.

Case 176.
 Place: Jaga.
 Date: Spring, 1954.
 Parties:
  a) *Defendant:* Ti Ama of Mogo.
  b) *Her husband, co-defendant:* Ij Auw of Jaga.
  c) *Authorities:*
    Ij Eka of Aigi, headman of the confederacy.
    Ij Jok of Itod, village headman.

Facts: The war between the Wa-Ti confederacy and that of Ij-Pi presented a dilemma to Ama. Should she help her blood relatives or be faithful to her husband? Once, after she overheard plans of a sniper expedition scheduled against her native village, she warned her relatives. A woman living in Mogo, who was loyal to the Ij-Pi confederacy, reported the treason.

Outcome: The husband, understanding the situation faced by his wife, refused to punish her. The authorities administered a public reprimand to the husband instead. The betrayed raid, of course, was canceled.

PART IV: KAPAUKU LAW

CULTURE, the buffer that mankind has created and placed between men and their environment, has been subdivided by Western thinkers. One of these traditional subdivisions has been called law. Law has been defined in many different ways and many theories have been advanced about its nature. Most of them are so contradictory, vague, and unpersuasive that many ethnologists omit the category of law when they describe and analyze a given culture.

Another reason why these authors make little use of the legal category lies in the fact that law has usually been defined too narrowly, so that in many "primitive cultures" there seems to be no law present. Radcliffe-Brown claims that law is absent in some primitive societies. Of the Yurok, for example, he says: "As the payment of indemnities is arranged by negotiation between the persons concerned and not by appeal to any judicial authority, the law of private delicts in the strict sense is not present" (Radcliffe-Brown, 1952: 216).

Should we apply Radcliffe-Brown's statement on law to the culture of the Kapauku, we would obtain an answer similar to his findings among the Yurok. Since there is very seldom an appeal to a rich man to decide a case and since the payment of indemnities is arranged ultimately by negotiations between the persons concerned, the Kapauku would have a culture void of law. Moreover, if we were to interpret the term "authority" in the customary Western way and look for a person, or a body of persons, with absolute power whose orders are followed as soon as they are given and whose acts, especially the decisions of disputes, are very formal, we would have to agree with some missionaries and some Dutch administrators that there is a virtual absence of authority, leadership, and, consequently, of law in this society.

The writer is of the opinion that the above statements rest on a misunderstanding of the essence of the concept of law that results from placing an undue emphasis upon the formalistic aspects of the legal process and upon descriptive characteristics peculiar to some cultures, which alone are believed to define a phenomenon as law. Law is conceived in this monograph as a functional, rather than a descriptive concept. A great majority of writers on law make this assumption although many of them fail to verbalize it and, consequently, lose sight of it as soon as they start to formulate a category of law. How else, for example, could it happen that so-called dead rules which are not enforced and are often even unknown to the public, being contrary to the actual behavior of the majority of the people, are considered together with the rest of the rules as the law of a country? Since the assumption of social control as a function of the institution of law constitutes the only common ground on which most of the current definitions of law meet, phenomena which do not exercise social control, such as the dead rules, will not be considered law. Instead of conceiving of a new category of law this writer will use for his analytical purposes the popular definition that appears in Webster's Dictionary. Thus the

248

following statement will delimit the scope of phenomena that will be called law: "Rules or modes of conduct made obligatory by some sanction which is imposed and enforced for their violation by a controlling authority; also, any single rule of conduct so imposed and enforced" (Neilson and others, 1940: 1401).

In the third part of the monograph this writer has presented 121 abstract rules, statements made to him by his informants about what should be done in situations in which the interests of different parties clash. Each presentation of a rule has been followed by pertinent cases, numbering in all 176. These inform us of what actually has been done in specific situations, regardless of the "proper" solutions suggested in the rules. The compilation of the cases and the rules represents raw material for the following analysis. It includes dead rules as well as those which are always enforced. It incorporates all kinds of disputes, religious taboos, peaceful adjustments as well as fights, cases in which headmen's decisions have been followed as well as those in which they were utterly disregarded. Our examples of clashes of interests have been drawn from various social groups, ranging from the family to the political confederacy and even the regional group. It is now our task to sift out the legal cases from the bulk of our material and analyze them in the light of the cross-culturally derived theory of law which has been mentioned in the introductory part of the monograph.

In this section, an attempt will be made to demonstrate the workability of a theory of law which should have cross-cultural applicability. Four attributes of law which the writer has abstracted from the legal cases of the thirty-two cultures studied will be presented. These attributes not only represent analytical constituents of the legal phenomena; they may also be used as criteria which help to differentiate law from other social phenomena, as for example from political decisions or purely religious taboos and observances. After this analytic endeavor our interest will shift to the dynamic aspect of law and the law's relation both to the smaller group in which it is upheld and to the larger society as a whole. Through this approach we will arrive at a theory showing the relativity of law and custom in the Kapauku material.

THE FORM OF LAW—A PROBLEM OF METHODOLOGY[9]

A following proposition has been derived from cross-cultural research: law is manifested by decisions of legal authority rather than by abstract rules or by the behavior of the litigants. However, for analytical purposes, it is important to investigate all three categories.

The Kapauku material on social relations presented in the second and third parts

[9] Before attempting an analysis of law, we must stress the assumption that all categories of phenomena including law which are constructed by embracing a number of facts do not exist in the outer world. They are, rather, constructions in our minds made for the sake of convenience. Justification for a category does not reside in its existence outside of the human mind but rather in its value as a heuristic device. There cannot be a sharp dividing line between categories. Instead, one must conceive of a zone of transition where the criteria of the neighboring categories overlap and where it is difficult to determine which one dominates the field.

of the monograph assumes three different forms: 1) the abstract rules which state what the relations should be; 2) the abstraction from the actual behavior of the people; and 3) the decisions of the native headmen about proper behavior. Thus the first problem that presents itself in the investigation of law concerns the form in which it is manifested. There are a number of possible solutions to this problem. Most of the theories of social scientists, however, have tended to follow one of three different paths of thinking which correspond to the forms represented in the Kapauku material.

Some social scientists have studied the abstract rules as they are to be found in legal codifications or in systems of rules which are embedded in people's memories and handed down from generation to generation. These scientists place emphasis on the abstract and impersonal nature of "principles behind manifestations of daily life." According to this trend of thinking, cultures that lack verbalized abstract rules, written or remembered, necessarily have no pure law (Kelsen, 1942: 51 and following).

Although the Kapauku have a very informal and rudimentary political organization, they have surprised the writer by their possession of abstract notions of proper behavior pertaining to different situations. Of these abstract rules, 121 have been listed in this monograph. Thus the Kapauku cannot be included in the category of "lawless societies," and it would be the 121 rules on which the study by social scientists would have to concentrate.

The present writer, who, together with Mr. Kelsen and most of the jurists, regards the function of the exercising of social control as indispensable for the concept of law, objects to the emphasis on abstract rules as a form of law for several reasons. In the first place, an abstract rule need not exercise the function of social control when it is believed to be outdated, obsolete, or regarded as an ideal which in actual life either cannot be realized or can only be approximated. We speak about dead rules which, since they are never applied in deciding legal cases, simply clutter many of the legal codifications. Because Kapauku culture is a very primitive one in which every change in behavior should easily result in a corresponding adjustment in the ideal counterpart, we would assume a "logical" absence of such dead rules. Let us look at the facts, however, and compare the cases with the pertinent rules.

Of 176 cases, only 87 correspond to a rule. In other words, in 89 cases which represent almost 51 per cent of the total, the actual results differ from the statements in the rules. The various reasons and the nature of the differences can be grouped into the following categories:

1. The outcome is more lenient than the rule because of alleviating circumstances: Cases 1, 29, 113, 121, 122.

2. The outcome is more lenient than the rule because of pity taken on the defendant: Cases 102, 103, 112.

3. The outcome is harsher because of aggravating circumstances: Cases 41, 120, 123, 124.

4. The outcome is harsher because the rule has been disregarded by the authority: Cases 150, 151, 152.

5. The authority is too weak to enforce the rule: Cases 54, 105, 119.

6. The outcome is harsher because the authority is the plaintiff: Cases 25, 62, 72, 153, 154, 156.

7. The outcome is unjust because the authority profits from the case: Cases 97, 104, 142, 143, 165.

8. The rule is not applied because of revenge taken by the plaintiff: Cases 66, 67, 84, 90.

9. The rule is not applied because of a duel: Cases 22, 86.

10. The rule is not applied because of a stick fight: Cases 40, 59, 118.

11. The rule is not applied because the culprit escaped: Cases 5, 10, 74.

12. The rule is not applied because the culprit was unknown: Case 63.

13. The rule is rejected by the authority: Cases 25, 33, 85, 125, 129, 130.

14. The rule is not applied because of a compromise for political reasons: Cases 26, 35, 37, 95.

15. The rule is not applied because of an interconfederational dispute: Cases 24, 28, 70, 76, 106, 108, 115, 127, 128, 139, 140, 141.

16. The rule is modified in a case of an interconfederational dispute: Cases 4, 16, 30, 36.

17. The rule is not applied because of self-redress: Cases 17, 82, 126, 135, 136, 137, 138.

18. The rule is not applied because of a special situation: Cases 50, 87, 89, 93, 114.

19. The rule is not applied because of the shaming of the plaintiff: Case 111.

20. The rule is not applied because of miscellaneous reasons: Cases 20, 21, 38, 60, 78, 101, 109, 158, 168.

The above survey shows beyond doubt that a study limited to rules would tell a student of law very little about actual social control among the Kapauku. If over half of the results of the cases do not comply with what the rules say, such a study could be called only an inquiry into the ideals concerning the settlement of disputes. It could, however, never be labeled a study of law, if by the latter we mean the institutionalized means of social control.

One may still defend an exclusive study of the rules by pointing out that the deviations in the results are due to aggravating as well as alleviating circumstances and to situations not defined in the rules. The rest of the cases which do not reflect corresponding rules may be labeled as showing injustice on the part of the authority. With reference to this defence, we may point out that the unverbalized, although legally relevant, circumstances would have to be studied in addition to the rules, an activity which would negate the emphasis upon the exclusive study of the rules. Furthermore, if "injustice" becomes regular, as in cases 139–143, then it is relevant to social control and also has to be studied. However, our main argument against the overemphasis on the rules rests on the presence of a few "dead rules" in the Kapauku mental codification of law.

Rule 100, which disavows punishment for a failure to pay interest, is not upheld in any of the five listed cases. In two cases, interest was partially paid (125, 129), in one it was promised (128), and in one it was taken by self-redress (126). Case 127 presents a dispute between individuals of two different confederacies in which political disunity precluded an enforcement of the rule. Case 129 especially illuminates the problem. The defendant is punished simply because of not paying fully the promised interest. Thus we may claim that rule 100 is an example of a dead rule in Kapauku culture.

Rule 112, dealing with disobedience in war, states that a reprimand should be the punishment for the delict. However, in two of our three cases (150, 151), the defendants are corporally punished as well, and in the third case (152) physical punishment was *forgiven* because the "authority, feeling sorry for him, refrained from corporal punishment."

Rule 101 states the right of a man to collect at any time a loan which provided the debtor with money for a bride price. However, in case 130, the creditor was reprimanded in public for using his right. Informants stated that the reprimand was proper and that every other offender would be punished in the same way. This is "because it is good to ask for such a loan only after the purchased woman bears a child." According to rule 101, however, an offender should not be punished.

In case 25, a boy molested a girl. Instead of being punished according to rule 21, he is actually rewarded for the deed by the authority. Since the writer's informants claimed that this is always the case, the rule may be regarded as a dead one.

Case 85 presents an interesting example of a conflict between a rule and the customary settlement of a dispute. Although the rule calls clearly for a full indemnity payable by the trapper to the owner of the killed pig, it is customary for only half of the value of the killed animal to be paid and for the owner to give to the defendant that quarter of the animal pierced by the spikes of the trap. Thus the customary settlement of the case is much more favorable to the trapper than the rule provides. Rule 55 is dead (never applied) because people claim that disputes are always settled in the same way as in case 85, rather than according to the wording of the rule.

Case 33 presents a violation of the rule defining an incest taboo. The outcome of the case not only contradicted rule 24 but it became a precedent for numerous violations of the same sort, which made the rule obsolete and resulted in an important change in social structure. Since no one would be punished any more for violating the rule, it belongs to the "legal past" of this community although it is still recited by many individuals of Botukebo as valid and proper.[10]

The result of a study concentrating upon Kapauku rules would, in the light of what has been shown above, hardly reflect the Kapauku system of institutionalized social control. Not only are some rules contrary to the customary results of the

---

[10] For fuller discussion of this case see the section on legal dynamics.

disputes, but many others are not applied or are in need of important qualifications, while the rules themselves are a "mental property" of relatively few of the older individuals in the society. Most of the younger and many of the middle-aged informants, when asked about these abstract statements, either referred the writer to a few individuals "who knew," or responded by reciting some of the outcomes of disputes they remembered.

When we return to cultures with written codifications of law, we find more reasons for not using the exclusive study of abstract rules as a means of revealing mechanisms of institutionalized social control (law). Thus rules stated in words are ambiguous because their interpretation may vary from individual to individual. What the judge says—what he conceives "the law to be"—is much more important for the outcome of a trial and consequently in its effect on the society than what is written in the code. There is no consistency between interpretation of a rule by a judge and the intent of the legislator. "To find the intention of the legislator" very often proves to be a hard task, especially when he died perhaps a century ago. To this verbal difficulty is added another when we deal with rules passed a long time before. Both the meaning of the phrasing of the law and the social milieu in which it exists change with the passing of time. This makes a rule even less safe as the ground for determining the actual institutionalized social control.

Finally, we may object from the historical point of view to the idea that a legal code, when present in a society, contains definite answers for all concrete judicial cases. We may even have serious doubts about the claim that people identify law with the rules in legal codifications. This claim was made by the "Legalists" in China in the third century B.C., and more than a thousand years later by the legal thinkers in Europe. Their opinion should be conceived of as showing only one of several possible roles codification may play in a society. Even in these two places there were times when rules were viewed not as solutions for given situations but only as a help to the judges—as a lead that might be followed. This, for example, was the case of the Law of the Twelve Tables in the casuistic approach of Old Rome. This was also the case with regard to most of the laws produced in China, save for the brief period of domination by Legalistic philosophy in the third century B.C. (Van der Valk, 1939: 13). In the two examples there was nothing comparable to the Western concept of the compulsiveness of written rules where a judge is obligated to apply these rules rather mechanically.

Similarly, the one hundred and twenty-one Kapauku rules presented in the preceding part of the monograph do not bind the native authority in his decision. Their role is comparable to that of the rules in China or in Old Rome—a help to the authority in settling disputes. It is easier to adjudicate a case by a decision referring to a rule, thus depriving it of an air of arbitrariness, than simply to state one's own opinion. However, when the authority felt that a decision satisfactory to all parties concerned would be one which did not comply with the appropriate rule, he would not hesitate to disregard it. Thus, a rule functions in the Kapauku process of settling disputes as a referential device rather than a ready-made answer applicable mechanically to corresponding cases.

The difficulties faced by the theoreticians who equated law with the abstract rule were clearly seen by Ehrlich (1913: 65, 323–4), and as a result he developed a second path for legal thought. He differentiated between rules and what he called the "living law," the actual behavior of the members of the society. The present writer would hesitate to conceive law simply as behavior because people's behavior lacks compulsion, and because the identity of the behavior is a fiction since individuals behave differently. In every society there are persons whose behavior is considered more important than that of other members of the group. Law, if considered as the actual behavior of all the members of a social group, would lack an ideal aspect which is so important in making people conform. The fact that the "living law" is identical with the behavior patterns of the culture makes this concept of law meaningless and superfluous. Furthermore, to follow Ehrlich's definition of the form of law would lead an investigator of the Kapauku culture to the conclusion that, since the majority of the people would and do steal money if the opportunity presents itself, the "living law" of theft is to steal rather than to prevent the thefts. This finding, in addition to its absurd wording, would fail to bring out the numerous trials and the extensive institutionalized punishments of the thieves.

The decision of an authority offers a third possibility for the study of law as an institutionalized social control. An individual, or group of individuals, decides each concrete case and his decision is followed for one reason or another. Some of the valid reasons in various cultures are fear of the authority's power, the people's conviction of their authority's superior knowledge, and their wish for security which is satisfied by a belief that the authority's justice will be applied consistently to all future cases. We may use Bronislaw Malinowski's idea and say that many people "having a long range view of the situation" comply with the present and to them unfavorable decision of the authority because they anticipate similar decisions in the future when it will be they who will profit (Malinowski, 1934: 36).

In our Kapauku situation, we face the problem of defining what actually constitutes a relevant decision. The description of the cases suggests by its wording that the authority passes decisions in a formal way so that a native trial would very much resemble one in our own culture. Nothing, however, would be more misleading than such an assumption.

The Kapauku "process of law" starts usually as a quarrel between the parties concerned. The individual, whom we would call plaintiff, accuses the other party, called defendant, of having done an injustice which causes harm to the plaintiff's interests. The defendant denies or brings forward justifications for his action. The arguments are usually accompanied by loud shouting which attracts the other people who gather at the place of the quarrel, which may be in the village or outside in a garden. The close relatives and friends of the parties to the dispute take sides according to their alliances, and start presenting their opinions and testimony by an emotional speech or by outright shouting. If this sort of argumentation, called by natives *mana koto*, goes on unchecked, it usually results in a stick fight (cases 40, 55, 57, 59, 118) or in outright war (case 16). However, in most of the instances, the important men from the village, as well as from allied communities, appear on the scene. First they squat among the onlookers and listen to the arguments. As soon as the exchange of opinions reaches a point too close to an outbreak of violence, the authority steps in and starts his argumentation. He admonishes both of the parties to have patience and starts questioning the defendant and the witnesses himself, as well as investigating other evidence which would lead to the identification of the criminal, such as remnants of bones, feathers, etc. found on the place of the crime or in the defendant's house (cases 62, 74). This activity of the authority is called *boko petai*, which loosely can be translated as "finding the evidence." After he secures all the evidence and makes up his mind as to the factual background of the dispute, the authority starts the activity called by the natives *boko duwai*, which means the process of making a decision and inducing the parties to the dispute to follow it. This process could hardly be compared in its form to the adjudicating activity of our judges. The native authority makes a long speech in which he sums up the evidence, appeals to a rule, and then tells the parties what should be done in order to terminate the dispute. If the disputants are not willing to comply, the authority becomes emotional and starts to shout reproaches, and makes long speeches in which evidence, rules, decisions, and threats form inducements. Indeed, the authority may go as far as to start *"wainai,* the mad dance," or change his tactics suddenly and weep bitterly about the misconduct of the defendant and the fact that the latter refuses to obey him. Some native authorities are so skilled in the art of persuasion as to produce genuine tears which almost always break the resistance of the unwilling party. A superficial Western observer confronted with such a situation may very likely regard the weeping headman as the culprit on trial. Thus, from the formalistic point of view, there is little resemblance between the Western court's sentence and the *boko duwai* activity of the headman. However, the effect of the headman's persuasion is the same as that of a verdict passed in our court. As we have seen, there were only five cases in our material where the parties openly resisted and disobeyed the authority (cases 54, 94, 105, 119, 168).

From what has been said, we can conclude that it is not the abstract rule that affects the Kapauku people but the actual decision of the headman. People conceive of righteous behavior as what the rich man, who is an authority, says and not that which is the content of the rules, although in the majority of the decisions the people assume that he complies with the rules. If we adhere to this as a form of law, we avoid the difficulties which were present in the two preceding theories. Moreover, if we consider the functional aspect as basic to the concept of law, the latter comprises only those phenomena which actually produce social control, and hence we have to accept the decision of the authority as the inevitable form of manifestation of law.

The following Kapauku statements stress the importance of legal decisions:

Ijaaj Bunaibomuuma of Botukebo, when asked about the importance of incest rules which prohibit marrying a girl of the same sib (rule 24) stated: "It is all right, of course (to violate the rule). It was prohibited in the past and the *tonowi* and relatives punished the culprits. Now Awiitigaaj (village headman) claims it is all right to violate the rule so I followed his decision and married an Ijaaj. People objected to my marriage but Awitigaaj, who himself married an Ijaaj, protected my own marriage."

Ijaaj Tajwiijokaipouga of Botukebo, when asked about the importance of abstract prohibitions, said: "They are good and we need them. But they are not always useful (practical). In the old days it was prohibited to marry Ijaaj people (to marry into the same sib) but now, since Awiitigaaj married an Ijaaj and decided it was all right, we agree with him. Obajbegaa people have just different ideas about the things (when they object to the practice)."

"People also say that it is tabooed to eat the fruit bat (totemic animal of Ijaaj sib). Many older men in our village ate it. Awiitigaaj himself agrees (with the practice), and nobody yet became sick. (As a matter of fact,) the bat has excellent meat."

The discussion above, as well as the evidence from the Kapauku material, tends to substantiate the general proposition which the writer derived from his cross-cultural research.

Law manifests itself in the form of a decision of a legal authority (headman, chief, council, etc.) by which a dispute is solved or a party is advised before any legally relevant behavior takes place, or by which approval is given to a previous solution of a dispute made by the participants before they brought it to the attention of the authority. This form of law has two important aspects. It unites the behavioral part that is played by the authority while passing the sentence, and the ideal part which is reflected in the minds of the people who follow the decision and regard its content as a revelation of the ideally correct behavior. A decision serves not only as a solution of a dispute but it represents a precedent and an ideal even for people who have played no role in the dispute. Accordingly a legal decision belongs to the behavioral component of the culture as far as the authority's activity of passing a decision goes, and to the ideal part of the culture as far as the "followers" are concerned. The first alternative concept or conceiving of rules as of the exclusive form of law lacked the behavioral part while the second, the "living law" solution, lacked the ideal part. This is one of the reasons why the writer has rejected these alternatives.

To sum up what has been said about the form of law, we may imagine a picture of the legal field which consists of several levels. The lowest level is composed of legal decisions. From this base, the principles of the decisions may be abstracted and will form, according to their degree of abstraction, the different upper strata. The abstractions from the decisions which belong in the field of law will be called legal postulates. They may be identical in content with the abstract rules, in which case we may say that the rules are enforced. Rules which are not enforced, i.e., dead rules, are by their definition omitted from the legal field, since they have no corresponding legal postulates.

The legal nature and importance of the enforced rules is neither denied nor diminished by the emphasis here on the idea that decisions form the base of the legal field. What we object to is the incorporation of the dead rules into the legal field, as well as the exclusion of the legal decisions and the denial of their paramount importance for the study of law as an institutionalized social control.

THE ATTRIBUTES OF LAW

The following proposition has been derived from cross-cultural research: if law is conceived as "rules or modes of conduct made obligatory by some sanction which is imposed and enforced for their violation by a controlling authority," then the analysis of such legal phenomena reveals a common pattern of attributes rather than one sweeping characteristic of law. These attributes if considered in turn as criteria of law separate it objectively from all other social phenomena.

Having discussed the form of law, we shall now analyze the legal phenomena and abstract attributes which they have in common. These attributes will also serve us as criteria for the more exact delimitation of the law's boundaries.

The decisions of an authority vary greatly and they embrace many facts that cannot be called law. In other words, we have to discover additional characteristics to differentiate legal decisions from political ones and from advice concerning non-sanctioned customs. We have also to distinguish law from purely religious phenomena and from the rest of culture. Social scientists have been searching for a single criterion of law which would constitute its essence. The most important early contributions in this respect have been made by Radcliffe-Brown and Malinowski.

Radcliffe-Brown (1952: 212) emphasized the physical sanction administered by a politically organized society as the basic criterion of law. Hoebel (1940: 47; 1954: 28) followed him in this respect. The emphasis upon the "politically organized society" led the former author to admit that there was an absence of law in some "more primitive cultures," and thus to limit the concept to cultures with a more formal political organization. The writer of this monograph agrees with the importance of the sanction criterion but is reluctant to accept the second proposition of "the politically organized society." This problem will be discussed later and an attempt will be made to show the universality of law and to refute the idea of a "lawless functioning group."

Malinowski selected as his main attribute of law the principle of obligation. The presence of obligation—that is ties between two parties—defines a phenomenon as law, punishment being inessential because conformance is achieved through mutual service based on expectance of future reciprocal favors (Malinowski, 1934: 30–42). This theory is much less workable than the one discussed in the previous paragraph, although it allows for the universality of law. N. S. Timasheff criticizes it by pointing out that although duels were obligatory in Europe, they were illegal (Timasheff, 1938: 871).

The present writer objects to Malinowski's view because law is defined so broadly as to include most of the customs of a society. For this reason the theory does not lend itself to being a workable tool for the ethnographer. Moreover there are many kinds of obligations, like moral or religious ones, that have to be differentiated from the legal. Consequently, a "legal obligation" must be defined more exactly and additional attributes are needed to set it aside from the other nonlegal cases.

We do not object to the above theories on the basis of their invalidity. Indeed, each of them elaborates a particular attribute which is important for our inquiry. The objection to these views lies in the fact that their attributes are insufficient for characterizing the essence of law. It is the contention of the writer, based upon the results of comparative research as well as upon the findings among the Kapauku, that not one attribute but rather a whole pattern of them which coexist in time form the core of the social phenomena which we call law. In the cultures studied, the writer has found four legal attributes which seem to be of importance: authority, true *obligatio*, intention of universal application, and sanction (Fig. 8). In addition a manifestation of a law has to have the form of a decision. This pattern of attributes, it is believed, constitutes the essence of law and may possibly provide an ethnographer with a workable tool.

THE ATTRIBUTE OF AUTHORITY

A decision to be legally relevant, or in other words to effect social control, has to be accepted by the parties to the dispute as a solution of the situation caused by the clash of their interests. An individual, or a subgroup, who possesses an influence which causes the majority of the members of the group to conform to his decisions, the writer calls an authority. We may ask whether we do not run the risk of making our legal concept nonuniversal by employing such an attribute. Many ethnographers have declared that there is genuine absence of authority in certain cultures. Some of them use expressions like "lateral social control" or "the group as a whole" (Yang, 1945: 134) when referring to the agency of social control; such expressions are virtually identical with a statement of the absence of authority, if by authority we mean a specific individual (or individuals). Let us investigate one such case.

Gusinde says about the customary laws of the Yaghan ". . . that they are faithfully followed is looked after by the group as a whole" (Gusinde, 1937: 628). Not being satisfied with the face value of the phrase "group as a whole" (*Allgemeinheit*), we may ask the question: who usually represents or speaks for this mysterious *Allgemeinheit*? The answer is to be found in a different part of the same monograph.

"There is never a shortage of men who because of their old age, spotless character, long experience and mental superiority, gain such an extent of moral influence that it is equal to a peculiar domination" (Gusinde, 1937: 803).

These strong men are called *tiamuna* by the people and they are active in the local groups (*Lokalgruppe*) that form the important units in the Yaghan social structure.

The picture in other cases of an alleged absence of authority is usually quite similar to this example. When we go deeper into our investigation, the *Allgemeinheit*, or absence of an authority, changes into more definite factors of social control.

We find particular individuals initiating action in the group, resolving problems, and occupying more or less definite positions of importance. The difficulty lies in the problem of what the respective author actually means by the term authority. The concept is usually not clarified and its meaning is taken for granted. Implicit in most of the statements of an absence of an authority is a definition that identifies the concept with a person of rather absolute power, whose acts, especially those involving the passing of decisions, are very formal. We may ask whether absoluteness and formality are the most important characteristics of an authority. The present writer has postulated that the essence of the concept does not rest with these descriptive characteristics peculiar to some cultures only. On the contrary, he believes that the fact that the decisions or advice of the authority are followed by the rest of the members of the group forms the only important criterion of the disputed term. The concept of an authority, therefore, is considered in this monograph not as a descriptive but as a functional one. Absoluteness and formality are only its specialized, nonuniversal attributes. An authority comprises one or more individuals who initiate actions in a functional group and whose decisions are followed by the majority of the group's members.

The postulate that an authority so defined is universal to all cultures is substantiated by the findings of psychologists in situations where the cultural factor emphasizing authority has been virtually eliminated. For example, Muzafer Sherif made experiments with the autokinetic effect (Sherif, 1947: 77–89). An individual was brought into a dark room where no lights could penetrate. A tiny lighted dot appeared to him in the darkness. Although this dot was fixed and motionless, the person observing it was under the purely subjective impression that the light was moving, for there was nothing with which the observer could compare the point of light to be able to observe a possible motion. The same experiment was conducted with other observers. After this, the observers were permitted to tell each other their perceptions and discuss their experiences. Thereafter they were asked to look at the dot once again and were told that this was done so that they could correct their observations and be more accurate. An interesting result was reported. The individual perceptions in the second trial tended to cluster in a narrow range, which was called by Sherif the group norm. For the purpose of this thesis it is important that the individuals within this "group norm range," who changed their original statements of observations very slightly, or not at all, were functioning as persons with authority. The rest of the group were merely their followers. This experiment suggests that there are always individuals differing in intelligence, assertiveness, temperament, and aggression who influence others and who are looked to as leaders.

Kapauku society is one of those considered by Western observers as having no individuals of authority.[11] However, even superficial observers had to notice a kind of reverence exhibited toward a man called *tonowi*, as well as the fact that some of

---

[11] See the discussion on *maagodo tonowi* under Political Structure in the Ijaaj-Pigome Confederacy.

the *tonowi's* wishes were respected by the rest of the group. In order to make a concession to those observable facts, the Europeans called this individual *"primus inter pares*, the first among equals."￼ We have discussed at length the attributes of this authority, his followers, as well as the different motivations for the compliance of the parties to a dispute with the *tonowi's* verdicts. In the preceding discussion, we have also shown his strange way of making decisions. In the description of our 176 cases of clashes of interests, we may notice that in 132 cases it was this authority— or the house owner and the husband in household and family cases—who passed weight-carrying decisions. In only three cases (54, 105, 119), the advice and solutions were not respected. Thus we may conclude that the Kapauku do have authorities who settle by decisions most of the disputes.

The objection of the Europeans to calling a rich man "the authority" is based upon disregard of the functional connotation of the concept. The attributes of the Western judge—the formality with which he adjudicates cases, the finality and absoluteness of his decisions, as well as the reverence and ceremony of the Western court—these purely descriptive criteria are held as a measure for deciding the presence or absence of an authority. The title *primus inter pares*, assigned to the Kapauku leader by some Europeans, exemplifies the above statements. The insistence on the functional definition of authority and the following analysis of its different attributes results from comparative research.

Various cultures give to their authorities special attributes that sometimes differ fundamentally. In one culture, an aggressive individual with absolute power may be favored, while in another, the opposite may be true.

These different attributes allow the authorities to be classified as different types. For our purpose we may be interested in two attributes: formality and extent of power. The strength of these attributes will change from case to case, and so we shall get two mutually independent and qualitatively different ranges of types. The extreme positions in the first range will be occupied on one end by a totally informal authority (with a minimal amount of formality) and by a strictly formal authority (with a maximal amount of formality) on the other. In the second range pertaining to extent of power, there will be a gradation from an authority with narrowly limited power to one with the most absolute control. The extreme positions should be considered ideal instances, approximated by only a few concrete examples. The examples will differ from one another according to the degree of the criterion measured (the formality or extent of power).

To give some tentative definitions of our ideal extremes, we may say this: by formal authority is meant an individual (or individuals) with his (or their) role, rights, duties, and activities defined by custom and/or law. The public and ceremonial parts of the action tend to be emphasized more than in the opposite extreme of informal authority.

The informal authority, on the other hand, has no ceremonial importance and little public emphasis. In his case everything tends to depend on the personality of the individual, on his skill and personal achievements, and on his conformity with the ideal pattern of legal authority set up by the particular culture. His rights, duties, and procedures are not defined by law or custom.

A limited authority is acquired by a procedure which is controlled by the society. Approval by the majority of the members of the society is necessary, or nomination by another person with relatively greater authority must take place. An authority of this type has very little power. If he breaks the law, he is punished either by the members of the society or by a superior. His power thus is checked by another authority or by constitutional law.

An absolute authority is different in many respects. His power is not limited by someone else. The subordination of his followers is emphasized in personal contacts. He is not checked to a marked degree by the other members of the society or by any other institution. The tendency is to see in such an authority the end and not the means for achieving something.

By measuring the two variables discussed above, we should be able to place each authority in a definite position that indicates his qualities within the two ranges. An authority then will be defined by the following possible combinations of the two measured attributes and their negatives: formal and absolute, informal and absolute, formal and limited, or informal and limited. The distance from the limits of the ranges can be designated qualitatively or quantitatively.

The Kapauku concept of *tonowi*, by the lack of emphasis upon the ceremonial aspects in passing a decision, by the dependence upon personal skill and the achievements of the individual, and by the fact that the rights, duties, and procedures of adjudicating cases are not explicitly defined by law or custom, has to be classified as extremely informal. The amount of power that a specific Papuan authority possesses, of course, differs from individual to individual. The average Kapauku authority is of the limited type because the acquisition of the position is controlled by the members of the group and the duration of the role is determined by the approval of the group's constituents. Custom and the rules provide a check on the amount of power wielded by the leader and prevent excessive arbitrariness. With respect to groups in a descending order of inclusiveness, we may generalize and say that a village leader would have more control over his followers than a leader of a lineage would have over the constituents of his unit. Thus Ekajewaijokaipouga, the leader of the Ijaaj-Pigome confederacy, would have the least power over Pigome people, more over Ijaaj people of the Gepouja lineage, even more in his own Jamaina sublineage, and most of all in the village of Aigii and his own household. In summary, we may call all Kapauku authorities informal with varying degrees of limitation in their power. Since the word headman has been used in current ethnographies to connote an informal native authority as differentiated from the more formalistic institution of chieftainship, the word headman has been adopted by the present author in translating the native word *tonowi*.

A Kapauku authority, however, does not limit himself to the legal field. In every instance, the headman is a political authority as well. Ekajewaijokaipouga, who has a reputation of being an excellent shaman as well as a legal and political authority, has a combination which lends him the greatest influence on his followers. Usually only in the most complex cultures such as our own do we find a specialized legal authority.

To sum up our discussion of the attribute of authority, we may say that the hypothesis of its universality, arrived at by cross-cultural research, has been substantiated in a culture where its absence was claimed by several observers.

THE ATTRIBUTE OF INTENTION OF UNIVERSAL APPLICATION

While analyzing the data arrived at from cross-cultural research, the writer conceived of the field of law as an ellipse surrounded by a zone of transition which separated the field from the rest of the culture (Fig. 8). Phenomena placed within the peripheral zone combined the overlapping criteria of the neighboring categories so that it was difficult to determine which ones dominated the field. Our attribute of authority, discussed in the previous section, constitutes the criterion which defines the lower boundaries of the ellipse and helps us to separate law from the neighboring field of custom. Repetitive behavior which does not form the subject of the authority's decision is simply custom. When we turn to the upper end of the ellipse, we find that our attribute of authority covering the whole field of law goes beyond it in this place and penetrates the adjacent field of political decisions, which is situated in Figure 8 above the field of law.

Since in the culture investigated both political decisions and legal judgments are made by the same authority, the Kapauku material shows a need for an additional criterion which would be effective in separating the legal and the political fields. This need is met by the attribute of legal decisions called by the writer the intention of universal application. This attribute, found to be present in all legal decisions, if applicable as a criterion of law demands that the authority in making a decision intends it to be applied to all similar or "identical" situations in the future.

In the decisions of Kapauku authorities, this intention is usually made explicit either by mentioning the pertinent rule or by using the obligatory-repetitive tense aspect while referring to the guilt and the punishment. When the decision is claimed to be made according to a rule, this incorporated rule constitutes the ideal. In the phrase, "*kou dani te tija*, one does not act like that," the verbal suffix -*ja* expresses not only the moral obligation "ought," but it also stands for the customary, repetitive action which may be translated as "used to." Thus this phrase, used in all the decisions which the writer heard, confirms the statement with respect to the ideal component of law which we have discussed while dealing with the form of law. Not only does the decision solve a specific case, but it also formulates an ideal—a solution intended to be utilized in all similar situations in the future.

The ideal component binds all other members of the group who did not participate in the decided case. The authority himself turns to his previous decisions for consistency. In a way, they also bind him. Lawyers speak in such a case about the binding force of precedent which is legal justice.

According to what has been said above, the following cases represent legal injustice on the part of the authority who failed to be consistent with respect to his past decisions because his own, or his protégé's, interests were at stake (cases 97, 139–142, 165).

In all the above cases the authority used his power to obtain personal advantages. Ijaaj Awïitigaaj of Botukebo certainly failed to emphasize an ideal when by sheer

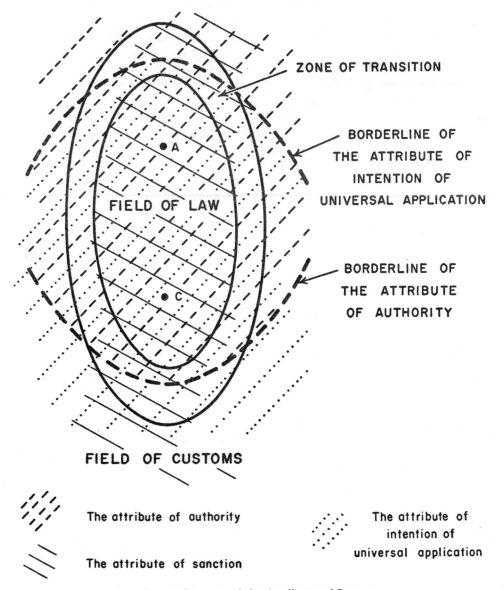

FIELD OF POLITICAL DECISIONS

ZONE OF TRANSITION

BORDERLINE OF
THE ATTRIBUTE OF
INTENTION OF
UNIVERSAL APPLICATION

• A

FIELD OF LAW

BORDERLINE OF
THE ATTRIBUTE
OF AUTHORITY

• C

FIELD OF CUSTOMS

The attribute of authority

The attribute of
intention of
universal application

The attribute of sanction

FIG. 8. Diagram of the Attributes of Law.

force of his following he repelled his creditors' requests for payment (cases 139–142). However, he failed to apply discriminatory "unjust" decisions in cases where his own interests were not involved (cases 105, 118, 119, 124). Because of the absence of the attribute of intention of universal application, the decisions in cases 97, 139, 140, 141, 142, 165 cannot be considered legal according to this theory. Kapauku informants agree, calling the decisions "unjust."

The reader, however, should be cautioned against an assumption that inconsistency with the precedent alone excludes a decision from the legal sphere. The decision in case 33 illustrates a radical inconsistency which being perpetuated and having the intention of universal application (the declaration that the formerly incestuous type of marriage was acceptable) does constitute law. It is the absence of this intention rather then of the inconsistency which excludes a decision passed by an authority from the legal field.

THE ATTRIBUTE OF OBLIGATIO

The third attribute arrived at analytically is *obligatio*. It corresponds to that part of the decision of an authority which determines the rights of one party and the duties of the other. Both parties, it has been contended, must be represented by living persons. A decision which does not fulfill this requirement is not considered legal. The *obligatio*, it will be noticed, is different from the popular concept of obligation which only includes duty. Our concept is a statement about a social relation and has two directions: one going from the privileged party to the obligated one, which is called the right; and the other from the obligated party toward the privileged one, which is called the duty.

For example, in case 57, which deals with a violation of a right of ownership of trees, the authority in his decision stated that the duty of the defendant was to stop asking his brother for a tree and to look elsewhere for the needed canoe wood. The decision contained the right of the owner of the tree not to be molested by the defendant's demands.

While this case states a negative right expressed in negative terms, many of the cases concerning ownership rights and contracts define the duty of the defendant as a positive action involving the payment or transference of some commodity. Thus in case 79, the authority decided upon the right of the pig owner to obtain an indemnity and upon the duty of the defendant to pay it. Since it is not always possible to induce the defendant to make a payment, either because of his resistance or lack of means, the plaintiff is given the right to have the culprit punished and the defendant has the duty to suffer the punishment. All of Kapauku defendants "sentenced" in the presence of the writer complied with the decision and passively received the scolding and beating. In cases 23 and 124, the defendants were squatting, looking at the ground, and receiving blows, reproaches and scoldings without trying to avoid them. It is notable in case 124 that the defendant appeared each morning in front of his house to face his prosecutors as well as those who were punishing him during the whole day.

A statement by the authority which gives one party a right, while not stating the duty of the other one, is not law even though both the attributes of authority and of the intention of universal application are present. The statement becomes law only when a duty on the part of someone is implied or included in the decision.

Thus in case 115, the duty of the culprit involving his liability for the loss of the pig was clearly recognized in the decision. The authority, however, probably because of political reasons, did not state the right of the pig owner to collect the indemnity. He only admonished both parties in the dispute to avoid violence. As a consequence, the plaintiff did not collect anything and had to leave empty-handed. This case does not represent the application of law because of the lack of our attribute of *obligatio* or the absence of a statement about the right of the pig owner. The recognition of the defendant's liability reminds us of the fact that we are not confronted with a case with a verdict of not guilty.[12]

Similarly, cases 139–142 demonstrate "verdicts" in which the authority acknowledged the rights of the creditors either explicitly or tacitly but, by using force and his headman's position, avoided his duty to pay.[13] Thus absence of the attribute of *obligatio* results in an inconclusive settlement of a dispute and prevents the decision, because of the lack of the ideal component (discussed in the section on the form of law), from becoming legal.

Another important characteristic should be noted while dealing with this attribute. The *obligatio* that forms part of the decision is necessarily a new phenomenon created by the authority. It should not be mistaken for the obligation incurred previous to the decision, an infringement of which brought about the suit and legal decision. This is because the person with authority, no matter how objective and just he may be, is in most cases unable to find out all the facts about the pre-existing obligation and its violation. What counts in a legal decision is not what objectively existed but what is stated in the decision to have existed, since this leads to the solution of the problem being adjudicated by the authority. The question of how far the actual facts differ from those included in the *obligatio*, and of whether the decision is therefore proper, belongs to the factual part of the problem of justice which is not our concern here. In case 81, for example, the confederacy's headman decided that Akoonewiijaaj was not guilty of the crime. This outcome was due to a lack of evidence about the crime, and it has little to do with the objective state of affairs. The writer's informants were convinced that Akoonewiijaaj committed the crime. Although according to the rules if he stole the pig he was obligated to restore the stolen property, the *obligatio* of the decision imposed a duty upon the plaintiff not to molest or accuse the defendant. Thus the actual obligation was opposite to the *obligatio* which was the duty and the right stated in the verdict.

[12] This case also makes it clear that the Hohfeldian concepts of privilege, no right, power, liability, immunity, and no power, being basically statements of latent and passive nature, are not attributes of the legal decisions that solve active disputes. Consequently they do not lend themselves as universal criteria of law.

[13] Cases 139–142 lack also the attribute of the intention of universal application.

The *obligatio* is a relation between two parties who are both represented by living individuals. Hence, all obligations toward the dead and toward the supernatural are excluded from the realm of law unless the interests of the dead or of the supernatural are represented by living people. It is an opinion of the present writer, who differs with Llewellyn and Hoebel (1941: 286) on this point, that a religious taboo "with no officials to enforce it" is not law, but a strictly religious phenomenon. If we were to include such taboos (where the privileged party is not represented by living people) in the legal field, this field would cease to exist because any kind of custom could creep in and break down its boundaries.

Cases 17 and 18 involve taboos imposed by shamans upon specific individuals. While in both examples the attribute of authority manifests itself in the person of the shaman, the attributes of intention of universal application and of *obligatio* are absent. The shaman did not say that in every similar (from the Kapauku point of view "identical") case he would impose the same taboos; in other words, he did not intend to apply his decision universally. Since *obligatio* is a relation between two parties, who if they are not human beings are represented by them, these taboos have to be considered religious phenomena. The same verdict has to be passed in case 20 which presents us with a violation of a totemic eating taboo. Although this taboo, by its universal application ("Any individual is tabooed to eat or burn totemic plants . . ." rule 12) comes closer to law in this respect, it lacks the attribute of authority as well as that of *obligatio* and has to be regarded as a purely religious taboo.

As a contrast to the above taboos, excluded from the field of law because of the lack of the attribute of *obligatio*, stand those which, being provided with the attribute, are to be classified as laws. Thus in cases 19 and 21, in addition to the violator of the taboos, there is present a plaintiff who has the right to have the culprit punished. While in the category first discussed, the punishment would always be left to the supernatural, and therefore be "more or less uncertain," in this type of taboo the plaintiff himself or a representative of his interests would see to the execution of the sanction.

Kapauku themselves have different attitudes toward the two sets of taboos which we have separated by our attribute. They would talk freely about their violations of the purely religious taboos. Indeed, some individuals would even boast about their disregard of supernatural prohibitions in order to show others their bravery and courage. The violations of the "legal taboos," on the contrary, are kept secret to the same extent that one does not boast in public about one's own crimes.

The attribute of *obligatio* separates religious customs, exemplified above by the first category of taboos, from religious law. The latter, in addition to the "legal taboos" discussed, includes all legal cases in which supernatural punishments either are added to the secular ones or take their place completely. Thus case 119 presents a decision which, possessing all the attributes of law and the headman's punishment by sorcery, is classified as religious law. Similarly, case 46 gives us an example of a religious authority who, in addition to being a shaman, is a legal authority as well.

Thus the attribute of *obligatio* functions also as a criterion which helps us to separate religious customs from religious law. We deal with the latter only when the interests of the supernatural are represented by a living individual such as a priest or shaman. The case will never be left to the decision and punishment of the supernatural only, as it may be in the case of a religious custom. A religious taboo is law only if all the legal attributes are supplied (an authority's decision, intention of universal application, *obligatio*, and sanction); otherwise it is classified by the writer as religious custom.

THE ATTRIBUTE OF SANCTION

The last but not the least important of the legal attributes is sanction. This criterion has played a paramount role in different legal theories; sometimes law has been almost equated with it. The writer does not attempt to underestimate its importance. Nevertheless, he would question the use of this attribute as an exclusive criterion and its superordination above the rest of the legal factors, the coexistence of which we have found as forming the essence of law. We have to realize that although many of the political decisions are provided with sanctions, they are not laws, for there is a lack of repetitive aspect, or, in other words, an absence of the attribute of intention of universal application.

As to the legal sanction itself, it has been usually conceived of as having a physical nature. In his early work, Hoebel has defined a social norm as legal ". . . if its neglect or infraction is met by the application, in threat or in fact, of absolute coercive force by a social unit possessing the socially recognized privilege of so acting" (Hoebel, 1940: 47). Hoebel means absolute coercive force when he writes ". . . the exercise of physical force to control or prevent action is the absolute form of compulsion . . . the characteristic feature of law, as distinct from mere force, is the recognized privilege of a person or social group to apply the absolute form of coercion to a transgressor when conduct deemed improper may occur" (Hoebel, 1940: 47).

In his later work Hoebel (1954: 28) gives the following substantially similar, definition: "A social norm is legal if its neglect or infraction is regularly met, in threat or in fact, by the application of physical force by an individual or group possessing the socially recognized privilege of so acting."

If we were to accept this definition of sanction, many of our Kapauku cases would not be "legal" and law would not be a universal phenomenon, for cultures exist where physical sanction is practically lacking. We may ask if the form of sanction is so important as to make the existence of law dependent upon it. Is not the effect (social control, conformity) of a sanction more important than its form? In this case, as in defining the concept of authority, the writer prefers a functional approach. He suggests that effective social control is the important qualification of a legal sanction. Some psychological sanctions, although of nonphysical nature, perform as strong a control as do physical sanctions. Ostracism, ridicule, avoidance, or a denial of favors—sanctions that are sometimes very subtle and informal—nevertheless may become more drastic than the corporal punishment to which we tend to attach over-importance even in our own culture.

The Kapauku, for example, consider being shamed by a public reprimand, which sometimes lasts for several days, much worse than anything except capital punishment. Case 124 shows that the reprimand was only secondary to execution in its gravity. In this case a notorious criminal was reprimanded for seven days during which the authorities were undecided between this kind of nonphysical sanction and the killing of the guilty man. The defendant sold most of his possessions in order to pay his debt and thus satisfy his creditors and put an end to the punishment. However, the later consequences of the shaming were even harder on the man than the seven-day long ordeal. All the villagers ostracized him, avoided meeting or even looking at him; and Gipemeide, the culprit's relative who shared his house, moved to another after the punishment of his landlord. "If they would beat me and take all my belongings it would be better than this," complained the unhappy delinquent.

In our sample of 176 cases, there are twenty-four which have reprimands as the sanction. Because all the other attributes of law are present, they belong in our legal field.

From cross-cultural research and the above discussion, it follows that a legal sanction does not need to be corporal punishment or a deprivation of property. The form of a sanction is relative to the culture and to the subgroup in which it is used; it may be physical or psychological. We can define a legal sanction as either the negative behavior of withdrawing some rewards or favors that otherwise (if the law had not been violated) would have been granted, or the positive behavior of inflicting some painful experience, be it physical or psychological.

In the following outline, the writer presents the various sanctions used by the Kapauku with the numbers of the cases in which they were applied. The reader is reminded of the simultaneous occurrence of different sanctions in one case, as well as of the fact that forty-four have been disqualified as legal cases on the basis of the absence of some of our attributes of law. The nonlegal cases will be given in parentheses.

Corporal sanctions. a) An execution. Capital punishment is administered either by a close relative of the culprit's sib, such as a brother, son, father, or paternal parallel cousin, or by the plaintiff or his close relative. A bamboo-tipped arrow is usually the instrument used for the execution.

Applied in eight cases: 2, 3, 15, 19, 31, 32, 170, 171; case 5 represents an unsuccessful attempt at execution.

Reasons for execution: Murder, sorcery, violation of taboo, incest, ungenerousness (in the case from the Paniai region), and instigation of war.

Comment: It should be noted here that the Kapauku executed the delinquents of these cases for crimes which, with the exception of incest, involved loss of life on the part of other people. This sanction is used in the village and on more inclusive group levels such as the confederacy. It is never applied on the family or household levels.

b) Beating with a stick. Sticks of various lengths and thickness are utilized. Most blows are applied on the head and shoulders.

Applied in 35 cases: 1, 11, 14, 23, 36, 44, 45, 61, 62, 64, 65, 68, 71, 73, 75, 104, 120, 123, 124, 125, 144, 148, 151, 153–156, 159–162, 164, 165, 167, 175.

Reasons for beating: Beating is used for all possible delicts, ranging from murder (case 1) to treason or a refusal to pay a debt.

Comment: There is no limitation on the use of this sanction to any group. In most of the cases, all of which belong in the field of law, the defendant accepted the punishment passively. On the contrary, in cases where the plaintiff unaided by the authority's decision beat the defendant (see below under self-redress), the defendant always fought back.

c) Slapping. The Kapauku slap a person over the ears with the palms of both hands simultaneously.

Applied in one case: 157.

Comment: Slapping is used mostly on children and wives for minor delicts.

d) Banishment. Banishment is always voluntary. It is an alternative to submitting oneself to punishment.

Applied in two cases: 10, 71.

Economic sanctions. a) Blood money. For killing a man, blood money is paid as compensation in order to avoid a war or capital punishment. The customary payment amounts to 120 Km.

Applied in four cases: 4, 7–9.

Comment: Blood money was used in cases of murder and manslaughter.

b) Indemnity. By offering an adequate indemnity, the defendant can avoid application of most of the other types of sanctions. Incest, most probably, would be the only exception from this generalization. The amount of indemnity varies according to the damage done to the other party. It seldom varies with the status of the plaintiff. A rich defendant, however, may be charged a higher indemnity than an objective estimate of the damage would suggest.

Applied in 14 cases: 12, 29, 36, 41, 55, 58, 61, 62, 75, 79, 83, 85, 87, (114).

Comment: The above cases comprise delicts against persons and against rights in things. There is not a single case where the parties to the dispute belong to the same family or household.

c) Payment of sums promised in contract. In this category are included cases in which the monetary stipulations made to one contractee have not been paid and where the verdict asks for such a payment.

Applied in 13 cases: 35, 99, (116), 117, 119, 122, 124, 125, (131), (132), 133, (134), 137.

Reasons for the disputes: The above disputes started because of the failure to pay rent, to pay a debt, to pay for goods, wages, or a bride price.

Comment: This sanction was used in cases where both contractees belonged to the same village or any of the more inclusive units.

d) Restitution. Here belong all the sanctions that pertain to the restitution of a commodity or money acquired by the defendant in a contract or through a delict.

Applied to 19 cases: 48, 49, 51, 53, 54, 56, 68, 69, 96, (97), 102, 103, 107, (108), (109–111), 112, 113.

Reasons for the disputes: Nonagreement about boundaries or a disagreement about the return of a payment or commodity.

Comment: Included are cases where both contractees belong to the same village or to any of the more inclusive units.

e) Destruction of property. This sanction is used only after the refusal of the defendant to pay what he owes or in a case when he has escaped corporal punishment. It is usually the plaintiff who destroys the property.

Applied in three cases: 34, 74, 146.

Reasons for the disputes: Adultery, theft, insubordination.

f) Confiscation of all property. This type of punishment is used in cases of treason when a man allies himself with the enemy and participates in a war against his own village. The Kapauku assume a fictional death for such a person, and his property is inherited according to the rules governing those who die intestate.

Applied in two cases: 173, 174.

g) Asking the return of loans. To ask a defendant for the return of a loan serves as a very effective punishment in cases of insubordination to the authority.

Applied in three cases: 117, 145, 147.

Comment: Two of the cases represent insubordination to the household authority and the third one constitutes insubordination to the village headman.

h) Ordering the cessation of offending behavior. This sanction is used against defendants who interfere with the rights of another party to the dispute. Such interference is always of the kind which has not yet caused damage, as for example, to dispute someone's rights or to make a claim which would preclude a right of another person.

Applied in two cases: 55, 57.

Reason for the disputes: Disputing the right to trees.

Psychological sanctions. a) Reprimand. This is the favorite sanction of the Kapauku and the one used against defendants who commit any of the delicts outlined in the third part of this monograph. It consists of intermittent public scolding, shouting of reproaches, and the dancing of the mad dance in front of the squatting defendant. The Kapauku consider this punishment the most effective of all.

Applied in 24 cases: 1, 4, 13, 29, 35, 39, 42, 64, 65, 67, 69, 121–123, 125, 129, 130, 150–152, 163, 166, 172, 176.

Reasons for the disputes: Any one of those discussed in the third part of the monograph.

Comment: Used in any group and by any type of authority.

b) Warning. Individuals who commit a minor crime but who otherwise have good relations with the authority are subject to this type of sanction. The warning is informal and it is given to the defendant in private.

Applied in three cases: 21, (24), 149.

Reasons for the disputes: Violation of a taboo, lying, insubordination.

Comment: Used in any group and by any type of authority.

c) Divorce. Divorce is used as a sanction against a spouse who has violated his or her marital duties. For details, the reader is referred to the section on divorce in the first and third parts of the monograph.

Applied in three cases: 43, 46, 47.

d) Passive resistance. The followers of an unjust or immoral authority can punish him by ignoring his wishes and by refusing to support the authority in his personal problems.

Applied in one case: 169.

Reason for the dispute: Absence of generosity.

Comment: This sanction may be used in all the groups and applied against their various authorities.

Supernatural sanctions. a) Punishment for the violation of a taboo. The violation of a general taboo (see first part of the monograph) is believed to be punished automatically "because Ugatame, the creator, determined so." Violations of taboos imposed upon individuals by the shamans are believed to be punished by the live spirits. Disease or death are the usual effects of such violations.

Applied in five cases: 1, (17), 19, (20), 33.

Comment: In cases 1 and 19, because other people's interests had been infringed upon, the violations also elicited corporal and psychological sanctions. In case 33, the secular sanctions were not applied and the incestuous marriage was proclaimed legal. However, the Kapauku who oppose intra-sib marriages believe in eventual punishment by the supernatural.

b) Sorcery. Killing by the use of black magic is a rare sanction in the Kamu Valley. Only in cases where all other means of punishment became impractical did the authority resort to sorcery (for more details, see the section on sorcery in the first part of the monograph).

Applied in one case: 119.

Comment: The defendant in case 119 was a wealthy man powerful enough to resist the authority. This sanction is never used within a family or household.

Self-redress. An action of the plaintiff by which he regains his property or punishes the offender without authorization by the legal authority is called self-redress. Such an action, if later approved by the authority, becomes legal.

a) Cases of approved self-redress (12 cases).

Property destroyed by plaintiff in five cases: (66), 67, 84, 88, 90.

A stick fight in three cases: 34, (59), 92.

Seizure of an offender's property in three cases: 82, 126, 138.

Killing in one case: 32.

b) Cases without the authority's approval (nine cases).

Beating in one case: (27).

Reproach in one case: (101).

Wounding in one case: (30).

A stick fight in two cases: (28), (40).

Seizure of opponent's property in four cases: (76), (77), (135), 136.

Comment: There seems to be no difference in the nature of the dispute between cases subsequently approved and those not approved by the authority. Because of the lack of the authority's approval, most of the cases in the latter category are not legal.

Cases without sanctions. a) Cases with verdicts of not guilty (eight cases). In the following cases no sanctions have been applied because the defendant was found either not guilty or because of a lack of evidence: (22), 25, 72, 80, 81, 89, 91, 158.

b) Absence of sanction because of a compromise (four cases): 26, 37, 50, 95.

c) Absence of sanction because of a war or a duel (two cases): (16), (22).

d) Absence of sanction because of an agreement between the parties (five cases): (52), (60), (93), (98), (100).

e) Cases without sanctions because of various reasons (18 cases):

No violation: (18).

Defendant escaped: 38.

The authority failed to take an action: (70), (115), (168).

Plaintiff surrendered his rights: (78), (106).

Defendant refused to obey the decision: 54, 94, 105, 118, (127).

Defendant made a promise: 128.

Defendant identical to authority; he rejected the claim: (139–143).

CONCLUSION

The four co-existing attributes indicate that a given decision actually is law. Forty-four out of our sample of 176 cases lack one or more of the attributes of law and therefore have to be disqualified as nonlegal cases. In the following paragraphs, we shall list the cases according to their lack of specific attributes.

The attribute of authority is absent in the following cases: 16, 20, 24, 27, 28, 30, 40, 52, 60, 63, 66, 76–78, 93, 98, 100, 101, 106, 108–111, 114, 116, 131–2, 134–5, 168.

The attribute of intention of universal application is absent in the following cases: 20, 22, 28, 59, 70, 78, 97, 106, 111, 115, 127, 135, 139–143, 165.

The attribute of *obligatio* is absent in the following cases: 17, 18, 20, 63, 98, 100, 115, 139–143.

The attribute of sanction is absent in the following cases: 18, 20, 24, 52, 59, 60, 70, 78, 93, 98, 100–101, 106, 108–111, 115, 127.

LEGAL LEVELS

The following proposition has been derived from cross-cultural research: law is not limited to the society as a whole. Every functioning subgroup of the society has its own legal system which is necessarily different in some respects from those of the other subgroups. The hypothesis of a uniformity of law and of the existence of a single legal system within a given society is herewith denied.

With the discussion of sanctions, we have completed our analysis of the legal phenomena into their constituent attributes. Now we have to investigate and solve the problem of where to look in a society for "legal decisions."

In addition to the society as a whole, with its authorities and their rules that traditionally have been called law, there are subgroups such as families, clans, and communities, which are usually omitted in the legal analysis. We have to answer the question of whether a given society has only one consistent legal system used by the different authorities present, or whether there are several such systems.

A society has often been defined as an organized group of individuals. This writer believes that we should use a more precise definition which would stress the fact that an individual usually does not participate directly in the life of the society as a whole. He is rather a member of a subgroup (or of several of them), through which he takes part in social activities. For this reason we may view society as a structured conglomeration of subgroups.

As has been already pointed out, the members of any functioning group, and therefore also of any of the society's subgroups, are organized into a hierarchial structure; in each case, an authority is present and he has followers. All these authorities make decisions having those legal attributes which have been discussed. So, for example, the decision involving a family in case 153, which resulted in a severe beating of the misbehaving boy, possesses the attribute of authority by virtue of the fact that the decision was made by the foster father as the family's head. The content of the decision forms an *obligatio*, the foster father being the party offended by the sex talk of his foster son. Intention of universal application was explicit in the scolding which accompanied the corporal punishment, as well as in the fact that the defendant had admittedly been punished for the same delict several times prior to this case. The sanction, in its nature and its harshness, is identical with those used by village, lineage, or confederacy headmen.

From the 176 cases we may conclude that the father's authority seems to be the most demanding. If we inspect the delicts of insubordination, we find that it is only within the family and the household that the authority requires services of an economic nature from his followers, a refusal of which services makes the follower guilty and liable to punishment (cases: 147–149, 155, 157–162). In comparison to these ten cases in which the authority asked for a service, there are only eight family cases where the defendant was punished for disorderly conduct (cases: 153, 154, 156, 163–167). In the village or on the more inclusive levels of the society, no services are asked; and only disobedience in war (cases: 150–152) or a refusal to comply with a legal decision (cases: 144–146) constitutes an offence against the authority.

Although among the Kapauku most sanctions may be applied in all types of groups, there seem to be a few notable exceptions. An execution is not a sanction permitted to the family or household authority. Although it is often a close relative who is persuaded to administer the punishment, the verdict asking for capital punishment comes from the village headman or from an authority of an even more inclusive unit. While slapping is seldom used as a sanction beyond the household unit, payment of blood money and indemnity, confiscation of all property, and sorcery are sanctions utilized only by the authorities other than a father and the head of a household.

We may claim that the law as identified by our four attributes is present not only on the society level but also in subgroups, so long as they are functioning units. The particular laws of a functioning group form a legal system. Many ethnographers assume that a given society has a single legal system. They either neglect legal phenomena on the subgroup levels or project these phenomena into the top society level and make them consistent with it. Instead of accepting this smoothed out picture of a single legal system in a society, the writer suggests recognition of the fact that there are as many such systems as there are functional groups. The legal systems of families, clans, and communities, for example, form a hierarchy of what we may call legal levels, according to the inclusiveness of the respective groups. We may speak about the family legal level, the clan legal level, and so on. A legal level may be defined as the sum total of all the legal systems of groups of approximately the same degree of inclusiveness. An individual is subjected not to just a single legal system, but to the legal systems (of the same, or different, legal levels) of all the groups of which he is a member.

Let us take an example from Papuan culture. A Kapauku boy who lives, let us say, in Kojogeepa, one of the villages of Ijaaj-Pigome confederacy, has to conform to the family law defined by his father. Because his father lives in the house of his older brother, the boy is subjected also to the decisions of his paternal uncle. At the same time, he is a member of the community in which the local headman Amojepa, together with the other headmen of the sublineage, defines the law. This law may differ in its content from the legal systems of the family or the household. The village, in turn, belongs to the Jamaina sublineage, to the Gepouja lineage, and finally to the Ijaaj-Pigome confederacy. Each of the legal systems of the enumerated groups, according to the inclusiveness of its respective group, belongs on a specific legal level. These are arranged in a hierarchy, with the level of the family legal system at the bottom and the level of the confederacy at the top. With respect to these legal levels, our 176 cases can be divided as follows:

> Family level: 30 cases.
> Household level: 8 cases.
> Village level: 56 cases.
> Sublineage level: 13 cases.
> Lineage level: 11 cases.
> Confederacy level: 21 cases.
> Interconfederacy level: 35 cases.
> Individual (religious taboos): 2 cases.

In the outline above, each specific case was assigned to the level of a group common to both litigants. This was done because the principle which allows a person to be tried by the headmen of his own group regulates the jurisdiction of the Kapauku "courts." The place of the crime does not influence the "court's" competence at all. Thus if the litigants were residents of two different villages which belong to the same sublineage, the case would almost always be handled by the sublineage's authority and, consequently, assigned to that level. The headmen of the villages involved function as advisors as well as jurors and with an importance secondary to that of the competent authority.

However, to this rule there are notable exceptions. Jurisdiction over married women and children up to approximately six years of age belongs exclusively to their husbands and fathers, respectively. Because of this, the husband or father is responsible for delicts of these individuals and it is he who has to stand trial if he does not punish or extradite the culprit (cases: 61, 62, 175, and esp. 176; extradition in case 23). Another notable feature of Kapauku jurisdiction lies in the competence of the village headman. This authority is entitled to try cases, in addition to those of his own village, in any other village of his sublineage. He does so either as a substitute for the absent village authority or as a challenge to an unjust village headman (cases: 58, 65).

Unlike the situation in our legal system, there is no subsequent appeal from the decisions of authorities. The only way to protest against injustice is to leave the group (cases: 72, 104). If, however, an authority becomes involved in the disputes to such an extent that he participates in or even starts a stick fight, the authority of the more inclusive unit adjudicates the case (cases: 12, 34, 50, 55).

At this point we have to consider the relations of the legal levels to each other. Two kinds of inquiry are necessary, into content relations and into relative power.

With respect to inquiry about content, we have to test a frequent opinion that there is a consistency in the content of law between the different legal levels. This consistency, if it is really present, may apply only to certain legal problems and be lacking in others. In such cases the inconsistencies may be conspicuous and go so far as to be contradictory. This problem is actually always a matter of degree rather than one of presence or absence.

There are some examples in the Kapauku material presented that show discrepancies between the contents of the legal systems of the various social groupings. Case 33 indicates how the law of incest has been radically changed in the Ijaaj Gepouja lineage by a decision. Among the Pigome people of Obajbegaa, marriage within the sib is still considered incestuous and the culprits may be punished by a severe beating at least, whereas the Ijaaj people tolerate such marriages. The Jamaina sublineage of the Ijaaj sib, which tolerates marriages within the sib, may punish a couple belonging to the same village who try to get married by flogging or shooting them with arrows. On the contrary, the people of Botukebo village, who belong to the Enona sublineage, tolerate village endogamy and prohibit only marriages between first parallel cousins. Thus, within the Ijaaj-Pigome confederacy, the law of incest differs from subgroup to subgroup. How inaccurate it would be to try to draw a single legal code for the subgroups even of a single confederacy!

On the household level within a single village, we find that different decisions are applied to the same or similar delicts. In cases 148 and 149, the discrepancy between the legal systems of the two households is due to the different personalities of the authorities. Ekajewaijokaipouga, the authority in case 148, is a kind but strict person who mercilessly punishes the culprit for disobedience by slapping and beating. On the contrary, Jokagaibo, the authority in case 149, having both a kind and placid personality, only lectures the defendant who is notorious for his laxiness, disobedience, and uncooperativeness. Thus, the same delicts are punished differently in two neighboring households.

Similarly, the family level shows a variation in its legal system (cases: 65, 153, 154, 158, 160–162). The almost identical delict of wives refusing to give food to their husbands is punished differently in cases 158 and 160. In both instances the husbands committed some injustice prior to the wives' refusals to obey. However, while Jokagaibo (case 158) did not punish his wives at all, Dege (case 160) severely beat his wife. Another example is given in cases 153 and 154. In both instances we are confronted with the extravagantly harsh training of a boy by his foster father and grandfather. In similar cases of breach of etiquette observed in four other families, the "culprits" went unpunished. Indeed, one father enjoyed a sexual joke his son made during supper on one occasion and rewarded him with a big smile and a friendly slap on the shoulder.

A striking discrepancy of family legal systems was also present in the household of Dou Enaago of Botukebo. While Enaago punished his young wife for mischief in the manner that Kapauku usually do, his father-in-law Jikiiwiijaaj, who shared the same household, was completely dominated by his wife. Not only did he never punish her but he himself was scolded on several occasions, and it was she who was the authority in the family.

The law of the society as a whole may not only be ineffective in bringing about a conformation in the legal content of the subgroups, but it also may become lost in the power of one level of the groups over another. In our Western culture, we are accustomed to the belief that the law of the state is the primary standard to which the individual looks for protection and security and to which he tries to adjust his behavior. Only after he has done this can there be control by a family or clique. In many other cultures the situation is different—the center of power is located in the lower levels, while the society level is so weak that frequently we can hardly speak about an authority and law.

For an example we may turn to the society level among the Kapauku. There is no authority in this society which would unite the inhabitants of two or more valleys. Not only do the Kapauku Papuans inhabit many regions, all of which are politically independent of each other, but even one region, such as the Kamu Valley, consists of many political confederacies which wage war against each other from time to time.

In our sample of 176 cases we have thirty-six which can be labeled according to the domicile of the parties to the dispute as "interconfederacy disputes." There are two more cases (82, 126) in which the disputes started between members of two different confederacies and ended, because of the plaintiff's seizure of some property of the defendants' co-villagers, as village disputes. Out of these thirty-eight cases, thirteen were adjudicated by the headman of the culprit's village and justice done to the plaintiff (cases: 4, 7, 36, 37, 68, 69, 79, 83, 123–125, 128, 129). In three additional instances (cases: 39, 112, 137), the culprit has been extradited to the plaintiff's party for further negotiations. Just action on the part of the authorities in the culprit's village was induced either by friendly interconfederational relations or through fear of the enemy's power. In five other cases, the disputes were settled peacefully without any authorities (cases: 106, 108, 111, 131, 132). However, in the seventeen remaining disputes the outcome depended primarily upon sheer force without any consideration for law and justice whatsoever. In eight of these cases the authority of the culprit's village refused to cooperate with the plaintiff's party or simply did not force the issue (cases: 16, 28, 70, 115, 127, 139–141). In two other instances the authority was not involved at all (cases: 24, 30), and in the last seven cases the plaintiff, not relying on interconfederational justice, seized some of either the culprit's or his relative's property by force (cases: 27, 76–77, 82, 126, 135, 138).

Thus when we consider that out of thirty-eight interconfederational cases, twenty-two were not legal, and that in at least seventeen of the latter, settlement by force was the outcome, we can see that there is not too much "law" beyond the confederacy. As a contrast, in the remainder of the 141 cases involving parties from the same confederacy, only twenty-four were "illegal." Moreover, the author has not included in the sample of clashes of interests twenty-four interconfederational disputes, all of which resulted in wars. Thus an anthropologist writing on the "law of the Kapauku" would in the strictest sense be writing about nonexistent phenomena. There is no law of the Kapauku society, but there is law within a Kapauku political confederacy. The sixteen interconfederational cases which have been solved legally were actually taken care of on the village level because the authority of the defendant's village had no jurisdiction beyond his own political unit. It is primarily at the confederacy level, and those of its subgroups, that we must look for the laws that are most responsible for social control among the Kapauku. Because of the amount of power manifested in the severity of sanctions such as execution, and the degree of control resulting from the possession of dependable followers, in the Kapauku society the center of power seems to lie at the sublineage level.

The center of power, of course, is not a static phenomenon. The relative amount of power at different levels diminishes or increases to the extent that the center of power changes its place. Among the Kapauku today, one finds an increase of the power of the village headman with a corresponding weakening of the position of the heads of families and households. This shifting of the center of power from these groups to the more inclusive level has been accelerated, if not caused, by contact with Europeans. Because the administrative officers as well as missionaries find it easier to deal with one or a few individuals rather than to explain the various problems to the multitude, and because the individuals whom they see happen to be usually the village headmen, these native authorities have started to assume more power and prestige than they possessed before. There is a tendency now in the Paniai and Tigi regions toward stabilization of the traditionally fluid village leadership pattern. Because a Papuan who becomes an agent of the white man receives not only periodical gifts and support from his European friend but is given also a permanent Malay title *"kapala*, the chief," his leadership is no longer entirely dependent upon his economic skill and his popularity among his followers. In the valleys controlled by the Administration, some Europeans went as far as to appoint an unimportant man to the *"kapalaship."* In this way the original emphasis on economic success and on the generosity of the native leader tends to be undermined, and the power and position of the household leaders who in the uncontrolled areas are regarded as potential village headmen, much weakened.

The conception of a society as a multi-level unit with as many legal systems as there are subgroups and with a dynamic center of power brings together certain phenomena and certain processes which otherwise would be put into different categories and treated differently. It helps us to understand why a man in one society is primarily a member of his kin-group or village and only secondarily of the state, while in another society the state may play the most important role. A gangster's behavior is not "absolutely illegal"; while it may be illegal on the society's level, it is at the same time legal from the point of view of the gang. The writer therefore, would qualify Hoebel's statement (1954: 27), which follows, on the basis of the above view. "There are, of course, as many forms of coercion as there are forms of power. Of these, only certain methods and forms are legal. Coercion by gangsters is not legal. Even physical coercion by a parent is not legal if it is too extreme. The essentials of legal coercion are general social acceptance of the application of physical power, in threat or in fact, by a privileged party, for a legitimate cause, in a legitimate way, and at a legitimate time. This distinguishes the sanction of law from that of other social rules."

We dare to say that it is inconsistent to make a qualitative distinction between the law of the state and the "criminal gang's ethics." Both of these phenomena contain all four legal attributes and thus belong to the same category; both should be classified as laws. It is unfortunate that in the West the concept of law has acquired a moralistic connotation.

LEGAL DYNAMICS

A proposition derived from cross-cultural research: customary law is not the only type of law in "primitive societies." Similarly, cultural drift is not the only cause of change in a "primitive legal system." Authoritarian law, such as decrees by a legislator and relatively abrupt legislative actions by a legal authority, are universal phenomena present to varying degrees in every society, no matter how "primitive" or "civilized."

Once again we return to the field of law conceived as an ellipse surrounded by a zone of transition. This time we are not interested in the analysis of the legal phenomena and in separating this field from the surrounding social phenomena. On the contrary, we shall try to find out in what way law is related to political decisions on the one hand and to customs on the other.

In order to accomplish this task we have first to investigate the traditional dichotomy between two types of law, the difference between customary law and the

FIELD OF POLITICAL DECISIONS

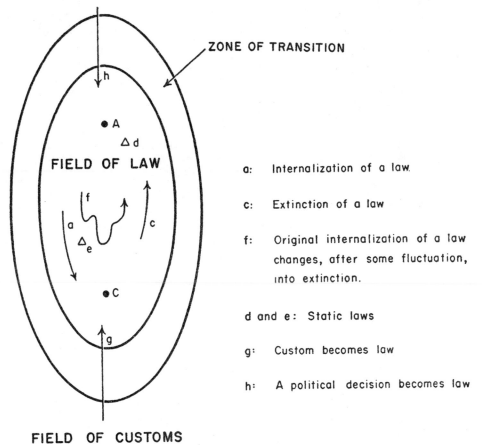

ZONE OF TRANSITION

FIELD OF LAW

a: Internalization of a law.

c: Extinction of a law

f: Original internalization of a law changes, after some fluctuation, into extinction.

d and e: Static laws

g: Custom becomes law

h: A political decision becomes law

FIELD OF CUSTOMS

Fig. 9. Diagram Illustrating Legal Dynamics.

decrees which represent the activity of the legislator. There are two foci inside of the ellipse marked by the letters "A" and "C" (see Fig. 9). "A" stands for the authoritarian type of law and "C" for customary law.

By customary law the writer means a law that is internalized by a social group. We call a law internalized when the majority of the members of the group consider it to be binding, as when it stands for the only proper behavior in a given situation. If such a law is broken, the culprit may feel guilty; he has a bad conscience or, if not, he at least has the feeling that he has done wrong—that he has behaved improperly. He would not like it if the other members of the society behaved in the same way as he did. Conformity to such a law is not much effected by external pressure—it is produced by a different, internal mechanism which we may call conscience in some cultures and fear of shame in others.

This is the type of law which the ethnographer has usually described and has claimed to be the property of the group. He has not recognized so readily that even in these well internalized cases, the individuality of the legal authority has played an important role in deciding, conforming, and changing, even if to a slight extent, the customary law. Without the authority's consent, in this writer's opinion the customary law would cease to be law and would become just a custom.

The majority of the 132 legal decisions (44 were disqualified as nonlegal), or a total of 114 cases, exemplify customary law. In all these cases the informants from the groups in which the decisions were applied agreed upon their justice. The informants' opinions in agreeing with the "verdicts of the authorities" are a manifestation of the internalization of those laws. If we compare the internalized legal cases with their corresponding rules, we find that forty-five decisions of the customary type do not correspond to their respective rules (cases: 1, 4, 10, 21, 25, 29, 33, 35–37, 41, 50, 54, 67, 74, 82, 84–87, 89, 90, 95, 102–103, 105, 112, 113, 119–126, 129, 130, 136–138, 150–152, 158). Thus there do exist customary laws which are contrary to the abstract rules of the society.

We may take as an example case 85. It has been already pointed out that the corresponding rule 54 requires the trapper to pay indemnity. However, this is almost never done and Kapauku headmen as well as a great majority of their followers believe that a compromise settlement, as exemplified in case 85, is a "just" solution.

The authoritarian law, on the other hand, is not internalized by a majority of the members of the group. A strong minority which supports the legal authority may have elevated such a law to be an "ideal" and may have simply forced the rest of the people to accept it. In some cases this kind of law is internalized only by the legal authority. An authority may even impose the law for opportunistic reasons, not believing himself that it contains the proper way of behavior. In other cases the law owes its authoritarian quality to the fact that there has not been sufficient time for its internalization. The opposing members of the group comply with such a law only under external pressure exercised upon them by the authority and the strong minority who may already have internalized it. The majority of the population feels no guilt in the event of the violation of such a law; there may only be fear of detection. These people consider the law to be unjust.

An example of an authoritarian law is the decision of the older brother Amojepa in case 65. He, as head of the household and family, decided that his sons and brothers could not take anything from his fields without special permission. For a violation of this law, he punished his younger brother by a severe beating. The majority of the members of his household did not agree that his decision and punishment were just. His law differed from corresponding laws of other families where it was permissible for the members of the household to help themselves to some fruit from the fields belonging to any household member, providing the food was taken for immediate consumption. Amojepa's household members were not the only ones who disagreed with the law. All the other people criticized the man's action and prohibition, and charged him with brutality. No matter how unjustified or even "criminal" his action appeared to the outsiders, in his own household it was perpetuated as "authoritarian law."

In our sample of 176 cases, of which 132 are legal, there are eighteen examples of authoritarian decisions (cases: 7, 26, 38, 47, 57, 62, 65, 72, 92, 94, 104, 118, 128, 153–154, 156, 160–161). Among these, eleven differ from the rules. Thus there are seven cases containing authoritarian laws which, although conforming to the rules, are held by the followers to be unjust (cases: 7, 47, 65, 92, 94, 160, 161). From what has been said above, we can conclude that the conformance of a decision with a given rule does not necessarily imply that such a decision will be considered just by the majority of the followers, or in other words, that it will constitute a customary law.

The difference between the two types of law is not a qualitative one. Rather, it is the degree of internalization that causes a particular law to be called either customary or authoritarian. There is a gradual transition between the two types.

The quantitative difference between the two foci is also emphasized by the fact that a given law can change from authoritarian to customary, a change which demonstrates the actual meaning of the word internalization. This process has two aspects. When we focus our attention on the individual, we study the internalization that takes place in his mind. When we think of the group as a whole, internalization consists of the increase in the number of individuals who have individually internalized the law. We may call these two aspects psychological and social internalization.

Psychological internalization starts when the individual is confronted with a new response to a given type of situation. The first part of the process is usually called learning. Miller and Dollard (1948: 25) describe it as a change in the individual's opinion by which a new response becomes dominant over the previously dominant response. We may suggest that the process does not stop at the point at which one response becomes dominant over another response. Indeed, the concept of internalization usually assumes subsequent changes in the newly established hierarchy. The dominant response may become more and more important and the rest of the possible responses progressively weaker until the latter become extinguished. If we visualize the hierarchy as a vertical sequence, the distance between the dominant response at the top and the next closest alternative may serve as a measure for the internalization of the dominant response at a given time. As the process of internalization continues, the gap between the two responses grows. On the contrary, if an alternative approaches the dominant response, the internalization of the latter grows weaker and extinction sets in. These changes may differ in speed and the situation may even become static for a period of time.

The degree of psychological internalization is indicated by the intensity of the individual's feeling as to how proper a response may be in a given situation and how unthinkable is the use of an alternative.

When we shift our interest from the individual to the society, we cease to emphasize the psychological aspect of internalization. Our main objective is to find out how many members of the society (or subgroups) have psychologically internalized a given law. Any increase in the number of those members may be called social internalization. When we distinguish between laws internalized by the majority and those by the minority of the people, we obtain the difference between customary and authoritarian laws. This quantitative difference, which seems to be an objective and precise criterion of the two categories of law is complicated, of course, by the fact that the internalizations of individuals differ one from another in the degree to which the law has been actually internalized. This makes the counting more difficult and certain standards (relative to the particular culture) have to be set up to determine the degree of psychological internalization.

The recently accepted law of incest which permits intrasib marriages (case 33) provided an opportunity of testing internalization among the population of Botukebo. Out of forty informants, twenty-three agreed with the new regulation of marriages, two gave evasive answers and expressed no concern with the whole affair, and fifteen condemned the new law as immoral and bad. Although this count gives an impression of uniformity in the opinion of people in one category, the acceptance as well as the rejection of the law differed in intensity as well as in motivation from individual to individual. Ijaaj Awiitigaaj, the headman who introduced the change, defended the almost complete freedom of choice in obtaining a spouse. He objected only to marriages between lineal relatives and siblings. Imopaj, who married his third paternal parallel cousin commented on the subject as follows: "All people should be permitted to marry as they wish. However, it is bad to marry one's first paternal parallel cousin. I would beat my younger brother if he would try to commit such a thing." Taajwiijokaipouga, whose sister married her third paternal parallel cousin, accepted that marriage but objected strongly to marriages of closer relatives than those of the fourth degree of collaterality. Another man objected to any marriage within the same sib: "It is bad. I would never marry my 'sister.' People are bad when they marry Ijaaj. I would beat my son or younger brother if he would try to marry his relative." A statement of an older Ijaaj man was even more antagonistic when he proclaimed that he would shoot his son with an arrow if he were to marry a girl from his own sib. Although the above informants differed in their opinion on the acceptability of an intra-sib marriage, they all, no matter how opposed they were to this idea, expressed the possibility that their close relatives might commit such an act. Dou Enaago, who recently married a Botukebo girl and went to live in her parents' house was unable even to conceive that his close paternal relative could commit such a crime. In other words, in his mind there was no alternative, not even an illegal one, to the old incest regulation. When asked about the new regulation of intermarriage by the Botukebo Ijaaj sib he exclaimed with horror: "Bad, bad, a 'sister' is never a spouse. They all are bad, their vital substance will deteriorate and they all will die because of their crimes."

The new law of incest has been internalized by the Botukebo people to the extent that 57.5 per cent of the informants who were questioned accepted it as proper, 37.5 per cent rejected it, and 5 per cent were indifferent. Because the sample included almost all the males of the community who were older than fourteen years of age and represents 22.5 per cent of the total population, of which 33.3 per cent are children, we may say that in this community the law is internalized. However, the last statement says little about the various degrees and qualifications of the psychological internalizations of the individuals.

A given law is consequently a dynamic phenomenon. On our chart (Fig. 9), the changing laws are represented by the different arrows. The movement (a) in the direction from "A" to "C" means that an originally authoritarian law was supported by more and more individuals until finally it entered the customary category and become socially internalized (Example: case 33). The opposite direction represents the process of extinction (c) by the progressive loss of supporters of a given law (Example: execution of an adulterous wife among the Kapauku). The speed of these movements may differ—a law may become almost static for a period of time (d and e) or fluctuate within a given range between the two foci (f).

A new law may originate in two ways. First it can enter the legal field from the realm of custom (g). This happens when the authority recognizes a custom as the basis for legal decisions. In our data this was most probably the case in the practice of giving the trapper a quarter of the pig that had been pierced by the spikes of his trap (case 85). The former law, still exemplified in abstract rule 54, required no such gift of pork to the owner of the trap. The law that originated as a custom recognized by the authority is popular and customary, but with the passage of time it may lose more and more supporters and grow increasingly authoritarian, supported only by a minority in the group. Here belong many of the cases of Western "outmoded laws" that are supported by a few conservatives and which may finally be abolished by legislation.

The second possible origin of law may be a direct creation by the decision of an authority, or transformation of a political decision into a law. In both of these cases the law starts as authoritarian. In the second case what was a political decision originally becomes law by the fact that some authority has supplied it with the intention of universal application by a proclamation, for instance, that the decision is intended to be applied in the future to all similar cases. An authoritarian law created in this manner may gain more and more appeal among the followers and finally become customary. It may happen that the authority will also abolish such a law by no longer making it the basis for legal decisions. If this happens and the law is dropped as unimportant, the practice which had been legalized will continue to exist as a custom for a period of time at least.

In this place we may give a striking example of the internalization of an authoritarian law in the Kapauku community of Botukebo. It was already referred to in case 33 as well as in this section and in the one on the form of law.

Ijaaj Awitigaaj, the headman of Botukebo, was a strong and wealthy man who had developed an extreme appreciation for beauty in individuals of the opposite sex. As any connoisseur would, he collected the most valuable specimens in his household by marrying ten of the most attractive women in the South Kamu

Valley. Because he discovered that the incest taboo which prohibited the marrying of an individual of the same sib would deprive his collection of at least one of its most extraordinary manifestations of female pulchritude, he did not hesitate to break the taboo. The manner in which this was done and the outcome are explained in case 33. However, Awiitigaaj, being a headman with many followers, set a precedent which has been followed by many Romeos of Botukebo. He himself agreed to the practice and confirmed it by marrying two of his second paternal parallel cousins. In order to give an air of legality to his actions, he proclaimed that it was permissible to marry girls of the same sib and village as long as they were not first paternal parallel cousins. He divided the village into two parts, which we may call "incipient moieties," so that all close relatives and first cousins had their residence in one of the units. He spoke with favor of marrying into the other unit. When he was asked about this innovation, he gave the following justifications and explanation:

"To marry an Ijaaj (same sib) is all right as long as she is *aneepa epee* (more remote than a first paternal parallel cousin). In the old days the people did not conceive of this advantage, but now it is *pio* (legal). I have introduced it. She (his first incestuous love) told me, 'Have sexual intercourse with me.' Who could resist? Adii people (who live to the south of the Kamu Valley) have started it (the incest violation) and so I thought we were the same as they are and I introduced the change. I married Ijaaj Enaago and Ijaaj Amaadii only after I have become *tonowi* so that other people were either afraid to object or they agreed with me. To marry *keneka* (the girl of the same sib) is not bad, indeed it is nice, in this way one becomes a rich man."

Since it was apparent that the justifications given in the presence of other people were rationalizations rather than a revelation of truth, the writer questioned the headman later when they were alone. Because of their "best friend" relationship, he was required by custom to tell the writer what he really thought. "Why did I marry my relative? Well, I will tell you but do not tell others. I liked her, she was beautiful." To the writer's question about his new incest taboo regulation which prohibits marriages of first cousins, he replied with a sly smile and a friendly punch under the writer's ribs: "Please do not tell others. They would not like me (for what I am going to tell you) and I would lose influence. It would be all right with me if first cousins were to marry. To marry your own sister is probably bad, but I am not convinced even of that. I think whoever likes any girl should marry her. I set up the new taboo (law) only to succeed in breaking down the old restrictions. The people are like that, one has to tell them a lie."

Thus an important change in the law of incest and consequent profound changes in the social structure were initiated in South Kamu by a single man because of his love for a relative. The new law at first was authoritarian because only few followers supported the headman. However, as time went on, more and more individuals accepted the law as just; and today the law is to be classified as customary in the village of Botukebo, where 57.5 per cent of adult males consider it as just.

Cases of adultery present us with another example of a change in the Kapauku law. Not many years ago an adulterous woman was usually put to death by her husband. This treatment is still reflected in rule 34. However, the Kapauku found it was not good to kill their women, because women cost lots of shells; so they punished them only by beating or wounding. "Rich men, because they have plenty of shell money, could afford to continue the old custom. However, even they finally changed to the present way." Our four cases of adultery (cases: 34–37) which are all of recent date reflect the changed situation. The above quotation from an informant shows that we deal in this case with a different type of origin of a new law. Since in the beginning only the poorer people refrained from punishing their adulterous wives by death, this practice first became a custom. With the lapse of time, the rich men and headmen accepted the custom themselves and incorporated it into their legal decisions. Thus an original custom of punishing an adulterous wife only by beating and wounding became law.

JUSTICE

In order to make the account of Kapauku law more complete, we have to say something about the phenomenon called justice. Since this field is peripheral to our interest, we shall be brief in its description. The writer found that the term justice may be applied to different notions. First there is the primary division of this concept into "the question of fact" and the "question of law" (Llewellyn and Hoebel, 1941: 304).

By "the question of fact" is meant the uncovering of all facts relevant to the adjudication of a legal case. A Kapauku authority who decides a case has first to find out about the nature of the dispute, about claims made by both parties, as well as about the facts relevant to the problem. While the claims are easily obtained from the shouting of the litigants, to find the truth about relevant facts is a laborious process which often requires ingenuity on the part of the native judge. The Kapauku have recognized this problem as separate from the adjudication activity of the authority and assign it a special term, *boko petai*.

In most of the cases, the native authorities relied upon testimony in order to obtain the factual material. Voluntary witnesses established the necessary evidence in thirty-nine legal cases (3, 5, 25, 26, 43, 48–50, 53–56, 71, 73, 75, 82, 84, 86, 95, 99, 104, 105, 113, 117–126, 128–130, 133, 169, 170). In legal case 83, a paid denouncer was used and in case 112 a special investigator was sent out to secure the evidence. A counter-spy helped to establish the guilt of the defendants in cases 175 and 176.

Testimony is seldom taken at face value. The personality of the witness is important in ascertaining the reliability of the material. Accordingly, testimony given in vague terms or made by individuals with dubious reputations is rejected as unreliable (cases: 23, 61, 80).

A special type of testimony is the confession made by a defendant. Among the Kapauku most of the defendants sooner or later admitted their crimes. In most of the above cases, where evidence had been first established by witnesses, the defendants finally confessed. Since escape or keeping quiet while being questioned is regarded as an admission of one's guilt, a confession is easy to make. In our 132 legal cases, 25 defendants openly confessed (cases: 14, 34–39, 41, 42, 44–47, 57, 65, 68, 69, 79, 85, 135–138, 155, 171). Three by keeping quiet in the face of charges admitted their guilt (cases: 61, 62, 79) and five individuals who became fugitives in order to avoid punishment thus admitted their guilt (cases: 2, 6, 61, 74, 94). An emotional and repetitive denial of charges is considered testimony and is often regarded as sufficient to stop prosecution of the defendant (cases: 80, 81). In some cases no evidence is needed because the crime was committed in the presence of an authority (cases: 144–154, 156–164, 166, 167, 172–174) or because the culprit was caught "in the action" by several people (cases: 64, 67, 87, 89, 90).

Inspection of some objects provides additional evidence. Thus the appearance of pigs was relevant in legal cases 107 and 112, while the destroyed crops of sweet potatoes were inspected in legal cases 102 and 103. The status of boundaries was examined in cases 51, 52, 91, 92, and the tracks of the culprits were followed in cases 62, 63, 74, 88. The bones and the feathers of the stolen animals were regarded by the Kapauku as *corpus delicti* in cases 74 and 79.

The Kapauku also use circumstantial evidence in solving obscure cases. Thus soft ground and the behavior of the defendant convinced the plaintiff as well as the authority that the defendant in case 4 murdered the victim. A death which occurs shortly after the offending of a known sorcerer is sufficient proof of the magician's guilt (case 15). The wife in case 66 charged her husband with the theft of her pork because she knew his taste for meat and because it was he who had knowledge of where it was hidden. The refusal to disclose the source of some inner bark which the defendant used for string-making was sufficient proof of her theft (case 72).

After the factual material is assembled and all the necessary evidence established, "the question of law" has to be solved by the authority. "*Boko duwai*, to adjudicate a case," is a Kapauku expression which would also be applicable to the activity of a judge who seeks a verdict. The problem of "legal justice" has many aspects. Various authors conceive of justice in different ways. The European legalists mean by justice a conformity of the verdict with the abstract rule. In the section on the form of law we established the fact that the Kapauku were not concerned about this type of justice. Out of the 176 cases of clashes of interests, the results of only eighty-seven corresponded to the rules. Contrary to the above type, primitive justice "rests on going practice" (Llewellyn and Hoebel, 1941: 305). It recalls the theory of "living law" advanced by Ehrlich which was discussed in the section on the form of law. There, the present writer objected to the undue emphasis on "going practice" and showed that the Kapauku do not regard the actual behavior of the majority of the people as normative.

"Legal justice" (Llewellyn and Hoebel, 1941: 305) or, in other words, the emphasis upon the precedent "which rests on demand for repetition in a new case of what was done officially before" is decidedly relevant to the justice of the

Kapauku. This conceptualization comes very close to the intention of universal application which was claimed as one of the attributes of law. However, the two concepts are not identical. The "repetition in a new case of what was done before" is the actuality, while the intention is only a thought on the part of the authority who passes the decision. Thus the unprecedented decision in case 33, although legal, was considered unjust at the time of its announcement. Accordingly, the Kapauku consider as unjust all cases which lack the intention of universal application as well as those which, although legal, introduce an unprecedented change in "legal practice" (example: case 33).

There is another type of justice which the Kapauku call "*uta-uta*, half-half." The meaning of the phrase comes very close to what we call equity. In other words, the Kapauku conceive of a tort and crime as upsetting an equilibrium which a decision should reestablish. This feeling about justice is reflected in many cases (especially cases: 84, 87, 88). The impossibility of enforcing payment of interest among the Kapauku is regarded by the writer as a manifestation of this type of justice. The notion is also applied in negotiations for peace. Only on rare occasions could hostilities be stopped when there were not an equal number of dead on both sides.

Internalization constitutes another way of conceptualizing justice. While the above concept of justice depended upon objective criteria such as equity, precedent, "going practice," in the case of internalization we measure justice by counting the individuals' feelings about a given law. While the above types of justice may be interesting and important philosophically (ethics), from the sociological point of view the recording of the opinions and feelings of the members of the groups is relevant. If we compare the internalization of the 132 legal decisions to the appropriate abstract rules, we obtain the following results:

1. Legal cases in which the decisions are just (internalized) and correspond to the abstract rules (76 cases): 2–4, 6, 8, 9, 11–15, 19, 23, 31, 32, 34, 39, 42–46, 48, 49, 51, 53–58, 61, 64, 68, 69, 71, 73, 75, 79–81, 83, 87–89, 91, 96, 99, 102, 103, 107, 117, 124, 133, 136–138, 144–148, 155, 157, 159, 163–164, 166, 167, 169–175.

2. Legal cases in which the decisions are just but do not correspond to the pertinent abstract rules (35 cases): 1, 10, 21, 25, 29, 35–37, 41, 50, 67, 74, 82, 84–86, 90, 95, 105, 112, 113, 119–123, 125, 126, 129, 130, 150–152, 158, 176.

3. Legal cases in which the decisions are unjust but correspond to the pertinent abstract rules (8 cases): 7, 47, 94, 118, 149, 160–162.

4. Legal cases in which the decisions are unjust and differ from the pertinent abstract rules (13 cases): 5, 26, 33, 38, 62, 65, 72, 92, 104, 128, 153, 154, 156.

The Kapauku distinguish between what they consider "legally just," expressed by the verbal suffix -*ja* (discussed under the criterion of intention of universal application and under internalization), and either what they call good or what they are ashamed of. To the latter we may assign the name morality. While justice is enforcible by law, morals alone cannot constitute a reason for convicting anyone. Thus, morality, for example, requires the father of a newly born baby to abstain from consuming food and to distribute all of it to the guests who attend the birth ceremony. However, he cannot be punished for not complying with this canon of morality. Similarly, although it is permissible, according to the law, to marry the wives of one's relatives who have deserted their husbands, one feels ashamed to do so because it is considered immoral.

If moral considerations are compared with feelings of justice by the informants with respect to the 132 cases, we obtain the following results:

1. Four legal cases in which decisions are just, but are considered immoral: 9, 14, 57, 130.

2. Four legal cases in which decisions are unjust but are considered moral: 62, 118, 149, 162.

3. In the rest of the 124 legal cases the presence or absence of morality and justice coincided.

If we compare the morality aspect of the 132 legal decisions with the corresponding abstract rules we obtain the following results:

1. Legal cases in which the decisions are considered moral and correspond to the pertinent abstract rules (76 cases): 2–4, 6, 8, 11–13, 15, 19, 23, 31, 32, 34, 39, 42–46, 48, 52–54, 55–56, 58, 61, 64, 68, 69, 71, 73, 75, 79–81, 83, 87–89, 91, 96, 99, 102–103, 107, 117, 118, 124, 133, 136–138, 144–149,155, 157, 159, 162–164, 166–167, 169–176.

2. Legal cases in which the decisions are considered moral but do not correspond to the pertinent abstract rules (31 cases): 1, 10, 21, 25, 29, 36–38, 50, 62, 67, 74, 82, 84–86, 90, 112, 113, 119–123, 125, 126, 129, 150, 151, 152, 158.

3. Legal cases in which the decisions are considered immoral but where they correspond to the pertinent abstract rules (9 cases): 7, 9, 14, 47, 49, 57, 94, 160, 161.

4. Legal cases in which the decisions are considered immoral and do not correspond to the pertinent abstract rules (16 cases): 5, 26, 33, 35, 41, 65, 72, 92, 95, 104, 105, 128, 130, 153, 154, 156.

In summary, we conceive of Kapauku justice as corresponding to the internalization of various laws. There is a tendency in this feeling of justice for it to coincide with the conformity of a decision to its precedent. However, this is just a tendency, for if the precedent itself had not already been internalized (was not considered just), the new decision although based upon precedent would be regarded as unjust also. Thus Kapauku justice should not be equated with the "rule of precedent." It should also be differentiated from Kapauku morality.

THE RELATIVITY OF LAW

The combination of the principles of legal levels with the ideas of authoritarian and customary law reveals the relative nature of the two latter concepts. The same law which is customary on the level of a more inclusive group at the same time may be authoritarian when considered as the law of subgroups that have not yet internalized it. The village headman of Botukebo, for example, radically changed the laws concerning incest (case 33, see also the discussion in the section on legal dynamics). While this law is considered just and proper in a majority of the families of Botukebo, thus making it a customary law of Botukebo, in some families the law is regarded as unjust and immoral although enforced by the heads of the families. Thus, if this new regulation of incest in these few families is examined, the law has to be classified as authoritarian.

The principle of legal levels brings out another important matter—the relativity of law and custom. A phenomenon on the level of the Kapauku confederacy may be called custom, as for example the services of an economic nature which the household members offer to the head of the household. This custom, however, which is never enforced on the confederacy or village levels, is certainly to be regarded as law if one focuses his attention upon the subgroup level of the household. Similarly, because there is no law on the level of Kapauku society as a whole (see the discussion on legal levels), we cannot speak about "laws of Kapauku society." All the phenomena which we have defined as the laws of various subgroups of Kapauku society have to be called customs when we discuss Kapauku society as a whole.

We may say, therefore, that law and custom are relative concepts which are relative to the level of investigation. If someone asks whether a specific social relation is law or custom in a given society, we have to ask in turn, "Do you mean law of the society, of the community, of the clan, or of the family?" The decision in favor of law or custom will be relative to the answer given to this question.

In this scheme of the relativity of custom and law, we may distinguish between those customs sometimes called neutral (Malinowski, 1934: 25) and which carry no sanctions in any of the subgroups, and those which are enforced by "social punishment." From this point of view, the latter are laws of the subgroups which have been projected into the level of the society. In other words, they are customs when treated from the point of view of the society as a whole, but at the same time they are laws if the point of view is that of a subgroup within the society.

This has an importance for legal dynamics. A customary law suddenly abolished by the authority on the level of the society will probably become a custom of the society because the people are not likely to set aside such behavior immediately. At the same time, the custom may continue as law on the subgroup levels.

CONCLUSION

In the monograph an attempt has been made to demonstrate by an analysis of the data from a Papuan culture the effectiveness of a theory of law developed from research on thirty-two cultures. In the first two parts the reader was made acquainted with the essential features of the Kapauku culture. This portrait of the neolithic way of life, reputedly without law and leadership, was followed by a description of 176 cases which involved some trouble or clash of interests. The main objective of this endeavor has been to provide suitable material for the analytical part. To conclude the monograph we shall summarize some of the theoretical findings and attempt to criticize the theory in light of the facts presented.

Library research on primitive law led the writer to believe in the virtual absence of abstract rules among the more primitive peoples of the world and induced him to conceive of law as decisions of legal authority. While the emphasis upon the actual decisions of an authority proved fruitful during the research and in the analysis of its results, the belief in the absence of rules among primitive peoples soon appeared fallacious in the light of investigation in the field. The writer was surprised by the abstract thinking of some of the more intelligent informants and shocked by finding a whole set of idealized abstract rules held as measures for good conduct. The postulate concerning the form of law, however, has been substantiated by the research; it is the legal decision rather than the rule which effects social control and merits primary attention in the investigation of law.

The comparative analysis of legal decisions revealed four co-existing attributes. The attributes that have been found important in the analysis are the following: the attribute of authority, the attribute of intention of universal application, the attribute of *obligatio*, and the attribute of sanction. In a definition of law these four attributes may serve as criteria of that concept.

It has been a postulate of the writer that any functioning group has its authority by whom the passing of a decision would constitute one of the attributes of law. This has been held important for laying boundaries between the fields of law and custom. Prior to the investigation, the Kapauku culture challenged the writer's postulate of the universality of legal authority. Several observers claimed an absence of any authority in the society. However, the writer, following a functional approach, defined the authority by the fact that his advice, decisions, and suggestions were followed by the rest of the members of the group and thus made it possible to conceive of the *tonowi*, the rich headman of the Kapauku, as a legal authority.

The attribute of intention of universal application separates law from the political decisions which also are made by an authority. It means that an authority intends to apply a given decision to all similar cases in the future. Although one can seldom find information pertaining to this attribute of law in the literature, the Kapauku verbalize the intention by referring to the abstract rules in their legal speeches and decisions, or by using the verbal suffix of the repetitive tense aspect -*ja*.

The attribute of *obligatio*, being a formulation of rights and duties between two parties who are either human beings or supernatural beings represented by living individuals, distinguishes law from religious custom and nonlegal taboos. Surprisingly enough, the distinction not only proved workable but it also coincided with two different attitudes of the natives. They talked freely—indeed, they sometimes even boasted—about the violations of the regulations we labeled "nonlegal taboos." Contrariwise, they kept secret their offences against what we call religious law.

Sanction is the last of our attributes of law. It is not exclusively of a physical nature but can be broadly defined as a positive infliction of pain or a denial of something that would have been granted if the rules of good conduct had been followed. In Kapauku society, the psychological sanction of public reprimand and the resulting ostracism is, except for capital punishment, more feared than any type of physical sanction. Thus this writer's objection to the conceiving of a legal sanction as being exclusively of a physical nature was upheld by the data.

Laws displaying these four attributes were found to be present in any functioning group and subgroup of interacting people. Each group of individuals, irrespective of its inclusiveness and composition, has its own legal system. Because of this, the assumption of uniformity of law and of the existence of a single legal system within a given society has been rejected. One who describes law in Kapauku society has to deal with the legal systems of the various political confederacies and their subgroups. Since there is no law present beyond a confederacy composed of a few villages, one who would write about the law of Kapauku society would, strictly speaking, describe imaginary phenomena. Society is viewed in this monograph as a structure composed of subgroups which in turn may be composed of subgroups, all of which have their authorities and legal systems. According to their inclusiveness, the groups form levels arranged in a hierarchy. Correspondingly, we have a hierarchy of legal levels consisting of the respective legal systems of the groups. The legal systems differ one from another in their content and relative power. Among the Kapauku, the family and village levels were the most effective groups in the field of social control. In the section on legal dynamics we have differentiated authoritarian laws from customary ones. While both types are upheld by the authority, the authoritarian law is supported only by a strong minority of the followers who consider it to be just, whereas the majority of the members consider customary law to be the only proper way of behavior. There is usually little need for the enforcement of customary law. We have demonstrated by means of the Kapauku material that authoritarian laws are by no means limited to civilizations. The fact that ethnographers, while dealing with primitive cultures, describe only the customary laws of people is most likely due to their personal interest and emphasis rather than due to the absence of the authoritarian type of law.

The internalization process has been proposed as the criterion for quantitatively differentiating between authoritarian and customary law. It has two aspects. Psychological internalization is the process by which a response (law) becomes dominant in the mind of the individual and thus continues widening its distance from an alternative response. Social internalization is actually a sum total of the psychological internalization processes of all members of a given group. Law becomes socially internalized as it gains more and more supporters. It is a dynamic phenomenon capable of changing from the customary to the authoritarian type or vice versa. The Kapauku material confirmed the importance of distinguishing between these two types of law on the basis of social internalization.

A combination of the idea of internalization with that of legal levels shows that the authoritarian and customary legal categories are relative concepts. The same law that is customary on the society level may appear as authoritarian when we look at it from the point of view of subgroups that have not yet internalized it.

The relativity detected by the recognition of legal levels extends even further and effects the differentiation between law and custom. A custom of the society as a whole may be at the same time a law of some of its subgroups, or even of a whole subordinate legal level, if it is recognized as law by the respective subgroup authorities. All depends on the focus of the investigation.

BIBLIOGRAPHY

ANONYMOUS
1938a. *Bij de Kapauko's van Nieuw Guinea* (Oost en West, vol. 38, no. 2, pp. 32–33, Den Haag).
1938b. *Kort verslag der verkenning van het Wisselmeergebied* (Tijdschrift van het Koninklijk Nederlandsch Aardrijkskundig Genootschap, vol. 55, pp. 320–325, Amsterdam).
1940. *Verkenningstochten van Pastoor Tillemans van de Mimikakust over de Wisselmeren naar de Etnabaai en terug naar Enarotali* (Nieuw-Guinea, vol. 5, pp. 153–161, Den Haag).

BIJLMER, H. J. T.
1938. *De Mimika-expeditie 1935–1936 naar Centraal Nieuw-Guinea* (Tijdschrift van het Koninklijk Nederlandsch Aardrijkskundig Genootschap, vol. 55, pp. 240–259, Amsterdam).
1939. *Tapiro Pygmies and Pania Mountain-Papuans. Results of the Anthropological Mimika Expedition in New-Guinea 1935–1936* (Nova Guinea, vol. 3, pp. 113–184, Leiden).

BOELEN, K. W. J.
1955. *Begrippen Stam en Tuma bij de Ekagis* (Nieuw-Guinea, vol. 1, pp. 1–6, Den Haag).

BRUIJN, J. V. DE
1939a. *Gegevens omtrent de bevolking in het Wisselmerengebied* (Nieuw-Guinea, vol. 4, pp. 259–271, Den Haag).
1939b. *Verslag van een tocht naar het brongebied van de Edere of Elegeboe-rivier in Centraal Nieuw-Guinea* (Nieuw Guinea, vol. 4, pp. 301–315, Den Haag).
1939c. *Verslag von een tocht van Enarotali via Itodah, Jamopa, Obaja, Kamero naar Orawja* (Nieuw-Guinea, vol. 4, pp. 259–271, Den Haag).
1953. *Korte Notities over de Verwantschapsterminologie en het Grondenrecht bij de Ekagi* (mimeographed, Hollandia).

CATOR, W. J.
1938. *Verslag van een tocht naar het Wisselmeer-district in Centraal Nieuw-Guinea* (Nieuw-Guinea, vol. 2, pp. 329–340, Den Haag).

DOBLE, Marion
1953. *Lessons in Kapauku* (mimeographed, Enarotali, Netherlands New Guinea).

EECHOUD, J. P. K.
1939. *Ethnographische gegevens omtrent de bevolking om an bij de Wisselmeren* (Nieuw-Guinea, vol. 4, pp. 121–137, 181–192, Den Haag).

EHRLICH, E.
1913. *Grundlegung der Sociologie des Rechts* (München, Leipzig: Duncker und Humblot).

EYMA, P. J.
1940. *Verslag van den tocht ten Noorden van het Paniaimeer* (Tijdschrift van het Koninklijk Nederlandsch Aardrijkskundig Genootschap, vol. 57, pp. 423–441, Amsterdam).

GALIS, K. W.
1951. *Bibliographie van Ned. Nieuw-Guinea* (mimeographed, Den Haag).

GUSINDE, M.
1937. *Die Feuerland Indianer—Die Yamana* (vol. 2, Mödling bei Wien: Publikation Anthropos).

HOEBEL, E. ADAMSON
1940. *The Political Organization and Law-Ways of the Comanche Indians* (Memoirs of the American Anthropological Association, no. 54, Menasha).
1954. *The Law of Primitive Man* (Cambridge: Harvard University Press).

HOGBIN, H. IAN
　　1934.　*Law and Order in Polynesia* (New York: Harcourt, Brace and Co.).
KELSEN, H.
　　1942.　*Pure Theory of Law and Analytical Jurisprudence* (Harvard Law Review, vol. 55, pp. 44–70, Cambridge).
KRECH, DAVID, AND R. S. CRUTCHFIELD
　　1948.　*Theory and Problems of Social Psychology* (New York: McGraw-Hill Book Co.).
LLEWELLYN, K. N., AND E. ADAMSON HOEBEL
　　1941.　*The Cheyenne Way* (Norman, Oklahoma: University of Oklahoma Press).
MALINOWSKI, BRONISLAW
　　1934.　*Introduction* (in H. Ian Hogbin's "Law and Order in Polynesia," New York: Harcourt, Brace and Co.).
MILLER, NEAL E., AND JOHN DOLLARD
　　1948.　*Social Learning and Imitation* (New Haven: Yale University Press).
MURDOCK, GEORGE P.
　　1949.　*Social Structure* (New York: The Macmillan Company).
NEILSON, W. A., AND OTHERS
　　1940.　*Webster's New International Dictionary of the English Language* (second edition, Springfield, Massachusetts: G. and C. Merriam Company).
RADCLIFFE-BROWN, A. R.
　　1952.　*Structure and Function in Primitive Society* (Glencoe, Illinois: The Free Press).
REDACTIE
　　1940.　*De tocht van den Adspirant-Controleur Dr. J. V. de Bruyn van Enarotali via Itodah naar Orawja* (Tijdschrift van het Koninklijk Nederlandsch Aardrijkskundig Genootschap, vol. 57, pp. 24–37, Amsterdam).
RHYS, L.
　　1947.　*Jungle Pimpernel* (London: Hodder and Stoughton Limited).
ROUX, C. C. F. M. LE.
　　1948–51.　*De Bergpapoea's van Nieuw-Guinea en hun Wooengebied* (Leiden: E. J. Brill).
SHERIF, MUZAFER
　　1947.　*Group Influence upon the Formation of Norms and Attitudes* (in "Readings in Social Psychology," edited by Theodor Newcomb and Eugene L. Hartley, pp. 77–89, New York: H. Holt).
SUMNER, W. G.
　　1938.　*Folkways* (in "Readings in Jurisprudence," edited by J. Hall, pp. 906–912, Indianapolis: The Bobbs-Merrill Co.).
STUTTERHEIM, J. F.
　　1939.　*Het een en ander omtrent de stam der Kapaoekoe's aan de Wisselmeren* (Koloniaal Tijdschrift, vol. 28, pp. 183–188, Den Haag).
TILLEMANS, H.
　　1950.　*Gebruiken op Nieuw-Guinea; regenverdrijving bij de bergbewoners van Centraal Nieuw-Guinea rond de Wisselmeren* (Nieuw-Guinea, vol. 11, pp. 88–96, 143–152, 183–192, Den Haag).
TIMASHEFF, NICHOLAS S.
　　1938.　*Law as a Social Phenomenon* (in "Readings in Jurisprudence," edited by J. Hall, pp. 868–872, Indianapolis: The Bobbs-Merrill Co.).
VAN DER VALK, MARK
　　1939.　*An Outline of Modern Chinese Law* (Monumenta Serica, Monograph no. 3, Peiping).
VECCHIO, GIORGIO DEL
　　1938.　*The Homo Juridicus and the Inadequacy of Law as a Norm of Life* (in "Readings in Jurisprudence," edited by J. Hall, pp. 929–934, Indianapolis: The Bobbs-Merrill Co.).
YANG, MARTIN C.
　　1945.　*A Chinese Village* (New York: Columbia University Press).

PLATES

EXPLANATION OF PLATES

PLATE 1. *A Young Informant, Ijaaj Akaawoogi.*

PLATE 2. *The Kapauku Country.*

Top, South Kamu Valley. *Bottom*, A canoe on Paniai Lake.

PLATE 3. *A Kapauku Village and House.*

Top, The village of Botukebo. *Bottom*, A Kapauku house.

PLATE 4. *Scenes of Food Production.*

Top, The intensive method of horticulture—sweet potato fields at Enarotali, Painai Lake region. *Bottom*, The slaughter of pigs at the pig feast.

PLATE 5. *Pictures of the Pig Feast.*

Top, Running to a pig feast. *Bottom*, Women gossiping at the pig feast.

PLATE 6. *Views of a Kapauku War.*

Top, Battle lines. *Bottom*, The *tuupe* dance.

PLATE 7. *A Tree Burial and a Kapauku Headman.*

Top, Burial. *Bottom*, Headman.

PLATE 8. *Kapauku People and Scenes.*

Upper left, An old man. *Upper right*, Mother and child. *Lower left*, Walking to a dance. *Lower right*, Young girl playing a jew's-harp.

A Young Informant

THE KAPAUKU COUNTRY

A KAPAUKU VILLAGE AND HOUSE

SCENES OF FOOD PRODUCTION

PICTURES OF THE PIG FEAST

VIEWS OF A KAPAUKU WAR

A Tree Burial and a Kapauku Headman

KAPAUKU PEOPLE AND SCENES